LOVE'S JOURNEY 2
The Red Thread

Love Without Boundaries Foundation
306 S. Bryant, Ste. C   PMB 145
Edmond, OK 73034

www.lovewithoutboundaries.com

Front cover photos (from left to right): Sisters—Kendal Elisa Qiu (age 4), Sanshui, Guangdong, and Kimi Jade YiNi (age 3), Yulin, Shaanxi. • Joshua Yu-Sheng (age 4), Nanjing, Jiangsu. • Isabelle (age 1), Yangchun, Guangdong • • Sisters— Abigayle Rose YuWei (age 4), Loudi, Hunan; Madeleine Grace XiaoXia (age 20 months), Changsha, Hunan; and Nathalie Tess QianYu (age 3), Tianmen, Hubei. • Brett Hua (age 5), Shantou, Guangdong.

Back cover photos (clockwise from top right): Sierra Diana WenJing (age 15 months), Shucheng, Anhui, with her special nanny. • • Mia (age 3), Yulin, Shaanxi. • Child at bath time on the back streets of Nanchuang, Jiangxi (photo courtesy Bill Brouwers). • • Siblings—Ethan (age 11); Anna Camille (age 4), Changsha, Hunan; and Emma Kate (age 2), Kunming, Yunnan. • • Chloe Borden (age 4½), Yangzhou, Jiangsu. • Lilliana Dawn ("Fu Xiu") (age 15 months), Gao'An, Jiangxi, with her proud granddad. • Brothers—Kevin (age 4), Guilin, and Matthew (age 6).

ISBN-13: 978-0-9794639-0-7
ISBN-10: 0-9794639-0-4

This past year was a joyous one for our family because once again we experienced the miracle of adoption. TJ Hao, a brave little two-year-old with the smile of an angel, became my seventh and final child on a beautiful spring day in Guangzhou. He has filled our house with so much laughter and noise, and I am the first to admit that I had definitely forgotten just how busy a two-year-old is and how stealth they can be with a permanent marker.

I never dreamed that I would adopt again. Since helping to found Love Without Boundaries, I have met hundreds of beautiful children and was just so happy each and every time one of them would find a family. But then there was TJ, a gorgeous little boy on a waiting child list, whom the aunties described as "naughty," "mischievous," "stubborn," and did I mention "naughty"? There was just no doubt at all that he was an Eldridge through and through, and all of our kids were thrilled at the idea of another brother to love. My daughter Anna, who had been adopted from China as a baby, threw her arms around us when we told her the news and exclaimed, "*Finally* someone else in this family that looks just like me!"

So once again our family found itself paper-chasing for adoption. Oh, the maddening joy of paperchasing! I had forgotten it well. I found myself scrubbing my house from top to bottom for social worker visits and tracking my documents hour by hour as they flew from the state capitol to the Chinese embassy. I agonized over being fingerprinted since the amount of typing I do each day had worn my ridges down smooth. I swapped homemade remedies to "puff up" my ridges with online friends and gave a shout of joy when the FBI said they passed. I paid so many visits to the notary public that I soon learned all about his family and even his favorite vacation spots. Finally the dossier, more precious than gold, was completed and on its way to China. Only then did we give a great exhale and settle in for the wait. Oh yes, the wait. I had forgotten about that agonizing period when each passing day seems like a month and when you start to create every scenario possible in your mind of why your family will never receive travel approval.

But then the phone call you have been praying for arrives, and your agency says, "Yes, you can bring him home." Life suddenly becomes a blur of packing and repacking and finally boarding an airplane to experience the miracle of becoming a mother again. All the paperchasing and all the waiting blurs into oblivion when your hotel room door opens and in walks an auntie nervously holding the hand of your new child, looking so small and so beautiful and so absolutely overwhelmed. I wanted to scoop him up and give him a huge bear hug, but of course I didn't want to frighten him; so I just knelt down next to him with a matchbox car and some cereal, all the while saying, "Wo ai ni—I love you." What a miracle adoption is. That I would be given the honor and privilege of being TJ's mommy is still such a *miracle* to me.

There isn't a day that goes by that I don't give thanks for my beautiful children. Every parent knows the feeling of looking at their own child sleeping and feeling absolute

> "*...every baby born on this earth has a purpose; so we must never forget those children who are still waiting for someone to believe in them.*"

wonder wash over them when they realize just how much they are in love with that angelic face. It is when I look at my children sleeping, however, that the emotions of my daily job get to me the most. How many children around the world go to sleep each night without a mother or father to tuck them in gently or to rub their back when they are afraid? How many children around the world can't run down the hall to Mom or Dad's room to crawl under the covers when the lightning storm begins and the thunder booms? How many children have a fever in the night and don't have a parent to cool their brow? I believe so strongly that every child on this earth deserves a family to love them, and that is why my job is both wonderful and heartbreaking at the same time.

It is so incredible to be able to know and love all the children in our programs but also very hard to know that so many are in need of life-saving surgery or medical intervention. There are thousands of children who would benefit from being in one-on-one foster care and so many older orphans who are in need of educational help and mentoring. All throughout China there are children with mild to moderate special needs who are just waiting for a family to say, "Yes, *you* are the child of my dreams." Meeting, holding, and knowing these wonderful kids in person has been one of the greatest blessings of my life, but knowing that so many of them might never know the love of a family makes me even more determined to improve their lives in every way possible.

This second volume of Love's Journey is dedicated completely to all of the children who are waiting to find their place in this world. Our first volume raised over $100,000, which we used to fund orphan surgeries, to build schools, to begin foster care programs, and more. I look at that first volume and know that hearts were healed and spirits were lifted because of a simple book. I hope as you read through this second volume, you will realize that, in buying a copy, you are now a part of bringing assistance to orphaned children. Once again all the proceeds from Love's Journey 2 will go to change the lives of children in China. While this book is a beautiful keepsake of the Chinese adoption experience, it is so much more than that. It is medical care, it is education, it is nutrition… it is *hope*!

I have learned in my work that the human heart has an infinite capacity for love. My own heart is filled with the images of all of the children I have met and held in China. I can pull up their faces in my mind, and each one is as unique and special as the next. I hope as you look at the photos in this book, you will catch a glimpse of the beauty and strength that I believe every child on earth possesses inside of them. I hope you will remember that for every child in this book who has found a family to cherish them, hundreds more are waiting for that same chance. I feel with all my heart that every baby born on this earth has a purpose; so we must never forget those children who are still waiting for someone to believe in them. I promise that if you take a chance and step out in faith to offer help, something absolutely wonderful will come of it.

Amy Eldridge, Executive Director
Love Without Boundaries Foundation

Contents

Editors: Sheri Russon and Amy Eldridge
Photo Editors: Carla Kennedy and Jolaine Chatham
Cover and Interior Design: Jolaine Chatham
Printed in the United States by Canterbury Press

Dedicated to all of China's children,
whom we hold forever in our hearts.

Discovering the Thread

Red. If ever there was a color associated with the country of China, red is the one.
There are red flags, red lanterns, red temples, red "lucky" envelopes, and, in the case
of those who make the decision to adopt from China, there is the "red thread."

Faith Anna Xia
(age 3), Gansu.

Catherine ("Catie") Alyssa FeiYun
(age 14 months),
Shangrao, Jiangxi.

Autumn (age 3),
Desheng, Guangxi.

Elizabeth ("Lizzie") YiMeng
(age 3), Changsha, Hunan.

Katarina ("Katie") Zishuang
(age 5), XinHui, Guangdong.

Kendalan MianYi (age 1),
Zhenghe, Fujian.

An ancient Chinese legend says that when a child is born, an invisible red thread connects that child's soul to all those people, present and future, who will play a part in that child's life. Many adoptive parents have embraced this belief, as they feel so deeply that their family was destined to be together.

Whether one believes in the legend or not, there is no denying that when a family makes the decision to open their arms to a child from China, they discover that there is indeed a red thread that now ties their hearts to their child's homeland. When one thinks of a thread, the first thing that comes to mind is something so tiny and small,

almost to be insignificant; yet the thread that ties adoptive parents to China is often as strong and unbreakable as steel.

There are hundreds of different reasons why people decide to adopt a child, but it is probably fair to say that in each case there is an ache in one's heart that someone who is supposed to be in the family is missing. In the case of Chinese adoption, that someone lives far, far away in a land that many of us have only read about in books. Our children were born in a country with a history 4,000 years old, a country filled with modern technology and yet ancient wonder and beauty. As their lives and ours join together, two histories and cultures begin to entwine.

Other Plans
by Jill McLaughlin

WE HADN'T PLANNED ON ADOPTING A FOURTH CHILD. We were sure our family was complete, and I congratulated myself on completing five years' worth of paperwork. However I still loved looking at waiting children lists. Every time anyone would announce a new list, I'd go and look at the children. I loved seeing the words "I found my family" next to a child, and I loved knowing new families were being formed.

I went to a new agency's website just to look at their recently announced list, but there were no pictures; only the gender, birth date, and special need of each child. One girl had the same birthday and special need as the child our family sponsors in foster care. Instantly I was curious to know if it was the same girl. I wrote an email to the agency but didn't send it. Something inside me said, "Are you sure you are ready to do this?" I subconsciously knew if I pushed the "send" button that nothing would ever be the same.

The next day my curiosity got the better of me, and I sent the email. I received a reply right away and discovered it was not the same child but the agency sent a picture anyway. When I clicked on the picture the first thing I thought was, "Oh! It's Emma!" Even though we hadn't planned to adopt again, we knew this child was ours.

As soon as we made our decision to adopt, everything fell into place with lightning speed. On May 24, 2006, we met a beautiful, terrified little girl. Once she recovered from initial shock and grief, an amazing child with an impish grin emerged. Emma was so happy to have a family! We have placed new family photos around the house. Emma loves to look at them and name each family member. Then she points to herself and repeats over and over, "This is Emma. This is Emma." When coming upon a family picture that didn't include her, she named each person and then said, "No Emma." She brought the picture to me and said again, "No Emma." I explained, "Emma was still in China." Her little chin started quivering. She pointed to the picture and repeated, "Emma was still in China," and burst into tears.

We likewise cannot imagine our family without Emma. Her enthusiasm is infectious. She is so loving and jumps into life with both feet. When I reflect on this whirlwind year I can't help thinking the best things in life are often unplanned and unforeseen. To quote John Lennon, "Life is what happens to you while you're busy making other plans."

Emma RunYu (age 3), ShiYan, Hubei—waiting for Mama and Baba to come.

Siblings—Jordan (age 9), Jamie (age 10), and Jenna Joy (age 22 months), Jiangxi.

Kai Yixing (age 18 months), Chengdu, Sichuan, with his big brother, Sullivan.

Red Note
by Cheryl Bonfils-Rasmussen

OUR DAUGHTER'S REFERRAL INFORMATION MENTIONED SHE WAS FOUND WRAPPED IN AN OLD COTTON QUILT AND IN THE POCKET WAS A RED NOTE WITH HER BIRTH DATE ON IT. I contacted Adele at blessedkids.com and asked her to call the orphanage for us and ask if we could have that red note. She was told that they may not be able to give it to us but that they may be able to show it to us.

I was amazed to find it folded up in the little photo album the orphanage gave to us. It is the oldest piece of my daughter's history and the only tangible link she has to her birth family. My Chinese teacher said that traditionally it is important to know the "Sheng Cheng Ba Zi" because it tells the date and time of birth. This information is important in the future when matching her with a young man.

It reads: "Sheng cheng ba zi, xiao nu sheng yu 2003 nian er yue, liu ri. Shang wu jiu shi. Xie Xie hao xin ren."

"Born, this little girl 2003, February 6th, at 9 a.m. Thank you kind heart person."

I Am in Love
by Sheri Marsh

OVER THE PAST 16 MONTHS, A RED THREAD STRETCHED FROM CHINA TO A FAMILY IN TEXAS in order to unite us with our daughter, Madison. I couldn't have asked for a more beautiful, loving, funny, happy, and adorable child. In just two

Madison Jia (age 13 months), Wuwei.

short days Madison wrapped us around her finger. I am so happy to have this little girl in my life. She wakes up every morning with a smile on her face that melts me to the core. I wake up thinking about her, go to bed thinking about her, and if I am away from her for just a moment, I miss her. She is my life.

The people of Gansu are lovely. While in China we went with our wonderful guide to the local department store, and everyone stared at all of the families. They love children and wanted to hold them and love them for the short time that we were there. They gave Madison snacks from the grocery section of the department store, and as we left I looked back at all the faces smiling at my daughter and knew that I would never forget that beautiful moment and would tell her about it as she grows.

We went to a Tibetan restaurant in Gansu; it was so much fun. The Tibetan people sing wonderfully and dance beautifully. They wear beautiful costumes with jewelry and colorful clothing as their everyday wear. They performed for us and served us dinner. Madison loved the music and had a ball watching these talented people from her home province.

(Last child on right) Madison Jia (age 13 months), Wuwei. Red Couch Photo at White Swan Hotel with travel group.

Maia (age 3), Dianjiang, Chongqing, with her squirmy 7-month-old brother, Jack.

Waiting
by Kelly Feichtinger

Wondering who,
Wondering where,
My child is waiting for me,
Somewhere out there.

I don't yet know your name.
I have not yet seen your face.
I only know that you were born to another,
In such a faraway place.

I long to enfold you in my arms.
To hold you close and tight.
I yearn for the day when I can be the one,
To rock you and kiss you goodnight.

My heart already loves you.
In my dreams, you are there.
You smile and call me "Mama."
Something I've been waiting so long to hear!

I pray that you are safe.
Please know that you are loved.
I've asked for Him to send his angels,
To watch over you from above.

Soon, I will hold you.
It's taking forever, it seems.
But for now, I'll be waiting,
And seeing you in my dreams.

A Deep Love
by Ann Stewart Zachwieja

The following essay is an edited excerpt from an email message I sent back to the United States from China.

WE HAD RECEIVED OUR DAUGHTER AND HAD MADE AN INCREDIBLE VISIT TO HER SWI, BEING THE FIRST FOREIGNERS TO BE ALLOWED IN. Our visit with the SWI aunties is one we will never forget. It gave us an understanding of the deep love they felt for our daughters.

Jiang Mei (age 1), Lian Jiang, Guangdong, with her beloved auntie.

"After the director arrived, we drove through the city to the SWI. Our group of parents and babies was ushered into a room where we sat around a table and heard speeches. As we were sitting in the conference room, the Chinese aunties suddenly swooped into the room and scooped up the babies who they had, just the day before, released to their new lives. I cry as I sit here and write about it. There is not one single doubt that our daughters were loved and cherished under their care. We were told that Mei had a special caretaker who was very attached to her, and we immediately knew who she was. She rushed to Mei, picked her up, and cried as she hugged and kissed her. When she knew that I was her new mother, we hugged and cried. I will never forget the experience of embracing the woman who took care of our Mei and having her hug me back so strongly.

Jiang Mei with Mom, Dad, and her auntie.

Mei happily settled into her auntie's arms, quiet and perhaps relieved to be back in the place she knew with familiar sights, sounds, and smells around her. Their eyes met as Mei drank her bottle, tears dropping onto her from her auntie's eyes. Their bond was evident, tangible.

There was another auntie who also couldn't take her hands off of Mei. The two just kept taking her back and forth from one another. Through my meager Chinese and the use of universal gestures, we were able to communicate enough for them to know that we will love and treasure Mei. We also understood that they truly cherished Mei. I walked hand in hand with them as we were leaving."

I look forward to the day I can bring my daughter back to honor her aunties and close the circle of their care.

The Seed Becomes a Flower
by Darlene Carroll

IT ALL STARTED MANY YEARS AGO WHILE ATTENDING CHURCH WITH MY FAMILY. I watched a family file into their seats with a young boy and girl of Asian descent. I wondered where the children were visiting from. Mom explained that this family adopted the children. She explained what adoption meant, and the seed was planted.

For years this seedling kept pushing to the forefront of my mind, but so many things kept my dream from becoming a reality. One night as I sat watching television, my husband looked at me and said that if we were going to adopt a child we had better get going as neither one of us was getting any younger. At the age of 45 the seedling began to sprout.

We decided we wanted to adopt a three- to four-year-old girl. Months later we finished all the paperwork, sent it off to China, and began the wait. The sprout began to bud.

Finally one day I got a call at work from our adoption agency. "We have your referral. She is beautiful!" My heart started to pound as a CD in the background played, "You Are My Miracle" by Roger Whittaker. Then the questions began to fly: "What size is she? How much does she weigh? How old is she?" There was silence for a second and then, "Your daughter's birthday is August 8, 2004; your daughter is nine months old. I know that you were asking for an older child. Is this a problem?" Problem? Not at all! It was God's will that Feng An Ni would be our daughter. I was in heaven. The flower was in full bloom.

Lesley Marie NingFeng (about age 6 months), Yongzhou, Hunan.

AnNi Rose (age 1), Fengcheng City, Jiangxi.

Sisters—Audra (age 13) and Sophia (age 3), Luoyang, Henan.

by Darlene Carroll

Within our yard upon a bench,
A delicate flower God has sent.
As this flower blooms and grows,
A mom and dad she will know.
To watch this flower come to life,
A mom and dad's pure delight.

Words to Live By
by Linda Lang

"The best and most beautiful things in the world cannot be seen or even touched. They must be felt with the heart."

We found Helen Keller's words to sum up so much of what we were feeling during the long wait for the referral of our daughter, Maya.

Maya LinXiang (age 2), Jiangxi.

A Beautiful Gift
by Amelia Mowery

THIS PAST SUMMER I WAS BLESSED WITH THE OPPORTUNITY TO RETURN TO CHINA AND SPEND TIME AT MY DAUGHTER'S ORPHANAGE IN FULING, CHONGQING, WITH OTHER MEMBERS OF OUR PARENT GROUP, FULING KIDS INTERNATIONAL. I so looked forward to holding the babies and getting a better feel for where my girls came from, as well as taking care of the business we had been sent to do.

After a busy week of meetings; playing with babies; assessing the progress of the "First Hugs" program that we have set up; and enjoying the sights, sounds, and delicious food in Fuling, I felt like I had the perfect experience and couldn't ask for more. Boy, was I wrong!

The night before we were leaving, a photo album that I had brought for the caregivers filled with pictures of children from both of our travel groups was making the rounds. The next thing I knew my older daughter's caregiver saw Kathryn's picture, read her Chinese name, and started to cry. This wonderful woman let me know that she was the one who held Kathryn, rocked her, fed her, and kissed her goodnight during the eight months she lived at the orphanage. In spite of our tears and very poor communication skills, we managed to share how much we both love her and how very grateful I am for the care she received. I gave her the pictures to keep, and she kissed them and held them close to her heart. She then showed me a picture of my baby that was taken the morning before we met Kathryn.

In this world of adoption we can never know for certain so many aspects of our children's life before we knew them. As parents we can't help but hope that they were loved and cared for in the months between their birth and our meeting them. I had always felt that Kathryn had been well loved, but the proof of that suspicion was the greatest gift that I could have ever received.

Kathryn FuDeYi (age 4), Fuling, Chongqing—in photo held by caregiver, Ming Hua.

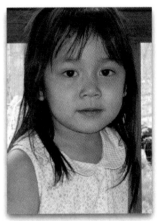
Above: Delaney Jia-Ke (age 3), Shantou, Guangdong.
Below: Lindsey NianChun (age 6), Pingnan, Guangxi.

First Meeting with Fallon
by Misty Woodhall

THE MOMENT THE KNOCK ON THE DOOR CAME I THOUGHT I WAS GOING TO FAINT. She was really here! Actually here! I was going to meet and hold my daughter for the first time. I was shaking so hard and crying that I was afraid I was going to drop her. Then in they came like a parading procession—Fallon held by a caregiver, the orphanage director, and close behind an entourage of nannies and caregivers. The caregiver who entered the room holding Fallon handed her to me and told us to sign a couple of papers. The procession was full of smiles and congratulatory nods towards us. Before we knew it they turned and walked out just as fast as they had walked in. My new daughter stared at me with as much wonder as I had for her. She then smiled and showed me those dimples. I knew at that moment that we would be able to overcome whatever was to come our way. She is my daughter! She is my Fallon!

Fallon Reece Xiu Wei (age 23 months), Xiushan, Chongqing, with Mom.

Jacqueline Fuya (age 3), Huangshi, Hubei.

Anna (age 28 months), Shantou, Guangdong.

Julia FuTong Rose (age 16 months), Wuxue City, Hubei.

Angels
by Betty Betz

BEFORE I KNEW MY DAUGHTER I USED TO PRAY EVERY NIGHT THAT ANGELS WOULD WATCH OVER HER, WHOEVER AND WHEREVER SHE MIGHT BE. On Halloween day 2002 I saw her picture for the first time on a waiting children list. While I waited impatiently for my paperwork to catch up with my heart, I changed my prayer. I now knew her name and where she was; so I started praying that angels would watch over her until the time that I could do it myself. I even sent her an angel necklace to let her know that someone was watching over her.

Little did I know, less than six months later, on the day I met my daughter, I would come face-to-face with the angels who had watched over her. As I met her foster parents and two other women, the story of how they had met unfolded. The two women had been allowed into the orphanage to work with the children—teaching them to count, color, sing songs, etc. One had spotted a small girl sitting quietly off from the rest of the children. Over time she earned the girl's trust and found her to be in need of medical attention. The women were allowed to take the girl to a local hospital where she received the medical care she so sorely needed, and the women also found a foster family to care for her. As the girl blossomed before their eyes, these women had a prayer of their own. They prayed that a Christian family would someday adopt the child and help her overcome her medical needs.

In the three years since I have learned that angels are indeed everywhere in the adoption community. And as my daughter sleeps tonight, around her neck is the same angel necklace I had sent to her before we met.

Sela Lian (age 9), Guilin— at the Magic Kingdom.

Stella Kate (age 18 months), Hunan.

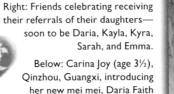

Right: Friends celebrating receiving their referrals of their daughters— soon to be Daria, Kayla, Kyra, Sarah, and Emma.

Below: Carina Joy (age 3½), Qinzhou, Guangxi, introducing her new mei mei, Daria Faith (age 15 months), Hengfeng, Jiangxi.

Madeleine Yan (age 23 months), Guiping, Guangxi, with sister, Emma Leanna (nearly age 7).

Marisa Gilana FuWu (age 2), Fuling, Chongqing, with sister, Roxana Halina Xinmiao (age 6), Dapu, Guangdong.

Timothy (age 5), Xinxiang, Henan.

Sibling love. Benjamin (age 1), Guatemala, and Lily RuiXiang (age 5), Ruijin, Jiangxi.

She Captured our Hearts
by Betsy Brundage

A FEW DAYS AFTER SENDING IN OUR INITIAL APPLICATION TO ADOPT A GIRL BETWEEN THE AGES OF FOUR AND SIX, I LOOKED AT OUR AGENCY'S WAITING CHILDREN PAGE. On it was the most beautiful four-year-old girl, holding a toy phone to her ear with a huge smile. She captured our hearts, and we contacted our agency to find out more about her, only to be told that a wonderful family had already found her. We never forgot the little girl, and, after seeing her photo, we knew that a waiting child with special needs was meant for us.

Four months later we were only a few days away from being DTC and anxiously awaiting our agency's next Waiting Children list. I checked the website and while the list hadn't yet arrived, a message had been posted a few days previously that the little girl with the phone was unexpectedly available again. I was on the phone to my best friend—a grandmother to a little girl from China—telling her I was just sure that many people were probably interested in this girl and we had missed our chance again. At that exact moment my other line rang; it was our agency asking if we were still interested in that little girl. I burst into tears, called my husband, and left work to run home and look at information the agency said we had to review before we made our decision—although in my heart she was our daughter from the moment the agency called. A little over three months later we got to meet our daughter, Annie, in person. She was as beautiful and amazing as we knew she would be.

Annie (age 5), Shantou, Guangdong.

Faith (age 4), Leping, Jiangxi, with one of her three big brothers, Nolan (age 7).

Seeds of Adoption
by Ann Marie Ronsman

THE SEED OF ADOPTION WAS PLACED IN MY HEART IN HIGH SCHOOL WHEN I SAW NEWS COVERAGE OF CHINESE ORPHANAGES. When Matt and I met and married, we had talked in abstract terms about adopting a child, most likely after having several biological children.

Our journey began when my husband forwarded to me a daily devotional from "The Purpose Driven Life" series. It was about adoption and about how we are all God's adopted children. I read it and then asked Matt that evening, "Does that email mean you want to adopt?" He answered, "No. Well maybe. Well someday." End of discussion.

A few weeks later I went to Barnes and Noble to get some books for our son Luke, who was 15 months old at the time. On the way to the children's book section, a book jumped off the shelf at me. It was a book about someone's Chinese adoption journey. I looked at the book and thought, "Well, it'll be good to read in case we adopt in the future." In the children's books with Luke, I bent down next to his stroller to look at some books with him. I picked up a book called "I Love You Like Crazy Cakes" and began to read it to him… only to find that it was a book about adopting a little girl from China. Strange!

A few weeks after that I was at a local community pool with Luke and some friends and their children. I had really been struggling with wondering, if we were to adopt, how our daughter would fit into our community. In walked about six moms with adopted daughters from China. I froze. Over the next hour or so I watched them with their daughters. The children were healthy, happy, and full of fun, and so were the mothers. I wanted to ask them about their adoption experience but didn't want to be too forward; so I left without approaching them. Matt and I prayed more and sent for information from some adoption agencies.

A few weeks later I was at the bookstore again, looking for adoption books. Sitting down in the

Siblings—Will (age 7); Ella Brooke ZhaoYi (age 3), Yuanling, Hunan; and Catherine ("Catie") Alyssa FeiYun (age 14 months), Shangrao, Jiangxi.

coffee shop, I started to read for a bit before going home. In walked one of the mothers from the pool and her two children (one biological and one adopted). I closed my eyes and prayed that God would give me an entry to speak to her if we were supposed to adopt. She sat down at the table next to me and said, "I see you're reading a book about Chinese adoption." I broke into tears. She proceeded to hug me and share with me her adoption story and how wonderful her experience was. At my car, I called Matt, and we decided we were going to adopt from China. I went home and called Holt.

What we didn't know at the time was not only would we be taking a leap of faith by adopting, but also that we would welcome a daughter with special needs into our lives. Once we learned what China considered special needs, we thought, "We can do that!"

On February 16, 2006, we learned that we had been matched with a daughter. Our daughter's special needs are glaucoma and a large port wine stain that covers much of her face. That is what you see—but she is so much more than her "special need." She is a bright-eyed, funny, joyful, and "spicy" girl. She fits into our family like a piece to a puzzle that had been missing. In her three short months with us she has bloomed like a little flower. She continues to astound us with her courage and her love.

We will always be grateful to the Chinese people for they have given us the gift of a daughter. Our very own miracle.

ABSOLUTELY PERFECT
by Amy Jones

THIS PAST YEAR HAS BEEN DEDICATED TO PREPARING OURSELVES AS A FAMILY IN EVERY WAY POSSIBLE FOR ADDING YOU TO OUR FAMILY, AND FINALLY THE DAY WE SEE YOUR PRECIOUS LITTLE FACE ARRIVED. I opened the attachment to see your chubby, sweet, precious face; a red sweater; and a little black hair. You were absolutely perfect, and I cried some more. The boys all went "ooohhhhhh" when they saw how sweet you were. It was all perfect—I was on cloud nine. When I hung up I called Daddy and gave him the details and sent your picture. By this time I wasn't crying anymore; I was sobbing. It was an amazing moment in my life—so much like giving birth to my boys. When Federal Express arrived the next day, the boys and I tore open the package to more pictures, with more hair and more adorable. I emailed the photos to your daddy at work and then called Grandma and told her, "I have the cutest baby in all of China." Grandma Jones agreed and blew the pictures up to 8" x 10" and framed them. She said, "I can't believe I can be so attached to a picture." Mya, you are already so loved. God's plan has been for us to be together since the beginning of time. You are a wonderful gift to our family already.

You Are Mine
by Kelly Feichtinger

I love you
Though I have yet to see your face.
You are mine.

I dream of holding you in my arms
My child from far away
You are mine.

I lie awake at night
Imagining who you will be.
You are mine.

I prepare our home and my heart
To receive such a precious child.
You are mine.

I pray for your happiness and safety
Until I can be the one to provide it.
You are mine.

I hold my breath
As we wait for the call.
You are mine.

I will the time to fly by
As we wait for permission to travel.
You are mine.

I feel as though my heart will burst
When you are placed in my arms.
You are mine.

You rest your soft cheek against mine
And sigh contentedly.
I am yours.

Nora (age 13 months), Chengdu, Sichuan— getting to know her new brother, Luke (age 2).

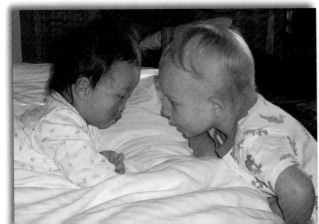

Forever friends—Mya and Mae (both age 10 months) Lianjiang, Guangdong— on their last day in China.

Aoife Nuo (age 18 months), Lin'An, Zheijiang.

Sofia Ruhai (age 2), Xiangtan, Hunan—reading a book with her stuffed animal imaginary playmates.

A WONDERFUL DREAM
by *Avara Yaron*

MY HUSBAND AND I WERE GREATLY INSPIRED TO ADOPT A DAUGHTER FROM CHINA AND AWAITED ONE LAST DOCUMENT TO COMPLETE OUR DOSSIER. Early in the morning of July 16, 2004, I had a dream that I gave birth to my daughter. In the dream we were having a huge celebration attended by both my family and my husband's family. Her delivery was smooth and easy, and the atmosphere was festive. I awakened feeling joyous and wondered if indeed our daughter had just entered the world. Later that day the long awaited final document arrived in our mailbox.

Months later, on January 31, 2005, my husband and I were at a trade show when our adoption agency called with our referral information. We learned our daughter's name, where she was living, when and how she was found, and her birth date. Chills ran through me and tears came to my eyes. The gatekeeper at the orphanage had found our baby on July 21, 2004. The staff guessed she was about three days old and assigned her the birthday of July 18th. My dream early on July 16th would have been late at night on the 16th in China. Maybe our daughter was born just as I dreamed it. We celebrate both days!

During the months of waiting for our daughter, I researched where in China I could find hand embroidery. I design a line of handbags and wanted to use embroidery for a new bag. The only concrete information I came across was a state run facility in Changsha, Hunan. When we received our referral we discovered our daughter was in Xiangtan, Hunan, and we would be staying in Changsha. We were in Changsha for a week, found embroiderers the first day, came up with a design, and placed our order. Our daughter was already working for the family business!

Above and left: Madeline Royal (nearly age 2), Guilin, Guangxi.

CATHERINE'S SMILE
by *Deborah Sorensen*

OUR FIRST PICTURES OF CATHERINE FROM THE WAITING CHILD LIST SHOW AN ANGRY AND CRYING TODDLER STRAPPED IN AN UNMOVING BABY SWING. In one of the photos she's actually glaring at the camera. There were four photos, all taken the same day, apparently, as she's wearing the same outfit and has the same unhappy expression in the same swing chair. We couldn't believe there wasn't one picture that showed her other expressions, but that was it. Holding that photo I thought, "I *know* this child has a wonderful smile, and one day we will see it."

With this belief firm in our hearts we committed to Catherine, named Yang Chang Huan, which means "always happy" in Chinese. We knew few details about her—only that she was two years old, born with a congenital cleft lip and palate, and that her lip had been repaired.

The irony of her name and the tear-stained face in the photos was not lost on us. As we shared the photos with friends and family, we would see them struggle to say something positive. Often they just said "*Whew*, I hope you know what you're doing!" Clearly they didn't think we did. Ten months later Catherine was in our arms, and we glimpsed her radiant smile for the first time.

Sisters—Abbie (age 3), Leizhou, Guangdong, and Katie (age 4), Sanshui, Guangdong—love music.

Quinn Lejun (born September 2004), Shantou, Guangdong— reunited with her auntie and her best friend at Shantou SWI.

Luke (age 6), Xi'an, Shaanxi; Catherine (age 4), Yangzhou, Jiangsu; and Delanie (age 10).

Sweet and saucy. Mia Kay Hui Na (age 2½), Fuling, Chongqing.

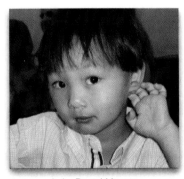

Luke Daniel Minmin (age 4), Xi'An, Shaanxi.

Sunny Xin (age 19 months), Shantou, Guangdong— on her baptism day.

Tia (age 3), Yongzhou, Hunan, with sister, Jada (age 2), Changsha, Hunan.

Katherine Jiao (age 4), Kunming, Yunnan.

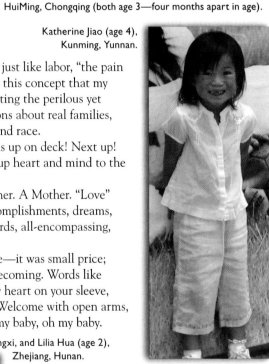

First day together. Sisters—Talia YuPing (age 4), Nanfeng, Jiangxi, and Lilia Hua (age 2), Zhejiang, Hunan.

Siblings—James Ezekiel, ShuYang, Shanghai, and Berea Abigail, HuiMing, Chongqing (both age 3—four months apart in age).

HOMECOMING
by Alison Reichstein

THE WAIT DOESN'T MATTER. "You'll forget," they say, just like labor, "the pain of waiting." I buy socks and try to get myself around this concept that my baby is real, will be realized in my life. I start navigating the perilous yet sweetly rewarding language of responding to questions about real families, and the great unknowns, and cultural differences, and race.

The chat rooms hold all the clues. "Our month" is up on deck! Next up! Getting real. Even the most cautious start opening up heart and mind to the soon-to-be presence.

Finally the floodgates open. In a rush I am a mother. A Mother. "Love" alone does not begin to express the challenges, accomplishments, dreams, and fears that culminate in the ineffable beyond words, all-encompassing, fierce, tender, adoring, grateful, enabling love.

What weight was waiting compared to this? None—it was small price; no price at all to pay for this wondrous, joyous homecoming. Words like "intertwined," "interweave," "interlace" entwine my heart on your sleeve, my heart in the crib next to me, in the next room. Welcome with open arms, never feeling whole again without this person. Oh my baby, oh my baby.

Within minutes of my raising the topic of a trip to bring home a sister from China, older-sister-to-be Talia was raring to go. (She suggested that we also bring home her brother, her other sister, and her daddy! Give her an inch...) We waited with yearning hearts to see where our next red thread would lead. Talia seemed to already know her sister and was impatient to get on that plane to China. Finally the day came when we all came together as a family. As you can see in the picture from our first days together, a sweetly smiling Lilia Hua took comfort in the presence of her sister, and Talia's proud, smug beam expresses her satisfaction of finally being with her baby sister.

Beautiful Little Girl
by Stacy L. Denham

Dedicated to our daughter, Myia, and family friend, Camille Beach

Beautiful little girl with eyes so brown,
Full of wonder as she looks around.

Along came a family with arms opened wide,
Telling their story with nothing to hide.

Beautiful little girl with eyes filled with tears,
How would she ever conquer her fears?

Along came a family, who traveled so far,
Just look and see how different they are.

Beautiful little girl with a face so round,
How happy she is that she was found.

Along came a family with hearts from above,
Who took her in and showered her with love.

Beautiful little girl with eyes so bright,
How happy she is to be held so tight.

Along came a family with a mother and father,
Waiting for this day to call her their daughter.

Beautiful little girl so full of love,
You were sent to us from the good Lord above.

Friends—Myia (age 17 months) and Camille (age 19 months), both from Changsha, Hunan.

The Most Incredible Gift of All
by Kim Beagle

For Kaylee (Yue Xiao Xi), Madison (Lin Chun Ming), and our third little angel who is still waiting for us in China

Adoption is an incredible, inconceivable gift.

Daily, we look at you and marvel, and realize how fortunate we are that God brought us together from two sides of the world to create our family.

Our hearts will always be grateful to your birth parents and the nannies in China who watched over you and loved you every day, while we were counting down the days until we could come get you.

Priceless treasures you have been since the moment those nannies placed you in our arms and you became ours.

The joy you bring to our lives is indescribable.

Indeed, the giggles and the smiles, the hugs and the kisses, the cute things that you say—they are little pieces of heaven.

Of all the many blessings in this life, there are none as precious as you.

Never did we imagine that our hearts could be this full… Never did we imagine that we could be this blessed… Never did we imagine that we could love you this much.

Below: Kaylee (age 3), Yueyang, Hunan—touching the face of her new sister, Madison (age 1), DianBai, Guangdong.

Left: Card created by Kaylee (age 4), to go along with a package sent to her orphanage.

Joscelyn Adell, YiYang, Hunan.

A Knock at the Door
by Joe Hampton

WHY, AT THE AGE OF 40+ AND A FATHER OF TWO PERFECT BIOLOGICAL KIDS, DO I FIND MY STOMACH IN KNOTS as I wait nervously in a hotel room halfway around the world from home? Why do I wonder, "Will you like me?" and "Will I love you?" Why do I ask, "Can I love you?"

A simple, soft knock at the door, and our world changed forever. So small, so vulnerable, so precious, and so alone. Your perfect face, your perfect hands. Such a tiny child wrapped in layer after layer after layer. Such courage, such bravery, such hope. At the exact moment your life and ours intersect, we meet and immediately fall hopelessly in love.

To all the "would be," "could be" dads who wonder "should I? could I?" the answer is "yes." Answer the knock. Open the door. Let life in.

MeiLi (age 22 months), QuJiang, Guangdong, with Mom—celebrating her first Easter with her forever family.

LULU
by Darlene Moitoso

I CAN REMEMBER THE FEELING I HAD IN THE CIVIL AFFAIRS OFFICE IN NANNING THAT LATE OCTOBER DAY IN 2005 as I was awaiting my first meeting with my 34-month-old daughter. It was something between terror and anticipation. I was exhausted from a nightmarish trip to China (having nearly missed the "Gotcha Day" altogether), which came after an exhaustingly long wait for our travel approval.

As I watched the room fill with little babies soon to be united with their families, I began thinking I was nuts to have ever done this. What was I, a single career gal, doing here in the remodeled floor of a place called the Welfare Lottery Hotel waiting for a little Chinese girl? What was I thinking?

Then I was called into another room, and there she was—the little girl I had named Miranda. She was tall, calm, and self-assured. She looked at me and pointed and said, "Mama." My heart melted, and I knew that this was what was supposed to be. I gave her a small doll, took her photo, and showed her a picture of herself. She yelled "Lulu" and squealed with joy (and Lulu she remains to this day). She had been so well prepared for this huge event in her life. She still had no clue, really, of the enormity of what would happen shortly, but I'll never forget the bravery she showed in that room. So willing to call me mama, so willing to give up what was known for what was promised. Those moments amazed me, and she continues to amaze me daily.

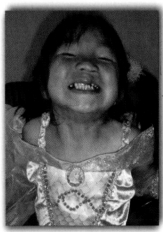

Lulu (age 3), Guilin, Guangxi.

媽

Piper Ling LuSong (age 3), Wuhan, Hubei.

Wan Wan, now known as Piper, was a very distraught two-year-old when placed with her forever family. She grieved for her foster mother, and it took almost a year for her to really settle in with her new family. Now Piper is a happy, joyful girl.

Big brother Cody (age 14) with his sisters—
Sierra (age 15 months), Fengcheng City, Jiangxi,
and Melaina (age 3), Nanning, Guangxi.

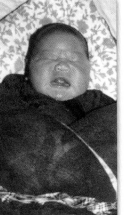

Newborn Emily Dana QianLei, Tianmen City, Hubei.

FAMILY OF FIVE
by Andrea Musgrave

I DIDN'T WANT ANY MORE KIDS. I had my perfect family of four—one girl, one boy. But then my daughter, Madison, was invited by her friend, Matt Eldridge, to go to China with him and his mom, Amy, on one of her early trips there after establishing Love Without Boundaries. Madison, then age 13, visited several orphanages on her trip to China. Something in her was stirred, and she came home with a mission—to get us to adopt a baby!

Frankly we told her she was crazy. However, with her heartfelt pleadings, the dreams started to come. I didn't always remember what the dreams were exactly, but I started searching the Internet about international adoption. It wasn't completely a farfetched idea for me. After all I'm adopted myself and had always imagined adopting.

Approximately three months after Madison's trip to China, our paperchase began. On October 24, 2004, we met our beautiful new daughter, Emma Xiu Yan Musgrave. We are now the perfect family of five.

Emma Xiu Yan (age 10 months), Xiushan, Chongqing, with Mom and Dad.

MOVING
by Chris Bowe

RECENTLY I TOOK OUR OLDEST SON, ADAM, ON A CAVING ADVENTURE. This was one of those experiences where we pushed ourselves to our limits from a mental and physical standpoint. We caved for over eight hours, and most of that time was spent in spaces I was sure I would not get out of alive. Adam can tell you that we were both very anxious. However the worst part of the trip was not the time spent crawling through the very narrow spaces, but the time sitting waiting for the group to catch up or right before entering a tight space. As long as I was moving, I was fine. Give me something to do physically, and I will put my head down and keep moving. But the time before the challenge, sitting and thinking about what lies ahead, really pushes me to my limits.

The adoption process has been much like our caving trip—although we were excited about each new adventure, the process pushed us to our limits. In each leg of our journey, from Beijing to Xining to Guangzhou, people reached out to us and touched our lives. It was evident our newest daughter, Anderson, was well loved and cared for throughout the orphanage and foster parent process. Our guides became part of our extended family, and everyone worked hard to make our adoption successful for us and Anderson. Looking back with our family well blended, the international adoption process was challenging, exciting, and so rewarding. Here's to keeping your head down and moving forward!

NEWS TO TREASURE FROM CHINA
Excerpted essay by Alison Skolaut

From a report from the Xi'an City Children's Welfare Institute:

"AN WEN LOOKS VERY LOVELY WITH HER LONG EYELASHES AND BRIGHT EYES. She has fair skin and two dimples on her face, which make her very pretty. An Wen is a gentle and obedient child.

"When she had meals recently, she stretched out her hands for the spoon, and tried to learn to feed herself. She likes to be praised. When the nanny praises her, she will show her small dimples happily, which looks very lovely. When she does something wrong, she will sit aside and lower her head, as if she knows that she is wrong.

"In a word, An Wen is a little, pretty and cute girl. We hope her to grow up healthily and happily."

Special cousins—Anna YanYi (age 2), Guiping, Guangxi, and Faith MeiLe (age 4), Leping, Jiangxi.

Olivia Danielle (age 3), Qinzhou, Guangxi.

Above: Siblings—Claudia (age 9), Gideon (age 2), and Reschen (age 8)—preparing gifts to send to their new sister.

Right: Gideon (age 2)—studying photo of his new sister, Evangeline ("Evie") Hope An Wen (age 2), Xi'An.

Katherine Guo Dan (age 9 months),
Yangjiang, Guangdong, with Dad and Mom.

FINDING PLACE
by Joy C. Lenz

I AM STANDING IN THE COOL, TILED COURTYARD OF MY DAUGHTER'S ORPHANAGE, HOLDING HER IN MY ARMS AND SMELLING THE SWEET SCENT OF HER HEAD. I have been her mother for three days now, but the heft of her 15-pound body is already familiar. Looking around at the courtyard and the surrounding buildings, I am filled with such a sense of peace. There are palm trees waving in the breeze off the South China Sea, and fountains and playground equipment make the space inviting. It is a good place to be.

In the months before we knew who Katherine was, I often tried to imagine the place in which she was living. I had hoped that it was a nice place, clean and full of love, but another side of me also worried about some dark and dreary orphanage straight out of Dickens. The minute we pulled up to Katherine's orphanage this afternoon, I knew that my greatest hopes for her early days had been realized. This orphanage is sparkling clean and full of lively children and healthy babies. It is a happy place. The nannies had called Katherine by name, cooing "Dan Dan" and kissing her hands. I knew without a doubt that she has been loved.

The director of the orphanage and the head nanny are talking with our guide. The guide looks up and asks the group of parents congregating near by, "Do you want to know where your babies were found?" I hold my breath a moment. Do I want to know? What if it is a scary place? Do I really want this information? But then, I *must* know. A finding place is a fragile link to my little girl's birth parents. I need to know. I look the head nanny in the eye and say, "Yes!"

The nanny consults a scrap of paper in her hand and then leads me down the drive to the front gates of the orphanage. She points to a spot on the pavement and says my daughter's name. I stand on that spot with Katherine in my arms and am filled with relief and a deep sense of gratefulness. She was left here, yes, probably only a few hours old and all alone, but that no longer seems terrifying. Her birth parents knew of this place. They left her where she would be found almost immediately. They left her in a place where she would be well cared for. They left her in a place that was so very safe. Standing in the spot where my baby's known history began, I *knew*, in the deepest part of my heart, that her birth parents had loved her. "Thank you," I whisper to the unknown souls who delivered my child into safety, "Thank you."

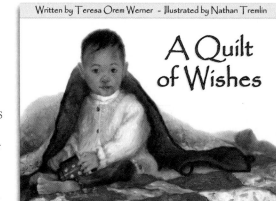

Written by Teresa Orem Werner · Illustrated by Nathan Tremlin

A Quilt of Wishes

Above: This touching adoption story was written by Teresa Orem Werner and illustrated by Nathan Tremlin shortly after Teresa's daughter's adoption from Changsha, Hunan, in 2004.

Below: Siblings—Jeffrey (age 7), South Korea; Natalie (age 2), Changsha, Hunan; and Andy (age 5), South Korea.

Friends—Kylie and Victoria Mei (both age 3) have an especially strong red thread that has pulled them together from Jianxin, Jiangxi, to the Netherlands, and all the way home to New York.

Red thread friends—Phoebe (age 4), Wanzai, Jiangxi; Alexandra (age 4), Danang, Vietnam; Frances (age 6), Gaoming, Guangdong; and Sophia (age 4), Zhuzhou, Hunan.

When the Winter's Done (©1999)
by Teresa Baldinucci

On a quiet Sunday morning in November 1999, I was writing in a journal I had started just after my husband and I realized our first child was in China. As I wrote, I found myself putting a poem down on the pages.

A tiny baby, far away,
on the other side of the world.
A precious child who, someday,
will be our little girl.

We're waiting here, your Dad and I,
until we get "the call"
that says that we're a family;
that love will join us all.

I watch the falling Autumn leaves
and each one's a little prayer
that angels will watch over you
until we can be there.

This Winter will seem very long,
the holidays less bright,
because our hearts will be with you;
we long to hold you tight.

But when the Winter's almost done
and Spring is almost here
good news should come from China
that our "family day" is near.

We cannot wait to meet you
for the first time, face to face,
(Who knew we'd find our daughter
in such a special place?)

WONDERING
by Barbara Gilbery

HAVING ONE OF MY WONDER DAYS! Every moment in the day when I find myself at a quiet time, I wonder when you'll come. Every night before I sleep, I look at the stuffed bear that is waiting for you and wonder when you'll come. Every few days I fret with head and heart that the "file" is lost. Every month that passes I work to keep hope renewed and push negative thoughts away. I wonder how to hold on. Everyone says "stay positive" and you will come. I wonder if I do this enough. I wonder how long I can keep on doing it. I have days of excitement of what will be and days of anger at crazy bureaucracy. I wonder how my head and family cope. I wonder that it is August already and months have flown by. I wonder that the waiting is passing while I wonder!

We're getting things all ready
for when we bring you home;
preparing everything you'll need
to keep you safe and warm.

Each day we're closer to you
our precious little girl.
Your Mommy and Daddy love you so!!
Already, you're our world!!

We haven't seen your face yet
or kissed away your tears;
we haven't held you in our arms
but still, we feel you near.

We know now what God always knew,
that someday there would be
a tiny child from China
who'd make us a family.

So hurry Winter, blow on by;
let cold gray days be past,
for Spring will bring our daughter home
into our arms, at last.

When Mother Earth brings forth new life
with warming from the sun,
Our family's new beginning starts—
When the Winter's done.

Callie (age 6), Hepu, Guangxi.

ON BEING "PAPER" PREGNANT
by Amy Dudley

THE ADOPTION PROCESS HAS BEEN SO VERY DIFFERENT FOR ME THAN MY PREGNANCIES WERE. When I was pregnant, the proof of my journey to motherhood was visible and the "milestones" were obvious to all. I shared every detail with eager family and friends, and I spoke with ease to strangers about my unborn children. With this "paper" pregnancy I find myself more introverted, more quiet. There are no doctor appointments, no ultrasounds and, really, no due date!

This pregnancy of the heart does have its miraculous moments, however. I keep them to myself, afraid of seeming crazy. After all, how do I explain to a stranger that, with one official LID email, I am the future mother of a child I do not know half a world away? How to explain the teary-eyed significance of one tiny hair bow hidden in my dresser drawer?

The answer is, I don't. Instead I gather moments like these to my heart and lovingly tuck them away. With each one my heart expands. Much like my pregnancies, I realize, I am making room to grow.

Written in Honor of Jadyn's Adoption
by Kim Rash
Submitted by Jacqui Moore

God Hears
Cry Touches Heaven
Desire Revealed,
    New Love Birthed
Three Hearts Are Now One

Nicole Doris Lin (age 4), DianBai, Guangdong— celebrating Chinese New Year.

Jadyn (age 3), Hebei. We sponsored Jadyn at the Philip Hayden Foundation and, when she became an amputee, worked to get her a prosthetic leg. She captured our hearts, and now we are a family sharing her rich culture and introducing her to our American heritage as well.

Right: Mia Han (age 17 months), Changde, Hunan.

Below: Sisters— Caroline Bin (age 7), Changde, Hunan, and Sarah Teresa (age 4), Guatemala—with referral photo of new sister, Mia Han.

After six months of prayers for a baby brother or sister, our daughters came home from school to a special surprise— news of their new sister, Han Han. Our oldest daughter immediately burst into tears, saying, "This is what I have been praying for." Several months later, the two older sisters flew to China to meet their much anticipated sister. On Han Han's Forever Day, Caroline looked at her mom and said, "I have happy tears."

Siblings—Blake (age 8) and Shannon (age 8 months), Suixi, Guangdong.

THE THINGS KIDS SAY
by Barbara Ingalsbe

MEGHAN, MY BIOLOGICAL DAUGHTER, AND I HOPE TO ONE DAY BE ABLE TO ADOPT FROM CHINA. One day at the hair salon, Meghan was chatting with the ladies there. After telling the women of her brother and numerous cousins, one of the ladies asked, "How many kids do you want when you grow up?" Meghan replied, "I don't want any 'cause I am adopting all of mine from China!"

Claire Gabrielle Mei (age 15 months), Hunan.

A FAMILY'S SPECIAL BOND
by Joanne Preston

WHEN I WAS IN MY LATE 30S AND BUSY WITH MY CAREER, I RECEIVED A GIFT IN THE MAIL FROM MY SISTER, PHYLL. It was a white t-shirt with a picture of a business woman looking at her calendar and shrieking "Oh my gosh, I forgot to have children!" She and I both laughed about it. She knew I wanted to have children someday and, being a mother herself, didn't want me to miss out on the joy of the experience. When my husband, Bruce, and I announced plans for our first adoption in 2003, Phyllis was, as always, wonderfully supportive. She and her daughter Kathie flew halfway across the country to be at our house before we arrived home from China. They filled our home with welcoming banners and flowers, stocked our refrigerator, and took care of us for the first week. It was a blessing.

For our second adoption in 2005, Bruce and I didn't think twice about asking them to accompany us. Although my sister was in the process of relocating across the country and my niece was in the middle of the busiest season of the year at work, both dropped what they were doing and came with us. Their presence on this trip meant so much. They held our hands, made us laugh, kept me sane and punctual, and took such good care of us. They watched over our daughter Laurie like mother hens, freeing Bruce and me up to bond with our new little Hayley. Before boarding our plane to China, Phyll pulled out a large canvas bag stuffed full of amazing toys and trinkets that delighted Laurie and captured her interest for hours.

Toward the end of the trip when my brain was turning to mush, these two were the voice of reason—always helpful, but never pushy. They advised me on my shopping: "Jo, you've simply got to buy these beautiful velvet dresses for the girls—they'll be perfect at Christmas." "Buy this tea, or I'll buy it for you. You know how you love green tea." I was tired and didn't want to shop that afternoon. I really wanted a nap. Ironically, as I sit here writing this, I'm sipping some of that wonderful tea, reliving cherished memories from the trip, and I am so grateful that I bought that tea. A final treat occurred the day we got home when my sister-in-law, Barb, flew in and took care of us for a few days—another blessing.

My family has been a rock solid support for me all my life. Our photos and written record of our two adoption trips will someday be a document of this familial love that I hope my two daughters will cherish. But best of all, they now have each other and the chance to give to one another the gift of caring, just as my family has given to me.

Friends—(Sitting) Lily (age 7), Anqing, Anhui, and Linnea ZhenQiao (age 4), Shanghai.

We kept this poem on our refrigerator as we waited for our referral. The wording is a little stilted due to the limited words in our magnetic poetry set.

we dream of a tiny baby girl
who lives over the blue ocean
we fly for you before spring
your mom dad and sisters
love to think of you
we imagine her home with us
our future dragon princess
all are so thank full

Three dear friends—Laurie (born April 2002), Nanning, Guangxi; Grace (born September 2001), Maoming, Guangdong; and Hayley (born December 2003), Huainan, Anhui.

Above: Chloe (age 21 months), Guiping, Guangxi, with Dad. Photo taken on the one year anniversary of 9/11.

Below: Siblings—(Clockwise from lower left) Lily (age 6), Anqing, Anhui; Jacob (age 5), Urumqi, Xinjiang; and Chloe (age 4), Guiping, Guangxi.

Friends—Connor XinYuan (age 7) and Jacob (age 6), both from Urumqi, Xinjiang.

Elizabeth LiHan (age 11 months), Hanchuan, Hubei.

She came to us on that day in China with this little yellow Chinese bottle tied with a simple string around her neck and the panda. Those were her only possessions.

Caitlin (nearly age 7), Changde, Hunan, with sister, Summer (age 1), Taihe, Jiangxi.

THE MOTHER'S DAY THAT ALMOST WASN'T
by Susan Huster

LAST MOTHER'S DAY, AND MY FIRST MOTHER'S DAY EVER, I ALMOST DID NOT RECEIVE MY WONDERFUL GIFT—A PRECIOUS LITTLE BABY GIRL FROM JIANGXI, CHINA. My husband and I, in our excitement, could not find the conference room in the hotel where we were to receive our babies. After endless months of preparing the dossier, more months of waiting, hour upon hour of anticipation, and traveling thousands of miles, we were within moments of receiving our little girl; yet here we were frantically riding the elevator up and down and running around corridors trying to find someone to help us find the conference room. We were so mad at ourselves and at each other. How could we be in this ridiculous situation? Could we possibly be fit parents if we could not even follow the simplest of directions? We were frantic that they would call our baby's name and no one would step forward to receive her. We finally landed in the hotel lobby and, to our surprise and relief, as the door opened a line of nannies and babies got on the elevator with us! We squeezed silently into the back of the elevator and rode up with all the babies. As the nannies and babies headed to the conference room, we nonchalantly slunk in behind them. Then we heard the sweetest sound ever. Our daughter's name was called, and we joyfully went forward to meet her— all our concerns and fears forgotten in the wonder of the moment.

Shelby (age 2), Ningdu, Jiangxi.

THE BEST DAY, THE WORST DAY
by Kathleen Brennan

IN AUGUST OF 2000 THE LAST LEG OF MY ADOPTION TRIP INCLUDED A SHORT VISIT TO HAWAII TO GET EXPEDITED CITIZENSHIP (a service that was provided to Americans living overseas). I was looking forward to a chance to relax and to get to know my new daughter without care or worry. That was the plan anyway. There are details and tears that I won't share, but I arrived in Honolulu jet-lagged, stressed, and, through no fault of my own, with my daughter's "Brown Envelope" torn open.

Upon arrival, Immigration and Customs would not accept the envelope. I was heartsick, not knowing if I would have to return to China and redo all the paperwork again. I was exhausted but clung to the slim hope that I could deliver the envelope directly to INS. That night on American soil was probably the most difficult night of our adoption journey. I was beyond tired and stressed, my daughter couldn't sleep, and I had no idea what the next day would bring.

The next day I waited in a beautiful outdoor waiting room with colorful flowers, sweet breezes, a fussy daughter, my tattered envelope, and a pounding headache. My appointment started with shocked disbelief that I would have been allowed to retain the documents in the envelope, and much tssk-tssking. But there were also warm smiles and reassurance that everybody makes mistakes. A lovely gentleman went out of his way to correct the mistakes, and I walked out of the office with an appointment for the following day for my daughter to become an American citizen. She also had her American passport within days.

I will never forget the kindness and warmth of the Hawaii INS staff. That night we celebrated the end of uncertainty, the eve of her first birthday and citizenship day. I have a beautiful picture of my daughter wearing a wreath of flowers that reminds me of that roller coaster day. If you exclude "Gotcha Day," the very best day and very worst day of my adoption trip happened on American soil.

Siblings—Jordan (age 8); Joel (age 35 months), Xianxiang, Henan; and Kenna (age 22 months), Guatemala City, Guatemala.

Siblings—Winter Hope (age 4), Yiyang, Hunan, and Wolfe Haowen (age 6), Nanjing, Jiangsu—holding hands after knowing each other for only a few days.

Kaziah (age 4), Hanzhong, Shaanxi—
enjoying a carousel ride with sister, Kalee (age 17).

Significant Dates
by Jeanna Trugman

When we received our referral for Brighton Noelle in August of 1996, we knew she was meant for our family by her birth date—March 18th. Her birthday falls right between her older sister's birthday of March 17th and her Dad's birthday of March 19th.

When we received the referral call for Briley Alexandra, we were not expecting it for another month. At the time we were getting ready to go out and celebrate our 20th wedding anniversary. I answered the phone and it took me a few minutes to realize why the agency was calling. Another daughter on a very special day. What a great gift for my husband and me to celebrate!

Dreams Come True
by Beth Edgar

Our adoption journey started many years ago while watching Oprah; yes, Oprah! My sister-in-law and I were relaxing, having no idea what an impact those 60 minutes would eventually have on our lives. As Oprah talked about China opening up adoption to foreigners we stopped chatting and hung on her every word. As the show ended we looked at each other and both said, "I want to do that someday." But, as often happens, life goes by and things we mean to do go undone.

My husband and I finally decided that we had talked about adopting long enough. We called a local adoption agency to start the process to adopt from China. There was only one possible hurdle. My husband had a hereditary kidney disease that could potentially be life-threatening. After a few weeks we got an email from the agency saying that China would not approve us to adopt. We were heartbroken.

Six months later we were at a birthday party for a little girl who was adopted from China. There were adoptive moms there and soon the conversation turned to adoption. I told one that we wanted to adopt from China, but because of my husband's possible health risks we could not. She turned to me and very matter-of-factly said, "That's not true; you can adopt from China." That woman will never know what a life-changing impact her few words had on our family.

I found a small agency called Children's House International and entered a request to be able to view a list of waiting children. I clicked on the link of one of the children and saw the most precious baby girl with a tiny little cleft lip. I emailed the agency and was told we could start the process to bring her home. With a letter from my husband's doctor, the health issue shouldn't be a problem. On January 29, 2004, my husband and I and our children boarded a plane bound for Beijing. We met our daughter and sister, Mei Mei, and thought our joy and our family was complete. It wasn't.

As I continued to be a part of our agency's online community, a little boy caught my eye. I emailed his information to my same sister-in-law who had watched Oprah with me. A few weeks later she and her husband submitted a letter of intent to adopt this little boy, soon to be named Seth!

Again a new list of waiting children came to our agency. There was one little girl who had a similar cleft lip and palate to our daughter's. My husband was having lunch with a dear friend a few days later, and she asked what was new in our lives. He told her that we would probably be adopting again. In her generosity she told us to begin and she would help us get started. We called our agency the next day and told them to start the adoption! Liza came home in September 2005. Her cousin Seth came home in November 2005—just in time for the three cousins from China to share a good ol' American Thanksgiving together with their families.

Brighton Noelle (age 10),
Zhanjiang, Guangdong,
with sister, Briley Alexandra (age 6),
Huazhou, Guangdong.

Parrish Elizabeth Cui (age 2),
Zhaoqing, Guangdong,
with Mom on her baptism day.

Meant to Be
by Pamela Wohlgemuth

The journey to my second daughter was truly an experience in trusting the legend of the red thread. In 2000, close members of my family and I met and took into our hearts my daughter, Callie. Her adoption, while truly earth shattering and miraculous for me, was pretty textbook as far as adoptions go. She quickly became the light of my life, and for 18 months we spent time getting to know each other and becoming a family. I then began the journey for my second daughter and what I thought would be another miraculous, yet relatively "routine," adoption. However, on this journey, which quickly became anything but routine, I discovered that the red thread really does exist, and it had wrapped itself tightly around my wrist and that of my tiny daughter waiting in Yangzhou, China.

September 11th changed so many things for my little family and me. We live in New Jersey, very close to the horror of that day. It created an urgency in me to complete all of my paperwork as quickly as possible. I had two guardian angels looking out for me, although I did not know it. As I frantically completed authentication, waiting and waiting for my 171, we drew ever closer to the December 1st deadline that China had set for single parents applying for adoption. What I thought was plenty of time turned into a disaster as the anthrax scare in the fall of 2001 paralyzed the New Jersey government. Envelopes sat in basements, everyone too afraid to open anything. My documents sat while my social worker frantically completed my home study in record time and sent it to Newark INS to be processed. By mid-November I was frantic, convinced that I would miss the deadline and be swept into the uncertainty of the new quota system. By late November I was convinced there was no way I would get all my documents back in time and sent to China by December 1st.

Then that red thread that I wore around my wrist gave a sharp yank. On November 29, 2001, as I was at work as an open heart ICU nurse and more than a little depressed, my social worker called me. "Pam, I just talked to INS in Newark, and your home study is approved. She is mailing your 171 today." I was shocked. I didn't know you could speak to a human being at Newark INS. But there was more. "It's a really good thing," Carolyn continued, "because we just got in a file on a little girl in Yangzhou. She is 15 months old. We didn't know who else to call because she has a heart defect. I know you are an open-heart nurse and figured you might just be right for her." I was speechless. The rest, as they say, is history. Chloe's heart defect was minor and had healed itself by the time I met her in China. She has since grown into a happy, healthy, and energetic 5½-year-old with the kindest heart I have ever seen. I never would have believed how many things had to come together to bring this little girl to me.

"Picnicking Pandas." Original artwork by Carmen (age 11), Kunming, Yunnan.

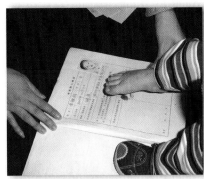

Left: Julia (age 3), Xian'An, Xianning— giving her red footprint for the adoption paperwork.

Below: Julia (age 3).

IMMEASURABLE JOY!
by Gretchen Haugh

喜

July 29, 2006

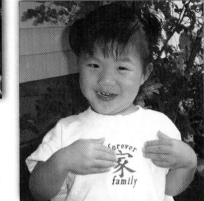

Siblings—Emily (age 3), Dingyuan, Anhui; Jessica (age 12); and Matthew (age 10)—at the beach in Montauk at sunset.

Grace,

For two years your family prayed over you. We prayed over your adoption, your health, your daily needs, and most of all that our family would bring you joy, happiness, and a hope filled future. After many prayers we traveled to China and received you on May 10, 2005. It didn't take long for us to realize that God had chosen to answer our prayers much differently than we had ever dreamed. Your smile, moments after receiving you, was the first peek into the gift God had blessed us with. Moments after your beautiful smile, you shared your "pre-moistened" crackers with me; they were the tastiest crackers I have ever had! You followed it up with a game of bear hugs and giggles. Mommy and Daddy were amazed that you had given us so much in our first hour with you. Your smile filled our hearts with happiness. You were so generous to share your food, and your hugs and giggles filled us with immeasurable joy! It hit me; God had chosen *you* to bless us with happiness, joy, and hope! Since your arrival home, you have continued to be a blessing to Mommy and Daddy, and your older siblings, Arthur, Austin, and Lillie. You are a walking, talking, smiling, running, laughing, giggling miracle from God! We are truly amazed at how God took our simple prayers for you and turned them into blessings for us.

Love, Mommy and Daddy

The many faces of Alana Peilan (age 10 months), Kunming, Yunnan.

Friends—Nichole and Megan (both age 2½)— both from Jiangxi.

100 Good Wishes Quilt: A Wish for AnLi Gute
by Grandpa and Grandma Gute

We gaze into the sky
and dream of you from afar.
We wonder when we'll get you home,
our beautiful little baby star.

Each day we say a little prayer
to our God from up above:
Please send our precious baby
all of Grandpa and Grandma's love.

AnLi (age 11 months), Lily (nearly age 12 months), and Sophia (age 14 months), all from Hanchuan, Hubei.

THE MOMENT OF FAMILY
Excerpted essay by Lana Harrison

I HAD TO WAIT UNTIL THE VERY LAST OF ABOUT 14 BABIES BEFORE MY DAUGHTER WAS GIVEN TO ME. I recognized her immediately, wearing the same outfit that I had sent her a couple of months earlier. At the moment she was placed in my arms, all of my worries vanished. This scared, tiny little angel held on to me for dear life, and I knew then that all was well with the world. The flood of emotions that I experienced at that moment equaled the emotions that I felt as my biological children were born. It did not matter that I had not carried this child for nine months. It did not matter that she was from another country, culture, and race. I was in love! This was my baby! We both hung on to each other and cried—each for different reasons; but eventually the reasons became the same: We were a family!

At age 3½ my daughter still holds on to me when she is sad or upset or just wants a hug. And when she looks at the picture of the two of us at that first meeting, she always comments on how she is holding on to me. I saved her outfit and can't believe that she ever wore it as she has grown so much. And my love, our love, continues to grow.

Sisters—Nicole (age 13);
Emily Jia-Zhen (age 6), Shantou, Guangdong;
Ashley Dang-Zhou (age 5), Yulin, Shaanxi;
and Katie Zhao-Qing (age 4), Yuanling, Hunan.

BECOMING A MOTHER
by Theresa Raphael

I HAD NO CLUE AS TO WHAT I WAS GETTING MYSELF INTO BY BECOMING A SINGLE MOM. But I was pretty sure I could handle just about anything except vomiting. I told anyone who'd listen that I could deal with tantrums, whining, potty accidents, etc. But not vomiting. All my life whenever I'd get one whiff of puke, I'd gag.

It happened on Adoption Day plus three, on the way to visit Lily's orphanage. On a day when I had taken such care to dress her in her new finery from America—a red button-down top, red and white pants, red shoes, and a red sailor cap. Who would expect a highway to be bumpy? And how did I miss noting the sum total of her food intake at the breakfast buffet that morning?

Lily, age three, was sitting on my lap in the car. It took me a half second to comprehend what was happening. I saw it first in the look on my sister's face. Then it was upon us: the congee, the watermelon, the fried rice, the cinnamon roll.

I was stunned. The driver pulled over to the side of the road. He and my sister were looking at me. I was waiting for one of them to snatch her off of me and apologize for this mishap! Another second went by before I realized that they were expecting me to handle the situation… that this was not someone else's kid… that this was not about me.

Lily, of course, was crying. I did my best to clean her off, using all the wipes we had brought. She calmed down but she stunk to high heaven. So did I. So did the car.

We arrived at the orphanage a few minutes later. So much for wanting to make a good impression. I kept catching whiffs of myself (they had spirited Lily away and we did not see her until we were ready to leave several hours later).

I no longer play act at being Mama. Somewhere along the way I realized I could not love another child more than I love this one. But when she vomits, I still have that second of waiting for someone to apologize… and clean it up!

Jillian Mei-Ling (age 5 months), Wuzhou, Guangxi.

Above: Grace Bai Lu (age 12), Dongguan, Guangdong— signing her own adoption papers and making it official that she chose to be in our family.

Below: Lily Rose Yang (age 13 months), Qingxin, Guangdong, with Mom.

THE NAME GAME
by Nadine Cox

THE RED THREAD SOMETIMES PROVIDES AN ASSURANCE THAT A CHILD IS MEANT TO BE OURS. As we waited for our second daughter's referral, we played "the name game." We posted a paper on the fridge and, whenever we heard a name we liked, my daughters and I would write it down and put a star by the favorites. The list was becoming quite long, but my husband, Bill, really didn't like any of the names we had chosen. Finally, a bit frustrated, I asked, "So what name do *you* like?" He replied that he had always liked the name "Lian." Okay, it was pretty, but I was not quite convinced myself.

The next few weeks passed slowly as we waited for our referral. Finally, while standing in the buffet line at our daughter's cheer banquet, the cell phone rang. This was "the call." We had a daughter! After finding out that she was 15 months old, the next question was, "What is her name?" Time stood still as I heard, "Ling Guang Lian." Guang (the same character as her big sister's) Lian—her chosen name was already Lian! My heart raced and tears flowed. This was my proof, my red thread, that this baby was meant to be our daughter. She has now been home just over a year, and I can't imagine calling her Olivia or Hallie or any of the other favorites on my list. She is, and always was, my Lian.

Lian Eliza (age 16 months), Shangrao, Jiangxi— sharing a final goodbye with Director Ye.

Abigail Grace (age 7 months), Nanchong, Sichuan.

ONE YEAR AGO TODAY
by Marla Husovsky

ONE YEAR AGO TODAY, WE WALKED DOWN A DIMLY LIT HALLWAY WITH 15 OTHER FAMILIES TO MEET OUR BABIES. As we walked down that hall, we heard a baby screaming and crying and joked that it was our daughter.

One year ago today, we held that same screaming, crying baby and tried to calm her, even as *we* cried tears of pure *joy*!

One year ago today, we promised to love her forever.

One year ago today, Kaitlynn Li-Jiang became our daughter forever!

Happy "Gotcha Day," Kaitlynn! Mommy and Daddy love you so very, very much!

Big brother Jacob (age 11) and Abigail Grace (age 3), Nanchong, Sichuan.

Kaitlynn Li-Jiang (age 6), Yunmeng, Hubei.

THAT MOMENT
by Margaret Cain-Miracle

MY WHOLE LIFE CHANGED IN THAT MOMENT. It was that moment suspended in time when they placed my daughter in my arms for the first time. There is nothing that could have prepared me for the overwhelming feelings that consumed me. My life had been preparing for this for so many years.

I have a distant memory of always knowing that I would adopt. I even remember announcing this to my family as a very young girl. I think it must have been a whisper deep inside my heart to prepare me for what would come so much later.

I remember the exact moment when my husband, Wes, and I decided to begin the adoption process. We were driving through the mountains on a beautiful spring day when we made the decision. Thinking back to that day, I still get the same chills of excitement.

The next months flew by while we chased papers and waited. I shopped and waited and shopped some more. We were the lucky ones. We waited just over six months for our referral. We knew the day that the call would be coming, and we both stayed home to be together. I will never forget when we heard, "You have a daughter, Xiu Wen, who is at the Xiu Shan Miao and Tujia Welfare Institute in Chongquing, China." Later that night we saw the first picture of our daughter, and she was so beautiful. I could not put down those first pictures until I had memorized every detail of her exquisite, tiny face. She looked so serious, and now the waiting was even harder.

We slept only a little the night before we met our daughter as the anticipation was building. That day is like a blur beginning with the flight to Chongquing and checking into our hotel. We rushed to gather our things and then there was the relatively short bus ride to the Civil Affairs office that seemed to take so very long. We were in the last group to go up the elevator to the office where we would meet our daughter. Then the doors opened, and there *she* was in the arms of her nanny.

Our daughter was not even ten feet from us. I wanted to run and grab her, but, as protocol dictated, *I waited*. I waited the minutes that seemed like hours for them to call our name. In that moment time stood still as we held Lily for the first time. I felt indescribable relief to be holding her along with joy, peace, and love.

It all seems so hazy now—my life before Lily. I watch her play and grow and laugh. Two years have passed since that first moment, and I continue to be in awe of my daughter with each new moment. I am so blessed to have this precious child in my life.

Lillian Christine Wen (age 2½), Xiushan, Chongqing.

Sisters—Lian Eliza (age 2), Shangrao, Jiangxi, and Jenna Grace (age 4), Guangchang, Jiangxi.

Alyssa Li, Yongzhou City, Hunan, with Mommy on their first day together.

IN OUR HEARTS…
by Tammy MacKinnon

WHEN I FIRST SAW ALYSSA SHE WAS CRYING IN HER NANNY'S ARMS. As I came into her view she immediately stopped crying and reached out her arms to me. It was as if she already knew I was her mother. When I was able to hold her for the first time, I knew she was exactly what my heart had been waiting for.

That initial touch of her face, the smell of her, the feel of her snuggled into me was a moment I will never forget.

Chris and I have two biological children, and every day we experience that intense love shared between mothers, fathers, and their children. It astounded us that one look, one touch, one moment with Alyssa was enough to bind us together with that same intense parental love. As we spend our days with Alyssa and our boys, we know God brought us all together because we are a true family—whether from the same biological parents or not.

Siblings—Dylan (age 7), Alyssa Li (age 2), and Caleb (age 9).

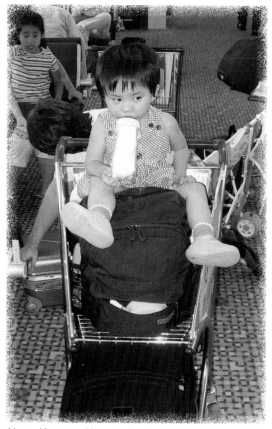

Above: Homeward bound. Veronica (age 22 months), Fuling.

This is in the Tokyo airport and we were headed back to Indiana. Veronica was 22 months old and actually quite heavy. The baggage trolley became a makeshift stroller that worked quite well.

Below: Veronica (age 2), Fuling, and Allyn (age 5), Qingyuan.

Since we brought Veronica home in 2004, I can't count the number of times we have been asked if they are sisters. "Yes, they're sisters."

EVERYTHING HAPPENS FOR A REASON
by Lin J. Kiger, Jr.

WE WANTED A FAMILY, YET WE COULD NOT CONCEIVE A CHILD. God obviously had a plan, and what an architect He turned out to be! Our lives would not be the same without Alexis Nicholle; she is the answer to our prayers. Barely 11 months old when placed in our arms, this little precious life was soon going to leave a lasting impression on everyone whose life she came in contact with.

Siblings—Chloe Xiaxin, Hefei, and Daniel Wenchun, Shihezi, (both age 4).

NOTES TO OUR BROTHER
by Thalia Suppan (age 8) and Wilder Suppan (age 4)

Excerpts from journal entries from our two older children, Thalia and Wilder, neither of whom are from China and both of whom are eagerly awaiting their new little brother, Kunzang Jian

Thalia

Hi Yue Jian! This is your big sister! We love you and we hope you aren't scared. I wanna ask the orphanage if there isn't a way to get you sooner and stay there with you at the place that you live so you can get settled in with us and so you can know that your true family is coming together. I know how to speak a little bit of Mandarin; so if you speak Mandarin, you can tell me hello and I'll understand. I hope you have a happy life and never get scared again. I don't know if you're scared right now, but I hope you never get scared again. Love, Thalia

Wilder

I love you. *Please*… I really want our new brother and if you could send him sooner enough than you possibly can that would be really helpful. And I love you, Mr. New Brother. I have been missing you. I really, really super love you and probably I'll be so excited that I'll tumble over you.

Connor Ian
(born January 2005),
Anhui.

Right: Chloe Nicole Lingxing
(age 6), AnQing, Anhui.

Below: Eleanor Lynne Jiajing
(age 3), Shantou, Guangdong.

Margaret Elizabeth Lewen
(age 17 months), Shantou,
Guangdong—enjoying a blanket
donated by the Waiting Children
China group as part of their
"Warm Cuddly Comforts" project.

MY RED THREAD JOURNEY
by MarySue Zekich

THE JOURNEY TO MY DAUGHTER BEGAN IN LATE MARCH OF 2004 WITH A LITTLE BIT OF LUCK AND A LOT OF FAITH. I was 44 years old and felt my life was incomplete. I had accomplished so many goals in my life but felt something was missing. That something was a child. I had researched different options of creating a family, but my heart kept bringing me to adoption from China. As you may know it is not as easy to adopt from China when you are single. The more research I did, the more I realized that the quota lists were long, and the process could take up to two years. But I knew it didn't matter how long it would take; this was the path I wanted. I knew in my heart there was a special little girl waiting for me.

Two months later I was scheduled to go to an adoption agency meeting. I remember the day vividly—it was raining, I had a broken foot, and I had been informed by the agency that they did not have any single spots available. You can imagine my heartbreak, but despite everything, including the hour drive to the agency meeting, there was something inside me that kept nagging me to attend this meeting. It was almost as if I were being driven to attend.

Once I arrived at the meeting, the office manager informed me that they had just been contacted and the singles list was going to open up in July. She made it clear that I had to get my application in right away. My heartbreak turned to rejoicing! This just might happen! My application was turned in within two days. That is when I started the first part of my journey and felt the first sign that everything would work out if I kept the faith. Since my heart was guiding this journey, nothing could go wrong. By the middle of July I received notice that I had a single's spot for 2005 and that I could start my dossier and have it submitted by December 1st.

Siblings—Chloe Hope (age 2), YuanJiang, Hunan; Alex (age 17); and AnnaLia (age 4), Fuling, Chongqing.

爸

ON SHAMIAN ISLAND
by Vicki Vogt

WE HAVE DONE THIS FOUR TIMES NOW. Four times we have prepared and waited for our newest daughter, each time taking a little longer to share the news with friends and family. Four times we have been asked the same questions, always beginning with the same word. "*Why* are you doing this at your age?" "*Why* when you already have five children 'of your own'?" "*Why* China?" "*Why* another one?"

Siblings—Jocelin (age 3), Jiangxi; Amelia (age 6), Zhejiang; Libby (age 8), Jiangxi; and Lily (age 9), Guangdong—with Dad.

Four times after the waiting and the travel and the much anticipated first meeting, we have arrived on Shamian Island, where the last anxious breath can be released. Each time the island feels more lovely and precious to me.

Is it the luxury of the White Swan that has captivated me? Or the friendliness of the Chinese shopkeepers hoping to entice us with gifts for the baby? Could it be the beauty and history of the old European buildings and the tree-lined streets? Maybe it is in the knowing smiles shared by new parents maneuvering strollers to their tables at Lucy's. Or could it be simply that in our four visits to Shamian, each time with a few more wrinkles and grey hairs, no one there has ever asked "*Why?*"

Sisters—Emma (age 3), Beijing, and Esther (age 3), Shenzhen, Guangdong.

Sisters—Lian (age 6), Fuzhou/Linchuan, Jiangxi, and Maya Grace (age 5), Daye, Hubei—with a 1966 MGB.

THE FOURTH BUNDLE
by Barbra King

EACH OF MY CHILDREN CRIED WHEN THEY WERE FIRST HANDED TO ME. My first three were warm, slick bundles of new life, each crying loudly as they were placed on my chest. Inside my heart nearly exploded with the joy of finally seeing them. Just this last September, my fourth warm bundle was handed to me. Arriving in full sob, she felt sticky and sweaty from the southern China heat. Again I could hardly contain the sweet wonder I felt as I was finally able to wrap my arms around this child. This little one, though, was not new to life. Only a toddler in years, she was much more experienced in loss than I. While her plaintive wailing spoke of grief, the careful use of the scrunched up tissue in her hand marked her as proficient in wiping her own tears. It was then that it hit me that adoption is a place where joy and sadness meet… a place where fear must be swapped with courage.

Above: Selah Dawn Qinglan (age 20 months), Guangxi, with her foster mom and forever mom.

Left: Sisters—Esther (age 5) and Selah Dawn Qinglan (age 2).

THE PARENT TEST
by Anna Tracy

WHAT LEADS SOMEONE TO ADOPT FROM A COUNTRY ON THE OTHER SIDE OF THE WORLD? To open up every detail of her life to a social worker, who until the moment she rang the doorbell of my home was a complete stranger? I sit across from her trying to stay relaxed while she asks me about my childhood and my relationship with my parents and how I manage stress and what I value in life. I lay bare my soul as I fret and worry whether or not I will be approved to finally become a mother. I open up the pages of my financial records, and I willingly walk into the police station to be fingerprinted and searched by the FBI. I do blood tests and criminal background tests, and each and every day it seems like someone else is deciding whether or not I "pass the test" to be a parent. I joke with my husband that if all the world had to go through what we do in order to become pregnant, there would be very few babies born each year!

What could possibly cause anyone to open her life to so many perfect strangers each step of the way? The promise of a child. The hope of a baby. The feel of a tiny hand in mine.

I would walk through valleys and up mountains and across the ocean to finally hold my baby in my arms. Ask me any question… I will tell you. Ask for any document or piece of paper… I will race to get it to you. Please just tell me I "passed the test" and that the child of my dreams can finally come home.

FULL CIRCLE?
by Janet Shoviak

SOMETIMES THE RED THREAD THAT SEEMS TO TIE US TO CHINA AND OUR CHILDREN CAN BE HUMOROUS.

In 1990, I married a guy that had a lifelong interest in cars. He decided to focus on one type: the British MG. MGs are small, relatively affordable; parts are available; and there are numerous clubs to join for information and socializing. I liked to drive a manual transmission anyway, and I always knew where he was—in the garage!

In 1999 and two MGs later, we found ourselves in our 40s, without children and wishing to become parents. After much contemplation, waiting, and paperwork, we adopted a baby girl from China in 2001.

Two more MGs later, we adopted another daughter from China in 2003. My husband had a little too much input with her name, as her initials are "MG."

In 2006, China bought the rights to the MG sportscar from Rover. China also announced that it would build a MG plant in Oklahoma. Hmm… could it be that one of our daughters will someday be an engineer for a Chinese-owned MG car company?

If anything, our girls will be able to use many tools, understand a car mechanic, and know how to drive a manual transmission! They are also good travelers on long car trips.

By the way, two of our MGs are bright red.

Brooke Yu Xin (age 11 months) and her cousin, Melina Fox Gao Yang (age 14 months), both from Wuhan, Hubei—united with their families on the same day.

Emily (born January 2005), Yifeng, Jiangxi.

The Long Road to Emma
Excerpted essay by Meredith Browning Bishop

SOME ADOPTION JOURNEYS ARE LONG. Mine was incredibly long. The paperwork difficulties we encountered paled in comparison to the events that happened after I got to China. Seventeen months after our initial application was submitted, we received a referral of a little girl in Xiamen, Fujian Province. She was 3½ years old—a cute little girl and the perfect age, or so I thought. After I met her, it was discovered that she had cancer, and I was unable to bring her home.

The CCAA worked to find another child for me. Upon meeting a second child—a four-year-old girl—whom I hoped to adopt, the orphanage director learned that the child was no longer available for adoption. Things were not going well. I returned to the hotel and waited.

I waited for two days. Then I got a call. Could I go meet another child? She was just 17 months old. The officials brought in a little girl who had the longest upper lip I had ever seen. Later I learned she looked that way when she was trying not to cry. It took a couple of minutes to risk putting my arm around her, but fortunately this time things did not fall through.

Over the next few days while we played the paper catch-up game, I explored this little girl. She was sick and unhappy, but medicine soon helped her feel better, and by day three she was standing while holding on to the bed, eating bananas by the bagful, and laughing like it was the first time. She had discovered life could be fun. At night I would rock her and stare at that funny little face that grew more beautiful before my eyes as she worked her way into my heart. I was and still am overwhelmed by how this happened—stunned and a little scared by the fact that I almost missed her.

My Emma was meant to be mine, and I can't even imagine any other family for her. I love her beyond belief. She is part of me—more like me than any of my other children. My Emma possesses a quiet self-possession rare in a child and an inner strength built on her complete faith in being loved as much as a mother can love. I do believe in that red thread.

Kameron ("Kammey") (age 4), Jiangxi, with mei mei, Brooke (age 18 months), Hubei.

Emma Li (age 17 months in May 1996), Xiamen, Fujian—being carried by her new mom.

Waiting for Emily
by Christopher and Cathy Treiber

Waiting requires hope and faith that soon you will receive
Expectations of a quick referral is what you need to believe
But time goes by and six months becomes a year
You wonder if you'll ever get a referral
That becomes your constant fear
A little baby girl somewhere in China is of what you dream
As you hear about the reports of more delays,
You just want to scream
To wait for such a treasure is an unbearable test
But we know that we've followed in the footsteps of all the rest
Who paved the way and whose journey took them across the sea
So that baby girls from China would have a forever family
So we pray for our daughter to heaven above
Until we can hold her in our arms and shower her with love
We'll continue to wait for our daughter-to-be
We've chosen her name
We'll call her Emily
She's alive in our hearts and soon we will meet
And then our family will be complete

Original artwork by Maya Alina HongLi (age 4), ZhuZhou, Hunan. According to Maya, the turtle is "swimming to China!"

I Had a Dream
by Malin Björkman

WHEN WE STARTED PLANNING ON EXTENDING OUR FAMILY, I HAD AN ODD DREAM. First it scared me, and then it made me warm.

In the dream we were contacted by Chinese authorities telling us that, yes, there was a child waiting for us, but we could only receive her if we moved to China. So what to do??? We sold our house, had a garage sale, and packed everything we would need to be shipped to China. We bought a house in China— a beautiful house on a slope, surrounded by some trees. We said good-bye to everybody and moved.

Upon arriving in China we again spoke to the authorities. They said, "Well done! You have proved that you'll do anything for your daughter— even move to the other side of the world; therefore she is now yours. You are free to live wherever you wish. This girl is yours."

The dream told me that no matter how much we longed for a daughter and a sister, we had to get prepared, and that, for such a precious gift as a child, there is no offering that is too big.

Ellen YuHua (age 3½), Loudi, Hunan.

Christina Joy (age 6),
Ji'An City, Jiangxi—at our
Chinese New Year Celebration.

Forever Family Day
by Tammy Osborne

Our hearts were forever filled with joy, love, and faith on that Forever Family Day in China.

Victoria Luci HaiJing (age 1),
Foshan NanHai, Guangdong.

Siblings—Nicholas (age 8); Ella YunLan (age 15 months), Gao'an, Jiangxi;
Claire (age 3); and Riley (age 6).

GOING TO GET ELLA
by Nicholas Fraley (age 9)

GOING TO GET ELLA WAS HARD BUT FUN. I'd say the hardest part was the long, never-ending plane ride. The funnest part was definitely getting Ella! I really liked it in China. I got to stay in a hotel room with my papa. We went swimming, ate, and so much more. The people in China were very kind to my whole family. They always wanted to take a picture with us. And trust me it got tiring. We had two guides; one was named Tom and one was named James. I liked them both the same. What I liked secondly was the big, bad Great Wall of China. When we first got Ella she peed on my mom. It was hilarious. Ella's real name is Gao Yun Lan. At least that was her name in China. To begin with we called her Lan Lan because she didn't know her name was Ella yet. I really love Ella even though she scratches me sometimes. I can't wait to go back to China again. My mom says that me and her can someday go back and volunteer in an orphanage together. I would really like that.

Ella YunLan (age 12 months),
Gao'an, Jiangxi—
on the red couch at
the White Swan Hotel.

THE FIRST RED THREAD
by Charlotte Halsema Ottinger

WHEN WE TRAVELED TO ADOPT OUR DAUGHTER, I DID NOT MEET HER FOSTER MOTHER. Instead a favorite ayi, or nanny, traveled with her on the 3½-hour journey to meet us. I didn't give it a second thought because I was so consumed with my own desire to start mothering my new child. I knew the framework of my daughter's early life: found at about six months, in foster care for two years, and then to the orphanage while she awaited her forever family. I did not take the time to consider who had shaped and developed this little girl's personality and sense of self.

Sarah Ning Na (age 3),
Changning, Hunan,
with her foster mother.

Shortly after coming home I started working on my daughter's life book. I sat staring at the pictures given to me by the orphanages—pictures of a little girl surrounded by groups of caring women. A picture of her dancing and singing for the younger children. A picture of my daughter with the man who found her and the orphanage director. These pictures were taken so that Ning Na would always remember their faces. But in this small stack of photos was another picture of my daughter securely snuggled on the lap of a short-haired Chinese woman with a warm face and understanding eyes. The closeness seemed different to me than the relationships in the other photos. There was a more intimate story written on their faces that I could not understand.

I soon came to learn that the woman in the picture was my daughter's foster mom, Luo Shuang Ying, who had cared for Ning Na in her home for two years—bathing her, feeding her, tucking her into the bed that had been in their family for generations, and loving her unconditionally as a member of their family. Ning Na called her "Mama."

Luo Shuang Ying also worked in the orphanage. When the orphanage administrator required that Ning Na move into the orphanage, Luo Shuang Ying continued to care for her there. She would take her on errands to the farmer's market and grocery store where she bought her Wa ha ha (her favorite yogurt drink) and little Jell-O snacks. She would take her home for sleepovers on a regular basis. Her love for Ning Na never changed.

In a quest for more information about my daughter's early life, I decided to write Luo Shuang Ying. I was thrilled to receive her response, but my elation quickly changed to feelings of compassion and guilt when I read, "Your letter eased my missing of Ning Na. Frankly, after she left, things related to her, such as the clothes she had worn or toys she had played with, would remind me of her. I missed her very much, especially when holidays come. Ning Na lived with me for a long time. We were very close. I treated her as my own child." I also learned that she did not bring Ning Na to meet us because the orphanage director said, "You might cry badly if you go." It was then that I began to

Three years later. Sarah Ning Na (age 6).

understand the intimacy of the picture. In the excitement of Ning Na joining our family, I selfishly did not consider the feelings of her foster mother. My heart hurt when I realized the sadness that was brought on by Ning Na leaving and the time and love Luo Shuang Ying had invested in raising my child—her child.

Ning Na and her foster family were brought together by fate in a way no less significant than how our own family was formed. Ning Na's rich story started long before we met her. I know in my heart that Luo Shuang Ying's love for my daughter is as genuine and strong as my love is for Ning Na now. I will continue to remind my daughter throughout her life how much she is loved by our two families—by a mama and a mommy. Even after five years Luo Shuang Ying and I continue to write, sharing the details of our lives and our children, but more importantly, preserving the first red thread in my daughter's life.

Sarah (age 2), Bengbu, Anhui—going back to visit her friends at the Bengbu SWI a week after her adoption.

Travel mates and friends—Mary Grace (age 11 months), Guangxi, and Lilliana Dawn (age 8 months), Gao'An, Jiangxi.

VISITING THE ORPHANAGE
by Lori Woods

WE WENT TO VISIT MY NEW 26-MONTH-OLD DAUGHTER'S SOCIAL WELFARE INSTITUTE IN BENGBU A WEEK AFTER I GOT HER. I was a little concerned about how she would respond, but it was truly heartwarming. As we got out of the car about eight children from her "class" at the orphanage came walking outside to meet her. She left me and mingled with them, sharing the community bottle, and voluntarily gave hugs and kisses to the nannies. She was clearly very comfortable. Then we went inside, where she sat on one of the potties and shared the community food bowl. For the first two years of her life this had been her world. When it was time for our short visit to end, she waved good-bye to everyone and happily came back to me.

Kate HaiYang (age 2), Guilin, Guangxi.

Waiting (words and music ©2004)
by Lance Musgrave

I don't know why the sun don't shine
I don't know why in this heart of mine
I think I may, I think I might
Just need to hold you tonight
But you're so far away
And I'm just waiting
Here waiting for you
And I'm

Waiting
Waiting for you
Waiting, till the time's through
Waiting, to come for you

There's a red thread
Tied from me to you
There's a red thread
That will get us through
So hold on, till I get to you
Just hold on, cause I love you
And I'm

Waiting
Waiting for you
Waiting, till the time's through
Waiting, to come for you

I think I may, I think I might
Just need to hold you tonight
But you're so far away
And I'm just waiting
Here waiting for you

Waiting
Waiting for you
Waiting, till the time's through
Waiting, to come for you

Left: Lynne
(nearly age 3),
Loudi, Hunan.

Right: Dad;
Hannah (age 12);
Morgan (age 14),
holding Merriella Grace (age 24 months),
Shantou, Guangdong; Mom;
and (front) Colin (age 9).

Below: Merriella Grace (age 24 months).

New sisters meeting for the first time. Abigayle (age 4),
Loudi, Hunan; Nathalie (age 3), Tianmen, Hubei; and Madeleine
(age 14 months), Changsha, Hunan, with Mom.

LIFE'S PUZZLE
Excerpted letter
by Wendy Petersen

August 25, 2005

Dear Son,

I have not had a lot of time to sit down and write to you from my heart, but I thought maybe I should take the time to do that now. As you grow up, you will hear us tell the story of "*you*" several times I'm sure, but you may never hear the story of my heart.

You will hear about our miscarriages and how those made us decide to adopt, but there is so much more I need you to understand. God gave me those years of difficulty in order to bring me to you, to give you a home, to give you a name, to give you a chance, and to give me a wonderful son. A lot of times, we can only see the bad things that are happening to us, and it is hard to see the Master's hand at work. You may often ask yourself, "Why me? Why did I have to be born with one hand and why did my birth parents leave me?" Honey, I have no idea, but I do know that God has something very big in mind for you. It is like having just one or two pieces of a puzzle in your pocket. You can pull them out, look at them, hold them up to the light, twist them, turn them, and study them until you are cross-eyed, but until you have the rest of the pieces, you will never understand the puzzle. God gives us just one piece at a time. Your hand, your birth parents, your orphanage, your foster parents, and we are all pieces in the puzzle of your life. We are all a part of the big puzzle. God holds the box with the photo on it. He designed the puzzle, He understands the puzzle, and He knows which pieces go in which order. I hope you will be able to look back on these pieces and say "Wow, God, look what you made!"

We are now about six months away from bringing you home. It will go fast. You have just been moved into foster care; so I hope you will now have a loving family to surround you. I feel your heart beat from here, son. I love you. I know God will take you under his wing and hold you until I can. Grow strong, little man.

Love, Mama

Brett Hua (age 5),
Shantou, Guangdong,
with Mom.

On adoption day we entered the same building we had been in on "Gotcha Day." He began to cry, and it tore at my heart and made me cry as well. I wondered, "Are you hoping you do get to stay with me, or are you hoping you don't have to?"

Our Dream (Waiting for Lucy)
by Karen Soanes

Her face we have yet to see
Her tiny body yet to hold
But our hearts are filled with a love
Yearning to escape and enfold

We see her in our dreams
And our love holds no bounds
As yet so unrequited
A vision that makes no sound
A life as yet to blossom
Our flower as yet to bloom
But our garden, plowed and ready
Our daughter will come home soon.

Sisters—Lucy Sue Lin Fu Dan (age 5), Hanchuan, Hubei,
and Susana Helen Fu Li Xin (age 2), Hengdong, Hunan.

Evelyn Elaine Fu Mei
(age 26 months), Jiangxi.

DEAR ABIGAIL-JEAN
by Karla Castens

May 9, 2005

It's very early in the morning, and I am sitting in your room on the floor. We leave for China later today, and I am very emotional. It seems like we have waited an eternity for this day—and now it is finally here. I am very nervous for the flight but more excited to start this journey.

I think of you in Dianbai, and you have no idea how much preparation is going on for your life. Your baba and I have you to think of now; we know this trip will be very hard on you.

This morning I pray for your safety. I pray that I can be the best mother I can be. I pray that you will grieve with us and let us love you and care for you.

I love you, Abigail-Jean.

P.S. See you soon, my sweet baby.

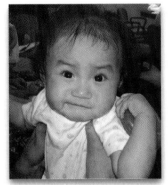

Julia (age 11 months),
Shangrao, Jiangxi.

Sisters—Katrina (age 10); Philicia (age 3), Jiangxi;
and Christina (age 2), Inner Mongolia.

Sarah (age 3), FengCheng, Jiangxi, with sister,
AnnieLynn (age 2), Ji'An, Jiangxi.

Jenna Zhao-Bin (age 11 months),
Yuanling, Hunan.

May 21, 2005

Tonight is the last night you will sleep in your homeland. We fly home to Minnesota tomorrow. I am feeling excitement because I want to have you home. I can't wait for everyone to meet you and love you like we do.

But I am also feeling much sadness as I know this is a choice over which you had no control. We will be bringing you back to China at least once, but it will be different, I know.

My deepest prayer is that you will know in your heart how much you are loved and wanted—and how you do belong in our family. I truly believe that God meant for us to be together. For some reason we were just divided by a great big ocean! But it worked out, and now we are together.

"Then from the same pattern,
    God crafted another person—a perfect match.
And he thought—Someday they will find each other.
And everyone will know they belong together."
–Anonymous

You have blessed my life, Abigail-Jean.

Love, Mommie

The Thread (©December 21, 2004)
by Tom Fisher

I woke up one morning and to my surprise
A red thread appeared right before my eyes
"Oh my," I exclaimed, "How can this be?
This tiny red thread seems connected to me!"

I remembered a legend about a red thread
That connects to the heart instead of the head
So I jumped to my feet and searched for the start
And found the beginning down deep in my heart.

The legend's from China, I grasped what it meant
I knew now for sure where the other end went
It says there is someone I'm destined to meet
A daughter from China would make life complete.

So a chase quickly started for a paper or two
Then three, then four, the pile just grew
The course was quite bumpy and to my dismay
It seemed over time that string started to fray.

The day finally came when we crossed the last "t"
The chase was completed, we were DTC
But then the excitement quite suddenly fled
When we heard the news of the long wait ahead.

The months spent while waiting were really aghast
That crazy red thread became tangled at last
But again it remained an unbroken cord
Whose tugging and tugging could not be ignored.

A referral then came with a picture of you
I saw through the tears what I already knew
The pull on my heart that was so discreet
Was coming from you and your tiny heartbeat.

To China we flew, our ends would now link
As soon as we hugged, our hearts came in sync
This tiny red thread perhaps in a way
Prepared both our hearts for our Gotcha Day.

That wasn't the end of the thread 'tween us two
We're both still connected; our love is quite true
We'll grow so much closer together each year
I love you my daughter, I'm so glad you're here.

Left: Mia Zhenzhen (age 1), Guiyang, Guizhou. This was our first glimpse of our daughter in the arms of her sweet foster mother.

Below: Mia Zhenzhen. I have a family!

Katie Yanyan (age 10), Jiaozuo, Henan.

WE'RE READY!
Excerpted essay by Brian Dekkinga

I AM THE PROUD FATHER OF TWO BIO CHILDREN, A BEAUTIFUL DAUGHTER, 22 YEARS OF AGE, AND A SON, 19. I can hardly believe it, but in ten short days, I'm going to meet my newly adopted daughter, age 18 months, in Nanning, Guangxi, China.

At this point the paperwork is done, the tickets are bought, the fees paid, the home study is complete, two governments have been satisfied, her bedroom is done, and we're ready to be parents! Although this little girl a half a world away has no idea, she is deeply loved already and will soon complete a family that is ready to welcome her with open arms.

Allie (age 3), Cenxi, Guangxi.

LOSS BEGETS FAMILY
by Kirstin Clark (from Wales)

THE LOSS OF A BABY OR CHILD IS THE WORST KIND OF GRIEF ANY MOTHER CAN EXPERIENCE. Yet it is from this kind of loss that my husband and I have the wonderful family we have today.

Our first son, Ifan Morgan, was stillborn in December 2000. His death was the catalyst of our journey to adopt from China. Little did we know that four years later, in December 2004, a mother was losing her newborn daughter, who was destined to bring us great happiness.

I risked my life again to have our second son, Gwion Morgan, who was born five weeks early, on the first of February 2003—the first day of the Chinese New Year of the Sheep. Our first red thread to China! On Christmas Eve 2004 our papers were winging their way to China.

Four days later our daughter was born. Within a couple of hours of her birth she was left outside the gates of Nanfeng Social Welfare Institute.

The wait seemed never ending, but seven months later we finally got an email from the agency in China saying we had been matched with a beautiful baby girl and giving us the medical details but no photos. The official paperwork with photos arrived from London two weeks later.

Seeing our daughter's photos for the first time was an indescribable moment. Gwion had helped us choose her name, Ceinwen, which means "beautiful and fair" in Welsh. Wen also means "color of the clouds" in Chinese; so we thought it was an appropriate name. The photos showed that she was indeed beautiful. We decided to keep her Chinese name, Jiannan, as her middle name.

Six weeks later we were in Nanchang, nervously waiting in a room in our hotel with two other families from the "Nanfeng 7" group. I recognized Ceinwen as soon as she was brought into the room; she looked just the same as she did in her referral photos. It was such an emotional moment. Gwion had been running around the room pretending to be a train but quickly came over to meet his new sister, and he was the only person for the first couple of days that she would make eye contact with. In fact she watched his every move and nearly a year later still does.

Ceinwen has settled into our family very well. Her personality came out very quickly—a confident, happy, chatty little girl who is always very busy. It has been nearly a year since Ceinwen joined our family in September 2005. Grief is definitely a bittersweet experience. Ifan can never be replaced, but if we hadn't lost him, we wouldn't have Ceinwen Jiannan. I wouldn't swap her for anything in the world.

I also remember that somewhere in China another mother has had to come to terms with her loss. I wish I could tell her that I know what she is going through, but I am so grateful that she left her daughter at the orphanage gate. Her loss has helped us with our loss more than she could ever know.

Mackenzie (age 2½),
Qingxin, Guangdong.

Sophia Rose
(born May 2004),
Daye City, Hubei.

Mei-Li Xiao,
Leizhou, Guangdong.

Flying Home in a Post 9/11 World
by Glen Sargent

Not only did our lives change while we were in China, but those of vast numbers of Americans did too. We received our daughter, Yuan Xin Yun (now Sophie), in Nanning on September 9, 2001. Before breakfast on our third day with her, we heard news of the terrorist attacks that have become known as 9/11.

Our first thoughts that September 12th in Nanning, besides being appalled at the unimaginable horror, were that we felt safer in China at that moment than we might in the U.S. The staff at the Mingyuan Xindu (aka Majestic) Hotel slipped a note under the door of each American staying there, expressing sorrow for the nation's loss and promising "to guarantee the safety of you and your family." The hotel offered CNN television coverage of the disaster, which helped acquaint us with more aspects of the day.

Days later during our stay, our travel group had a short religious service at a room in the hotel, both in honor of our new responsibilities with our children and in memoriam for persons who died in the terrorist attacks.

Of a more practical concern we were worrying about whether our flight home would occur as scheduled. All inquiries that we made from then on throughout the trip pertaining to our September 21st departure were favorable. The plane took off from Hong Kong that day pretty much on time, with about 60 passengers scattered around a jumbo jet. There was ample room to spread out, and we were grateful for that.

The flight home was uneventful. When we landed at Newark Airport, it was incredibly quiet, with no crowds flocking along the hallways. Clearing customs had never been quicker for us. The airport itself was eerie for another reason.

We had flown out of it on our way to Hong Kong on September 4th, exactly a week before the airport became the origin point of some of the 9/11 activity.

Someone Is Waiting (©2004)
by Carolyn Cain

Somewhere, someone is waiting,
Though I can't see your face, I know your heart.
'cause God has knit us together, even though we're far apart.
And until you can be here safe in my arms, I will trust,
That somewhere, someone is holding you close and keeping you warm.

My thoughts, my prayers are for you
Father, love her, protect her, I know You do,
And until that perfect timing when our hearts and eyes will meet.
I will rest knowing that You are there… I will trust,
That somewhere, someone is holding you close and keeping you warm.

If time could stand still, our love would bridge the ocean
But know that until then, that even an ocean can't keep me from you
Hold on, little one, hold on.
And until you can be here safe in my arms I will trust,
That somewhere, someone is holding you close and keeping you warm.

This song was written while waiting for the referral of our first daughter from China. One of my prayers was that she would have someone in her life that would provide the love and physical touch she needed until she could be in my arms. When we received her referral, my heart soared when one of the pictures was of her being held by a woman. I knew then that my prayers had been answered.

MiKayla Hui (age 3), Hunan—playing with Dad.

Jade (age 20 months),
Nanchang, Jiangxi.

Lauren (age 5 months),
Xiushan, Chongqing.

Hello, Everyone!!
Excerpted essay by Bryan Clark

We survived food poisoning, U.S. Customs and Immigration, dirty diapers, jet lag, cold meals, sleep deprivation, ketchup deprivation, money deprivation, language barriers, interesting menu selections, and everything else associated with traveling 8,000 miles to another continent and becoming instant parents. You all should try it sometime too.

But we're home—and we have our girl!!!

THREE CORDS OF A RED THREAD
by Mike Mahathy

WE RECEIVED OUR SECOND DAUGHTER FROM CHINA IN KUNMING ON JANUARY 10, 2005. She is our darling Hannah, or Jiao Jiao as she was called by Director Zhao of the Dongchuan Children's Welfare Institute. Our journey to Jiao Jiao started in January 2001 in Foshan where we stayed during our trip of a lifetime when we received our first China daughter, Olivia. We were able to visit children at the Foshan Social Welfare

Right: First photo taken of Hannah (age 33 months), Dongchuan, Yunnan.
Below: Smiling sisters—Olivia (age 5), Zhanjiang, Guangdong, and Hannah (age 3).

Institute. Stepping out of the elevator, our hearts were touched by children, especially the toddlers. I reached down to the floor and gently pulled a toddler girl toward my heart. I chose her because she seemed so lonely. I cried as I held her. I had all the reason in the world to be happy after receiving Olivia. Yet still I cried. After a few moments I reluctantly released the dear toddler back to the floor and left the room. As I looked back at the child, I saw teardrops slowly flowing down her face.

Back home in America, Olivia brought me much joy. It was a wonderful time. Yet from the day we returned home, I hoped to go back to Foshan and adopt the little girl who had captured my heart. I knew that would be a huge challenge. Specific children cannot be requested for adoption. I knew my wife had no desire for another child. In late 2002 I lost my job, and it took almost six months to secure another position. Thoughts of the girl from Foshan almost vanished; yet the memory of her was tethered to my heart by a red thread. I could not forget her. Weeks passed into months. I enjoyed dear Olivia more and more, and people who know me will testify to that. Nonetheless my heart would say, "Mike, do you love the child from Foshan?" "Yes," I would reply. My heart would say, "Find her. Bring home your daughter." Finally in early 2004 the time seemed right, at least for me, at least to look for her.

Drawing by Olivia (age 5), Zhanjiang, Guangdong.

How would I find her? I had very few contacts in China who might help. I asked the agency we had used for Olivia's adoption for assistance. I was unable to get any information from the agency. I asked a friend in Guangzhou if she would look for information in Foshan. I gave her a picture I had taken so long before. My friend went to Foshan and inquired about the toddler. I soon learned from my friend that the girl had been adopted. I was very happy for the child and her new family. I was also sad. I had waited so long to find the darling daughter of China in Foshan. I so wanted to bring her home. That could not be. I later learned the girl's name and information on where her family lived through an Internet group of Foshan adoptive families. I was so happy.

The Foshan daughter had tied a cord of red thread through my heart from her tears. It would never be broken. She prepared the door of my heart for another daughter. A fire now burned in my heart for another daughter. I searched the Internet for pictures of children who were waiting in China for families. I received an urgent email from our agency on July 23, 2004. They were searching for a family to adopt a girl from Dongchuan. Another family had been matched but the adoption was not approved. As soon as I read the email, I knew the girl was my next daughter. At that very instant the Foshan red thread was knotted from my heart to the girl from Dongchuan—Fu Jiao. Jiao Jiao was neither an alternative nor a replacement for the beloved Foshan toddler. They are both daughters of China bound by a red thread of love that speared my heart.

Thank you, darling child from Foshan. From the sadness of your tears, you gave me hope, courage, and love. Even though we may never meet again, you sewed a red thread of love in each of our lives. May our cords of love endure!

MERRY CHRISTMAS
by Suzanne Alvarez

IT WAS A WARM TEXAS EVENING AS MY HUSBAND AND I SAT IN OUR CHURCH LISTENING TO OUR PASTOR TALK ABOUT INFERTILITY. He and his wife had a heart for infertile couples as they struggled for 17 years before they were blessed with a baby. My husband and I were called to the front of the altar to be prayed over by the pastor and the elders of our church. As they laid hands over us, our pastor said he received a word from God and the word was "Merry Christmas." We left the service that night with renewed hope, knowing that we were to become pregnant for Christmas. But four Christmases came and went and still no baby filled our arms. We rationalized that our pastor must have heard wrong and went on with our visits to the various fertility doctors, hoping that they would fulfill our deepest desire to become parents. When the doctors failed, we decided that there had to be a child out there that needed a family as much as we needed to be parents. Our hearts turned toward China. Within three months our paperwork was logged in at the CCAA, and we began the year of waiting. It was a warm fall morning when the referral call came in. The voice on the other end said just two words, "Merry Christmas." I was too stunned to speak, and she went on and gently said, "Suzanne, your daughter was born on Christmas Eve." It took four years, lots of frustration and tears, and finally paperwork sent halfway around the world, but God had not forgotten us, and our pastor really had heard just the right words.

Sisters—Isabella (age 3), Gabriella (age 5), and Annabella (age 15 months), all from Guangdong.

Emily (age 13 months),
LaiBin XingBin, Guangxi.

Sisters—Sophie (age 2), Shangrao, Jiangxi,
and Mia (age 3), Yulin, Shaanxi.

THINKING OF YOU
by Rachel McKellar (age 12)

Monday, June 26, 2006

Dearest Carrie,

I *love* you with all my heart. I don't even know you yet, but I love you already! I've seen pictures and think you're beautiful, but I don't really think it matters. Whenever I think about you, I feel all warm inside. I really can't wait to get to know you! I really hope that you will feel safe, happy, and at home here. We are all working very hard to get you, especially Mom and Dad! I pray for you as often as I can.

You are very special. Don't forget that. Your Heavenly Father loves you very, *very* much! Never, ever forget that!

Love, your (big sister)
Rachel McKellar

WHERE ARE YOU?
Excerpted essay by Stephanie Tait

WHERE ARE YOU, SWEET PRECIOUS CHILD OF MINE? So many keep asking me about you. I feel so alone as I rattle off my wanderings to them, knowing they don't understand what it feels like to be searching for a little face that is seared into my heart but whom I have never seen. How can it be that it feels as though I have lost what I never had? But I am not alone as I search for you—and neither are you, sweet child. He is holding us both close to His heart, and His strong hands are working to bring us together. Hold on, because one day we will be together. Hold on tight, sweet child, and so will I.

Mariah, Zhanjiang, Guangdong, and Emma, Kaiyuan, Yunnan (both age 5)—having fun at Dillon International's 2006 China Heritage Camp.

Drawing by Cassandra (age 5), who drew about 30 of these ladybugs on small scraps of paper as a token of good luck for finding her little sister in China.

Best friends from the beginning. Sisters—Ruth Elizabeth (age 2) and Caitrin Jin (nearly age 3), Maanshan, Anhui.

FAMILY STORY
by Heather Johnson

IN 2002, AFTER YEARS OF TRYING TO CONCEIVE, WE DECIDED TO ADOPT. I found the paperwork daunting. Every time I thought we were finished, another problem popped up. I had difficulties with our doctor and ended up changing doctors and going off of a medication that I long had used before completing the paperwork. Finally the paperwork was filed in May 2003, and we anxiously entered the waiting phase of our adoption. We were told that the wait could take anywhere from 12 to 18 months; so we didn't immediately start actively preparing. We felt that we would have more than enough time. We couldn't have been further from the truth.

In June I visited my new doctor again and learned that I was pregnant. People asked, "Are you still going to go through with the adoption now that you are having your own?" This question infuriated me as if it wasn't for the adoption, I wouldn't be having "my own." If I hadn't been going through the paperchase, I wouldn't have changed doctors, gone off the medicine, and become pregnant. We started to prepare for our life with two children, knowing that we had made the correct decision to proceed with the adoption, but nervous at the prospect of having two who would be close in age.

Our baby was born three months early, but we never once thought to change our decision about the adoption. Upon meeting my baby for the first time, I looked up and on the wall next to Ruthie's warming bed was a picture of a Chinese orphaned child. It was almost as if Ruthie's sister was in the room, like an angel, to guide her through the uncertainty of the next two months in the NICU. I left the room convinced that it was my sign from God that the adoption was the right thing to do.

Ruthie came home from the hospital on January 20. On January 22 we got the phone call confirming that our baby in China was ready to come home too. Having had a premature baby, doctors recommended that one parent stay home with her and another travel to China to bring home our other child. My husband, accompanied by my father, traveled to China. On March 16, Caitrin Jin (Ma Wei Jin) officially became a member of our family.

Since Cait arrived home, she and her sister have been tremendously close. They have helped each other developmentally. Ruthie was behind in her physical abilities. She was a late crawler and a late walker. Cait liked to move toys around to encourage Ruthie to walk or crawl to get them. Cait was a late talker, but somehow Ruthie always knew what she was saying. Years later, the girls continue to complement one another.

Sisters—Meghan FanLi (age 3), Changsha, Hunan, and Rachael LuDang (around age 15 months), YiFeng, Jiangxi.

THE STORY OF MY BABY SISTER: RACHAEL LuDANG
by Meghan FanLi Landers (nearly age 4)

ONCE UPON A TIME THERE WAS A BABY WHO WAS LOST IN THE FOREST. She cried because she couldn't find her mommy or daddy, and she was scared. We were a family of three—Mommy, Daddy, and me—Meghan. We went on a long plane ride all the way to China and stayed in a hotel. When we saw the baby, we gave her hugs and kisses, clean clothes and a ba-ba (bottle), and she stopped crying. We called her Rachael and became a family of four—Mommy, Daddy, me—Meghan, and Baby Rachael. We went on a plane ride again all the way to Oklahoma.

The End

Sisters—Sami Angeni Saltanat (age 8), Almaty, Kazakhstan, and Jaimi Anela YangShuang (age 3), Xiangtan, Hunan.

Brotherly and sisterly love. James (age 1), Taiwan, and Meigan (age 5), Zhanjiang, Guangdong.

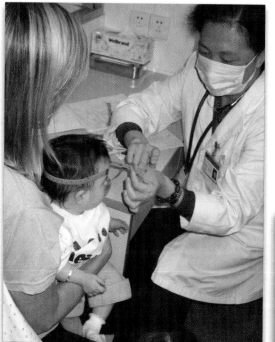

Above: Sophie YaQing (age 1), Xiamen, Fujian. I hope I measure up!

Right: Proud new sisters— Ellie Min Lee (age 4), Guangchang, Jiangxi, and Sophie YaQing (age 1).

愛

WHY?
by Kimber Graves

IT'S COMICAL, REALLY, HOW WE ASSUME THAT ONLY THREE-YEAR-OLDS USE THAT WORD. "Why do you paint your hair, Mommy?" "But why do you have white hairs in your head?" or "Why is Emma looking at me?" But it is not a word reserved only for those under three feet tall!

Over the last couple of years many people have asked us "Why?" "Why are you adopting again?" Or recently I fielded the question, "Why mess up your comfortable family with adopting an older child who might have issues?"

One of the top five life-changing events for me was adopting Anna. Coming face to face with the stark reality that children in our world go to bed night after night without anyone to tuck them in, check under the bed for monsters, or greet them in the morning caused me to evaluate even further what my priorities in life were. I want to be able to look back over the course of my life, knowing that some of it was *hard*, and I didn't always get what I wanted, but that my life was *good* and blessed.

I knew back in 2003, as I stared into the eyes of so many orphaned children, that I simply couldn't return to America the same person I was when I had left. We went on to adopt Emma, who was a bit older than Anna had been, and had a special need. God stretched us a little with this next adoption. These two little girls bring spice and sweetness and excitement, and, yes, frustration to our lives.

And then came Elli. Six years old. Two years with a foster family whom she will no doubt grieve deeply when she leaves them. Why would we want to do this? Because she is lovely; because when we looked at her face, we knew she was our daughter; because we have room in our hearts and our home; because life is about more than me; because her amazing big brother, Ethan, challenged his parents by saying, "How could you possibly say no, Mom and Dad?"

Will it be a breeze? Likely not. Will her joining our family cause some temporary turmoil? I expect so. But how many wonderful things in life come easy? Not many that I know of. I read a great quote recently that sums it all up for me:

"Life is not a journey to the grave with the intention of arriving safely in a pretty and well preserved body, but rather to skid in broadside, thoroughly used up, totally worn out, and proclaiming, "Wow, what a ride!!!"

SOMEWHERE IN CHINA
by Maureen Rielley

IT WAS A DAY I WOULD NEVER FORGET. I was standing in dinner line at camp; my mind was far away from the exciting news that was soon coming to me. Suddenly a young boy walked toward me and handed me a note. I thought to myself, "What could possibly be in this note?" The message in the note was a message that would change my life forever. The note said, "Little brother from China, four years old." I could not believe what I read! This was really going to happen. As I looked out the window into the distant setting sun, I realized that somewhere in China I had a little brother. I thought about him in his orphanage at that same moment. Was he in his bed or was he playing with his friends? I wondered if when he awoke the next morning he would know that he had a sister somewhere in Kansas.

Forever sisters—Dominique Xi (age 5), Xinyu, Jiangxi, and Taylor Xiu (age 3), Nanjing, Jiangsu.

Sisters—ZoraLin MeiHe (age 4), Taishan, Guangdong, and RaeAnne YuQi (age 6), Guigang, Guangxi.

Alina (age 4), Zhangjiang, Guangdong, with brothers, Zander (age 5), Xiamen City, Fujian, and Cameron (age 7), South Korea.

FIRST LOOK
by Sheryl Brewer

OUR WHOLE FAMILY—ERIC, ALEX, AMANDA, AND I—CROWDED AROUND THE COMPUTER and at 1:36 p.m. laid eyes on our precious baby girl for the very first time. It was a moment that stood still in time and is forever etched into my heart. I remember saying, "She is so perfect," and laughing and crying at the same time. She seemed so familiar, like I had always known that sweet little face. This really was the child in my dreams! Just like in "The Grinch," we felt our hearts grow ten sizes that day!

Linzi (age 2), Wuwei, Gansu, with Dad and brother, Alex (age 12).

THREE MOTHERS FOR YUYU
by Marji Hanson

YUYU'S FOSTER MOM AND DAD AND HER WAI PO (MATERNAL GRANDMOTHER) MET US IN THE HOTEL LOBBY SATURDAY MORNING AND RODE IN THE VAN TO THE AIRPORT TO SAY GOOD-BYE. WE had to say good-bye to YuYu's grandma at the hotel because she was taking care of the new baby Xiao Zhen (YuYu's mom) had recently started fostering. That was so hard to pull away from the curb with her grandma watching us leave, knowing that she will most likely never see our YuYu again in her lifetime. YuYu was nine months old when she went into foster care and very thin and sickly. Her grandma practices traditional Chinese medicine and is convinced that she brought YuYu back to good health and cured her hepatitis. Either the medicine or the love and attention made a difference in YuYu's life, and I owe her grandma more than I can repay.

I still can hardly write a word about YuYu's parents without getting weepy. They adore this child, and so do I. YuYu was matched and was supposed to have been adopted in October 2001; she would have been 14 months old. But then came 9/11 and no one ever came for her, and her parents weren't told why. Then her blood work was interpreted incorrectly and her mom had to take her in four more times for blood draws, which made Xiao Zhen angry and so sad that they were hurting her baby and she couldn't say no to the requests. Then the years went by and they loved her more and more deeply and started to worry about her future. They talked to the SWI about adoption. Even their teenage son came up with a plan: He would do well in school and go to university to earn a good career position. His parents only had to support YuYu until he could get a good job to take over her support. Then they got the news that I was coming for her. They told me that they were not unhappy, but relieved. They told me they were content for her future and were only concerned that I would love her. On the ride to the airport, Xiao Zhen was holding YuYu; she had not shed a tear up until now. Then, with tears falling down her face, she reached for my hand across the bench seat, and Matthew said that she wanted me to know that she could stop worrying about YuYu. She stood and watched us go through airport security— me crying buckets, of course, YuYu happy to be on her way back home—until we couldn't see them anymore. The loss and gain of adoption, the pain and joy, all in her eyes. There will be three mothers who will always be thinking of YuYu.

Kathryn Marta Rui Yu ("YuYu") (age 5), Nanning, Guangxi— saying good-bye to her foster parents at the Nanning airport.

Emily ("Emmy") Ann Zhao-Ren
(age 2), Wuwei, Gansu.

Wendy Fu (age 4), Jiangxi.

Chinese culture class. (Clockwise from top)
Miriam (age 5), Chongqing; Ella (age 3), Yuanling, Hunan;
Meilyn (age 5), Yueyang, Hunan; Jolene (age 3); Lily (age 4),
Ruijin, Jiangxi; and Autumn (age 3), Yizhou, Guangxi.

Building a family. Mom and Dad; Anna Bai Ling (age 2), Changsha, Hunan; Rebecca (age 23);
Adam (age 22); and Shoshana Beth Xishun (age 23 months), Chenzhou, Hunan.

Next Christmas
by Tasha Moon

Next Christmas
There'll be more gifts to buy,
More excitement,
More celebrations.

Next Christmas
The house will be a little more full,
A little less clean,
A lot more bright.

Next Christmas
Our laughter will be louder,
Our smiles wider,
Our joy deeper.

Next Christmas
We will cuddle you tight,
Stroke your black hair,
And shower you with love.

This Christmas
Hopeful eyes will look at the moon,
And dream of you,
And of having you home
Next Christmas.

RED THREAD DREAMS
by Michele B. Levin

I ALWAYS WANTED TO HAVE A FAMILY THAT INCLUDED ADOPTION. I drew little paper dolls and cut them out with my cousin when I was ten years old. My play was that the dolls were little orphaned children. I read books by Pearl Buck and admired her. I watched Vietnamese children being rescued and raised in my community in the 1970s. When a friend started an adoption agency, I told her we would let her know when it was time for us to adopt. The years passed by and responsibilities overwhelmed us. It never seemed to be the right time.

In September 2002 our country was talking about how we had to live our life now, and discussions were everywhere about how can we move on. I was in a contemplative mood too. I bumped into a colleague that I hadn't seen for several years and in a warm conversation catching up she mentioned she had a kindergartener. My children, Rebecca and Adam, were in college and I was able to proudly relate their achievements. I then saw Jackie walking home with her kindergartener, her adopted daughter, Suki, from China. I thought, "I always wanted to do that!"

The thought wouldn't leave me, and a few days later I broached the topic of adoption again with my husband, Murray. I said, "I usually don't ask for much…" He called our friend who had the adoption agency, and two days later we filled out our first papers. I knew the country for us was China. China was always kind to the Jewish people and, being the daughter of a Holocaust survivor, this connection and return of kindness was always in my adoption dream.

One of the forms asked whether we were requesting to bring an "orphan" or "orphans" into the United States. Murray and I looked at one another and decided our child may be children; we checked off "orphans." We were so excited and immediately in love with our Chen Xishun when her picture arrived, but she was only one child! Why was there only one?!

We bought baby items and gifts to give to those we would meet in China. I made a 100 Good Wishes quilt, and we waited with new friends in a DTC computer group. Less than ten days before our travel time, we received a heartbreaking call. Our little Xishun was in the hospital and was very sick. She was no longer able to be offered for adoption. We decided to keep to our travel schedule and accepted the referral of Zhang Bai Ling. We got a message from Xishun's orphanage, "Tell family not to give up on baby." We weren't going to give up on Xishun. We just needed to open our hearts to our new daughter waiting for us in China, Bai Ling. With the help of many unnamed people, Xishun was able to get well, and we returned to China to adopt her as a special needs heart baby.

Anna Bai Ling and Shoshana Beth Xishun love to hear their stories. I start "A long, long time ago I dreamed of you when you were only paper dolls…"

A Well Worn Book
by Karen Moore

I REMEMBER THE DAY AS IF IT WERE YESTERDAY. It was the day after "Gotcha Day," and you were standing by the bed in the hotel. You were looking down at the pages of a well worn children's book. It was a hand-me-down given to you by your foster mother. Some of the pages were torn and some had scribbling on them. Huge tears rolled down your cheeks as you looked at the precious book; yet you did not make a sound. How brave you were—only 2½ years old, taken from the foster family you spent the last year with, and given to two crazy foreigners you could not understand. All you had in your possession was the beautiful handmade dress your foster mother crocheted for you, a jacket, a little yellow backpack, a handmade doll, and those two old worn books.

What were you thinking, my darling baby girl? Were you remembering the times your foster mother would hold you on her lap and read those books to you? How sad and helpless you must have felt. Did your birth mother have this same helpless feeling as she placed you under the banana tree?

At that point I made a vow to myself. In addition to my undying love and a safe and secure home, there was another gift I would give you: your independence. I want you to grow up with all the educational opportunities I can possibly give you so you can become a confident, independent woman who is in charge of her life. Never would I want you to feel as scared as you were then. Never would I want you to feel that others are in control of your destiny. That will be your responsibility alone. Finding the new coloring book and crayons I brought for you, I knelt down next to you and slowly distracted you away from the old books to the new coloring book. Within a few moments you were happily coloring away.

That's right, my brave little girl—just as you turn aside from the old books and accept the new, you must also use that spirit to embrace your new life. I quietly picked up the old worn books and put them away with your other treasures. Some day when you are older I will give you back these treasures so lovingly given to you by your foster family. And perhaps when you look at those old worn books again, they will make you smile.

Bliss Chunjie Marie (age 9 months), Hunan—looking up at her new mother.

Our Forever Family

Family photos of Emma Mae Qiu (age 2), Guangxi.

Left: Referral photo of Kevin (age 10), Nanchong, Sichuan.
Below: Brothers—
(Top to bottom) Clay, Hank, and Kevin (age 10).

A New Mother's Prayer
by Molly Moates (March 28, 2006)

A New Mother bows her head to pray
Trusting in God through this adoption phase

Realizing He has the perfect plans
She places her confidence in His hands

A New Mother's Heart reaches out to China
With an overabundance of pure Love

To her much anticipated Baby Girl
A heavenly Gift from far above

A New Mother and Child remain many miles apart
But once joined together both will gain a new start

A New Mother continues to dream of that special day
And waits patiently to bring her Baby Girl home to stay

But until that moment arrives
A New Mother bows her head to pray

That both birthmother and child
Be healthy and safe each and every day

Karlin (age 7), Guangxi—receiving gifts from her foster family.

Book created by Karlin (age 8), Guangxi.

Someone New
by Karlin

We're going to China to get a little sister!
OH!

going to China

ORPHANAGE

flying back home

THE END

LOVED IN CHINA
by Kelly McElwain

Gabriella Chen
(age 20 months),
Dingyuan, Anhui.

THIS BEAUTIFUL LITTLE GIRL IS MINE. I can say that because so many people have helped us become a family. As a single woman I knew that undertaking this journey of adoption would be difficult but worth it all. I never imagined the people along the way that would help me and my daughter in different ways and worlds apart come to each other.

I always knew I wanted to adopt a daughter from China. As I got older and remained single, I decided I would be doing it without the benefit of a spouse. I was introduced to the "special needs" program by a woman named Kelly from the 38th agency that I contacted in early February 2005. It sounded daunting; yet she felt it was something I should consider. I am so glad that I did. After the mountains of paperwork that so many friends helped encourage me to climb and the anxiety of the home study, I was contacted again by Kelly in September with the news that she had a file she knew was meant for me. She emailed me Chenshuang's information, and I was immediately in love with this little girl. Oh, those eyes! I of course said yes, and the waiting began. My friends and family were there to support me. We had fundraisers to defray some of the cost of the process of the adoption, and they helped me to prepare my home and my life for her.

Unbeknownst to me Chenshuang was having her own support team prepare her for life with me. In trying to raise funds for me, a friend found a connection to Love Without Boundaries. Through emails it was determined later that they were taking care of my daughter in China through their foster care system. When I first laid eyes on my child she was being held by the woman that had been her foster mother for the year that I was trying to get her home. I cannot tell you how special it was to know how loved she had been in her Chinese home. I have photos of her foster family to share with her. I will have photos of her from before we were a family because someone else cared enough about her and me to take them and save them for us. We cannot thank anyone enough for all that they did for us on our separate journeys to each other. I just know that we intend to make the most beautiful journey of our lives together as thanksgiving for all those who have given to us.

The red thread that connected us was crossed, knotted, and strengthened by so many people that, although this beautiful little girl, Gabriella Chen, is mine, I am willing to share her amazing little self with all of you, as you have cared for her too.

Cousins—Hannah Elizabeth (age 2) and
Sophia Grace KeLe (age 2), Qujiang, Guangdong.

Allison (age 34 months), Qingxin.
A Chinese policeman is captivated by her laughter.

Grace (age 10 months),
Loudi, Hunan, with Mom.

WHAT I WILL NEVER FORGET…
by Karen Firstbrook

LOOKING OUT MY AIRPLANE WINDOW AT CHINA BELOW ME, and with utter astonishment realizing that in just ten minutes I will be in the same country, under the same moon, on the same ground, as my daughter. *Finally.*

The feeling of complete isolation as we seemed to be the only Westerners in a city of 3.1 million Chinese people for 48 hours. *Lonely.*

Watching the rice fields and villages pass by as we drove to the countryside, realizing that these cinder block homes that look deserted really were inhabited by families, making their living working those fields, washing their clothes in ditches filled with rain drainage, and hanging those same clothes to dry out their windows as the rain continued to fall. *Humbling.*

Walking down the hallway in the hotel and seeing others from our travel group for the first time. Total relief. Others are here! More are coming. The sense of community and camaraderie began. *Relief.*

Those last few minutes before we boarded the bus for the Civil Affairs Office. It was like waiting in the doctor's office to see if you really are in labor. Are they going to send me to the hospital? I think today is the day! And then you're told, "All aboard!" and off we go, to all become parents together! *Amazing.*

Standing in the room at the Civil Affairs Office, thinking our babies are just outside. I don't think I can breathe one more time. I don't think I can wait one more second. Oh, but wait, they aren't here yet. Let's wait just a few more minutes, a few more breaths. *Torture.*

Taking Katie Mei into my arms for the first time. This big lug of a baby—hot, sweaty, screaming, terrified. All other thoughts left my brain. All I could think of was love her, comfort her, protect her, help her. *Overwhelming, all-consuming love.*

Back at the hotel with Katie Mei we washed her up, changed her clothes, and sat her on our lap.

It was just like that first night home from the hospital with the girls. Now what do we do with her? *Familiar, yet terrifying.*

Waking up Tuesday morning and lying in bed with Ron, he said, "This is just like Christmas morning. You know, when you wait for your parents to wake up so you can unwrap your gifts. I can't wait to unwrap this baby and find out what she's like!" *Sweet anticipation.*

Hanging out in the playroom and watching all the other babies happily sit on the floor and play and talk and coo, while Katie Mei sits on my lap, unsure and full of attitude. Another mom lures her onto the floor with the promise of bubble fun. And suddenly it happens. I hear her laugh. I see her smile. It's as sweet and beautiful and wonderful and precious as I knew it would be and as I longed for it to be. *Magical.*

Watching quietly from the corner as a newly adopted 3½-year-old daughter struggles to bond with her new parents. Smiling as she begins to play ball and catch and bubbles, the laughter and the smiles begin. And then we hear it, "Momma." She has done it; she has started to recognize her new mom. And tears, laughter, and joy erupt in that room. *Priceless.*

Lying in bed with my daughter across my chest. Looking into those beautiful eyes, her hand on my chest. Long-awaited moment. I know there will be more to come. But for that moment, all the paperwork and stress and waiting and longing melts away. We knew it would, but now it has happened. God is good. *Very good.*

Shei Lin (age 3), Hefei, Anhui.

Rebekah MeiLyn (age 22 months), Fenyi, Jiangxi.

The One I Waited For
by Kenda Hall

It started as a dream God placed deep inside my soul;
I knew that we would need you to make our family whole.
But waiting for God's timing was as hard as it could be;
Some days I wondered if the dream would ever come to be.
For days turned into months, and months turned into years,
And there were times the thought of you would only bring me tears.
But most days I could hear God whisper softly in my ear,
"Keep waiting and believing and one day she will be here."
Then we began our journey down the road that led to you
A very different journey than what many families do.
Our road was lined with paperwork and standards we must meet,
It took months but one day all the papers were complete.
We took them to the post office, it was a joyous day.
Then we waited and we waited and we waited and we prayed.
We prayed for your dear birth mom who paid the highest price.
Selflessly she let you go, a loving sacrifice.
We prayed for your kind caretakers who loved you as their own,
And for your sweet director who made your orphanage a home.
But most of all we prayed for you, our daughter far away
That angels would surround you and protect you through the day.
That you would want to laugh and love and learn and all the while
Somehow you would feel our love across the many miles.
Then one great day in our mail a package did arrive
We stared at your sweet picture and we cheered as we cried.
Before we knew it, we were on a plane across the sea
Anxious for the moment that very soon would be.
Finally, the day came that forever changed our lives.
From the moment that we saw your face we knew that it was right.
God's timing had been perfect, He had led us straight to you
You are the only one who could make my dream come true.
And I want you to know that no one could love you more
For you, my precious girl, are the one I waited for.

Jamisen (age 1), Chenzhou, Hunan.

An Unfinished Story
by Kathy L. Davenport

Excerpted from memoir first printed in the February/March 2006 issue of "Adoption Today"

I HAVE PICTURED HER IN MY MIND MANY TIMES: her olive skin and almond-shaped eyes, her petite framed body. This is the little girl I will travel to the other side of the world for. Her culture will become mine, and mine will become hers. We will blend our lives in ways that will change the two of us forever. This innocent child, as yet unknown to me, will become my daughter. This is a story waiting to be told.

The waiting time is the most difficult of all as fears and doubts creep into my thoughts. What if I am not a good parent? Am I too old for this? Am I prepared for the major changes my life is soon to undergo? And for me, the chronic worrier, the thoughts are sometimes bizarre. Tom says he believes I lay in bed at night worrying about not having something to worry about.

For now, though, I try to put these dark images behind me as Tom and I look to the future with faith and hope. Every news article about China attracts our attention, while any mention of adoption causes us to stop and listen. And every time I see an Asian child, I dream of my own little girl who will call me Mommy.

Somewhere on the far side of the world, another woman will give birth to a child. Because of the circumstances, whatever they will be, she will make the most difficult decision of her life. Her decision will unite us across the world with the love for a child, both her daughter and mine. From this union, a beautiful story will unravel. I only know the beginning now because the story is unfinished. My heart eagerly anticipates the next word, line, and chapter, for this will be the story of a lifetime.

Hope Noelle AiFu (age 22 months), Fuling, Chongqing.

Above: Lane ("Lanie") Gabrielle JiJie
(age 3), Datong, Shanxi.

Below: Madison ("Maddie") Noelle Wanjun (age 7), Nanping, Fujian,
with red thread best friend, Natalie Ting (age 5), Yuanjiang, Hunan.

THE ANSWER TO THE QUESTION, "WHY?"
by David Cline

WHY ADOPT A CHILD WHEN YOU CAN JUST HAVE ANOTHER ONE OF YOUR OWN? Why China? Why another girl? Five girls, are you crazy?

All those questions have crossed our minds too. And a lot of "what ifs." But as I sat up late one night last summer, I gained the perspective I needed. I was reading in our camper on the lake, and the girls and Shelly were already asleep. I read a familiar passage, "Where your treasure is, there your heart will be also." I asked myself what that really meant to me. What really is my treasure?

It didn't take long to figure out that for me my treasure is my kids, my wife, and the relationships with the people I love. That to me is real treasure. I began to ponder my life: where I had been and where I was going. Then I realized I will never be rich, never be famous, or may never be great in the eyes of the world… I realized that those things were not important to me. But my life will count for something.

Shelly and I asked ourselves if we were willing to open up our lives to a child we had never met. I wondered, "What does an adopted child really need?" Would she need designer clothes, an Ivy League education, or a wedding that would be featured in the society page? You wouldn't believe how many people have said to me, "Wow, that means five college educations and five weddings! Are you nuts?" That's when I began to think about children in orphanages around the world who have no home or family of their own.

So we took an inventory of our lives and realized that we had a little extra room, extra clothes, plenty of food, and a whole lot of love to give. Then the decision was easy. Shelly and I believe with all our hearts that God gave us a passion for adoption and for the children in China. We believe that God has called us to this journey and so far it has been an incredible ride.

As for all the money and the weddings and the stuff, we believe that God will provide for our every need. And we believe that the blessings we receive from our daughter will far outweigh the blessings we give to her. After all, it is the adventure and the journey in life that makes life worth living.

Sisters—Kenna FuQian (age 2), Jiangjian, Chongqing,
and Kiley HanLu (age 3), Harbin, Heilongjiang.

Siblings—Katie ("Tong Tong") (age 5), Xinhui, Guangdong,
and David Xuefeng (age 3), Chengdu, Sichuan.

BECOMING A FAMILY
Excerpted essay by Sharadon Smith

AS A LONG-TIME SINGLE PERSON, I LOVED MY JOB AND CIRCLE OF FRIENDS BUT CONTINUED TO HOPE FOR THE CHANCE TO BE A MOTHER. In my mid-thirties I decided to do something about it and started the adoption process. I chose China because I had lived in Singapore and had fallen in love with Asian children.

The wait seemed to take forever, but I did have one wonderful distraction. I began to date a co-worker's cousin. When we started to get serious, I told him, "I may look single, but I come with a child attached." He looked a little bewildered until I explained about my adoption that was in the works. Luckily Edison loves children and was willing to be part of the adoption.

Trying to plan a wedding when you don't know when you'll get the "adoption call" was tricky. I have always believed God watched over us because it turned out that we were married one day in Idaho and left the next day for China to pick up our daughter, Tessa Mei-lin. We always joke that she was our honeymoon baby. When she was placed in my arms, we looked deep into each other's eyes. Hers seemed to say, "Hi, Mom. I've been waiting for you." And mine said right back, "Hi, Daughter. My arms are right where you belong."

Sisters—(Second from left) Katy (age 3), Yulin, Shaanxi, and (far right) Molly (age 1), Zhangzhou, Fujian, with cousins, (far left) Mariah (age 11) and (third from left) Makayla (age 7).

Ava Rae Cheng (age 4), Yueyang, Hunan.

WE'RE A FAMILY NOW, AGAIN!!
by Kevin Jenkins

WE'RE A FAMILY NOW!! Stacey and I were married in June 1997. Stacey's son, David, then age six, was our ring bearer. We shared our wedding night, the three of us, playing games in our living room. This was the best night of my life, until the next night, then the next, and so on. We're a family now!!

As Stacey and I discussed adoption in the years to come, my response was always the same: "I feel perfectly content with our family just the way it is right now, but I know that I will also be just as happy if we adopt." I am the youngest of six children and have always loved the camaraderie between us. Stacey shares a wonderful kinship, in addition to the same birthday, with her only sister. We both knew that with David's big heart he was the perfect big brother for a little sister. Adoption, here we come.

We're a family now, again!! Ava Rae Cheng Jenkins completed our family on August 31, 2003, at age 11 months. This was the best day of our lives as a family, and then the next day, then the next, and so on.

Katy (age 4), Guangxi, with Mom.

MEETING MY DAUGHTER
by Stephanie Petkie

AFTER A YEAR AND A HALF OF WAITING AND WONDERING ABOUT OUR CHILD, WE ARE MIRACULOUSLY LEFT WITH ONLY A FEW REMAINING MINUTES. My eyes fixate on the clock while tears start trickling down my face. I am overcome with emotion. I feel excitement and relief. Years of infertility and longing are finally behind me. In 30 minutes I will meet and hold my new daughter for the first time. My dream is coming true.

As we drive to the government building where our babies are waiting for us, I hear some of the other expectant mothers chatting. On our last flight from Hong Kong to Nanning, many of them took the time to carefully write down an elaborate list of questions to ask the caregiver of their child. I wrote down a few questions too and reminded myself to be sure to have them answered when I received the baby.

After a short bus ride, we arrive at the government building. My attention immediately goes to the sound of hammering and drilling inside the building where workers are busy remodeling and repairing rooms. Our facilitator leads us into an empty room surrounded with numerous flags representing China and other countries. The room is also adorned with a large red, roped wall hanging. Red is very lucky in China, and the wall hanging immediately reminds me of the red thread legend and the destiny that has brought us all together. Outside the room, a few minutes later, we see nannies standing in a line holding babies—our babies. "Which one is mine?" I wonder. They are all so beautiful.

The moment is surreal. Before I know it, one of the beautiful babies is placed in my arms. I gaze at her tiny body in my arms and then at those big, frightened brown eyes looking up at me. I am holding my daughter. She is perfect. I drink in her beauty, her almond-shaped eyes, round cheeks, and pouty lips. "We have a baby," I tell my husband. "We are parents."

I never did ask the caretaker any questions because I never saw the person carrying my daughter. My eyes only focused on the little beauty placed in my arms. I couldn't see anything else except for her. After all the years of yearning for a baby, I knew that God had blessed me. She was the one that I had waited so many years for—the perfect one for me.

Siblings—Christopher (age 17) and Tiana (age 2), Hanzhong, Shaanxi—hunting for Easter eggs.

Raines' first Easter with his family. Edie (age 4), Guixi, Jiangxi; Rosalie (age 5), Jiaozou, Henan; and Raines (age 2), Kunshan, Jiangsu.

Hanna Bu Yun (age 3), Fuzhou, Jiangxi.

WAITING
by Claudia Progelhof

AS WE WERE WAITING FOR OUR FIRST DAUGHTER, HANNA, A POEM HUNG IN MY CUBICLE AT WORK, and I would read it a thousand times a day in the hopes that she would feel our love and know that we were coming soon.

Now as we wait for our second daughter, it once again hangs in my cubicle at work, and I read it every day at least a thousand times and send my kisses to a faraway land. Hanna and I now look at the moon at night and send kisses to "baby sister."

A HAPPY ENDING!
by Kathy Lowe

OUR THIRD DAUGHTER FROM CHINA, KENZIE, WAS DEFINITELY MEANT TO BE OURS, and for that I will forever be grateful to God, her birth family, and the family who, through circumstances I will never know, disrupted her adoption in China. I know that might sound strange, but I know this child was meant to be ours, and she needed to find her way to us.

When Kenzie first became available for adoption, we couldn't have been chosen to be her family because we were already in China adopting our second daughter, Abby. When we returned home with Abby, I still had a gnawing inside that someone was missing from our family picture. I started looking on agency waiting child lists, thinking we might find our daughter there. Five months later the new lists came out, and there she was! I knew she was ours, but there were several obstacles that we had to overcome. We hadn't been home the typical six months we needed to be to submit a dossier, Kenzie was only two months younger than Abby, and financially I was wondering if we could swing it. Every challenge was surmounted, and we started paperchasing. In the meantime we were told that this child's adoption was disrupted in China. We did as much research as we could on disruption and her special need. Nothing scared us because we knew she was ours.

Kenzie has been home almost a year now, and she is a ray of sunshine and the light of our lives. Her health is perfect, she is thriving, and she is home with her forever family. There is a happy ending to a difficult beginning for her. We found each other and that's what is important.

Yalei (age 2), Nanfeng County, Jiangxi, with brother, Vasile (age 5), Romania— looking at the koi pond at the White Swan Hotel.

Sisters forever.
Kylah (age 4), Yongzhou, Hunan; Kenzie (age 2), Fuling, Chongqing; and Abby (age 2), Pingxiang, Jiangxi.

WAITING FOR ZACH
by Kimberlie Meyer

WE FIRST MET ZACH THROUGH HOLT INTERNATIONAL'S CHILD SPONSORSHIP PROGRAM. We had signed up as sponsors in 2002 because our niece was adopted from China through Holt. We requested to sponsor a girl of any age from China. We were matched with three girls in very quick succession. When the third girl, Hua, was adopted in July 2003, we were sent a picture of a lively little boy, Jin Zhenfei. Zhenfei was two years old at the time. He was so cute, he captured our hearts immediately. We had started to think about adoption as a way to start our family. We said to ourselves, "Too bad we can't adopt Zhenfei. He's our boy."

Each quarter we received an update about Zhenfei with a picture. His updates indicated he was healthy and happy. Every time we got our sponsorship update I would open it up, dreading that he was no longer "ours" and relieved to find the latest information about him. The update in March 2004 indicated he had started school and cried the first day when his foster mother dropped him off. In July 2004, at age three, he had learned to like school and got along great with other kids. He liked to play football (soccer, we assume) with his foster father and the neighborhood children. He liked to sing and dance when happy. He liked to draw and color. Once again we remarked, "Wish we could adopt Zhenfei."

Later that month we started our own adoption journey. We applied to a local agency for their China program. We knew that most likely we would be adopting a girl of just under or slightly older than a year. We were thrilled! In September my mother came to visit us for my birthday. One day she looked at Zhenfei's picture on our refrigerator and said, "Why can't you just adopt him?" I explained to my mother that we would love to, but he was not available for adoption.

Fast forward to November 13, 2004: Our dossier documents were coming together, and we were greatly anticipating a daughter. That afternoon I received the latest issue of Holt's monthly magazine highlighting adoption. I flipped open the magazine, and it opened to the "Waiting Child" page. In the bottom right corner was a picture of a little boy with the name "Zach" typed across the top. My heart almost stopped. It was our boy—Zhenfei. I looked at the description for the birth date just to make sure it matched. Yes, it was the same. I ran into the kitchen and pulled the picture off the fridge to double-check once more. Yes, it was definitely our boy. My husband was there, and I said, "Look! It's our boy. He's available for adoption!" My husband took one look and said, "We need to call them about adopting him." No hesitation, no doubts. We called that evening but were disappointed to find out that the person we needed to speak with was out of the office. She would call us the next week.

Our talk with Holt's director of the Waiting Child program left mixed feelings. On the one hand, we heard more about his situation and his particular "special

Zachary Paul Zhenfei (age 4), Guiping, Guanxi. This photo was taken in early winter 2005 as Zachary experienced his first snowfall and winter ever.

need." On the other hand, she mentioned there were other families interested in him, and the fact that we would be first-time parents was a concern when adopting an older child. My emotions ran the gamut from desperation that we *had* to be his family, to nervousness about adopting him at almost four years old, to relief that if we were not chosen to adopt him then he would at least have a forever family. After a couple weeks' consideration and reviewing his medical records, we decided he was, after all, our boy if Holt's Waiting Child Committee would choose us.

Meanwhile we waited. We amused ourselves by discussing what we might name him. In the end we decided Holt had it right. Zach means "God has remembered." So we chose the name Zachary because God has certainly remembered.

On August 23, 2005, Paul and I traveled to China to start the last phase of our journey to our son. Seven days later in Nanning, Guangxi Province, we met our son and became a forever family.

"Our son." That's a phrase I never thought I would say. God has truly remembered.

Lilli Mali MeiHui (age 8 months), Suichuan, Jiangxi.

Top 11 Reasons for a "Wait"
by Tessa Hill

11. Simplifies hair maintenance as there is less hair since most of it has been ripped out

10. Allows time for more things to be repeatedly put in and then pulled out of a suitcase (i.e. Packer's Neurosis)

9. Keeps relatives who are going to help while you're away in a confused uproar over their schedule

8. Allows time for more people to ask, "So have you heard anything??????"

7. Continuously postpones any vacations that could possibly sap "Pearl Money" (i.e., money for China trip)

6. Allows more time to act like an "expert" on APC (what else have you got to do?)

5. Results in more time to eat fortune cookies and get a "good one"

4. Gives more shopping time for cute little baby things, which you can't pack because of reason #10 (see above)

3. Keeps your schedule simple: "Can't plan anything for the next nine months because I heard I *might* be going to China this year!"

2. Results in looney, obsessive, irrational behavior in the "Waiter"

1. Creates great bond with fellow adopting families who are the *only* ones in the world who understand!!

FIRST MEETING
Excerpted email by Elizabeth Lambe

OUR NEW DAUGHTER HAD BEEN ON A HOT BUS FOR OVER AN HOUR AS THAT IS HOW LONG IT TAKES TO GET FROM XIANGTAN CITY TO CHANGSHA. She was immaculate—dressed in shorts, shirt, socks, and little sneakers. She was very quiet, but not crying, and just sort of sat there looking at us. The nannies were all dressed up for this special occasion. We talked to a guy who works at the orphanage and some guy who is with the local CCAA (the adoption branch of the Chinese government.) One of them seemed to know her quite well and told us her nickname is Xiang-Xiang, pronounced Shei-Shei. We think it is cool she has a nickname. Anyway she was totally quiet, looking at us with big eyes—first me, then Steve; going back and forth. We gave her a cookie and eventually a bottle, which she took, but she didn't talk or make a sound or anything. The first real reaction we got from her is when we went to dinner. I gave her a piece of chilled watermelon and her face lit up. You could tell she thought I was pretty weird looking but had some darn cool snacks. She had six teeth and was clearly teething. Then later at dinner, after eating a piece of broccoli, she made some cooing sounds and sort of perked up. When we went back to the room, the party began. She was rolling around on the bed, laughing and smiling. She loved it when we played "peek-a-boo." A totally cool little girl. We couldn't believe it. We were expecting the worst and it didn't happen… at least so far.

Leah (age 15 months), Xiangtan, Hunan.

Discovering the Thread
by Ruth Mayo

FOR 16 YEARS MY HUSBAND AND I HAD TRIED WITHOUT SUCCESS TO HAVE CHILDREN. We had given up hope of ever being parents. One night I went to a needlework meeting. I started talking with a woman who was new to the group, as was I. She told me she had wonderful news. Her paperwork had gone to China so that she and her husband could adopt a baby girl. She was so excited. She went on to tell me all about the process. I went home very excited and told my husband, "Guess what—we can adopt from China!" We had looked into adoption ten years before, but it had not been the right time.

My husband was really surprised. We discussed the matter at length. For some reason (maybe the shorter wait), we decided to adopt from Cambodia instead of China. It was not meant to be. We put in our paperwork in November 2001, and Cambodia shut down adoptions to the United States in December of 2001. We decided to start the China adoption process.

We received a referral in March 2004 for our daughter, Christina, from Zhangye SWI in Gansu Province in northwestern China. She was 10½ months old when we met her in Lanzhou on April 18, 2004. She is now three years old and waiting for her baby sister or brother from China.

My best friend from college told me one day recently, "I never thought I would hear you say that you were going to adopt from China!" When she met me the only trip I had ever made out of the state of Virginia was to Florida to Disney World when I was 12 years old. I had lived in the same house in rural Virginia until I went to college at Virginia Tech when I was 18.

My wonderful husband gave up his dream of a red sports car when he became a daddy at 40 years of age. He jokes that for his midlife crisis he went to China to adopt a wonderful little girl. We can't wait for our referral for our second child.

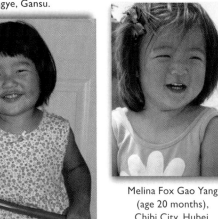

Christina Hui (age 3), Zhangye, Gansu.

Melina Fox Gao Yang (age 20 months), Chibi City, Hubei.

Lydia Ann XiuAi (age 12 months), Xiushan, Chongqing, with her mother.

Mikayla (age 4), Qidong, Hunan, with brother, Robbie (age 12).

Much Wanted
by Teri Waite

A FEW MONTHS AFTER THE BIRTH OF OUR FOURTH AND FINAL CHILD, A BEAUTIFUL LITTLE GIRL, I sat in my son's room and cried as I packed up all the little clothes I had been saving for our next son. We knew before the birth of our daughter that we wouldn't be able to have any more children, but my heart ached for the son I knew was missing from our family. His name was to have been Connor. Most people would say that four children is enough, that I should be content with the children we had, and I was, but I had long felt that we would have a second son. I grieved the loss of that child I would never know. The years passed, and I was mostly content with my life, except for the fleeting ache in my heart when I held the newborn sons of my friends and family.

Then in April 2001 I met a woman who had adopted a beautiful little girl from China. I was enthralled as she talked about her experiences. As I went home that day, I was not thinking of adoption but wondered how I could get involved in helping orphaned children in China. I went online and got involved with some charities working in China and the China adoption community. I was reading posts on the APC Yahoo group one day when I found the story of a little boy who captured my heart. His name was Yuan, and a charitable organization was reporting on the heart surgeries they were performing on him and a few other children. I followed the progress of these children and found myself returning often to stare at the picture of this tiny two-year-old boy. I didn't know at first that he was our son; just that there was something special about him. One day I found myself thinking, "I wish we could adopt him." And then it hit me: "Why couldn't we?"

A pre-identified adoption is not for the faint of heart; as a matter of fact, we were discouraged by almost everyone we talked to. However our agency agreed to try, and, after many, many months of waiting, hoping, and praying, we were finally able to bring our then 3½-year-old son home in August 2002. He is a wonderful addition to our family.

Even though the name Connor had become quite popular, I knew that was his name, and I never considered changing it to something else. When we were in China, many times people would ask us what Connor meant. I had to admit I didn't know. I didn't realize that the meanings of names held so much importance in China. It wasn't until we got home that I looked it up and found that Connor means *much wanted*.

Siblings—Linnea ZhenQiao (age 4), Shanghai, and Connor (age 7), Urumqui, Xinjiang.

Written at 2:30 a.m., by lamp in the hotel bathroom, hours after adopting Molly Feng
by Edorah Frazer

They told us she might scream for days.
They told us she might withdraw, shut down, implode.
They told us she might have scabies, boils, rashes,
    fevers, infections, worms, Mongolian spots.
They told us she might fear us, reject us, or simply
    not care.
Instead, she sparkles.
She sings and dances.
She's patient and kind.
No one prepared us for this.
We wash each other with blessings.

Olivia Joy
(age 16 months),
Jianxin, Jiangxi—
wearing sunglasses
on her head
just like Mom.

QUIETLY WAITING
by "Daddy Bob" Dickey

BEST I REMEMBER, WENDY WAS JUST ABOUT AGE 14 THE FIRST TIME SHE TOLD ME SHE WANTED A BABY OF HER OWN. As a typical father of a teenaged daughter, I worried about that for the next half dozen years or so. When she married the high school buddy who had always been her best friend and became her sweetheart, I just knew I'd be a grandfather in short order. But I waited. Quietly. Mostly.

And waited.

They tried and tried and went to all the different doctors and tried all the different treatments. I think I remember some mention of "eye of newt and tongue of frog," but I could be mistaken. Then one evening Wendy called to ask me, "Dad, how would you feel about us adopting?"

Hmmmmmmmmmmm. Let's see. I'm adopted, my wife's adopted, my son-in-law's adopted. Nope! No problem here.

And so the process began. With all its high and lows, its anticipation and trepidation. Ending in the second most important adoption in my life: Kaylee's. The only words I have left are, "Thank you, Lord. Thank you."

Kaylee, Fuzhou, Jiangxi—"reading" to her granddad.

ANGELS AMONG US
by Sherrell Blankenship-Brown

AFTER A LONG, TUMULTUOUS TRIP HOME FROM CHINA, WE ARRIVED HOME IN COLUMBIA, SOUTH CAROLINA, AND MADE OUR WAY OUT TO THE RECEPTION AREA. Sixteen-month-old Mary Clare Miaoma, already a girl who believed in making an entrance, decided that instead of being carried, she would stomp her squeaky shoes the long length of hall that separated the airport gates from her waiting fan club. My husband and I took turns pointing out friends and relatives we could see way down at the other end, and we both wondered who those two little polyester-clad women were that waited with them. Must be friends of my mother, we agreed. We were surprised when they were among the first to greet us. One touched our daughter's rash-inflamed cheek and whispered, "God bless you little one." The other touched her hand and promised her a long and happy life. Sometime later in the day it occurred to us to ask who those two well-wishers were and discovered that everyone assumed they had been friends of someone else in our welcoming party. They are not in any of our pictures, nor did they make the videotape. My head says these were two nice ladies who recognized a moment of joy and wanted a little taste. My heart instead sings angels—angels sent to welcome our daughter to her new life in this new place!

I believe in angels. I saw one in the orphanage doctor as she danced around the room with our new daughter trying to comfort her so that we could eat the meal they had arranged for us. I saw another in our driver who was so moved by the grief of our child that he went out and brought back a tablecloth to wrap her in so that she might be warm, feel secure, and sleep. I saw them in our travel mates when they discreetly offered us money after my husband's wallet was lost. I saw another in our wonderful guide, who cared for us so thoroughly and lovingly says good-bye each month to all those precious gems of her homeland. And I see that angelic spark in my daughter as she rests her head on her baba's shoulder, as she shrieks with joy at the sight of her grandfather and says "I wuv you" to her PoPo, and as she is lifted into the arms of my best friend. There are angels among us and in us. Of this much I am certain.

Mary Clare Miaoma (age 2), Huazhou, Guangdong—
indulging her creative side.

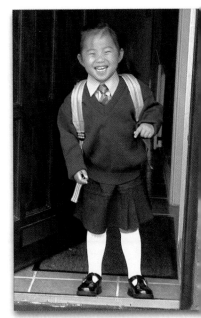

Katherine (age 4), Chenzhou, Hunan.

Sarah (age 4), Jiangxi.

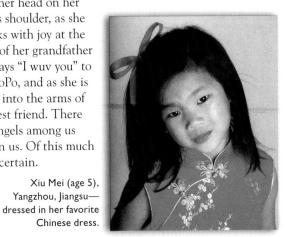

Xiu Mei (age 5),
Yangzhou, Jiangsu—
dressed in her favorite
Chinese dress.

GUO DONG RUI
by Susan Knispel

THE RED THREAD CONNECTING ME TO MY DAUGHTER HAS INCREDIBLE RESILIENCY. I was single and in my mid-forties when I started the journey to bring her home. I started the paperwork with excitement and anticipation. It was then that the red thread started to stretch. Although I did everything needed to obtain my birth certificate in the correct form, it was greatly delayed. I planned to go to New York City to get it certified but changed my mind and decided to mail it instead. It was September 11, 2001.

Referral photo of Lia Emily Rui, DaYe, Hubei.

The horrific events of that day really tested the strength of that thread. The county office where my birth certificate needed to be certified was right outside the World Trade Center. It took a number of weeks for that office to be open for business again. I felt so guilty worrying about a delay when so many lives were lost that day.

Then the CCAA announced a plan to limit the number of single parent adoptions. I was in a panic. It now appeared impossible for me to meet the deadline of getting my dossier logged in at the CCAA before December 1, 2001, in order to avoid the new quota system. My I-171 had to come from Newark, New Jersey, where processing adoption paperwork was taking a back seat to issues of terrorism. I spent hours begging for documents to be sent to me, pleading for rapid processing times, and becoming teary-eyed in front of a variety of bureaucrats. At last my dossier was logged in at the CCAA on November 30, 2001. It was a miracle.

Fourteen months later I received the referral of my daughter, 16-month-old Guo Dong Rui, born in DaYe City, Hubei Province. Ironically she was born in September 2001. Little did I know that the path was not yet quite clear for the two of us to become a family. Just before leaving for China, my fingerprints expired, and I had to rush into Philadelphia to be re-fingerprinted. SARS was casting a serious shadow. The Iraqi War was declared. Security was tight, nerves were frayed, and everyone was tense. However the red thread to my daughter was strong and survived all challenges. On March 24, 2003, Lia Emily Rui and I met for the first time, and the following day we became a family.

Lia Emily Rui (nearly age 4), DaYe, Hubei.

Now at age 4½, Lia is a preschool graduate headed for kindergarten. She loves swimming, gymnastics, and dancing. She is incredibly smart and has a wonderful sense of humor. I cannot imagine my life without her in it. The red thread leading us to one another had many twists but now is taut and strong.

Sisters—Olivia Susanne Fuyu (age 3), Suichuan, Jiangxi, and Sophia MeiLin Yuxi (age 1), Yugan, Jiangxi.

Katia Chun (age 3), Yangchun.

MOTHER'S DAY 2004
by Virginia Richard

A BABY GIRL IN AN ORANGE GINGHAM DRESS, WRAPPED CAREFULLY IN A CROCHETED BLANKET MAILED TO HER FROM A GREAT DISTANCE WITH LOVE FROM HER MOTHER SHE DID NOT KNOW IN BALTIMORE.

A mother who stands emotionally with her three-year-old in her arms as the babies enter the room one by one, holding closely a child she knows and loves while waiting eagerly for a child she loves but has never seen.

A baby girl carried into an office room at the Civil Affairs Office in Guangzhou, China, not knowing that her mother, grandmother, and big sister are waiting for her.

A mother crying, holding two beautiful daughters in her arms and grateful that she has the privilege to be the mother of Chun Hua Liang.

A baby girl, fearful and timid as her mother, grandmother, and sister embrace her, mourning and silently overwhelmed by the strangers who cry and gently touch her.

A mother and baby girl are proclaimed a family, joined together on Mother's Day.

Twin beauties—Olivia Wu and Elyse Ting (age 13 months), Loudi, Hunan.

The nannies, assistant director, and Sissi, our local guide, brought Baby Madeleine—Madeleine Gisele Tai (age 12 months), Taihe, Jiangxi—to our family.

They Also Wait
Anonymous

TING WAS AN EIGHT-YEAR-OLD GIRL THAT I FIRST MET WHEN SHE WAS JUST FIVE. She had a bubbly personality and a ready smile, and each time I returned to her orphanage she would follow me around as I did my work. I loved being with Ting and would hoist her onto my back whenever possible for makeshift "horsey rides." I always tried to get her to laugh because her giggle was so low and cute.

Over the years Ting had watched baby after baby be adopted. The new parents would excitedly visit the orphanage, and Ting would watch them proudly holding their new child. She always made a big impression on everyone who visited, and more than one parent came back from China to tell me about the adorable little girl they had met there.

Ting was enrolled in one of our school programs, and so I visited her regularly to do the updated reports. One day she and I were sitting together as the teacher told me how she was progressing. She was coloring a picture and would stop to answer the questions I had of her, such as her favorite subject, her favorite color, and what she liked to eat. At the end of our talk, I asked Ting if there was anything else she would like to tell me. Shyly Ting nodded that there was. With a quiet voice, she looked up at me and said, "Please, I would like a mama of my own."

With a lump in my throat, I promised this beautiful child that we would do everything possible to find her a family. Just a few short months later, her picture appeared on an adoption agency list, and a woman who saw it chose Ting as her daughter. I gave the orphanage the wonderful news, and they immediately told Ting that a family was coming for her. And so, while the family in the U.S. gathered papers and permissions, Ting quietly waited. While they sent off their dossier and prepared for a new child, Ting waited some more. Over and over she asked, "When is my mom coming? When is the day?" To an eight-year-old girl, "the wait" is very hard indeed.

Now whenever I hear adoptive families discussing the truly difficult time of adoption known as "the wait," I try to remind myself that the parents aren't the only ones waiting. On the other side of the earth are thousands of children who are hoping that tomorrow might be the day that they, too, are chosen for adoption. They wait and they dream for a "mama of their own."

Best friends—Sydney YunLing and Chloe YunQiu (both age 2), both from Zhuzhou, Hunan.

Hubei
by Linda Mitchell

Hope survives abandon.
Unknown daughters grasp broken red threads as
Born-again parents, once lost now found, journey
  with blankets, bottles, and arms ready to
Exchange paperwork for little ones in split pants,
  showing cautious stares and courageous smiles.
Indescribable pain births unimaginable joy into family.

Best friends—Sophia Cai Lan (age 3) and Lily Ke Yan (age 4), both from Zhuzhou, Hunan.

Amelia Rose (about age 10 months), Lianjiang, Guangdong, with Mommy.

The Red Coat
Anonymous

LITTLE YAYA WAS JUST THREE YEARS OLD AND HAD ONCE BEEN GIVEN A RED COAT BY A VISITOR TO HER ORPHANAGE. She loved this red coat and wore it all the time. The aunties would joke with her that it was her favorite thing in the world.

One day the orphanage staff needed to photograph another child who was being sponsored for surgery. They wanted Zhen to look as beautiful and colorful as possible; so one of the aunties went and got YaYa's red coat for Zhen to wear in the photos. When YaYa saw Zhen wearing her coat, she started to cry really hard. Everyone could hear her sobbing even from outside the room.

As Zhen was having her photos taken in the hallway, YaYa ran to the metal gate at the door and cried some more. The aunties tried to move her back into the room, but she used all her strength to hang onto the gate and kept crying.

The aunties scolded her and said, "YaYa, you must share your red coat. You cannot be selfish." But still she continued to cry.

Finally one of the aunties listened to what she was saying and realized that YaYa wasn't crying because she didn't want to share. She was crying because she wanted her photo taken too. YaYa said over and over, "Take *my* picture!" You see, she had realized at the tender age of three that in order to have a mommy and daddy come to take you home, you first had to have your picture made. YaYa wasn't crying because she wanted a simple red coat. She was crying because she wanted a family of her very own to love her.

First meeting of Kori Song (age 14 months), Chenzhou, Hunan, and her mommy.

Referral photo of Emma Grace ShaoLiu (about age 5 months), Gaozhou, Guangdong.

Crista (age 2), ZhuZhou, Hunan—enjoying the spring flowers.

Katherine Jiao Merritt (age 3), Kunming, Yunnan.

EMMA'S DELIVERY
by Vicky Long

THE DAY WE RECEIVED THE PICTURE OF OUR DAUGHTER IS ONE WE WILL NEVER FORGET. We dreamed about her for months, and the time had finally come to see her face. We had received "the call" the day before and our agency had sent her referral overnight by FedEx for our review. All we knew was that she was seven months old, had big round eyes, fair skin, no hair, and was named Gao ShaoLiu. We had not seen her, but we were already in love.

We arranged for our three children to be home when the referral was delivered by FedEx. At 10:30 a.m. we heard a truck pull into the driveway, although the delivery was not scheduled until 4:30 that afternoon. The poor driver looked as if he was being ambushed. Our daughter was in charge of the camera, and one of our sons had the video camera. When my husband met him in the yard, the gentleman asked us if there was money in the envelope. My husband told him no, but that it was better than money. He explained about our new daughter's picture being in the envelope. The driver congratulated us and was kind enough to let us take his picture.

We all rushed inside and tore the envelope open. Inside was a picture of the most beautiful baby we had ever seen, shaved head and all. We knew instantly that this was our daughter.

Now, almost a year later, we remember that day with laughter as we recall the excitement we all felt. I don't think our FedEx friend will ever forget it either. He was able to meet our daughter for the first time just a few months ago as he was bringing information about her new brother, also from China. He told me we were the only family that has ever asked to take his picture when he delivered a package. I reminded him that it's not every day he gets to deliver a baby.

Passport photo of Emma Grace (age 17 months).

My Daughter (©2000)
by Holly Hardcastle Bombria

My daughter awakens in the morning.
She is welcomed to the new day…
By arms
That are not mine.

My daughter cries from hunger.
She is fed and nourished…
By hands
That are not mine.

My daughter is tired
She is laid down for her nap…
By hands
That are not mine.

My daughter is wet.
She is changed or placed over a potty
By hands
That are not mine.

My daughter is laughing
She is amused by a toy that is held…
By hands
That are not mine.

My daughter cries and then feels loved
She is held and comforted…
By arms
That are not mine.

I miss and long for my daughter.
I am so unspeakably thankful
For arms… and hands…
That are not mine.

Best friends—Rory (age 2), Hanzhong, Shaanxi, with brother, Henry (age 5).

TO OUR DEAREST NOAH
by Yvonne Ferrier

OUR JOURNEY TO YOU IS QUITE A STORY. Below is part of a post that was made about you right after we became your family. We hope every time you read it, you smile and are filled with love knowing that you were and are *so loved* long before you knew it!

July 2006

This has been one emotional roller coaster, but I can see now how all things really and truly happen as they are supposed to. I have been watching "Dylan" since December 2004 when he was on another agency's list. We were waiting to travel to pick up our son at the time. I had a friend who was looking at this list; so I'd sit on the phone with her and look at all the sweet faces. I thought "Dylan" was so incredibly adorable and thought he would be snatched up so quickly. Well, we traveled to get our son, came home, and this sweetie was still waiting. His file went back to the CCAA, and I was heartbroken wondering what would happen to him. I couldn't understand why his family didn't find him. We began the paperchase again to adopt our daughter. While we were in the middle of our wait, "Dylan" popped up on CHI's new list of waiting children. I could not believe it. I called my friend and told her he was on CHI's list and I was so happy because I knew he would find his forever family now for sure. CHI always does an amazing job finding these sweeties their families and I knew he was in good hands. He did find a family, and I was so happy for him. Every

Noah Paul HuaYue (age 4), Shenyang, Liaoning.

once in awhile, I would pop in to peek at him and smile, knowing that he was coming home.

We traveled to pick up our daughter, came home, and all was well. I felt for the time that we were complete and adopting was not on my mind. One day I logged on to the CHI group to lurk and what do I see but that "Dylan" needs a new placement! My mind was on overload. I knew we didn't have the money for any more adoption fees right now, and, wait, hadn't I said we felt complete and adoption was not on my mind right now? However I was scrambling and trying to figure out how to make this work. This sweet boy had been on my heart for so long now; there had to be a way to bring him home. I emailed the adoption agency immediately. I was desperate!!!!!! My husband and I talked and talked and talked and figured and figured and figured. Then I had someone tell me, "Where there's a will, there's always a way." Finally, finally, finally we heard the words we were waiting to hear: We *are* "Dylan's" family!!!!!!!!!!!!!!!!!!!! Does life get any better than this?! Just seeing "My Family Has Found Me" next to his name made me smile and cry happy tears. It has been a long road for this little sweetheart, but he's finally coming home.

To our sweet angel, hang on just a little bit longer. We love you from the deepest part of our hearts and pray that you will sleep tight wrapped in our love every night until we can get there.

We love you, Noah Paul! Take our hands and together we'll take this next step in your journey. We are privileged and honored to be a part of your life! Don't be afraid, little one; spread your wings and fly. We are here to watch you, guide you, catch you, and love you! Your heart is safe with us, always!

Wrapping you in our hugs and love,
your Forever Family,

Daddy, Mommy, Cody, Jordan, Gracie, and Tyler

Above: Friends forever—Lynzie and Shali (both age 3), both from Bengbu, Anhui.

Below: Siblings—Kyle (age 14) and Shali (age 2), Bengbu, Anhui.

Maddie (age 2), Zhanjiang, Guangdong.

THE GREATEST EXPERIENCE
by Brad Ellis

I WAS FIRST INTRODUCED TO MY DAUGHTER, MADELINE EVA ELLIS, OR MADDIE AS WE CALL HER, ON JULY 7, 2005—not in person but in a picture posted on the waiting children page of Children's Hope International's web site.

That day I returned home from work just like any other day. I walked to the office to find my wife, Camille, in her usual position, in front of the computer with the telephone to her ear. Only on this day it was not her mother she was talking to. When she saw me enter the room she frantically waved her arms for me to come and sit down. Camille showed me the picture of the 2½-year-old little girl with cleft lip and palate. My wife informed me this was the girl she wanted to be our child, and, as adamant as she was, I was not going to tell her no.

As with many of the people who find their way to international adoption, it had been a long and difficult road to this point. We attempted to have children biologically, but that was not to be. We tried the domestic adoption process, but that was to us like putting your name in a hat and hoping you would get drawn. After multiple disappointments we decided to go with international adoption. We knew what the final outcome would be—we would have our daughter.

We prepared and submitted our dossier and began our wait. Anyone who has gone through the adoption process knows this is the hardest part. It seemed like forever. The days felt like weeks, and the weeks felt like years. Finally the call came with the news that we were about to go get Maddie.

When we arrived in Guangzhou, I was very nervous. After so many attempts at becoming a father had come up short in the past, I would not sleep well until I had my daughter. We awoke the next morning to begin the day we had been waiting for. At the Civil Affairs Office in Guangzhou, we stood in the room for just a brief moment before a beautiful little girl appeared from around the corner. We recognized her immediately. She was wearing a traditional outfit with a pink flower in her hair and a package of her favorite cookies in each hand.

Like us she was nervous and afraid. Neither of us knew what to expect. She couldn't fully understand what was happening, but she was old enough to understand her life had changed forever. I had only been a father for a matter of seconds but did not want to lose my composure and scare my new daughter. We kneeled down with the stuffed Elmo we brought for her. I reached out to give her a piece of chocolate, but she would not take it from me. At that point she burst into tears, the first of several episodes of tears to be shed before she fully accepted us as Mom and Dad.

Magic Seven
by Wendy Ritz

When I was in second grade, there was this purple reading book that I loved. It was called "Seven Is Magic." I lugged that thing around on weekends and actually lost it one time in the barn for a week. Anyway that title has never left me. Is the number seven magic?

Last night I was in the frozen section at WalMart. I got a call on my cell phone. It was Stefani from CHI. Now, the first thing that she asked me was, "Is everything okay at your household?" "Ummmm… well, it was when I left." Then Stefani offered me a pure miracle. There was a little girl, seven years old, who needed a home. I was stunned. I sat right down in the butter section at WalMart. I could not believe it. This precious child was just home from China, and the placement did not work out. Would I go get her? Could I leave now?

I simply cannot wrap my mind around what is being offered to me. I'm leaving as soon as I post this to meet my daughter. What a surprise adoption! As you can imagine my household is in a state of shock. Our families do not know. What will everyone think when I show up at church next Sunday with her? We truly have nothing prepared—no clothes, no bed, no toothbrush, no *money*… nothing—but I have faith that this will work out. As I leave to get *my daughter*, child number seven, I can't help but think that seven is magic. However magic truly has nothing to do with this. She is another miracle. Another gift from God to cherish and love. Please remember me in your prayers as I drive to get her. Please pray for Yao—to go through so many transitions at age seven is just heartbreaking. She needs all our prayers.

Siblings—Fallon (age 7), Fuzhou, Jiangxi; Whitney (age 12); Shae (age 3), Qujiang, Guangdong; Dakota (age 13); Rylan (age 1), Taiwan; Cooper (age 5); and Skye (age 3).

Above and below: Sisters—Leah (age 4), Huainan, Anhui, and Lauren (age 3), Shangrao, Jiangxi.

Twins—Kenna and Michal (age 2), Maonan, Guangdong. Give me a kiss.

Meili's Aunties
by Lori Melton

Gaoyou was our destination that day in February 2004 as we traveled to visit the place our newest daughter, Gao Fu Fan, now our Meili, had called home. Gaoyou, Jiangsu Province, by Chinese standards is a small town. I read that there are almost 900,000 residents. The streets and sidewalks were very crowded. It's very typical on Chinese streets to have a four-lane road with six or seven lanes of traffic. Gaoyou was no exception. It certainly didn't seem "small town" to us. The street the SWI was on was narrow and fairly busy. A gated fence sat very close to the street, separating it from the SWI. As we drove through the gate and into the narrow parking lot, I was feeling so emotional. I had so wanted to make this trip. I wanted to see the place my daughter had lived; I wanted to meet and more importantly personally thank the ayis who had cared for her. But I was about to step into the reality of my daughter's life. I was about to step into the reality of all the children whose families never find them. I wasn't sure I could bear it.

I dreaded getting out of the van for fear my emotions would overtake me. I was so slow to get out of the van that by the time I did, most of the bags of gifts we had brought had been unloaded. Several ayis met us in the parking lot and helped unload the toys and clothes we had brought for the children. One of the ayis was older than most of the others but seemed very young at heart. Her hair was cut short, but stylish. She was cute with a few freckles and a gentle face. Her smile lit up her eyes! She ran towards Meili, obviously thrilled to see her again. It was very apparent to me that she loved my new daughter a great deal, and I let her take Meili from me. I surprised myself by doing so because I swore I would never allow that to happen. But the love she felt for Meili was so obvious in her eyes that I couldn't deny her the opportunity to hold my daughter one last time. She held her close, rocked her and hugged her, and said something over and over to her. She fussed over Meili, and it was very clear that Meili was enjoying being with her again. There was something about that moment for me. I saw the love she had for Meili. I witnessed it. Until that moment I would have told anyone, "Yes, the nannies love the children. How can they not?" But now, I can honestly say, "Yes!" I saw the love in their eyes, I saw her hold on to my daughter, I saw her cheek-to-cheek with Meili just like I have done so many times since.

She continued to carry Meili as we were escorted upstairs to a fairly large reception area/playroom. There were so many ayis there. Many weren't wearing their white lab coats; so I wondered if they had come in on their own time. Most of them wanted a chance to hold Meili. They couldn't seem to get enough of her. I saw them reach up into her little snowsuit to hold her hands. I saw them watch her intently until it was their turn to hold their former charge one last time. We thanked the staff for the care they had given Meili. They thanked us in return. Pictures were taken; some names and information jotted down. I allowed the ayis to hold Meili while we were given our tour. Although I desperately wanted my baby in my arms, I knew this time would help give those women closure. I felt I owed them that much. When the tour was over, we were politely escorted to the parking lot where it appeared we were expected to depart quickly. I didn't want to leave. I wanted to stay and spend more time at the SWI and with the ayis. I wanted to get to know them. I wanted to laugh with them as they relayed to me stories about my new daughter. I wanted to hang on to this moment, the very last moment of my daughter's current life before she began her new one. But of course that wasn't possible. Some of the ayis followed us to say good-bye. I made a point to thank and hug each one. At least I think I thanked them. I'm not sure if the giggles were brought on by my pronunciation or by their apprehension over the hugs given them by this silly American woman.

Meili's special auntie took longer to say good-bye and seemed to appreciate the hug from me and even hugged me back. We smiled at each other through our tears. I made it partway to the gate and turned around and ran back and gave her another hug. We shared a love for my daughter that I could feel and I think she could too. We got in the van, and I wanted to sob. I hurt for the ayis, and I hurt for Meili. I just tried to take in everything that had just happened. I wanted to remember every little detail so I could one day share it with my daughter. I want her to know how much she was loved. The Gaoyou SWI doesn't have all the latest toys or technology. They may not be able to keep the heat turned up in the winter and they can't give the children fancy meals. But they do give of themselves. They *do* love these children.

Abigale (age 17) and Gretchen (age 13)
with sister, Beth (age 2), Yangjiang, Guangdong.

A Dream Fulfilled… Twenty Years Later
by Kitty Larochelle

My husband and I discussed adoption as an option for our family even before we were married. The exact date of that discussion was February 23, 1985. After having four sons we knew it was time to fulfill our dreams, and we finally wrapped our arms around our daughter on February 20, 2005!!! She has filled our house with love and fun. We truly believe that she was made for our family.

While childbirth is an act of nature, adoption is an act of faith.

Six sisters pretty in pink.
(Back) Hannah (age 10), Dongyang, Zheijiang;
Lilee (age 8), Yiwu, Zhejiang;
Savannah (age 6), Phnom Phen, Cambodia;
and Annabella (age 5), Wuhan, Hubei.
(Front) Maya ("Lulu") (age 3), Shantou, Guangdong;
and Jaci ("Monkey") (age 2), Shantou, Guangdong.

Siblings—(Back) Timothy (age 15); Christopher (age 17); (Front) Nicholas (age 8);
Karina (age 2), ChongRen Jiangxi; and Jonathan (age 9), with siblings—
(Right front) Jared (age 8) and Kaylin (age 2), ChongRen, Jiangxi.

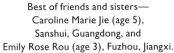

Best of friends and sisters—
Caroline Marie Jie (age 5),
Sanshui, Guangdong, and
Emily Rose Rou (age 3), Fuzhou, Jiangxi.

Kayla Jun (age 15 months), Chenzhou, Hunan, with nanny.

Sisters—Kristi Lily (age 4), Sibu, Malaysia; Kayla Jun (age 6), Chenzhou, Hunan; and Jordan Chao (age 2), Fuzhou, Jiangxi.

Zoe Michael (born December 2005), Jiangxi.

OUR DAUGHTERS' CAREGIVERS
by Sheri Russon

A BEAUTIFUL SMILE AND PINK-FLOWERED PIGTAILS—TWO PHYSICAL EVIDENCES TO ME THAT MY TWO DAUGHTERS FROM CHINA WERE LOVED BY THEIR CAREGIVERS BEFORE COMING INTO OUR FAMILY.

Our daughter Kayla Jun (Yan Jun) was adopted in July 2001 at the age of 15 months. We made a life-changing visit to her orphanage in Chenzhou, Hunan. One of her caregivers—a beautiful, young woman with a most memorable smile—lit up when she saw Yan Jun. She immediately reached out to hold her, and pictures of Kayla and her nanny show a very contented little girl—quite the contrast from the worried forehead in her referral photo which I have learned to recognize as a signal that things are not right. When it was time to leave and we were waiting for a van to pick us up, Yan Jun's nanny sought us out again and brought an extra bottle and a bowl of food to share with Yan Jun in their final moments together. Her nanny's beautiful picture always reminds me of the love she shares with me for my daughter.

Our daughter Jordan Chao (Chao Yang) was barely two years old when adopted in May 2006 in the Jiangxi Province. She had spent most of her life in foster care. When we first received her, she looked oh-so-cute with pink flowers with bells wrapped around pigtails. She carried a package of boxed drinks with her. She was very serious but started smiling and laughing a little before the end of the day. Three days later we drove two hours to see Fuzhou, the city where our daughter was from. We could not visit the orphanage but went to see the orphanage grounds. A Chinese woman came up the alleyway and handed me a box of drinks for Chao Yang. Our guide was not close by; so when she came back I had her ask the woman who she was. She said she was the daughter of our new daughter's foster mother. She said she and her mother had come to the orphanage every day since the day Chao Yang left, waiting and hoping that we would come. Her mother had left a short time before but had asked her to stay just a little while longer. With my heart bursting, I was able to thank her and give her a small gift for her mother, as well as a page of pictures of our family—which I hoped would show both of them how much we love our children and how much we would love our new daughter.

I will forever be grateful to these two women, as well as all of the other loving and kind caregivers, who truly love our children.

A SPECIAL PICTURE
Excerpted essay by Susan Rousso

MEA KEEPS A PICTURE OF HER CAREWORKER HOLDING HER—TAKEN WHEN SHE WAS SEVEN MONTHS OLD, PRIOR TO OUR VISIT TO FULING—ABOVE HER BED. She took this picture of her careworker on her fourth birthday to school to include her in the first four years of her life celebration that was conducted for her at the school. She always says her careworker wore pink because it was Mea's favorite color and that her careworker knew that (and perhaps she did, although it was the color of all of the careworkers' jackets).

This October we are going back to China for the first time since Mea left. Her careworker is still there. I am certain Mea will first hug her cautiously when she first sees her and then hug her freely as we leave to come back home.

Sisters and best friends—Jaedyn (age 5), Maoming, Guangdong, and Naomi (age 4), Xinyu, Jiangxi.

Jordan Chao (age 2), Fuzhou, Jiangxi.

The Red Thread
by Louise Holden

The Chinese have a saying,
It's about a thread that ties,
The hearts of people not yet met,
'Cross oceans and 'cross skies.
The thread may sometimes tangle,
But however long it takes,
For those whose destiny is to meet,
The thread will never break.

Sisters and friends—Lilianna (age 8), Shenzhen, Guangdong, and Amelia (age 4), Hepu, Guangxi.

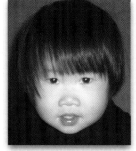

Isabella Patricia Lin (age 2½), Jiangxi.

Sisters—MacKenzie YinYing (age 14 months), HuaiHua, Hunan, and Kendra Wenyu (age 6), QingCheng, Guangdong.

THOUSANDS CHEERED
by Sharon Manuel

LITERALLY YOU COULD HEAR THOUSANDS OF PEOPLE CHEERING AS I GOT OUR REFERRAL CALL! It's true. On April 18, 2005, my husband, our first daughter, Kendra Wenyu, and I had walked down to the main road a couple of blocks from our house to watch the Boston Marathon runners as they passed by. There were hundreds of runners passing every minute and thousands of people lining the road to cheer them on. We were just headed home when my cell phone rang. "Sharon, we got it! Your referral is here. She is beautiful. She is in Hunan. And her birth date is March 27, 2004. Her name is…" Well I could hardly hear because of all the cheering. Okay, the cheering was for the runners, but that's our story and we're sticking to it.

We ran home, Kendra Wenyu screaming all the way, "She's a baby girl, she's a baby girl, I have a sister," and me crying. I called back while sitting at the computer. I could watch my new daughter's sweet and beautiful face come on the screen from the emailed file. Oh, I was just shaking. So happy and amazed! Last April we walked over to watch the Marathon again; this time with two daughters.

Drawing by Kendra Wenyu (age 6), QingCheng, Guangdong.

Daddy and his girls. Lenna (age 2) and Abigayl (age 15 months), Yuanling, Hunan.

Siblings—Noah (age 27 months), Changsha, Hunan, and Elisabeth (age 35 months), Hengfeng, Jiangxi.

MY BEAUTIFUL BLESSINGS
by Karen Kakishiba

IF SOMEONE WOULD HAVE ASKED ME IN 1990 WHAT MY LIFE WOULD BE LIKE IN 2006, I WOULD HAVE NEVER PICTURED MY LIFE AS IT IS NOW. I am a single mother of two beautiful little girls: Kristen (eight years old) and Kylie (four years old). I practice medicine in a private office. I live in the same town in which I was born and raised. I look at my journey to this point and realize that God had this plan for me.

Kristen Kai (age 8), Wuzhou, Guangxi, and sister, Kylie Xiao (age 4), Changning, Hunan—having fun with Mom.

I had always expected that I would have children, but I expected to have a traditional family with a husband and two children. However my husband and I divorced while we were in the middle of trying to adopt a child from China. While I was married and unable to conceive, I felt God was letting me know that children were not in the picture for me. Then when we decided to adopt and later had to stop the process, He was obviously telling me I was not to have children with my ex-husband.

When my divorce was final, I was able to start the process for my first daughter. I worked hard to complete the dossier and had it in China by July 1998. I finally received the call in February 1999, and I was so excited to finally be a mom. I knew God had chosen the perfect child for me.

Kristen, formerly Wu Cai Sha, was placed in my arms on April 6, 1999. She was beautiful. She didn't cry or smile. All she did was study my face. She just kept looking at me as if to say, "I know this face." We bonded immediately, and she didn't want to go to her grandmother, who also had been waiting for years, to be called "Bachi."

Kristen and I came back to Yuba City, and I expected our life to be just the two of us. After Kristen was home for about six months, I began to feel as if China was calling me again. I had the support of my family and the finances were available; so I finally started the paperchase again in September 2000.

Kylie, formerly Ning Xiao Hua, was handed to me on October 30, 2002. She was almost 12 months old and developmentally delayed. She was quiet and seemed very sad. Early on her only spontaneous smile was when she would stare at the ceiling. It was as if she was smiling at someone; many of us believe she was looking at her guardian angel. Over the next several months Kylie began to blossom. After about two months she also stopped staring at the ceiling. I think maybe her guardian angel felt she was finally home.

I thank God every day for my beautiful blessings.

MEANT TO BE
by Paula Swett

YEARS AGO MY HUSBAND HAD A VASECTOMY AFTER THE BIRTH OF OUR THIRD CHILD. I immediately knew we had made a mistake and longed for another child. My husband immediately knew that he did not and was quite happy. For seven years I longed for a child. I prayed. I talked to my husband about adopting, fostering, or a vasectomy reversal. He was opposed to it all. Finally it came to the point that our marriage was almost beyond repair. Still we entered marriage counseling and wanted to make things right.

In marriage counseling we both saw how selfish we had been. My husband finally understood how important having another child was to me. In my mind I saw a little girl from China. The question became did we want a vasectomy reversal or should we adopt? The reversal would cost $3,000 and had a 50% success rate. The adoption would cost around $20,000 but gave us an almost 100% success rate. We prayed and felt we needed to give the reversal a chance.

In February 2004 my husband underwent the reversal procedure. We were so excited and so sure we would soon be pregnant. Two weeks later we started trying to conceive our baby. Months went by and it became clear that we would not be conceiving a child as the reversal had failed. We were devastated. I had promised that if the reversal failed that we would be done. That was it—no more babies.

Christmas of 2004 came, and I was still so depressed. Our neighbors had just returned from China with their new little girl. After hearing their story and seeing the baby, our hearts were so touched by her. The next day we decided to adopt from China. We had come full circle.

It dawned on me the other day. The same month we began trying to conceive a child, a child was conceived in China. The child who was conceived was our daughter, 21 months before we held her for the first time. All along she was meant for us even though she came from another country. When we started our paperwork we did not know that we would adopt a baby with cleft lip and palate. We did not know that we would find her on our agency's special needs list the month that we were ready to find her. Nor did we know that we would be chosen to be her family. But I am convinced that God knew all along… and the invisible red thread led us to her.

Lilia Dorothy (age 18 months), Jiaozuo, Henan— enjoying a treat with Mom.

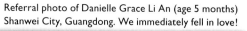

Counting the days— At the very end of January, after filling in the waiting child forms with CCAI, we received a picture of a beautiful little girl with white hair and blue eyes. We said yes and began the wait for all our paperwork to come in. A month later, I was already going slightly crazy with the wait and made this picture. This photo is of her paperwork and the shadow of the abacus falling upon it.

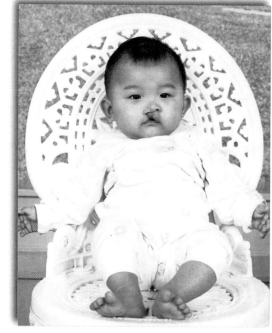

Referral photo of Danielle Grace Li An (age 5 months) Shanwei City, Guangdong. We immediately fell in love!

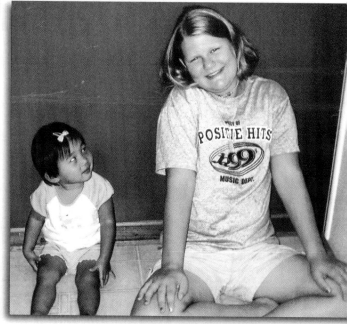

Danielle Grace Li An (age 19 months), Shanwei City, Guangdong, with big sister, Megan (age 11).

MY SISTER
by Megan Swett (age 10)

MY SISTER'S NAME IS DANIELLE. We adopted her from China. We decided to adopt her on my birthday. It was the best present I've ever had. I've never had a sister, and I have always wanted one. I guess God and my parents decided this was the best thing to do. I am so happy that I will finally have a sister. I will love her with all my heart. My mom and dad are going to China, and we don't get to go with them when they get the baby. I want to be the first one to hold her. I am very excited. I will play with her every day. I will dress her once in a while. I will love her like a real sister.

I love you, Danielle—no matter what.

Sisters—Hannah Zhipan (age 7), Xinyu, Jiangxi; Rachel Zhiheng (age 4), Chenzhou, Hunan; and Abigail Lihuan (age 2), Yangxi, Guangdong

WORLD CUP IN CHINESE
by Sarah Daetwiler

OUR FAMILY OF FOUR—ME, MY HUSBAND, AND OUR TWO BOYS, AGES NINE AND FIVE—traveled to China in July 2006 to become a family of five. Our beautiful Anna was waiting for us in Guangdong province.

We stopped in Beijing first to sightsee for three days. The Chinese people were tremendously kind. They loved our boys and frequently talked to them about soccer since the 2006 World Cup final was taking place.

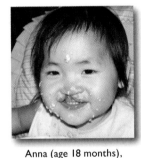

Anna (age 18 months), LeChang, Guangdong.

Unfortunately for us jet-lagged folks, the finals were televised at 3:00 a.m. The next morning I asked our breakfast waitress if she knew who had won. I erroneously assumed she knew English. After we both gave up trying to understand one another, she found a supervisor, who politely asked what I wanted. I again asked if she knew who had won the World Cup. She considered my question, then perked right up. "Yes!" she said, and disappeared.

She and the waitress came back to our table a moment later, confidently handing me a bottle of Tabasco sauce! They had been so patient with my non-breakfast request and accompanying soccer charades, so I accepted it and ate my hardboiled egg doused in hot sauce as if that was exactly what I'd wanted all along.

Tabasco sauce is now and forever more known as "World Cup" in our house, and our laughter in remembering is another continuing gift to us from China.

THE PLAN
by Nancy Haddad

I WANTED TO BE A WIFE AND MOTHER MY ENTIRE LIFE. It's funny that I never really dreamed about the husband while dreaming about the kids. I had a wonderful single life with lots of friends and activities, but no relationship ever seemed to be the one. I always said, "I think Mr. Right took a wrong turn." I never really minded not being married and liked dating, but when I hit my 40s I was having a very hard time with the fact that there were not going to be children in my life. My nephews and godchildren just weren't filling the yearning. One day I saw an article in the *Denver Post* on single women adopting from China, and I went for it.

Bringing my first daughter home was truly a dream come true. I didn't want to burden my daughter with being my main companion and confidant and felt that she needed a sister. China wasn't available to me at that time due to single quotas unless I wanted to adopt from the Waiting Child program. I just didn't feel comfortable with that. I found an agency that said, "We have an Asian child in a Russian orphanage that just might fit into your family." I did not want to adopt from Russia, but I saw Tracy's picture and video and I thought, "That is Marney's sister"; so I went for it again! I was sure that my family was complete.

One year later a little face was staring at me from a Waiting Child brochure from my Russian agency, and I thought, "He looks like Marney and Tracy rolled into one. He should be their brother." I really did not think an agency would allow me to adopt again. I was 50, single, and had two children. But I thought that I really had to give this a try, and if it was not meant to be, okay. He has been with us almost two years!

Then came the nagging feeling that just one more boy—and a boy from China—would really balance our family. By this time I was 52 and retired. Would anyone really let me bring home another child? I started searching the lists of waiting children from China (of which I was so afraid just a few years back) and did some serious soul-searching on what special needs I was capable of handling. I found Yang Fu Shun, soon to be Jack, and the process began again.

A friend said after visiting with us, "You really planned out your life well. You're still young enough to enjoy your kids, and you get to stay home with them." My reply: "This wasn't my plan. I was going to marry a rich man and be pampered for the rest of my life!" I believe that this is God's plan. All those years of praying for children, and look at how He blessed me!

Ethan (age 11) with new sister, Elli Yuan (age 6), Liuzhou, Guangxi.

Lorelle Yan (age 3), Yangjiang, Guangdong, with Mom.

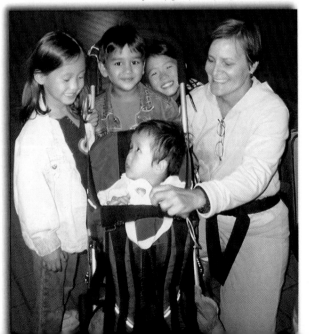

Arriving home. Tracy Aselya (age 6), Krasnoyarsk, Russia; Samuel Khalim (age 3), Moscow, Russia; Marguerite ("Marney") Hualin (age 7), Hanchuan, Hubei; with Mom and new brother, Jack (age 2), Yunyang, Chongqing.

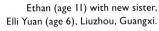

A WISH COME TRUE
by Dana Gong

I WAS DIAGNOSED WITH SYSTEMIC LUPUS ERYTHEMATOSUS. Although my prognosis was good, I was told to stay out of the sun and not have children biologically. Having had an elementary school friend who was adopted from Korea and having babysat a three-year-old Korean adoptee, I decided, at the ripe old age of 15, that I would adopt my children.

Fifteen years later, while traveling in China, my husband and I happened across three new adoptive families. With adoption in our future, I rushed over to meet them and to learn of their experiences. Among their comments, however, were "China has very strict regulations. With so many waiting families, I am not sure they will let you adopt with a chronic illness." Needless to say I was devastated by this news. However my husband and I decided to investigate further and found some agencies, while a little hesitant, that were willing to give it a try.

Although we spent months living and breathing the paperchase, on September 27, 2004, my husband and I took time to celebrate our one year wedding anniversary. Like a birthday or New Year's, I looked at our anniversary as a time to reflect on the previous year and a time to be excited for the year ahead. As we were getting ready to cut the top layer of our wedding cake, I wondered, even though there was no candle, if I got to make a wish.

Months later when our referral arrived, we were greeted by a photo of our beautiful daughter. As we read the referral further, we saw a date at the bottom of the paperwork: September 27, 2004—the exact day of our anniversary. In May 2005 Natalie was placed in my arms, and my wish came true.

Referral photo for Natalie Lauren Minpei (age 4 months), Tonggu, Jiangxi.

Three beautiful sisters—Lilee (age 9), Maoming, Guangdong; Parker (age 6), Huazhou, Guangdong; and Carsyn (age 3), Wuchuan, Guangdong.

Siblings—Mark (age 9), Luke (age 15), Carrie (age 12), and Christy LiWan (age 8), Shantou, Guangdong, with Mom and Dad.

MUCH WANTED
by Suzanne Damstedt

Dear Wan,

I am hoping that I will not have to write you very many more letters. It is not because I don't like writing you letters, but that I write them because I am not with you. In a few weeks I will meet you, and then you will come home with us. This letter is a little different from the ones I have been sending to you at the orphanage for the last 2½ months. Those letters tell you a little about me and include pictures, cute cards, or a small puzzle. I send you those letters for several reasons. One is so you will learn I am dependable and that you can trust me as your mama. Another reason is that I hope it will help the time pass for you, and that you can look forward to receiving a letter every week.

Since you are eight years old, you know we are coming for you. When I first found out you had received the photo album I made for you and that you now knew we were coming, tears came to my eyes for gladness that you were happy to know you would have a family. I know you will remember your life in China and in the orphanage and that you will remember people there and maybe some of your language. It will take a lot of courage and work for you to learn all the new things you will need to learn. I hope you will see it as a wonderful thing to have a family and a home, even though you will have to leave all that you know in your life now. I want you to know that I already love you.

This letter is a little bit different because I want to tell you some of the wonderful things that have happened to bring you and me together. When your father and I got married, I wanted to have eight children. We brought six children into this world and decided that six was a good number to have. About a year or so ago your father mentioned to me something about adopting, but I wasn't ready for that yet. But in January, your older sister was invited to go to China with a friend of mine who was adopting a little girl from China.

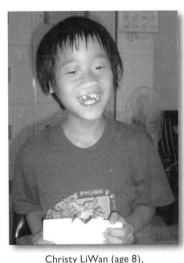

Christy LiWan (age 8), Shantou, Guangdong.

Sisters home at last! Hannah (age 6), Anhui; Hollie (age 3), Hunan; and Heidi (age 2), Hubei.

Your sister brought home books about Chinese adoption, and I started reading them. Before your sister even left for China, without even remembering that your dad had asked me earlier, I approached him about adopting. Two days later I called an adoption agency. Two weeks later I first saw your picture and wanted you to be my daughter. Since that time we have done a lot of work to get everything done so that we could come and get you. Soon we will be there to bring you home.

While you have been in China, living your normal life and going to school, I have been preparing to have you come. I have been so lucky to learn a few things about you from people who have actually met you. Your education sponsor, Saja, wrote to me: "Wan is very cute. I paid lots of attention to her in August. She can speak a bit of English. To me she said, 'Hello, how are you?' and 'thank you' after I gave her some Kentucky Fried Chicken. She is very talented, a great hula-hooper. I am so, so happy you are adopting this child!" Another lady who met you, Peggy, wrote to me, "I definitely remember Wan. She really stood out in my mind. I've seen her dance and also viewed the hula hoop video. Very cute. I remember thinking that this little girl would do so well with a mommy who knows how to mommy. I'm so excited for you and for her." Janice, who saw your picture, wrote, "She is adorable! Her eyes really sparkle, don't they?" These are wonderful things I was able to read about you. But perhaps one of the sweetest was written by the woman at the orphanage who wrote the following: "She is so lovely. She need many love. I think if she has a mom who love her, she will be more lovely than ever before." I have seen solemn pictures of you that were taken in January and then happy pictures of you taken in June, holding things I have sent you. You are even more lovely with your happy smile. I believe her words are true; having a mom and a family will make you more lovely than ever before.

Someday, Wan, I believe you will probably read this letter, after you have learned a new language and have come to know and love us. I hope you will treasure the things I have shared with you. But when that day comes, I hope that it won't be the letter alone that touches your heart, but the knowledge that we love you and wanted you to be in our family.

I love you,
Mama

Emily (age 6), Shantou, Guangdong—catching a fish on a fishing trip with her daddy.

Our Family Prayer
by Marcus Richard Dix

Hear our prayers, please Lord today
An unborn child, is for whom we pray.
Tiny little hands and big beautiful eyes
A child so innocent of any shape or size.
Curious minds with hearts of gold
Your wonderful gifts, this child to be told.
Bless us, Lord, with the sound of joy
The angelic melody of a little girl or boy.
The sound of footsteps we long to hear
Please, Lord, let us know that you are near.
Send us an angel, Lord, so pure and sweet
The promise to cherish this child,
   is a promise we'll keep.
We thank you, Lord, for all that you've done
Please find us worthy of a daughter or son.
Amen

Emma Li YuXiang (age 27 months),
Zhuzhou, Hunan.

Anna Xin Chun (age 3),
Kunming, Yunnan.

Jayna (age 2),
Nanning, Guangxi.

THIRD AND LUCKIEST MAMA
by Monica Keen

Dear Cece,

Today I learned about your fantastic memory.

The other day in email I received a picture from another mom in our adoption group. It was a group photograph from your orphanage in ShaoWu. In the photo you are a tiny baby held in the lap of your nanny. The two of you are surrounded by other children, some babies like you with their nannies and other big girls and boys too. But the two of you are near the center. It was a new picture to me and one I was happy to get. I printed it out but did not show it to you right away.

When we picked you up in China, your orphanage director gave us a disc of photos. They are of you and your orphanage sisters and brothers and your nanny with her shy but strong face, you snug on her hip. You had seen them but didn't respond to them. I guessed the images were forgotten by you and hadn't shown them to you in nearly a year.

Today when your auntie was over, I brought out the new picture I had printed. I was excited to show her, and you came over to see what we were looking at. You pushed your little head in between us and gazed. Then your finger pointed and you said "Mama" as you looked carefully at the small printed face of the woman who cared for you those many months. My heart flipped and flopped; much was in it—ache and jealousy, sadness and loss, and more for me and for all of us. But your primal memory! How marvelous!

I knew then that I was truly your third mama. Not your birth mama, or your ShaoWu mama, but your third and luckiest mama! The one to know you always after. I pray for your other mamas. They have lost so very much, and I've been given all.

Love,
Your mama

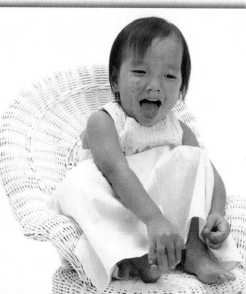

Above: Joy XiuYang (age 3), Xiushan.
Below: Hope XiaoHong (age 2), Hepu.

Cecilia ("Cece"), ShaoWu, Fujian, and cousin, Leah (both age 2½)—born one week and 4,000 miles apart.

MY PRECIOUS LITTLE GIRL
by Melissa Widenhofer

WELCOME TO THE WORLD, LITTLE ONE! Even though we won't be with you on the day of your birth, our hearts reach around the world to you, and we are praying for you and already loving you. We love you and know that, although we don't know your name or what you look like, God does. He formed you in your mother's womb and has a very special purpose for you—only one of which is to be woven into a very special part of the fabric of our family. He has joined us by an invisible red thread!

I started this journey toward adopting you more than a year ago. I don't know the exact moment when the adoption seed was planted, but once it was in my heart and mind, I knew it was something I had to pursue. I had been ensnared by your red thread!

I began to do a little checking on the Internet and reading stories of other kids and families who were brought together through adoption. I went to several seminars held by adoption agencies and learned about the adoption process. I approached your daddy and explained that this was something I felt God had placed on my heart. I knew the idea might be a little "out of the box" for him, especially since we were so busy with your brothers; so I just asked him to pray about it. The red thread was strengthened.

About that time Daddy took a new position at work. We attended a small gathering of people he had been working with and met their spouses as well. Within the first three minutes of arrival, we met a couple who had just returned from China with their little girl. We then discovered that another family had adopted from Guatemala five years earlier and that yet another couple had just begun the adoption process. We were surrounded by families created through adoption!

Referral photo of Lia Ruth Qiafu (age 4 months), Loudi, Hunan.

Daddy mentioned that I had been investigating international adoption, and one of the moms said, "I can tell from the look in her eye that she's been bitten by the adoption bug, and she's not going to give up on this." Daddy just smiled and said that maybe this was God's way of giving him a nudge. That beautiful red thread began to wind its way around Daddy as well.

Many months passed. I continued to pray about this and ask if it was the right thing for our family. I felt such a strong pull toward adoption that I could only explain it as the hand of God—and the tug of that red thread.

Some time later I asked Daddy what his recent thoughts were on adoption. His reply was immediate, "Let's do it!" I was ecstatic! The very next day, I gathered all the information I had collected and began to narrow the choices. We chose an agency and decided our daughter was in China. We were fully entangled in that unbreakable red thread.

I got right to work gathering the mountains of paperwork required. I filled out forms, sent requests for birth and marriage certificates, and scheduled appointments. I was a woman on a mission and flew through that part of the process. During this time I felt a strong urge to pray for your birthmother. I can't imagine how she must have felt. Was she excited to give birth? Would her heart break when she knew she couldn't keep you? I knew without a doubt that she loved you beyond measure. I prayed incessantly for both of you. You see, she's an essential fiber in that treasured red thread.

So far each step in the process has been exciting since it pulls me one step closer to you. We are so close to the paperchase finish line, and I can't wait to send off our dossier. I'll send it along that ever-stretching red thread all the way to China where it will reach you and pull us together at last.

I love you,
Mommy

A red thread wish, "Red Thread of Love," created by Dianne Jacobsen, grandma of Lia Ruth Qiafu.

Sisters—Willow (age 5), Gaoming, Guangdong; Lily (age 6), Shantou, Guangdong; and Camille (age 4), Tuanfeng, Hubei.

Forever sisters—
Xia Lu (age 9),
Jingmen, Hubei,
and Yue (age 5½),
Bengbu, Anhui.

ANTICIPATION
by Jacque Gaudette

THIS ADOPTION FROM CHINA WILL BE OUR FOURTH. I know the signs—the not sleeping, the worry, the anxiety, and the stress. I am a good friend of "what if." And even an acquaintance of "OMG!!!" I am also very close to "What am I doing at my age?" Because I know these feelings so well, they hang around during much of the adoption process, showing up at odd times and places.

As the time for my travel approval gets closer, things change a little. Other things start happening. I become short-tempered, pace a lot, sleep less, or I can hardly wake up in the morning except to run to the computer and see if anyone has heard anything. I join more groups or visit old groups where I have not posted in a while—just in case someone hears something; just in case there is word, rumor, or innuendo. "Someone saw posted somewhere that…" are words I start to live for. If my computer has a problem, I will move heaven and earth, and my computer tech, to see it is fixed. During those few hours of downtime, I am so, so sad. Now I do not turn my computer off at night in case it won't come up in the morning. When I leave my home, I make sure I am carrying my cell phone where it belongs: close to my heart. I also check it every ten minutes—just in case.

If people are foolish enough to ask me how I am, like at the grocery checkout line, I leave them dizzy with my tales of getting our new son. I forget simple things, like dentist appointments, hair appointments, and husbands waiting at work to be picked up. Most of these things are on my calendar, but it seems its only function is for me to go back over the day we realized he should be ours, the LOI day, his birthday, and of course the PA date. It is a good thing I do not have a job outside my home; otherwise, I would not have a job. The one I am doing here could use some help. My floors are sticky; my laundry is piled; and I am unmotivated to clean, fold, or cook. My friends seldom call. They know all I want to talk about. My children have to repeat "Mama," "Mama," "MaaMaa" any number of times to get my attention.

Having been through this before, I know all will return to normal once I am home. I also know it gets worse, culminating at the White Swan, where I become a person I do not know—tired beyond words, wanting nothing more than my own soft bed, and kisses from all my children as I tuck them into their blankets before restful sleep. Yes, this adoption thing is not for the faint of heart.

Friends—Grace Han Ping (age 2), Yongzhou, Hunan, with Sophia Cai Lan (age 4) and Liliana Ke Yan (age 4), both from Zhuzhou, Hunan.

Chloe Elizabeth YunQiu (age 11 months), Zhuzhou, Hunan— at the Orchid Garden in Guangzhou.

TWO THAT ARE TWO
by Debra Byrne

AFTER OUR BIOLOGICAL DAUGHTER, TIFFANI, WAS BORN IN 1995, WE WENT THROUGH MANY YEARS OF UNEXPLAINED INFERTILITY. In September 2003 we felt God telling us our daughter was in China. We applied to our adoption agency and began the paperwork. Seven months after our dossier went to China, we were referred a beautiful baby girl in Sichuan, China. She was born one week after we decided to adopt from China. In November 2004 we flew to China and met our daughter Abigail Grace Yu. She was perfect. Abby was 14 months old when we met.

Six months later we applied to our agency to adopt another daughter. We were planning on adopting another non-special needs child. Then we were introduced to a precious photo on our agency's waiting children list. We fell in love. We were nervous because this little girl was three months younger than Abby but still felt like she was our daughter. Nine months after we applied to our agency, we were in China. We met our daughter Jadyn Mei Shu in March 2006. She was scared but perfect. Jadyn was 26 months old at "Gotcha Day."

It has been a challenge raising two two-year-olds, but it has also been rewarding. It is great to see Abby and Jadyn play together. They have bonded and know that they are sisters. Our 11-year-old daughter has been an awesome help to us. Tiffani is a wonderful big sister and loves her baby sisters to pieces.

I never thought that I could love another child as much as I loved our first daughter, but I do. I'm so thankful to God that He brought us all together.

Emma Grace Tinting (age 4), Qidong, Hunan.

Evan Alrich Cheng Jun (born March 2005), Nanjing, Jiangsu.

THE FIRST NIGHT
by Sue Morano

AS I ROCKED EMMA TO SLEEP, I THANKED GOD FOR THIS PRECIOUS GIFT—THE BABY I HAD WAITED AND PRAYED FOR, FOR SO MANY YEARS. In a song in the musical "Les Miserables" there is a verse that states, "To love another person is to see the face of God." Well, God was there with us that day as I handed Emma to my husband. He created another family, one of many that day in China and across the world. What a wonderful gift, one we will cherish everyday.

Sisters—Jadyn (age 2½), Shanggao, Jiangxi, and Abby (age 3), Nanchong, Sichuan.

Haiku
by Noriko Lovasz

The wait

Yearning, waiting, stress
Will our baby ever come?
Hope and love abound

The call

One hot summer day
We finally got the call
We have a daughter

In China at last

The wind at our backs
Climbing up the Great Wall steps
In China at last

My sweet Megumi

My sweet Megumi
You are the light of my life
Now I am complete

One year later

It has been one year
Unimaginable joy
Time has new meaning

Forever bond

Some things are fleeting
Like cherry blossom season
But you're forever

Megumi Doris Ping (age 1½), Chenzhou, Hunan, with her "pop-pop."

Left: Brothers— Silas Emmanuel (age 5), and Téo Charles Quanxiang (age 2), Guizhou, holding photos of his sisters waiting to meet him back home.

Right and below: Book written by Talia (age 8) about the adoption of her little brother, Téo.

喜

BONDING
by Tim Chauvin

BONDING WITH YOUR NEW CHILD IS A PROCESS MADE UP OF MANY SMALL EVENTS. This is just one that brought Mattie and me closer together.

For some reason Mattie chose me as the only human allowed to touch her on her first night with us. I could happily live with that for a while, and it fell to me to get her to sleep. After several unsuccessful attempts I finally settled Mattie down. However each time I tried to lay her down, she bolted awake and screamed… really loudly! Once Mattie was awake the entire process had to be repeated.

Eventually it became apparent that the only way anyone was going to get sleep that night was for me to hold her the whole time. I finally tried to just gently lay back on the bed and hold the hopefully still sleeping Mattie on my chest. It worked, and I, too, nodded off.

Unknown to us at the time, Mattie is a climber—even when asleep. As the night wore on she crawled upward on me. I dared not disturb her; so I just laid back, and after each of her little climbs upward we would both sleep a bit longer.

Eventually Mattie had crawled her way to my head. She didn't weigh much, and since most of her upper body was borne by my pillow, I could stand it. I figured we both needed the sleep and decided to just live with this until morning. All was going well until I heard this gurgling sound emanating from my new daughter's nether regions—quite literally beside my head. Before I fully comprehended what this might portend, Mattie delivered nearly the entire contents of her gastrointestinal passage in one large, warm, semi-solid, and aromatic mass. Said mass was separated from my nose (and the side of my head for that matter) by a thin layer of flannel and the straining fibers of a disposable diaper. "Aromatic" barely begins to describe what, at some time in the recent past, had entered the other end of Mattie's gastrointestinal tract, presumably as food.

Lying there, as my eyes watered and I struggled for clear air, I silently went through a whole list of never before considered questions. Do I dare wake the noise machine now on my head and thereby everyone else within 100 yards? Should I trust the structural integrity of the burgeoning diaper? How much will a Huggies hold and for how long? Will flannel pajamas contain the contents should diaper failure occur? How long can I really hold my breath? Do I chance getting an earful of something besides noise? There was so much to consider.

While I was contemplating all this, Mattie decided things for me by waking on her own and, of course, bellowing. The added strain of her now fully employed diaphragm forced what little remained in her bowel outward, and it was then that the structural limits of her diaper were surpassed. For the uninitiated, flannel pajamas will hold far less than a disposable diaper.

Of such small events, lifetime bonds are made.

Last year my parents went to China to bring back a new wondrous little boy. His name would be Téo; but when he was in China his name was Quanxiang.

They went to the Great Wall of China!

They went to a place where they sold fish, crocodile legs, snakes and frozen birds(and they were to eat!)

Finally the day came that would change our lives forever, the day that we were to meet Téo!

Dec. 14th, my parents came HOME! I was so happy I cried the moment I was in my daddy's arms.

So that's how it happened: Love's Journey to us. THE END.

Lauren Kennedy Ji (age 4), Beijing.

Above: Jordan Samuel YouFu (age 20 months), DaTong, Shanxi.

Below: Jillian LiQiao (about age 7 months), Ganzhou, Jiangxi—being held by a woman who lived in the senior section of the SWI and who came over to hold Jillian daily.

DIFFERENT TRIPS TO THE SAME PLACE
Author Unknown

DECIDING TO HAVE A BABY IS LIKE PLANNING A TRIP TO AUSTRALIA. You've heard it's a wonderful place; you've read many guidebooks and feel certain that you're ready to go. Everyone you know has traveled there by plane. They say it can be a turbulent flight with occasional rough landings, but you can look forward to being pampered on the trip.

So you go to the airport and ask the ticket agent for a ticket to Australia. All around you excited people are boarding planes for Australia. It seems there's no seat for you; you'll have to wait for the next flight. Impatient, but anticipating a wonderful trip, you wait—and wait—and wait. Flights to Australia continue to come and go. People say silly things like, "Relax. You'll get on a flight soon." Other people actually get on the plane and then cancel their trip, to which you cry, "It's not fair!"

After a long time the ticket agent tells you, "I'm sorry, we're not going to be able to get you on a plane to Australia. Perhaps you should think about going by boat." "By *boat*!" you say. "Going by boat will take a very long time and it costs a great deal of money. I really had my heart set on going by plane." So you go home and think about not going to Australia at all. You wonder if Australia will be as beautiful if you approach it by sea rather than by air. But you have long dreamed of this wonderful place, and finally you decide to travel by boat.

It is a long trip—many months over many rough seas. No one pampers you. You wonder if you will ever see Australia. Meanwhile your friends have flown back and forth to Australia two or three more times, marveling about each trip. Then one glorious day the boat docks in Australia.

It is more exquisite than you ever imagined, and the beauty is magnified by your long days at sea. You have made many wonderful friends during your voyage, and you find yourself comparing stories with others who also traveled by sea rather than by air. People continue to fly to Australia as often as they like, but you are able to travel once, perhaps twice. Some say things like, "Oh, be glad you didn't fly. My flight was horrible; traveling by sea is so easy."

You will always wonder what it would have been like to fly to Australia. Still you know God blessed you with a special appreciation of Australia, and the beauty of Australia is not the way you get there, but in the place itself.

Bryndan (age 3), Tuanfeng, Wuhan, with her big sister.

Cleo Eileen Yi Qiao (age 3), Chenzhou, Hunan.

BECOMING A MOM
by Kimberly Pollinger

WE ENJOYED TWO LOVELY DAYS TOURING BEIJING WITH OUR TRAVEL MATES, OUR NEWFOUND FRIENDS, AND OUR GUIDES. We climbed the Great Wall, ate Peking duck, and marveled at the sites. It felt like one big vacation, but always in the back of my mind was Monday morning—the day I'd become a mom.

We were in the bus on our way to the Forbidden City and our guide said "We have a big surprise. We are going to meet the babies tonight!" My mind screamed, "*No, No, No!* I haven't had a good night's rest, I don't know how to make a bottle yet, I'm not ready!! Monday, it's supposed to be Monday." As crazy as it was, after waiting so many years and months and days and miles of journey, I was not ready for this surprise.

We flew into Changsha that night. With my mind racing, at the appointed time we were the first family to arrive. We walked past one baby, another baby, and there she was, fast asleep. My calm, steady husband gently woke her up. Big brown eyes studied these two strangers. I held her, and she looked into my eyes and my heart steadied. Here she was, and suddenly, completely, I was her mother and my husband was her dad, and we were the family we were supposed to be—that is until we three return to China to become four.

"Soul sisters"—Kendall Tian and Jia Li-Leigh (both nearly age 4), Changzhou, Jiangsu. Kendall and Jia had cribs side by side in Changzhou, share the same date of birth, and now live in the same neighborhood.

Yan (age 2), Shenzhen, Guangdong.

Above: Fuzhou, Jiangxi sisters—Stephanie, Angelica, and Samantha (all age 9).

Below: Rachel (age 6), Jinjiang, Fujian, with University of Texas China Care President, Teresa Lo—at a play group activity.

A Waiting Mother's Prayer
by Wanda Penney

A woman looks toward the sky,
Breathes a prayer and gives a sigh.
I wonder if my child will be born today.
Keep her safe from harm, dear Lord. Hear me pray.

For I can't be in China, when my daughter arrives at birth,
Another woman will have the joy of seeing her face first.
But this woman surely faces what must be a heartbreaking day,
When she must make the dreaded choice—to give this child away.

Although I cannot be there when your life gets its start,
You're already my sweet daughter; you're always in my heart.
Through time and all eternity, there'll be a bond to share,
With someone that I'll never know, yet still, I'll always care.

And I'll always be so thankful for this woman I won't see.
She gave me my sweet baby girl, so we're bound eternally.
And even though it's not possible to see my daughter for a while,
A promise I'll make to my darling girl, my precious little child.

Although it isn't possible for me to see you first,
I'll be there for your growing up, when life's at its best and worst.
So when your nose is running or you scrape your little knee,
And at times you're feeling upset because maybe you've been teased.

When you have your kind heart broken, or if you just need a friend,
Know that I'm your mother and on me you can depend
And we'll be bound together, through ties of family love,
While another woman sighs and looks up to the sky above.

She'll wonder how you're doing and hope that things are good,
For the precious child she couldn't raise, but wishes that she could.
And we'll remember her in prayer, that God will mend her heart,
And help her understand that His plan was written from the start.

For this was always meant to be; my daughter you are mine,
A family bound by love and prayer, is a family for all time.
And family ties are bonds so strong, not made of flesh and bone,
But deep in hearts, where love is true, that's where families are born.

OUR LITTLE LINEBACKER
by Kimberlee Stout

WHILE WE WERE WAITING FOR OUR REFERRAL, WE OFTEN JOKED THAT IF WE WERE TO BE REFERRED A DAINTY LITTLE GIRLY GIRL WE WOULD ALL BE IN TROUBLE. You see, we have three sons—Nicolas, Ryan, and Jacob—so there is a lot of testosterone in our house. Our home tends to be a place with much activity and a great deal of noise. On the amazing day when the FedEx truck finally delivered our referral package, we were quite surprised to discover that our daughter looked more like a linebacker (albeit a gorgeous one) than a feminine little girl. We were instantly in love.

A week later we took our paperwork to a Chinese professor at a local university so that we could have some of the untranslated parts read to us. Contained in the narrative describing our daughter's personality was a sentence that read, "Lin Tong loves to ride in her walker and bang up against the other baby in the foster home and then she laughs and laughs." Yes, she most definitely was ours. We knew right then that she would fit perfectly into our wild and crazy home. And without a doubt she has.

Siblings—(Back) Nicolas (age 16). (Front) Ryan (age 13); Caroline Grace LinTong (age 3), Xiaonan, Hubei; and Jacob (age 10).

Left: Together at last. Siblings—Julia, Ben, Stephanie, and Katherine SiJuan (age 2½), Nanning, Guangxi.

Below: Katherine SiJuan (age 25 months)— playing with big brother, Ben, on their first day of meeting each other.

FOREVER LOVE
by Ohilda Bombardier

Written in my journal while in China just hours before receiving our beautiful 22-month-old son, Kai, from YiWu, Zhejiang

Kai, I just want to tell you, sweetie, while we count down these last hours and minutes, that we understand the immense changes that you will be going through these next few weeks. We've heard you are very attached to your nanny, and I thank God for that. That means that she has loved you and cared for you as best as she could. And in turn, I am praying that you have been able to reciprocate that love to her. Baby boy, please know that we will love you eternally. There is no bond stronger than that of mother and child. You were conceived in my heart, and I have felt every second of every day that I have waited for you that you were meant to be ours. We love you with such an intense, powerful love already that I cannot imagine it getting any stronger, but I know it will. And yes, there will be many tough times, but we will make it through together as a family. That is what families are for. And you, my little one, are now and always will be a part of ours. I love you more than words could ever say, and I am counting down the minutes until I can look at your sweet face, give you kisses, and feel your soft skin!!

I love you so very much, Kai!!!

Mommy

Adrian Wen Kai (age 22 months), YiWu, Zhejiang, with sister, Amanda (age 11).

LAUREN NICOLE
Excerpted essay by T. Lynn Large

SIX YEARS AGO I NEVER THOUGHT I WOULD BE A FATHER AGAIN. Vicki and I had one child—a son who was now 22 years old and moving out on his own to face life. The goal of every parent had finally been reached. Now it was time to really start enjoying life. We could travel or go out to dinner whenever we wanted and didn't have to be responsible for anyone but ourselves.

That night at the beach, after a day sunbathing, playing in the waves, and just walking leisurely on the beach, Vicki turned on the TV. Just as I walked into the living room, a JC Penney's commercial was showing us consumers how we could change a spare bedroom into the most beautiful nursery. It wasn't the beautiful furnishings that caught Vicki's eye but the ending. The couple weren't having a baby but meeting their new Korean daughter at the airport. "I'm surprised you never wanted to do that!" Vicki said. "I didn't know you'd want to" was my reply.

That started a conversation that not only lasted through dinner but throughout the next few days. By the time we were ready to return home from our vacation, it had been decided that a little girl from China would be added to our family. From the time we decided to adopt Lauren, she was real to us. Even though it would be almost two years before she joined us physically, she was a part of our family from day one.

It was important to me that Lauren would always know how much she was loved during the entire adoption process. I started keeping a journal about not only the process but also about family events, world events, and most importantly about feelings that Vicki and I had during our wait. When we picked out a name, just days after filing the adoption application, everyone said we should wait to see her picture so her name would match her. But we already knew that she would be Lauren Nicole.

After waiting more than a year for our referral and to travel, Lauren was placed in Vicki's arms in the lobby of the Central Hotel in Nanjing before we even had a room key. With new pajamas and freshly bathed, she smelled just like a baby should. She immediately cuddled up to Vicki as if she knew that this was her forever mommy. Much to my delight, as soon as she was handed to me, she laid her little shaven head on my shoulders and smiled before falling to sleep.

Every night after prayers, Lauren asks to hear the story of how she came to be our little girl. And, yes, everyone agrees that the name Lauren Nicole fits her perfectly.

Maggie Mei (age 2), Changsha, Hunan.

First meeting. Caregiver explaining to our new daughter, Esther Ming Yao (age 2½), Qingdao, Shandong, that we were her mama and baba.

Siblings—Hannah (age 10); Abigail (age 8); Samuel (age 3½), Wuhan, Hubei; Miriam (age 5½), South Korea; Rachel (age 4½), Lu'An, Anhui; and Esther (age 2½), Qingdao, Shangdong—celebrating Esther's official adoption day in court.

Esther Ming Yao (age 2½), Qingdao, Shandong—being held by her dad on the way to have her adoption photo taken.

Just moments after meeting Esther, we were whisked off to take a photo for the adoption. Esther was still in shock and so frightened. She had just stopped crying when I snapped this photo.

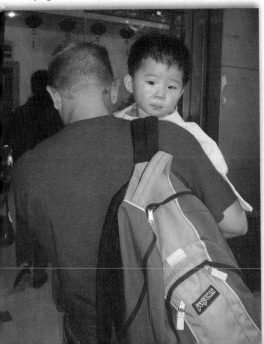

Audrey Eugenia Xiajie (age 5), Yueyang, Hunan, with sister, Ava Grayce Xiangchen (age 2), Kunming, Yunnan.

MADELYN'S STORY
by Tamara Murphy

WE BROUGHT TEN-MONTH-OLD MEGHAN HOME AT THE END OF 2002. A couple of years went by, and Meghan started asking for a baby sister. Shortly after that, in the middle of Thanksgiving festivities, I started having the dreams—dreams that there was a baby in our upstairs guest room, and she kept calling me "Mama!" I couldn't get the dreams to stop; they just kept getting more vivid. So I got an application from our agency and gift-wrapped it to give to Dad on Christmas Day. I really wish I would have had had the camera with me that day! It took him a month to say "yes," but then we were off on our second adoption journey. And the dreams stopped.

Our paperwork was logged in China in September 2005. At that time the wait to referral was only six to seven months and had been for over a year. Of course the China adoption program slowed dramatically immediately after our paperwork was filed; call it "Murphy's luck."

I began to feel that I had not done all I could do to bring Meghan's baby sister home. On Chinese New Year I sent additional paperwork to our agency stating that we'd be open to a "waiting child." In my mind every child has a special need—the need to be in a loving family—and every child has been waiting too long.

Much to my surprise we got a call from our agency on April 26th, exactly three months after I sent in the last paperwork. "I have a file for you to look at—a beautiful little girl named Yi Li Ying. She has a repaired cleft lip and is from the same province as Meghan." An hour later we told the agency "yes"; this was our Madelyn! An hour after that we gave Meghan her little sister's picture.

By the way Madelyn was born on December 9, 2004—the same month I was having those dreams.

Left: Emily Xiao Zu (age 15 months), LeChang. This day was the happiest day of our lives! It was such a pleasure to be able to meet the wonderful caretakers of Emily's orphanage and to share our appreciation for all they do to help these wonderful children!

Below: Emily Xiao Zu (age 19 months).

Above: Jada (age 4), Gaoming, Guangdong.

Below: Kina (age 2), BaiHai, Guangxi.

Last night in China. Julia Rose Honghui (age 9 months), Zhuzhou, Hunan.

It was my sister Robin's doing, really. I learned about international adoption while she and her husband waited for the referral of their darling Meredith in 1997. I was the first family member to see them on their way home from China, and I was instantly smitten with my lovely niece. "You could do this too," said my big sister. And so I did, four years later, with my sister at my side. "Xie xie, Sis, for leading the way."

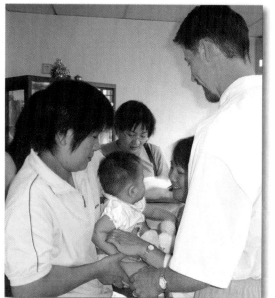

First meeting. Jane May Xiaoshu (age 9½ months), Leizhou, Guangdong.

TODAY IS THE DAY!
Excerpted essay
by Scott and Meri Butler

WE WOKE UP EARLY AND FLEW FROM BEIJING TO GUANGZHOU. We checked into the White Swan Hotel. After settling in the hotel for two hours, we headed for the Civil Affairs Office to meet our babies. We were brought into a waiting area. In a matter of minutes, they started bringing in the babies.

We were the third couple out of eight. The nannies from the orphanage brought in the babies. We showed our passports, and they handed her to us. It was the most incredible experience we've ever been through.

We're probably biased, but Jane is just perfect. She went right into our arms without a fuss. We both held her, and she seemed so happy. We waited until all the babies were united with the parents and then started the "paperwork trail."

We finished up around 5:00 p.m. and went back to the hotel. It is unbelievable to walk into the same room you left three hours ago and come back through the door as parents.

Today has been so incredible. It's hard to describe the feeling.

THE VIEW OF BABY DAY FROM GAMMA'S EYES
by Kay Collier McLaughlin

TODAY I WOULD BE THE PHOTOGRAPHER. It is a job I know well, although I normally do not try to juggle two digital cameras and a video camera all at the same time. And, despite the fact that I have covered many important stories over the years, this time it was Mom to the impending new mother and Grandmother to the new baby trying to stay on assignment, despite my heart in my throat and the tears I shared with all of the group who gathered in that office building in downtown Guangzhou, China.

We waited—the sounds of the babies drifting across the hall from a nursery. Then suddenly, after all of the prayers, preparation, persistence, endless paperwork, and the utter vulnerability of it all—they called her name, and Diane stepped forward and held out her arms. MaryChun Rong Collier Slone rested her head against her mother's heart.

There is a moment in virtually every medium when the skills of the novice are so finely honed that the swing of a racket or forward thrust of an arm exemplify the word athlete, the sweep of the bow defines the violinist. I do not think there is a more awe-filled moment than to be with a parent moving into his or her role, as all of the awareness of responsibility, the depths of love and the sheer connectedness between parent and child transform two lives. Half a world away from the places we know as home, I watched in wonder and thanksgiving as Diane took the physical step to complete the emotional and spiritual journey she had begun so many months ago—mother to MaryChun.

Later, as Chinese nursery tunes played softly, I watched MaryChun's tiny fingers lifting Cheerios from her mama's palm. When the tired tears rolled for this little one, who had traveled seven hours by bus with her nanny, one could only wonder at the greater journey of her heart—and the trust with which she laid her head on her mama's shoulder. Just when we thought she had fallen asleep, she pulled herself up in the wooden crib to peer at her mama, who was busy at the computer. And, for a second or two, a smile lit the small, solemn face.

Here at the White Swan, we join an incredible chosen family, with hundreds of thousands who have come before us, and all of those who are waiting on their love's journey.

It has been a momentous day. MaryChun is with us. We feel the excitement, the love, and the support of all those "with us" back home. We are so very blessed.

Love,
GammaKay with Diane and MaryChun

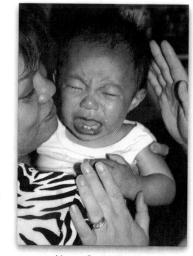

Above: Sophia Fei Ling (age 11 months), Guangchang, Jiangxi— meeting her family for the first time.

Below: A much happier Sophia (age 1½).

MaryChun (age 16 months), DianBai, Guangdong, with Mama.

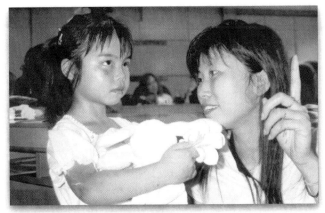

Christina Leanne DiFang (age 5), Changde, Hunan.

Lillie (age 8), Maoming, Guangdong—cast as Marta in "The Sound of Music."

Sophie (age 3), Huaibei, Anhui.

Sisters—Emma (age 22 months), Yingtan, Jiangxi, and Grace (age 4), Kunming, Yunnan, with Mom.

AN OLDER CHILD
Excerpted essay by Sue Huntress

SUCH EXCITEMENT! We have finally arrived in Changsha and are more than ready to meet our newest daughter from the Changde SWI. But where is she? In an effort not to panic, I let my mind drift back over the last several years, and a revelation hits and brings peace. We have been blessed with the strength of the red thread in our previous adoptions, and it won't fail us now.

Our first encounter with the red thread involved our oldest daughter. After several failed infertility treatments, we had given up hope of having a child. Unexpectedly we received a phone call from a family member saying that an acquaintance of an acquaintance had just delivered a baby girl and would we like to adopt her. We found a wonderful attorney who united us with our daughter in a short amount of time.

Our attorney worked with us again when we used the agency she represents to adopt our second daughter from China. While we were in Guangzhou completing our daughter's adoption, our agency had another group there receiving their children. One couple was adopting, not an infant, but a toddler and I was smitten. I was just knocked over and in love. Why couldn't we give a child a bit older a future? The family never knew what effect their adoption had on me, and we occasionally see the little girl at agency events. I yearned to adopt a third, older child. Ron knew of my wishes but did not know how strong my feelings were. While believing our family was complete and that there was no way to talk Ron into another adoption, we attended agency and adoption events and enjoyed being a family of four.

Then one day the red thread wound its way around our hearts again. While at an agency picnic, I checked out the waiting children referrals, and there she was—an adorable four-year-old little face with a wonderful smile and a twinkle in her eye that just called out to me. Talk about love at first sight. *but*, I thought, Ron would never, ever agree. I was disappointed, but we had never kept our feelings a secret, and I knew he was right—we had a full house with two daughters already. I also knew the budget was already stretched a bit. So I went and played with the girls on the playground at the park.

Imagine my surprise when I walked back to join my husband and there he was talking to our attorney—and he was looking at the same little girl's picture!!!!!! Before we left the picnic that day, we asked for additional information, and soon the process was under way to complete our third daughter's adoption.

Now shaken from my thoughts, there she is—scared and beautiful beyond belief! She has on a pale yellow dress, the color of the magnolias she has wound in her hair that falls almost to her waist and a bouquet she is clutching like a lifeline. Our family is complete!

The Picture
by Nathan Ruffolo

This picture, the first family picture you've ever
    been in.
The beginning of a brand new life.
Your first time out of the orphanage.
People crowding around tiny computer monitors
    to get the first glimpse.
Trips around the city will follow.
More pictures will be taken.
People will watch those too with enthusiasm.
They will marvel at your face.
They will laugh at the stories.
They will sit in anticipation of your arrival.
The day will come.
More pictures will come.
They may look nicer.
You may look happier.
Everyone may be better dressed.
People love them all.
But none will ever be the same.
None will ever cause the same excitement.
None will ever hold the same significance,
    the same importance.
This is the first.
Your first picture.
The Picture.

First family picture. Maya YaFei (age 13 months), Guiping, Guangxi, with Mom, Dad, and brother, Nathan.

Maley McKenzi
(about age 14 months), Fuzhou,
with her cat, Snowfah.

Delaney Liu (age 4),
Guigang, Guangxi.

Best friends—
Lucy and Laynie
(both age 3),
both from Guangxi.

BREATHLESS
by Jennifer Bedell

DADDY AND I WAITED IN A SPACIOUS CEREMONIAL ROOM. A platform was front and center and on it were an American flag, a Chinese flag, and a podium. Lining the sides of the room were the flags of many other countries, and we were reminded that hundreds of other families from around the globe had stood there before and that hundreds more were likely to follow. But this was our time. Six families, each with different stories and from different parts of the United States, who first met only days before, were now gathered to share this momentous life experience. We sat in a row of chairs that ran the length of the room, and behind us sunlight streamed through large windows and was reflected in the polished wood floor. Nervous laughter and excited chatter were balanced with silent pondering as only moments of waiting remained of the many months already endured. Now, along with much-practiced diligence, heightening anticipation and irrepressible joy abounded.

Such was the atmosphere when the announcement was made that you and your friends had arrived and were waiting in the hall with your nannies. For an instant I was speechless and breathless. That I would soon hold you for the first time was wholly overwhelming, and it was with considerable effort that I focused on the opening comments. Your caregivers demonstrated unmistakable love and concern for you as they shared advice and insight for easing your transition.

Then the doors opened, and the nannies entered carrying you and your friends. I was mesmerized by the sight of six tiny girls dressed alike in traditional Chinese clothing. Our most recent photo of you had been taken seven months ago, yet I recognized you immediately. Your eyes searched the room and found nothing familiar; so you settled into a bewildered, uneasy silence. One by one the families were called forward to meet and hold their daughters. Soon the room resounded with strong and varied emotions.

Our name was the fourth to be called. At last I held you, darling daughter, and marveled at your astonishing beauty and how eagerly and intensely life can be experienced. Some of my impressions were fleeting, gone almost before there was time to acknowledge them, while others became imprinted in my memory and promised to remain, perhaps forever. These moments can't be contrived or even duplicated but rather are incomparable blessings from God.

Sixteen months ago you were born during the same week that Daddy and I felt the stirring in our spirits that led us on our journey to you; today we know the fulfillment of finding someone intended for us since the beginning. And so we found ourselves at once completing one journey and embarking on another.

Ryleigh Gyll BaoXin (age 13 months), XinYi, Guangdong.

Libby Mae He (age 3),
Yangchun, Guangdong.

TUESDAY, FEBRUARY 21ST, 2006
by Stacey Teague

WHAT CAN BE SAID ABOUT A DAY THAT CHANGES YOUR LIFE FOREVER?

We left for the Guangdong Government building around 2:20. One of the people in our group had forgotten their gifts; so we were running late. The energy on the bus was incredible!! Everyone was buzzing with excitement!!

When we got to the government office, we were told to go to the fifth floor. We all went up as fast as we could, peering around corners, hoping for a peek of our girls. Eleven families brought together for two incredible life-altering weeks. We were ushered into a small room just big enough for all 11 families.

We no sooner had turned around and they were saying, "It is now time to present the babies!" Tears started flowing from me, and Mark was videotaping like crazy! The experience in that room is almost indescribable. Most babies did not cry but just looked around. When it was our turn we stepped forward and through the door came our little little girl—Xin Hong Bao, our brave little girl. She was smaller than I pictured but still had the same little triangle of hair that I had looked at and longed to stroke for the past six weeks while waiting for this moment. She didn't cry but stared with big dark eyes at her new family. Instantly she became a daughter, sister, granddaughter, niece, and cousin. She is ours.

Referral photo
of Lyndsay Li,
Fuzhou, Jiangxi.

Lyndsay Li (age 18 months)—
playing by a mountain creek.

Mommy Again at 45
Excerpted essay by Jan Jansen

I WAS ALWAYS HAPPY WITH MY ONE BEAUTIFUL SON. I had him young, and having more children was never a priority. I married a man with four children in 1994; so my quiver was not empty. For some reason that I could not explain, when I turned 38 I had this undeniable desire to have another child.

Five years of deep prayer and many, many confirmations of us being parents again came and went, and yet there was still no pregnancy. My heart was broken waiting for my miracle child. Slowly my husband and I began to get confirmations that we were supposed to adopt, running into people who were in the process of adopting or who had been adopted themselves. Both of us began to remember seeing a little Chinese girl in our spirits over several years, but neither of us knew who she was and had never mentioned it. When we finally made the decision to add to our family through adoption, God quickly provided. When we needed $1,000 for our home study, a lady walked up to us at a church meeting. She said, "I don't know why but God told me to give you $1,000." This happened every time we needed money to proceed with our adoption.

Throughout the process God showed me the amazing spirit of adoption. He led me by the hand and taught me that adoption is not a second choice but a wonderful miracle. We received our miracle on April 3, 2006—Mercy Rain, age 12 months from Chongqing, China. When I saw her picture for the first time in January, I couldn't believe what love I felt. When we held her in our arms for the first time, it was indescribable love. I know now that she was ours before the beginning of time. I believe God knew she was our child long before any of us were ever born.

Lianne (age 7), Mayme (age 7), Hannah (age 8), Marena (age 7), all from Jingdezhen, Jiangxi—celebrating the girls' 7th "Gotcha Day Reunion."

Sophie's Home at Last!
by Cindy Mansfield

MY HUSBAND, MIKE, AND OUR SON, JOSHUA (17 YEARS OLD AT THE TIME) TRAVELED TO CHINA TO BRING OUR SOPHIE HOME. I stayed behind with our daughter, Caroline. The wait for that phone call from Mike saying he had Sophie in his arms seemed to take forever. When he finally called, the first thing that struck me was that he sounded just like he did when I gave birth to our older two children. His voice was so full of love and emotion and joy at this little bundle of joy that God blessed us with.

Ten days later Caroline and I were waiting at the airport for them to arrive home. Finally I would have my new little girl in my arms!

I was standing at the bottom of the escalator with a doll and Cheerios in hand. When I saw them at the top of the escalator, I screamed—despite trying not to. I noticed that Sophie looked at me and then back at her dad, who was holding her, then back to me and just stared at me. Later Mike told me that he told Sophie, "You will know your mommy; she will be the one screaming when she sees you."

These two memories are the ones I hold so dear of that magical few weeks of our journey to Sophie. Now, though, is the best part. Our journey to Sophie is over. Our journey with Sophie has just begun, and it is just as wonderful and magical as was the journey to her.

New sisters—Hannah (age 8), Jingdezhen, Jiangxi, and Rylee (age 2), Guiyang, Guizhou—enjoying lunch at the White Swan Hotel.

Sophie (age 21 months), YiWu, Zhejiang, with Dad.

A Journey Full Circle
by Michelle Matlack

Anticipation
A smile a mile long
Tears of joy
Tears of pain
Strange people
Confusion
What's happening to me?

Long awaited
A journey
Two countries
Two families
Miles apart
Language barriers
Memories forgotten
Memories created
An old name
A new one
Is this right?

Hearts break
Hearts soar
Wondering
What does she look like?

Sadness forgotten
Happiness emerges
Sparkling eyes
Inquisitive hands
A gentle giggle
This family, my family loves me.

Common bond forged
You may never know
Does she look the same?
Does she remember us?
Questions left unanswered
But trust tells you she's okay.

Grace Anna Lu (age 1), Guangxi, BeiHai.

Kaleigh Xiao-Zhou (age 11 months),
Xuwen, Guangdong.

FINALLY, OUR BABY
by Whit Brown

KARYN AND I DID NOT HAVE CHILDREN, AND WE WANTED A FAMILY SO BADLY. We had tried the various medical procedures, and none of them worked. We decided to forego further medical efforts in favor of adopting from China. We both wanted a girl, and, when we saw Internet pictures of the girls in orphanages, we felt this was what God intended for us.

Our log-in date was June 27, 2005. We originally thought we would have our referral in six months. As December approached, the time frame increased to eight months. Then in February 2006 it was changed to ten months; then in April it became 13 months. It seemed like every time we got close the waiting time was increased.

Meanwhile we set up her room and tried to remain busy, but in the back of our minds we hoped the referral would come soon. We started checking the China Center for Adoption Affairs site every day, sometimes two or three times a day, hoping it had been updated. Friends who had adopted from China kept encouraging us to be patient. I ran into a friend in a parking lot who said she and her husband experienced a similar frustration on their first adoption. But, she told me, if they had gone any earlier, they would not have gotten Anna Marie. That helped tremendously. We kept waiting, knowing that God had already picked our child and was watching over her.

Finally, after a year of waiting, we learned we had been matched with a beautiful girl. On June 26th Karyn called me at work and said, "Are you sitting down? We have a daughter." Our agency had just called and confirmed. They said, "Karyn, she is just precious, just precious!"

The next morning Federal Express delivered our packet. Karyn brought the packet to my work, and my hands were shaking as I looked through the envelope for pictures. And then I saw her—and my heart was filled with love and amazement. I was glowing! I could not believe how wonderful the feeling was. Three pictures of the most precious little girl! Her Chinese name was Xu Xiao Zhou. She was age 11 months and from the Xuwen Orphanage, Guangdong Province. She was perfect! We named her Kaleigh Xiao-Zhou Brown. It wasn't a name we had considered, but it was the right name for her. Suddenly the 13 month wait was nothing. Our friends were right. God had picked out our daughter, He had matched us, and it was just a matter of time. We learned regardless of how long you must wait, it is so worth it! You *will* be matched with *your* child, just as we were.

Katie (age 17) with baby sister, Grace (age 13 months), Yangzhou, Jiangsu— at bath time at the White Swan in Guangzhou.

For My Dear Little Grace
by Katie Conrad

Looking into your face
brings joyful tears to my eyes,
for I know I must be
seeing an angel in disguise.

You fill my heart with joy
and my mind full of gladness,
Just the presence of your existence
makes sense out of madness.

You are meant to be our baby
through the red thread and God above,
You will soon be home with your
family who will shower you with love.

You have touched so many lives
and are loved by so many,
Though you may not know it yet
the love that exists for you is plenty.

Beautiful, bouncing baby girl,
No hair yet but soon will have her first curl
Soon you will be walking, talking, playing.
Then reading, writing, learning and praying.

God has watched over you
with gentle love and care,
and soon we will meet you...
Can't wait to see you there!

We both have polar bear hair!
Thomas AnAn ("TomAnAn") (age 2½), Hangzhou, Zhejiang.

Courtney (age 9), with sister, Cassidy (age 3), Chongqing.

Cribmates at the Yangchun SWI, Guangdong.
Page Jin and Libby (both age 3) remain best of friends.

THE POSSIBILITIES
by Marcia Armstrong

THE INSPIRATION TO ADOPT COMES IN MANY FORMS. A simple thought breaks through a busy life, ceaselessly nudging the prospective parent out of a comfort zone and into the path of change. Other times, a celestial whisper reveals the potential of what could be. Or destiny arrives in the recollection of a long-ago dream lying dormant until just the right moment.

Adoption holds so many possibilities. A first child. A sibling. Love and laughter all rolled into one little package. Yet often there is an initial shadow of doubt. Can this adoption really happen? Is there really a child for me out there? Yes, it can. Yes, there is.

So begins the phase of hurry-up-and-wait. There's so much paperwork to gather and so many hoops to jump through. So much waiting for stamps, seals, approval. There's a new vocabulary to conquer with new words and phrases, acronyms never heard of. Referral, dossier, authentication, courier, LOI, PA, DTC, LID.

Then, the collection of precious paper is sent to the Chinese Center for Adoption Affairs and the wait intensifies. Finally, a phone call! There's a child just for you! And suddenly, the child you have been dreaming of has a name and a picture. New mothers and fathers tape the photos to the refrigerator, or frame them for an office desk, stopping often to gaze at their new son or daughter. They admire the beautiful eyes, the dark hair. The younger children in the photos gaze back, lying on their bellies or sitting astride toy rocking horses. Older children pose hopefully near playground swings and in front of colorful murals painted on orphanage walls. Young or old, the look is the same. "Hurry to China for me," the sweet faces beckon.

Such potential! Such possibility!

Chloe (age 16 months), YiFeng, Jiangxi—learning to blow bubbles from her daddy.

Mom and Abbie Xuan Shan (age 10 months), Shangrao, Jiangxi—on their first day together.

Friends—Rachel (age 2), Yangjiang, Guangdong, and Caroline (age 4), YouXian, Hunan—having a great day playing at the San Diego Zoo.

A BIG SURPRISE
by Debra Harrop

WHILE IN GUANGZHOU ADOPTING MY DAUGHTER, I GOT A GRANITE ETCHING OF OUR "GOTCHA DAY" MEETING. It turned out great! My sister, Rae, decided she would also like some granite etchings of her children. She didn't have photos with her and placed her order after returning home. I later decided that I wanted to adopt again. I thought that I would like to adopt a boy around five years old through the Waiting Child program. My agency (the same one that I had used for my first adoption) just happened to have my future son on their current waiting children list. Rae traveled with me again, along with her daughter, Kylie. I wanted to carry on the granite etching tradition, and so off to Sherry's Place we went. As we turned the corner to her shop, my sister yells, "Oh, my God, it's Kylie!" I immediately thought that Kylie got hurt or something and rushed over to them. When I got there I saw what she was yelling about. Sitting right there was an oil painting of the picture of Kylie my sister sent five years prior to get the stone etching! We both about fainted. My sister kept telling anyone who would listen that the subject of the painting was her daughter! We didn't set out to buy oil paintings, but, needless to say, Rae bought the painting and it now sits proudly in their home. Unfortunately we didn't get to meet the artist, but this is a memory that Kylie, Rae, and I will always cherish.

Riley's Poem
by Patty Smith

I dreamt about you last night
You lay in my arms, I held you tight.
You giggled and cooed as I stroked your hair,
It felt as though you'd always been there.
Your perfect smile, precious and sweet
I knew our family was now complete.
Chosen by God it was plain to see
A perfect match for our family.
And now this dream is soon to come true
In a few short months we'll be holding you.
Until that time may God keep you strong
And may you always know you were loved all along.

Siblings—Shana (age 10); Mason (age 8); Brady (age 23 months), Jingmen, Hubei; and Riley (age 3), Fuzhou, Jiangxi.

Anna Claire LuYi (about age 13 months), Yifeng, Jiangxi, with Mom.

We Always Knew
by Liberty Sieberg, big sister to Vivi from Guangdong and Bella from Jiangxi

All our lives
we always knew,
for you were
waiting there.
In our hearts
you have remained,
for always and eternity.
As we sat and watched
the world go by,
you lay there
waiting for us,
through tears
and laughter,
joy and pain.
Nothing will stop
us from seeing you
for that first time.
We will travel
a million miles
just to hold you
in our arms.
No matter what
you look like, act like,
or sound like,
we will never stop
loving you.

WONDERING
by Stephanie Shea

Dear "Baby,"

I wonder where you are, what you are doing, and if you're even born yet. Your daddy and I have been plugging away at our paperwork, and it is almost done. What a good feeling that is! It's so hard to believe that we will be holding you in our arms very soon. It seems so off in the distance right now! I just pray that in the meantime you are loved and that God will watch over you and protect you. Sometimes I feel scared about all of this. I wonder if I will be able to meet the unique and individual needs of all of our children. I do know that God will give us the wisdom, love, and patience for all four of you. I also know that your brother and sisters will love you immensely. I bet they will fight with you too, but that's to be expected!

I just want you to always know how much you were prayed for and wanted! Your daddy and I prayed for and longed for all of our children. As a mommy I think it is normal to feel a little scared and nervous before the arrival of each child. I am also feeling a tremendous amount of joy and excitement about meeting you. This time I will not be meeting my new baby in the delivery room but in a beautiful place called China! This is truly the journey of a lifetime in many ways, and I am so thankful that God has laid this on our hearts and guided us along on this path.

I love you,
Mommy

Emily Grace Jiezhi (age 9 months), Gaoming, Guangdong.

Siblings—Andrew (age 3); Madeline (age 5), holding Anna's picture; and Rebecca (age 3).

THE LOVE OF A "MAMA"
Anonymous

YAN HAD ENTERED THE ORPHANAGE WHEN SHE WAS JUST A BABY. She didn't have any other memories except living in the "big house." She remembered wishing she had a mom and dad, but by the time her orphanage began doing international adoptions, it was too late for her. She was 14 and past the age when she could be chosen; so she turned all of her attention and time to helping the babies on the third floor. There was one little baby in particular that made her heart feel happy. Baby FuFu was so tiny. She was the littlest baby Yan had ever seen. She was so tiny that regular baby clothes didn't fit her, and so she spent most of her time in a small scrap of material for a diaper and a tiny white t-shirt.

Each day Yan would go and rock FuFu and sing to her. She fed her bottles and changed her diapers, and she would sit on the floor of the orphanage with her knees bent up and rest FuFu against them. Yan's eyesight was bad, and so she would bring her face as close as possible to Fu's, so that she could stare intently into her beautiful eyes. "You are not alone," she would tell her. "I will always be here for you."

With the love and care of Yan, Baby Fu grew stronger each day. When she would see Yan come through the door, she would get so excited and kick her little legs as if to say, "Pick me up!" And of course Yan did. She carried Fu with her everywhere she went. One day little Fu ran a very high fever and had to have an IV. Yan sat patiently beside her crib, singing to her and rubbing her arm. She ran cool water on a washrag and wiped Fu's brow. She did not want to leave Fu's side, even in the middle of the night. Like a loving mother, Yan tended to baby FuFu. Everyone in the orphanage could see the love they shared, and whenever a visitor came for the day, Yan would proudly show off baby Fu to them.

The orphanage had filed adoption papers for Fu, but no one wanted to tell Yan that someday "her baby" would be going to America. News came from Beijing that a family had been found and would be traveling soon, and still the orphanage staff was reluctant to tell Yan the news that her baby was leaving. Finally, just a few days before the adoption, the vice-director broke the news to Yan that her precious Fu would be leaving. When she heard the news, Yan broke into tears and ran upstairs to the room she shared with the other older girls. She sobbed inconsolably and refused to come down to eat. Finally one of the aunties was able to get her to speak, and Yan told her that she felt like her heart was breaking in two. "I cannot bear to be away from her," cried Yan. Patiently the auntie tried to explain how happy they all were that little Fu would have a family to love her forever, and they asked Yan to be brave and to be happy that baby Fu would know such joy. Yan promised she would try, but on the day of the adoption she could not bring herself to say good-bye to Fu as she got in the van that would take her to her new family. Instead she fled in tears once more to her room, vowing never to fall in love again because it simply hurt too much to say good-bye.

In America Baby Fu bonded quickly with her new mother and father, and her new parents commented over and over on how happy they were that she got such good care in China. But the orphanage workers knew the full story on who gave the greatest care. They think of little Fu and know that she was loved completely by a gentle and caring 14-year-old orphan who had never known the love of a mother herself. Yan gave Baby Fu the most priceless gift she could… the tender and unconditional love that every child deserves.

Mary Frances FuWen (age 2), HuangMei, Hubei.

Mackenzie Joel's Smile
by Tina Biggs

A smile lit up my room
And danced in my heart so light.
It came and sat down so close
As if to hug me tight.

Then the light suddenly went out.
The smile could no longer stay.
My heart tore open and the dance poured out,
And it took my breath away.

Another smile was left behind
And I watched as it grew brighter.
But where is the dance that was in my heart
To sit close and hold me tighter?

I searched for more light to fill my room
And the brightest of lights shown in the distance
But the smile seemed as if it were worlds away
Do I dare even take a chance?

A smile lights up my room.
Worlds are together that once were apart.
It danced in and sat close as if to hug me tight,
And it gently closed the hole in my heart.

Sisters—Faith (age 18 months), LinXiang, Hunan,
and Grace (age 4), Phnom Penh, Cambodia.

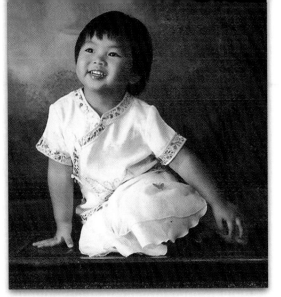

Above: Laurel Rae Fu SiYa (age 3), Guaghan, Sichuan.

Below: Elise Joy Zhao Fu Dan (age 5), Dongchuan, Yunnan.

Li (age 4), JinOu, Fujian, with his dad.

A Remarkable Trip
by Pat Alford

Our experience in China to adopt our son Li was a remarkable and memorable experience. It was like a dream vacation and we brought home the best souvenir ever!

We have a large adopted family with children from Korea, Honduras, China, and the "foreign state" of Texas. Our children from Korea were escorted to us. Two came with Korean women; one came with a missionary friend. We traveled to Honduras, China, and Texas for those adoptions, and we can honestly say our China experience was the best!

Since we were adopting a boy with special needs from an orphanage deep in the mountains of Fujian Province, we did not have the opportunity to travel with a group. We did not see any other adoptive parents until we reached Guangzhou. It would have been nice to meet more English-speaking friends; however we did enjoy having our own interpreters and guides.

We discovered how warm and considerate the people of China are. Everywhere we went we tried to communicate how blessed we felt to be in their country adopting our son. They, in turn, communicated to us that they were thankful that we were giving Li love and a home in the U.S.

The sightseeing was wonderful, but we especially liked being with the people. When we were in Honduras to adopt, there was always a sense of fear and uncertainty. In China, however, we felt safe and extremely comfortable.

Our trip to Li's orphanage was very emotional. We wanted to bring all of the special needs children home with us! While in JinOu we were treated to a Chinese feast with dignitaries from the town and orphanage. They were toasting us because we were the first foreigners to ever visit the orphanage at JinOu, and they were so happy that we had come to give a little one his forever home. We wanted to toast them because we felt so blessed to be Li's parents.

Even though we missed our family back home, it was difficult leaving China not knowing if we would ever have the opportunity to return. Our dream is to one day go back and do work in some of the orphanages and possibly help other children as they wait for their forever families.

Sisters forever! Jaelyn, Changchun, Jilin, and Kaia, Foshan Nanhai, Guangdong (both age 2½).

Right: Brotherly love in Tiananmen Square, just before flying to Guiyang to be united with their new sister. Ethan (age 4) and Nicholas (age 5).

Below: Phyllis Ting (age 2), Guizhou.

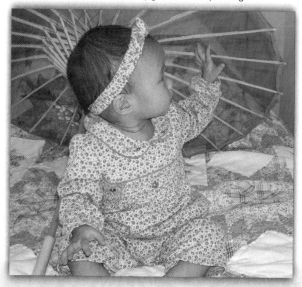

Lydia Anna AiDuo (age 12 months), Fuling.

Babies From China
by Jennifer Boitnott

Babies from China, what does it mean?
Rosy round cheeks, soft black hair,
Delicate silk parasols and giggles everywhere;
A touch so gentle with two tiny hands,
And a bond so strong that every parent understands.
Love unbounded that no heart could have foreseen,
That's what my baby from China does mean.

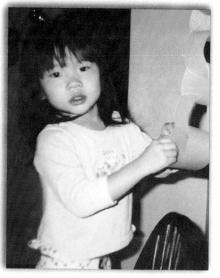

Gracie Elizabeth (age 3), Gaozhou.

When I was in China to adopt my second child, my agency would not allow me to bring my daughter. I came up with several ideas to keep her busy and help her with separation while I was away. One thing I did was create a chain with a link for every day I was gone. Every morning she removed one and saw that it was getting shorter and that I would be home soon.

OUR DAY OF JOY
Excerpted journal entry by Bruce Thomas

IT WAS QUICK. After a two year pregnancy it all happened very fast. Monday morning we climbed aboard a bus and drove across town to the Civil Affairs Office. Arriving we could see women holding little babies through the second floor windows.

They ushered us into a board room with a bunch of Disney characters on the wall. A civil affairs officer came in and gave us a few last minute pointers: Don't give them cold water or ice for the next few days, keep them bundled up, and don't expect anything—each child is different.

Then the Wuhan Orphanage director came in holding a baby. I thought she was going to give a little speech as well. "Bruce and Lise, do you recognize your baby?" We were the first called! I was stunned. Lise took Wu Dong Xia, and I took a picture. I had a grin that hurt and tears. Of course our new daughter, Autumn, immediately starting crying, very upset.

Soon we had eight crying babies in the room. Most were older, around 18 to 24 months. Only one other child was younger at 13 months. Dong Xia stopped crying after about five minutes and just looked at us. By then I was holding her, and she put her head against my chest and let out a big sigh.

Three minutes later she was crying again. It came and went for the next half hour. The director gave us the camera we had sent and some formula that the orphanage uses. Then she gave us a photocopy of the note that was left with Autumn when she was abandoned. She also gave us a handwritten note of her daily routine.

On the bus trip back she fell asleep in my arms, but once back at the hotel she awoke. Up in the room she snuggled with me for a while. Soon she was playing with a toy and giggling. It was a wonder to hear.

The next day we went back to do the official signage and make it complete in the eyes of the Chinese government. Autumn started crying as we drove up but then settled down. They gave us a chop with her name on it, a gold coin, a photo book with more photos of Wu Dong Xia at the orphanage, and a small bronze wine pitcher— a traditional gift in this part of China.

We have a child! And we love her deeply.

Christopher (age 6)— holding the referral photo of his new sister, Cimberli.

Cimberli (age 2), Dingyuan, Anhui.

Joslyn (age 17 months), Shantou, Guangdong.

Waiting Mummy
by Helen Haines

Like all the other mummys,
I'm waiting in a queue,
'til time goes past, when at last,
I'll be a mummy to you.

You do not know I'm waiting,
And you're not expecting me,
But I am trying to be patient,
Although patience is not my thing.

It seems forever and a day,
The wait 'til you come home,
It seems so very far away,
And I feel distant and alone.

I know that when the time does come,
All the wait will be forgot,
When I can hold you like a mum,
And tuck you snuggly in your cot.

This promise I will make to you,
When you come home to me,
That will be the day my love,
You complete our family.

With all my love,
Mummy

Ashelyn ManShu (age 1½), FengCheng, Jiangxi—playing peek-a-boo!

Above: Pencie Si-Yan (age 17 months), Qingyuan, Guangdong.

Left: Ada Li-Yan (age 3½), Lishui, Zhejiang.

Maud Yang Tong (about age 11 months), Yangxi, Guangdong.

Double trouble. Sisters—Emma-Grace (age 2) and Annabelle Ning (age 3), Xianyang, Shaanxi.

Lily Isabella Li (age 22 months), Maonan, Guangdong.

Pierce Robert Beijing (age 1½), Kunming, Yunnan.

Rose Fu Ying ("AiYing") (age 23 months), Laibin, Guangxi.

ANNABELLE NING
by Shelli Craig

IN LATE 2002 I WAS PREGNANT WITH MY THIRD CHILD. Unfortunately that pregnancy ended at ten weeks' gestation when we discovered at a routine ultrasound that the baby had no heartbeat. I was devastated. I had known people who had this happen but hadn't grasped the pain it causes. I mourned for quite a while and even sent off for a birthstone memory bracelet from a group that provides comfort for moms who have had a miscarriage.

Several months later I discovered I was pregnant again. This pregancy resulted in a 10 lb. 1 oz. baby girl named Emma-Grace. As the months went by we realized we wanted more children, but I had decided to have a tubal ligation after Emma-Grace's birth. We were led to adopt by a friend who was researching international adoption for her family. After seeing the list of children, we decided to adopt through our agency's Waiting Child program. We were drawn to two children, but one in particular was just calling my name. I would dream of this child. I thought she looked like my birth daughter! Finally our agency's decisions were made, and we were matched with our gorgeous girl, the one of my dreams: Annabelle Ning from Shaanxi.

Several weeks into the adoption process it hit me. I had put away all the grief from our baby that died. The baby's due date was within days of Annabelle's birthday! As the time came for us to travel in December 2005, I got a package in the mail. I had no idea what it was until I read the letter inside. I had forgotten about the bracelet that I had ordered in memory of the baby we had lost. It came on the day before we left for China for our new baby! I felt a chill that I will never forget. We will never forget the baby we lost, but every time we look at our Annabelle Ning we think of how lucky we are to have her to love.

DOUBLE HAPPINESS
by Sandra Tooman

WE TRAVELED TO CHINA IN SEPTEMBER 2005, EXPECTING TO ADOPT LILIANA AND RETURN TO THE U.S. AS A HAPPY FAMILY OF THREE. On the day of Liliana's adoption, the orphanage director told us that she may have a twin sister, who was very upset after Liliana left that morning. They wanted to keep the girls together and wanted us to adopt the other child. We were excited at the possibility of adding Liliana's beautiful twin to our family. We were just not sure if it would become a reality. Paperwork needed to be adjusted, DNA testing performed, and we were scheduled to return home in a week.

We met Lauren on a bus as we traveled to a Medical Center in Hefei and had a DNA test performed. It was amazing how much the girls looked alike. The doctor told us he would try to get the results to us before we were to leave China the following week. We were able to visit the orphanage the following day and spend a small amount of time with Lauren. We had to proceed from Hefei to Guangzhou as if they were not twins until we received the results from the DNA test. It was so hard to leave her behind, but in our hearts we knew we would be returning for her.

The day before we were to return to the United States, we received the wonderful news that the girls were twins. Instead of flying home, we flew back to Hefei and that same day adopted our beautiful daughter Lauren. We have been truly blessed with not one but two incredible daughters. Our family of two became three and then four. Life is definitely full of sweet surprises!

Twins—Lauren and Liliana (age 2), Chaohu, Anhui.

My New Family Nationality
by Molly Vechart

Just a couple years ago,
Not too far from this spot,
My mom found a book,
It was called "Shaoey and Dot."

It was all about China,
And Chinese adoption,
Shaoey's family became a part of
Music singer, Steven Curtis Chapman's.

At that moment she just knew,
In her great and loving heart,
There was at least one baby girl,
Out there in that world apart.

She talked to my dad,
And he thought and prayed,
He finally said sure,
And then we all hurrayed!

One and a half years later,
Something awesome made me cry,
My mother got the call,
We were getting twins! Oh, my!

Just the day after that,
We received something in the mail.
There was paperwork and pictures
Of two beautiful baby girls.

Molly (age 14) with her new twin sisters— Anna and Emma (age 11 months), QianJiang, Chongqing.

Only two months later,
And my parents already were
Off to amazing China,
"We'll be okay," said Mom, "I'm sure!"

They were gone for two whole weeks,
It seemed like eternity,
But when the first day of school came,
We all shouted, "Finally!"

For on that special night,
United we all would be.
All of us together would make,
One big, enormous, very happy family.

After we got to the airport,
The minutes went by very slow.
We all just couldn't wait,
For our parents and sisters to show!

Then all of a sudden it happened,
Just in a blink of an eye,
My parents and sisters came through the doors,
Everybody broke down and cried.

So in case you weren't listening,
I'll give you a summary,
About my big, long poem,
And my complete family.

My mom and dad went flying,
Over stormy seas.
And after they came home,
My family was part Chinese!

Sisters and "virtual twins"—Maggie, Nanjing, Jiangsu,
and Katie, Loudi, Hunan (both age 3).

Above: Le Dan (age 3), Shantou, Guangdong—
standing in front of the Forbidden City.

Below: Le Dan waiting at the big police station in Guangzhou.

A 40-Year Wait
by Ann Smith

IN THE '60S, WHEN I WAS 12 YEARS OLD, MY MOTHER AND I WATCHED "THE INN OF THE SIXTH HAPPINESS" STARRING INGRID BERGMAN AS GLADYS AYLWARD—the British missionary who went to China and, during WWII, saved 100 Chinese orphans. I asked my mother if we could adopt a Chinese orphan. She said she didn't think it was possible but maybe someday.

Forty years later that someday arrived. I asked my husband what he thought about the idea of adopting a baby from China. He said it was absolutely the right thing to do. We should do it today. Where did we sign up? Oh, and by the way, I should be the one in charge of all the paperwork. I set about gathering documents.

One month later, my older son, who was a United States Marine, received his deployment orders. He was being sent to Kuwait. Though the war had not yet begun, we all felt it was only a matter of weeks. My son was going to war. It was a terrifying thought. The night before he was to leave, our family went out to dinner. I kept thinking this might be the last time I ever see my son. I might never see him again. Even the possibility was profoundly devastating.

While we were having dinner, it was the next day in China. It was the day my daughter was born. Here in Ohio, I was grieving the potential loss of my son. In China, my daughter's birthmother must have been grieving too.

While my son was away, our paperchase came to a halt; I didn't have enough room in my brain to concentrate on the details of our documents. At last he came home. After a huge sigh of relief, I said to my husband that we could now continue with our paperwork. I said mentally to my unknown daughter across the world, "Mommy and Daddy love you. We'll be there as soon as we can!" That same day in China my daughter's finding ad was published in the newspaper: "We found a baby girl; if she's your child, please come and get her." Well, she *was* our child and we did go and get her. It took 40 years, but I was finally able to adopt my beloved daughter from China.

MY BABY SISTER
by Anna Rauh (age 9)

"SHE IS SOOOO CUTE!" I whispered as I stroked my new baby sister Maria's soft arm.

Just a couple of hours before, we had stepped off the last and final plane, and I realized that we were in China. I waited until the city bus took us to our hotel, the Majesty, in Nanning, China. Nanning was the city where I was going to get my new baby sister.

It was Saint Patrick's Day, and we were worn out. We were just settling into our hotel room, talking, and arranging our clothes in the dresser, when Lydia, our guide, came in to our room and said, "It's time to get your baby! Grab a bottle and a diaper and come out to the elevator lobby. Everyone in our group that is adopting a child will be there."

When we got out to the elevator lobby right next to our rooms, there were seven Chinese caretakers all lined up, each holding one baby. The nanny that had Maria was crying when she handed her to Mama. I was soooo excited! I hugged Maria because she was so cute; in fact I wanted to eat her up! I finally had my baby sister!

After that I walked happily back to our hotel room with Mommy holding Maria and Daddy right beside me. She was so cute in Mama's arms with her hair sticking straight up as if there was a magnet on the ceiling, and with her hot, soft arms hanging helplessly at her sides.

Boing! Boing! went the soft toy basketball that we had brought as I bounced it on the floor. Crinkle! Crinkle! went her beady butterfly as I waved it in front of her. Maria did not want to play. She was too tired to play.

Sisters—Anna (age 10) and Maria (age 4), Pingnan, Guangxi.

After Mama gave Maria her milk, she put her in the hotel room bed and Maria fell asleep. I stepped over next to the bed and watched her. I knew she was *my* baby sister. I felt so overwhelmed with joy that I could have just squeezed her until she popped!

This changed my life because now I have my very own, cute, little baby sister that I will love all my life.

Zoe Annalise (age 13 months), Desheng, Guangxi— with her parents on a river cruise.

Wow!
by Laura Tate

I lost most of my old self
when the plane hit the tarmac
in Hong Kong.
At least there could have been a funeral
for closure,
some parting words,
a song,
but there was no time.

Only diapers and bottles
and sleep deprivation.
Soon, I was Mama,
but this only helped a little.

Then, *wow!*
wow, God!
I lost my life and found it
being Mommy.

This exotic black-eyed flower,
this beautiful daughter
jumped into my heart
with her skinny legs
wearing a flouncy, floral
church dress.

She wiggled into my soul one night
like a happy, raging fever
and made my bones
laugh out loud.

PICTURING MAYA
by Karen

IMAGINE THAT YOU HAVE A PICTURE IN YOUR MIND OF WHAT YOUR CHILD WILL LOOK LIKE. You base this picture on what you looked like as a baby, what your partner looked like, what you think the conglomeration of the two of you would look like.

Then you find out you are infertile. You push that picture away. When you decide to adopt, you instead refocus your pictures on Chinese babies that you have seen—your friends', those in your Yahoo groups, online. Your picture is fuzzy and blurred—more the promise of something, the idea of it.

Then you receive photos of a baby—your baby. She is not a newborn, not a young infant, rather a baby with a blooming personality nothing to do with you. She already looks like a little person; she is smiling, shining. You grow attached to these photos after a few days. Absolutely this is who your daughter is. Your thoughts about her revolve around who she is in these photos, even though

Kaylie Scarlett Fuyan (age 10 months), Gao'an, Jiangxi— at the Buddhist Temple in Guangzhou.

you know they are a few months old and that babies change quickly.

Then you receive another photo; your baby is a month older. A different photo—a more serious photo. People actually question whether this is your daughter. Yes, you say. You can tell from her ears, her eyebrows, her tiny pursed mouth. You've studied these pictures, every inch of them, 'til your eyes grew bleary. Her face changes so much when she smiles, people say. And so you have another layer to your daughter, to your thoughts about her—now you can see her both ways: smiling, not smiling.

And now another two photos come. These have been taken barely over a week ago, on your wedding anniversary! They show your daughter at her present age—almost 13 months—and she is standing by herself, wearing a sundress and squinting in the sun. You print the photos and stare. The colors are so vivid. Your girl looks almost grown up, light years away from the baby you "know," but she is the same baby; you can see that when you place all of the pictures in a continuum. And you realize how much you have missed—the pictures you don't have, everything inbetween.

Your husband walks over and says, "We've watched her grow up in pictures in the space of two weeks." As if someone has pressed fast forward—presto, chango!—your daughter has emerged. And she is beautiful. She is everything you want. She seems almost a different person than the one in the first few photos; now her own person. She is gentle, kind, and brave. She doesn't like crying, but she likes giggling. You read that she is already saying "mama." At first you laugh nervously; later you can't sleep because of this small (huge) news.

And now you say: Okay, this beautiful girl is my daughter now. Here. And you point to the picture and try to convince yourself that it will be okay that you have missed these moments. That there will be a hundred million other moments and that she won't do too much more growing before you can go and make her yours.

Sisters—Leah Chun Ming (age 7), Huainan, Anhui, and Tea Heng Juan (age 5), Guilin, Guangxi—on the Great Wall.

A Letter to the Child
Submitted by Cheryl Bonfils-Rasmussen

YOUR BIRTHPLACE, HENG FENG COUNTY, IS SITUATED AT THE NORTH EAST OF JIANGXI PROVINCE. It is at the joint of Fujian Province, Zhejiang Province, Anhui Province, and Jiangxi Province. Total area of the county is 655 km squared with a total population of 200,000. The town is a key transportation point.

It was set up at the railway junction of Zhegan railway and Hengnan railway. 320 National Highway, Shangde Highway, and 311 Highway bypasses the town.

The county has a glorious history, and it hosted the local Zhegan governments during the second civil war. The county has rich mineral resources. So far more than 40 types of minerals are found here, such as lithium, nicbium, tungsten, zinc, and coal. It's known as the national "underground treasure."

The natural environment of the county is excellent. Situated in the sub-tropical zone, the weather is very pleasant, with plenty of rain and sunshine. The mountains are green, and the waters are clear. The quality of water, air, and plantation are among the top of the country.

Child, your hometown is rich and beautiful, and its people are smart.

Headmaster (Director) of Orphanage, Heng Feng County, Jiangxi, China
Zhiyoung Huang

Above: Daddy and Mei Li Quan (age 3), Hengfeng, Jiangxi—heart to heart. It took a while to convince him that we should adopt a child. After all he was 52 and already had two sons ages 20 and 15. It is moments like this that make my heart smile soooo big!

Below: "A butterfly for my sista" waiting in China. Drawing by Mei Li (age 3).

Above: One-year adoption day anniversary. Ana Rose Cai Mi, (age 22 months).

Right: First moment together. Ana Rose Cai Mi (age 10 months), Maoming, Guangdong, with Mama.

My Waiting Child
by Amy Heymann

I was not there the first time you laughed.
I missed the first bottle, I missed the first bath.
I did not witness your first steps.
You're growing so big without me.
I hope I will be there to teach you to trust.
You'll learn to speak my mother tongue.
You won't be adopted when you're young,
but you'll know the love of a family.
God has not forgotten every tear
you have cried alone, my waiting child.
And I have not forgotten that you are there.
My days would be empty without you.

Li Zhi (age 19 months), Bengbu, Anhui.

This photo was created for our December 2005 Christmas card. We were DTC December 12th for our daughter in the NSN program. January 3rd we accepted a referral for our daughter Amy-Hui Carmichael through the waiting child program. She joined our family forever on April 3, 2006.

Visual Memories

Yellow Pajamas
by Jodi Edwards

You may have wondered why I love you best in yellow pajamas. There are two reasons: When your Aunt Dayna and I were little we had these matching fuzzy yellow pajamas. I loved those pj's! Your aunt later told me that they were her favorites too! They were just so comfy, soft, and warm. I remember thinking that when you finally came, I was going to look for yellow pajamas for you too—so you would feel that same comfy, soft, warm feeling.

The second reason is probably even more important though. The very first moment I saw you, guess what you were wearing??? That's right! Yellow pajamas! It was a pretty amazing moment. It was March 18, 2002. We had just flown from Beijing to Nanning, and our plane was late. This made the moment even more tense and exciting because we were supposed to meet you for the first time that night at the hotel—not exactly something you would want to be late for!

I know the adoption officials had visions of a very structured and orderly meeting. First they would check all of the parents into their respective hotel rooms. Then the babies would arrive. They would bring them to a room somewhere and calm them down; then one by one bring each baby to their new mommy and daddy. But our lateness put a little glitch in their plans.

We arrived at the Nanning International Hotel, and they took us to the desk to check in. They said the babies weren't there yet but would be arriving shortly. Just as our guide told us that, there was quite a commotion at the entrance door across the immense hotel lobby. The babies had arrived!! And we were still waiting in line to check in—not tucked away in our hotel rooms as planned. Our guide sternly told us not to go over to the babies, but some of the other mommies and I did at least walk over to the entrance of the check-in area. You were still very far away, but I saw you right away. You were one of the few babies who weren't crying. Your huge eyes were just taking it all in, looking very serious and a bit scared too. Clear across the lobby I could tell it was you. There was no mistaking those beautiful eyes! There you were, my precious Emily—all huge eyes and yellow pajamas. I'll never forget that "first glimpse." It's forever etched in my memory.

So now you know why Mom is always trying to get you to wear your yellow pajamas. It just brings back that soft, fuzzy, warm feeling of seeing you for the very first time!

Yangjiang, Guangdong, sisters reunited. Amy-Hui and Katherine (both age 2).

Forever friends—Allie (age 3), Yangxi, Guangdong, and Alyson (age 2), Guangchang, Jiangxi.

Aubrey MeiLing (age 3), Qujiang, Guangdong.

New sisters—Aslynn Brooke XinYu (age 3) and Ava Marie XiaoE (age 4), both from Changsha, Hunan.

A Helpful List on What to Do While You're Waiting
by Ben Gerber

1. Freak out the neighbors by getting in shape for your baby. This can be done by wearing any sort of baby carrying device; filling it with sacks of sugar, flour, or a protesting cat; and then wandering around the neighborhood for hours on end muttering "testing this darn…" and "never stand up straight again…" Cats are particularly effective if you wish to test your first aid skills as well.

2. Get a raise. This can be done by spending countless hours at work reading adoption stories. Plan this so that your boss strolls into your office just as you are sobbing like a baby after reading your fifteenth "Gotcha Day" story in a row.

3. Practice your acronyms. This can be done by speaking only the following for a 24 hour period: "DTC, 1600A, BCIS, DW, DOR, CCAA, CCIA, I-171H, DH, CAWLI, FCC, DD, DS, DOT." You may not need to do this if you work for the government.

4. Now that your paperchase is done, you may feel a certain something lacking from your life. Volunteer to do the neighbor's taxes. Fill out forms for random background checks on local officials and document everything in your daily life. Detail such things as the decision-making process that goes into buying either coffee ice cream or vanilla ice cream. Have friends write you recommendation letters to bring to your auto mechanic before you have your oil changed.

5. Practice your socialization skills. Find total strangers who are obviously new parents and ask them about the method of birth, how much the hospital stay ran them, and why they chose to have a child in such a manner. This is best done while wearing good running shoes and with a lawyer on retainer or physically present.

6. Attend first time parenting classes. You will be one of the only couples or singles there who are not actually pregnant. If you are a woman, stuff a pillow up your shirt to fit in better. If the class gets boring, pull the pillow out and take a nap. If you are a man, you should also stuff a pillow up your shirt. This won't accomplish anything, but I find the concept of a man with a pillow up his shirt at a first time parenting meeting amusing.

7. Practice packing. Take your entire closet and organize it to fit into a 19" by 21" travel case. Then add medicines and foods. Try to fit other items as well, such as your pets, neighbors, or possibly Johnny Depp.

8. Memorize important phrases, such as the "Unafraid" song from "Mulan II," and "Mary Poppins" in its entirety. This won't help you in China, but—trust me—they'll be committed to memory by the time your child is three anyway; so you might as well just get it over with.

9. Go away for a while. If you're planning on a ten-month wait until you receive your referral, I recommend leaving now and returning sometime around May. Trust me, you'll thank me for this later.

Anna Man Lian (age 4), Yueyang, Hunan—performing fan dance at a Panda Academy recital.

CONNECTING
by Brenda Morehead

I WOKE UP AROUND 3 A.M. THE SECOND NIGHT ANNA WAS WITH US IN CHINA. She and I were sharing the hotel bed. I glanced over at her next to me and was surprised to see her eyes wide open and fixed on me. Just staring. Studying. And silent.

And I stared back. For several minutes we just looked at each other. I wondered if she was checking to make sure I was still there. Maybe she wasn't yet convinced the whirlwind of the past 24 hours was real.

But it was real. In fact those few minutes we spent looking at each other were more powerful and moving to me than any other moment during our China trip. No words were spoken, but we connected—mother and daughter. I think we somehow conveyed to each other in our own quiet way that everything was going to be okay.

Siblings—Jake (age 12); Meisha Ya Qian (age 3), Xinhua, Hunan; and David (age 9).

OUR RED THREAD THAT WASN'T
by Terri Nalls

I THOUGHT THE PAPERWORK FOR MY SECOND ADOPTION WOULD BE EASIER, AND IT WAS EXCEPT THAT I COULDN'T SEEM TO MAKE MYSELF PRINT OUT THE LETTER OF REQUEST TO CCAA. My first daughter was from Qichun, Hubei, and I thought I would request that my second daughter come from there as well. It seemed like a no-brainer; heritage trips later would be easier to one place, they do only foster care there, etc. I typed up the letter, and it sat in my computer for six months while I paperchased. I just couldn't print it out. Each time I hesitated. Each time it just didn't feel right. Finally on the night before I was ready to mail off my dossier, I retyped the letter and took out the request. I mentioned that my first daughter was from there but didn't make a formal request. In my journal that night I wrote, "I decided to leave it to fate. With that decision, I printed it out easily and took it to be notarized. Ahhh, that peaceful feeling when you know you've made the right decision. It's like God was sending me a message." Little did I know then just how true that would turn out to be.

Eight months later the referrals for my group started to come in. When I received the news of my Jiangxi daughter, I was so very happy and checked online for my travel mates' referrals while I waited for that first picture. I was amazed to see that people in my agency group were getting referrals for Qichun! I was just devastated. How could they not refer me a child from Qichun when they were matching that orphanage with my agency group? I cried and thought the red thread legend just didn't work for me! As the email came through with my new daughter's picture, I got myself together and tried to be happy about seeing it. My older daughter and I sat at the computer to see her baby sister. Mykayla did her usual "awwww" and then said, "This one is *ours*!" Oh, she was so right! All of my anguish over seeing referrals to Qichun just melted away when I saw my daughter. She flew like a dagger straight into my heart! It's so clear to me now why I couldn't print that letter—because *my* daughter was in Jian, Jiangxi!

Becoming sisters. Mykayla Lin Chunchao (age 3), Qichun, Hubei, and Marissa Li Shui Ting (age 13 months), Jian, Jiangxi—meeting for the first time.

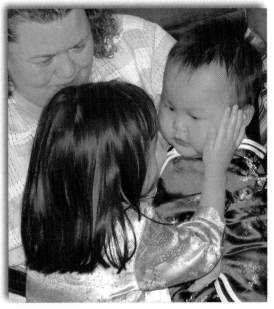

OUR ADOPTION STORY
by Maria Hansen-Quine

OUR ADOPTION STORY BEGAN 33 YEARS AGO WHEN MY HUSBAND'S PARENTS DECIDED THAT THEY WANTED TO ADOPT A LITTLE BABY BOY FROM KOREA. Found at the doorsteps of a stranger's home in a little basket, barely hanging on, being unable to keep any food down or weight on, that little baby boy is now my amazing husband and the proud father of two adopted daughters and one biological son! Thirteen years ago the story continued when we first met and started dating. It was immediately clear that we both shared the same passion for having children through adoption. Twelve years later, with one biological child and one domestically adopted child, we thought we were done having children! To our surprise, our precious little Faith crept into our hearts, as well as the glaring reality of the 80 million orphans in the world needing forever families. It became unbearably clear to us that God cares *so* passionately for each one of these orphans and that He demands of us to do the same, and that we in doing so had the ability to make one of them be our little girl! So now only one year later from deciding to bring home our little Faith and being home now for only five months, we have learned that our "special needs" little girl really is special indeed, and that somehow, for a reason unknown to us, God deemed us special enough to be her mommy and daddy!

Faith (age 3), Shangrao, Jiangxi; Isabella (age 4); and Matteus (age 1), with Mom and Dad.

Mia Hai Man (age 2), Foshan NanHai, Guangdong, with brother, Luke (age 4).

THE CHILD OF MY DREAMS
by Jennifer Embree

FINALLY, IN THE FALL OF 1999, I DISCOVERED THAT I WAS PREGNANT. We were overjoyed! Weeks later I had a dream about my child, as many pregnant women do. The strange thing was that the child in my dream was not a little boy, as I was carrying, but an infant girl in a white dress. She had large, almond-shaped eyes, creamy beige skin, and a head full of shiny black hair. The dream left me a little bewildered, but I chalked it up to hormones.

Years later we received our referral for eight-month-old Hai Man from Foshan NanHai Social Work Institute in the Guangdong Province. When I saw her picture two days later, I marveled at the little face looking back at me. She was the little girl of my dream, meant to be a part of our family. I knew it in my heart, more surely than I know that China is on the other side of the earth. After years of great heartache, my daughter was finally born into my heart.

MY JOURNEY TO LILY
by Maureen Sharp

THE VERY FIRST ACTION I TOOK THAT SOLIDIFIED MY COMMITMENT TO ADOPTING MY DAUGHTER WASN'T APPLYING TO OR SIGNING WITH AN AGENCY; IT WAS BUYING A TILE ON THE HANDS OF HOPE WALL. I had been reading the email lists regarding China adoptions for a few years when someone posted, yet again, rumors of shutdowns for singles hoping to be adoptive parents. The timing must have been just right because this propelled me to action, and I realized that, at age 44, I needed to get going if I was really going to be a mommy. I began to really consider the changes to my life if I adopted a baby girl from China, what I would want to give to her, and also what I wanted to give to China.

At this time Love Without Boundaries and Angel Covers were in full swing with their project to raise money for orphans by building a wall holding tiles honoring children adopted from China and those staying behind. The project was called the Hands of Hope Wall, and it really struck a chord with me. I knew that if I ever had a precious Chinese daughter with me here, I wanted a memorial for her to remain in the country of her birth, leaving a little part of her there. For years I had hoped that I would meet the man of my dreams and have a daughter I could name after my grandmother, Lillian Day, and so I sent a check and my request for a tile to read "Lily Day Sharp, My Future Forever Child" to Love Without Boundaries. I do not spend $50 lightly; so I felt that I was truly committed.

Then I corresponded with the generous, late John Harrah, co-founder with his wife, Jackie, of Harrah's Family Services, about the validity of this change for single adopters. Even though I wasn't a client, he patiently answered my questions and was very supportive of my chances of adopting. I knew that Harrah's had a reputation for "going to bat" for their clients, and, lacking confidence in myself, especially as a single, I thought that I might

Sisters—Alice Rose (age 4), Anqing, Anhui, and Zoe Nicole (age 7), Huainan, Anhui.

need an agency that would do that. It was months later, in June 2004, that I went with a friend to meet the Harrahs at their adoptive families reunion in Hershey, Pennsylvania. It was a great experience, and I am pleased to say that they were willing to work with me. I submitted my dossier in February 2005 and was matched with my perfect daughter, Lillian MeiQiang Day Sharp, formerly Qian Mei Qiang, in early October 2005. It was a dream come true.

My mother and I left for our trip in late November, earlier than we needed to, so that we could go early to Beijing and see the Hands of Hope Wall. I wanted a photo of Lily's tile for her life book. Our guide met us at the airport, and we went directly to Langfang Children's Village. Spending a little time with the children in care in the House of Luke was wonderful and made me feel closer to Lily and her caregivers than I had when I got her referral information. My mother and I were both very overcome seeing how open, trusting, and anxious for approval and affection those sweet kids were. I hope their families have found them. Though the wall was up and some tiles were on it, Lily's wasn't; so instead of her tile, I have a picture of the gentleman from the Philip Hayden Foundation laughing and pointing at the spot where her tile will be. I was given my precious daughter on December 6, 2005, and she is the most fabulous, beautiful, brilliant, brave, and funny little angel of a daughter I could ever wish for. I love my little Lily more than I ever thought possible. Someday when we return to beautiful China, we will visit the city where she was found, the people who loved her and cared for her at her orphanage, and her tile, from the mommy who wasn't one, on the Hands of Hope Wall.

Missy Kenny-Corron on her wedding day, with her mother.

Leah Mei Ai Xin (age 2½), Fuling.

Left: Referral picture of Lily MeiQiang, Qianjiang, Chongqing.

Below: Lily MeiQiang (age 13 months), with Mom and Grandma.

家庭

A Turning Point
by Missy Kenny-Corron

In December 2003 we lost my mom. It was a tough time, and I still miss her very much. She raised us by herself, and being our mother was her number one job. The next few months were a haze of sadness and trying to settle her affairs. Naturally it was also a period of reflection, and I began to wonder if the life I had was really as complete as I thought it was. I had a feeling that there was something I should be doing that I had not had the time to contemplate. I realized that the reason we had worked so hard on our dreams was to make a better life for our family. We had all the really important qualities that make happy families but no children to share it with. I finally began to think of something that Greg and I had talked about before we were even married—our wish to adopt children. We knew that Greg's cancer diagnosis (he is now considered cured) and my age (40) meant that biological children, though possible, were probably not very likely. We knew that there were children who needed families, and we would be happy to provide a loving family for children through adoption. Through the loss of my mother came the birth of our parenthood.

Chloe Rose XinYing (nearly age 1), DuChang, Jiangxi, with Mom. Photo taken only an hour after meeting for the first time.

Ava ZiSha ("ShaSha") (age 20 months), Shangrao, Jiangxi—
being dressed by her foster mother for the last time.

FOR SHASHA'S FOSTER MOTHER
by Valerie Martin

THE WEEK AFTER WE RETURNED HOME I DEVELOPED THE DISPOSABLE CAMERA I HAD SENT MONTHS BEFORE. I had no idea that your parting with the child we share would be included in the photos, and it was against better judgment that I opened the package while I was still in the store. As I paged through them my heart stopped, and my tears began as I saw you and ShaSha and the grief and tears on your face the morning you said good-bye and dressed her for the last time. I realized only then how much you loved our daughter. As I quickly left the store to be alone with the priceless photos, over the sound system came the "Ecclesiastes Song" with the lyrics: "A time to dance, a time to mourn… a time to laugh, a time to weep… to everything there is a season, and a time for every purpose under heaven." It was so appropriate as I thought about our ShaSha giving both of us happiness and sadness. Your heartbreak brought our joy.

I realize as I watch her during the day how much you taught her—as she washes her toys in the bathtub, blows on a warm cup of milk, or kicks a ball. Our lives have been blessed by your sacrifices during her first 18 months of life, and I know that the grief ShaSha felt after adoption was directly because of how much you cared for her. Thank you for loving her; thank you for pouring your life into hers. We will never forget you.

Sincerely,
ShaSha's parents

ShaSha had only been taken from her foster mother of 18 months that morning. She grieved so hard for her when she saw it was night time. She knew then that we were not going away. The following is what I wrote to family and friends: "Please pray for Ava. It's nighttime now, and ShaSha is grieving very, very hard. She speaks a bunch of words in her Shangrao dialect, but we can't understand them. She keeps crying hard and calling for her 'Ama' and a few other words only she knows. It's the most helpless feeling in the world. There is no way to ease her suffering except to plow through it and try to come out the other side. All the reading in the world does not prepare you for seeing your child hurt this badly because of your presence. My brain knows what all the parents before me have said, but my heart can't process the possibility of her someday feeling secure with us. She is exhausted (okay, we all are) from her crying, but she can't seem to let go of her fear enough to fall asleep." She cried and cried and cried and did *not* want to be held, touched, rocked, walked, or put into her crib or my bed. So we sat her up in front of my husband, and he gently pulled her back against him. She banged her cups a little, and, after a half-hour of not crying, her body gave into sleep.

Thoughts from

I REALLY FEEL LIKE SHE IS MY OWN CHILD, AND I SOMETIMES FEEL THAT I LOVE HER EVEN MORE THAN MY OWN CHILDREN. When I had my own children I did not spend much time caring for them since my family helped me. I think the foster care program is a life-changing experience for children and their foster families. We never realized that there are so many kids needing families to care for them and people like me can help a little bit. We just wish we could help more kids like Lingquan.

We think Chinese people should foster orphans as an opportunity to contribute to society and loving a child who is in need. I think it is a good thing to foster a child. They bring us much joy, although it will be heartbreaking when they are adopted. But we know it is good for these children to have a happy life and have a family of their own. As adults we can handle our emotions better.

I personally think foster care is important to society since if the children are not well loved, they might not survive their health problems. Even if they do they might be hurt emotionally by lack of love and they might grow up to be a problem for society. It is important to the child to experience family love while they are young and have a happy childhood. In the family we spoil them. We should discipline them, but it is hard.

When she first arrived at our home, Lingquan had just had major heart surgery. She seemed fragile and helpless. We felt we would do anything to make her better. We have loved her since then. I will be very sad to see her adopted, and I will miss her for the rest of my life.
by Yang Bao Yuan

I AM A NEW FOSTER MOTHER. I feel that this child has brought a lot of joy into our family. We have not had a baby at home for the past 23 years! We have really started to love this baby. I feel that since she has no parents to love her, I will be her mother to love her as much as possible. I feel that having her in our family really helps the baby, and we have developed a strong bond. I feel that this is a way to devote our love to a child who needs it. We will do our best to take care of her while she is under our care. We will be sad to see her adopted, but we will be happy for her at the same time. If it is possible we want to keep this baby in our family forever.
by Ding Rui Ying

WHEN I FIRST HEARD THERE WAS A FOSTER PROGRAM IN OUR VILLAGE, I COULD NOT BELIEVE I COULD HAVE A BABY TO LOVE IN MY HOME. I have one grown son who is in the military, and my house is empty. I first got to foster a child named Ting. She had not wanted to eat in the orphanage, and she was quite small. When she first came to me she was very quiet and would not smile. She looked very much like a bird who had fallen from her nest. I gave her rice porridge and pieces of banana. I walked with her outside to show her the sun.

Foster Parents

When she waked at night afraid I put her in my bed. Slowly she got used to me and then would meet me with a smile in the morning light.

I love Ting as my daughter. She became happy and strong. When she left for America, I was so sad in my heart but happy that she would have parents to love her forever and give her any dream she had. I still miss her. I have one photo of her that I keep on my table. I still have her little yellow jacket as well.

Anonymous

MY FIRST FOSTER CHILD IS AN OLDER GIRL, AGE EIGHT. She was not strong and did not walk well when she came to my home. I decided to help her get stronger and learn to walk so she could go with me outside. Each day I fed her three eggs and steamed fish. Each day I helped her walk across my apartment and told her to try harder and be strong so she could be like regular kids. Each day she took more steps. One step. Two steps. Three steps. Then 20 steps! Now she goes to market with me and proudly carries home the vegetables. She is a good girl. She likes to help me cook the dinner, and she likes to sing songs to us at night.

I am happy I can help this child. I wish her much happiness and hope a family will come to adopt her. She is a lovely girl.

Anonymous

MY HUSBAND AND I LOVED BEI WITH ALL OF OUR HEARTS. She was the cutest girl we had ever seen. We had one son who is grown and no daughter and so I loved having a daughter. I would brush her hair until it was like silk and put tiny clips in her hair to make her look beautiful. I would knit her sweaters. She loved the color red.

Bei would laugh with her whole body. My husband would take her outside, and she would run after the chickens. When they would flap their wings she would laugh and laugh. Then we all would laugh at Bei's big smile. We got a bunny for Bei to chase as well.

When I first heard Bei was going overseas, I cried and could not stop. I did not want to lose my daughter. My husband told me my job was an important one to get her healthy and happy for the new family coming.

One day my friend in the orphanage brought a photo to me. Bei's family had sent a photograph to China and a small toy, and I was then looking at the faces of Bei's new family. The mother and father looked very kind in the picture, and there was an older boy who would be Bei's new brother. I liked thinking of a brother for her, to help her in life and to take care of her. I am glad I have this photo. I try to close my eyes and think of her new life. I wonder if she is happy. I wonder if she still laughs with her whole body when she sees chickens. I wish for her a life of joy. I wish for her the kind of joy she brought to me and my husband. We will never forget this child. We will always love this child and think of her each day.

Anonymous

IN GRATITUDE TO A FOSTER FAMILY
by Joe and Erin Lore

LOU FU RUN (GRACE) BECAME PART OF OUR FAMILY ON NOVEMBER 28, 2005. She has brought tremendous joy and laughter to our home. Her dimpled smile brightens up anyone she comes across. We believe her happy, bright personality is, in part, a reflection of the care she received during the first 10½ months of her life.

Grace's journey began in Loudi, Hunan. Born on January 5, 2005, she was soon brought to the Loudi Social Welfare Institute. Early in her life Grace was fortunate to be selected to live with a foster family. She lived with her foster parents until we were able to bring her home.

Meeting Fu Run for the first time was magical. Upon hearing our guide call out "Run Run," the nanny handed our daughter to my husband. Watching the tears of joy run down Joe's face as he nestled his baby girl into his chest was a moment I will never forget! Although Fu Run played with Joe during lunch that first day, it took approximately four days for us to gel as a family. From that moment on we truly believe Grace knew we were her "mommy and daddy" and we would be a family forever.

We believe it was the love and nurturing of Fu Run's foster "mama and baba" that helped mold her into the person she is today. Grace is extremely loving, kind-spirited, and funny. She was relatively quick to welcome our open arms and love. We would wish that every orphaned child in China has the opportunity to become part of a foster family. It is our hope that in the near future, foster and forever families are able to communicate with each other. We would like to tell Fu Run's foster family how much we appreciate them for loving her the way they did. They are in our hearts and prayers as it is our hope that someday they realize what a beautiful little girl they helped to create. They will always be a part of our family!

Nana caring for foster child.

NANA
by Julie Flynn Coleman

ON A VISIT TO CHINA TO SEE OUR FOSTER CARE FAMILIES AS A REPRESENTATIVE OF LOVE WITHOUT BOUNDARIES, I WAS FILLED WITH JOY to see the children turn away from me, the stranger, to the comfort of their foster parents. I watched as they were tenderly reassured or gently bottle-fed in the arms of those who cared so completely for them. A warm feeling enveloped me as I tracked up and down the many stairs of the buildings the families lived in. As I entered the last of the homes, I thought I could not witness anything better than what I had already seen that day.

We entered the apartment—probably the smallest we had been in. It was a very simple abode—poor by monetary standards, but, oh *so* rich in love. The older foster parent was feeding the baby on her lap. When she saw me, Nana quickly put the child's "new" jacket on, wanting her child to look resplendent in fancy clothes for visitors. She held on to her girl and with true Nana pride turned to show her off to the world. It brought me right back to Ireland and the way my mom beams with pride over my girls—her "can do no wrong" grandchildren! The feeling of love and pride in that room at that moment was palpable! We stayed briefly and took a photo—one of my favorites to this day—of a Nana totally in love with and proud of her girl. As we exited the stairwell onto street level, I looked up and saw Nana and granddaughter wave good-bye to us from the window. The moment will stay with me forever.

GRANNY
by LWB Foster Care Volunteers

RECENTLY ONE OF OUR BABIES WE WERE TRYING TO HELP IN HENAN WAS VERY, VERY SICK. Little Fei was in and out of the hospital with tonsillitis and pneumonia. He would be discharged, only to get sick again. He wasn't feeding well and was very weak. Over and over he was taken to the doctor, but he just couldn't seem to get healthy.

LWB decided that the baby would have the best chance of becoming stronger if he was in a one-on-one foster care setting; so an ad was placed in the local paper asking for possible families to come forward. "Granny" was one of the first people to respond. This elderly woman rode on her tricycle for ten km from her apartment to the orphanage in order to submit her application to "love a baby." When she met Fei she was so taken with him that she asked to take his measurements, and the next day she again made the ten km journey by bike, but this time she carried with her a new baby blanket that she had custom made the day before for Fei. Once again she pleaded with the staff to please be able to be his foster mom. The orphanage was so moved by her dedication to help that they chose her to foster little Fei. The day she took him home, he was still very fragile. But in just one month, he was healthy and strong. His foster mom was determined to make him the healthiest little boy possible and so was feeding him eight times during the day and two to three times at night as well!

Granny is so in love with her foster son and is giving him very special care. When her neighbors heard that she was caring for an orphaned baby, they all came to visit and fell in love with him as well. Now they have all donated clothing for Fei. All of us at LWB are so grateful for the tender care that our foster parents give the children. For many children foster care is simply essential and allows them to truly bloom and grow.

The special love of a foster mom.
Ai Ying Rose (age 18 months), Laibin, Guangxi.

LETTER TO JING RU
A letter by foster mother, Yao Xiao Wei, to our daughter, Yang Jing Ru
Submitted by Terrie Watch

July 29, evening, 2005

I am not your biological mom, but I feel like I am. You will have to know that in Guilin, China, there is your mom and daddy and sister and brother who will always love you. In our family, Mom had you since you were four months old, and Mom gave you everything that is good and that you like. Now you are one year and seven months old. Now you are going to your new momma and daddy.

We are going to miss you, but we know you are going to have a better living environment that will change your whole life. We are happy for you. Your Chinese momma is very young and your Chinese baba is very handsome. And so are your sister and brother. We have a family picture for you to take home. We are hoping one day we can meet again.

Now you are leaving. You will never know how much your dear momma has cried. Every time when I think of you leaving, I cry. Now you are going to really leave us in a few days, my tears are dry. I really wish I could keep you, but we can't.

Dear child, when you grow up you may or may not see this, but it is your story. And you have to understand that your Chinese momma has a low education and it's not easy for me to write things down. Now I am writing this and you are in my arms, sleeping. In another five, ten, or twenty years will you remember that there is a Chinese momma? Any time you have a chance, please write to me or come to visit. I wish that you grow up quickly. Be a good girl. A China momma blesses you all the time.

Dear child, let me kiss you again.

Aunties with a newborn.

Wren Liliana Xuege (born August 2001), Chengdu, Sichuan.

SEVENTH MOTHER
by Nancy Fontaine

I WILL FOREVER BE GRATEFUL TO ALL THOSE WHO TOOK CARE OF MY LITTLE GIRL FROM CHENGDU, SICHUAN PROVINCE—MA XUE GE. Through the love of the important people in her life, Ma Xue Ge, now known as Wren Liliana Xuege Fontaine, developed into one strong and loving little girl. The first moment I held her in my arms, we were both very nervous and unfamiliar with each other. For me, the depth of my love was immense. For Wren, her eyes spoke a thousand words. To her at that moment, I was yet another mother. In her three short years, Wren was just being introduced to her seventh mother. This fact hadn't yet dawned on me at that moment, but it howled loud and clear that evening in our hotel room. Although she was sweet and quiet and endearing, Wren had great anxiety with her new mother. In fact she cried her heart out wanting her "mama," and that woman was not me. As I held her close, my heart broke with

Loving auntie.

Left: Olivia (nearly age 5)— holding Alexandra's referral picture.

Below: Alexandra FuXiang (age 12 months), Bao'An, Guangdong—During our visit to the Bao'An, Shenzhen SWI, we met Alexandra's favorite caretaker. The love this nanny felt toward Xiang Xiang was plain to see. It broke my heart as we said good-bye and she walked away crying.

Auntie and children.

Siblings—Emily, Wuzhong, Jiangsu, and Jacob, South Korea (both age 6).

"Hi, Ayis!"
by Emily Champoux (age 7), Huaying

To my Chinese family:

Ni hao! How are you doing? Are you doing great without me? I am still missing you, and my family too, at China. But we are going to meet you some day. I hope that you will remember my face and my hair because my mom sent a picture of me.

I think about you feeding me. And I think about you all the time when I sleep. My mom at this house tucks me in at night and loves me. She gives me Chinese food sometimes, but Dad doesn't like it.

Emily—that's me. I have a family now. I have toys that are great. I wonder if the babies have the toys that I had at the orphanage. I have a brother that's named Jacob. He's funny and silly, and he talks all night sometimes. He's a great brother. And I have a sister named Jamie. She acts so pretty and sometimes she gives me pretty makeup. I have this brother named Matt. He is funny and weird, and he has two frogs that make noises.

You know my mother, she went to the orphanage to adopt me. And we have a video of my dad when I was little—he was sleeping and I was messing his moustache up. Thank you for taking care of me. I liked it. I love you.

the sudden realization that I was her seventh such mother. I thought about all of them—her birthmother, the first nanny in the orphanage, her first foster mother, another nanny after she was brought back to the orphanage when her foster mother couldn't care for her any longer, her second foster mother, and the next orphanage nanny when she was brought back to wait for me three months before I came to get her. Huge tears fell down my face in gratitude for all that these women had done for my daughter, in sadness for Wren's grief, in fear that she would be forever angry at me, in joy that I was finally able to hold my precious new daughter, and in infinite wonder at how much this little soul had endured. At that moment, I repeated my solemn vow that Wren's seventh mother would be her forever one.

Daniel Jia-Tuan (age 3), Shantou, Guangdong— being held by his nanny.

Daniel Jia-Tuan (age 3), Shantou, Guangdong, and Noah Yue-Nan (age 3), Hengshan, Hunan— enjoying TV with Dad. There is always room on Daddy's lap.

Thoughts

Jian Chao
During our time together, you have brought all of us so much joy. Hoping that under your father and mother's protection, you will grow up healthy and happy. In your life from now, may you continue to grow in courage and strength.
Miss You. Your Ayi
Jiang Hai Xia

迷潮：

和你相处的这段日子里，你给我带来了许多快乐。望你在爸爸妈妈的呵护下，健康快乐的成长在往后的生活中定会更加勇敢、坚强。

想你的阿姨：
蒋海霞

Dang Jian Chao
The precious one to Ayi's heart. You are about to leave the Ayi that loves you most at Hope Foster Home to go to a faraway country to meet your father and mother. Ayi is happy for you. I hope from the bottom of my heart that you will pass each day in health and happiness.
Your Ayi that will miss you forever.
Mu Gui Rong

29th August Sunday
I HAVE HAD A DOUBLE DAY'S REST. I am on duty tonight. I have never had a double day's rest since I got this job before now.

On entering the children's building, I feel very hot. Crossing into the office and putting off my back pack, I rush to see those babies, even though I am sweating all over. At this moment I feel a sudden understanding in my heart of my feelings for these babies. I do *love* them!

In the infant room Qin is still so pink with a pair of round black eyes looking at me. Mei is eating her little hand—so delicious! Xiao Zi is so quiet and doesn't want to draw too much attention. Fei and Gui fall asleep right after they have had their bottles. They are gaining weight. I am so happy to be part of them growing. Lovely Di is sleeping soundly now. I don't want to wake her up; so I just put my hand so softly on her head to wish her good dreams.

You are Always on my Mind
AT THE BEGINNING WHEN MIN LEFT THE BABY HOUSE, I COULD ALWAYS FEEL THAT SHE IS STILL WITH ME. I couldn't believe that it wasn't true. Later I tried to make myself understand that she wasn't here any longer; yet I told myself and believed in my heart that Min will be back one day!

I always have a feeling she is with me, although she is at the other side of the earth. I talked to my mother and father about her. I mentioned her to the other aunties. I shared with my friends my sweet memory about her. I want everyone to share this happiness with me. I want everyone to know there is such a bright, healthy, and happy child in the world named Min.

Bathtime
IT IS HOT IN THE ORPHANAGE THESE DAYS. The active, fun loving Mei is always sweating. Bath is one of her favorite activities. Look! Every time she sees the aunties take other kids to the bathroom, her eyes follow the auntie until she is out of sight. It seems like she is saying, "You forgot to take me!"

This time it is Mei's turn. I hold her up and she seems to know that it is bath time, waving, kicking,

from Ayis

and laughing happily. Once in the tub, she laughs happily again, very contented.

I bathe her slowly, trying to drag the minutes to let her enjoy this *cool* moment. For a while she turns to look at me, very satisfied! "You are so cute," I say tickling her. She giggles and raises up her legs to spat the water. Spat! Spat! Water drops are all over me. She is laughing, I am laughing. I believe even the water is laughing. You are happy; so am I. Oh, Mei! A lovely child.

Farewell

TUAN WILL BE LEAVING FOR THE CITY TOMORROW. She will soon go to America after the related process is done. That's incredible to me! She has parted from one and another although she is still such a little thing. In fact she is still too young to understand all that is happening, and I think that is a good thing.

In the daytime I devote myself to feeding the kids, trying hard to ignore this matter. In the evening Tuan went to bed early. She was sleeping soundly. I was on duty that night. To my surprise I had difficulty sleeping. Morning came and I woke up very early. Tuan had already woken up too and opened her eyes, big and round. I avoided looking into her eyes, afraid of my feelings. The milk was sent to the room and I took a bottle and began to feed her. "Be happy forever," I whispered to her.

She would not drink the milk. She stopped and pushed the bottle away to look at me. I cannot believe it. She understands what I am saying and looks into my eyes. Soon she will see golden hair and green eyes instead of mine. They come and take her to get ready. Soon the staff runs to tell me, "Hurry up. Tuan is getting on the bus. Go and say farewell."

I really didn't want to go. I did not like to say good-bye to her, yet my heart was fighting. When I went downstairs, Tuan is in a lucky red cloth. She looked happy and excited to see me, kicking her legs to say, "Come hold me." But it is time to go up the stairs of the bus. Watching the coach leaving, I feel an emptiness inside. My heart is heavy. Be happy, Tuan. I now understand what a mama feels for her child.

Dang Jian Chao
You are an especially good girl, my precious one. Ayi's heart is so warmed by the fact that you have found a home and parents. Wishing you happiness as you grow up.
Your Ayi who will always miss you.
Chen Gui Qin

党建潮：

你是一个特别听话的宝贝，

阿姨忠心地祝福你有了家和爸

爸妈妈，希望你幸福快乐的成长，

永远想念你的阿姨：

陈桂琴

Daughter Jian Chao, Beautiful angel, Ayi can't bear your departure. Ayi will never forget the joy your intelligence has brought her. Now that you are going to another country, who knows when we will be able to meet again. Ayi wishes you lasting peace.
Your Ayi, Wei Yan Hua

女儿建潮：

美丽的天使，阿姨会永远记住你

离开，你的聪明伶俐和快乐的笑

脸给阿姨带来了许多欢乐，阿姨

永远都不会忘记，今后你到异国他

乡，不知何时才能相见，在这里阿姨

祝福你一生平安，长大以后前途无量

你的阿姨：魏艳华

Weaving the Fabric

According to legend, the red thread is already established when we begin
our adoption journeys. Families are pulled along the thread as they wait,
working their way through the twists and tangles that they find along the way.

Abigail Mae-Xiao
(age 9 months),
Gaozhou, Guangdong.

Anna Chuan Wei
(age 2½),
Jiangxi, Fuzhou.

Gabriella Grace ShaoRan
(age 15 months),
Gaozhou, Guangdong.

With a referral, the thread is carefully knotted and secured
to the fabric of a family. After a long journey overseas, the
farthest end of the thread is discovered. With one final tug,
parents suddenly find a son or daughter in their arms, and
at last it is time to start making those very first stitches.

We no longer cling to that single thread for dear life.
We are home now. Slowly, almost imperceptibly, hearts and
lives are woven together into a rich tapestry. Starting with
the simplest needlework around the edges, we work our way
inward. With each stitch, the thread becomes stronger, the
fabric more complete, creating a work of art that is more
precious than anything we could have imagined.

The red thread becomes entwined with those of sisters,
brothers, grandparents, aunts, uncles, cousins, and friends.
We are now adoptive families, transracial families, families
of children finding their place in a new country. To many
we are unique and colorful, and people often take notice of
us. To those who will take the time to look closely, they will
find real beauty. We are true families, lovingly stitched by
hand and richly blessed.

Aubrey Rose Feng
(age 14 months),
Huazhou City, Guangdong.

Jenna Mei JiaTao
(age 12 months),
Qichun, Hubei.

Ashley (age 14 months),
Yangjiang, Guangdong.

Emily (age 7), Wuzhong, Jiangsu,
with brother Jacob (age 7), South Korea.

Lily YongLi (age 4), Zhuzhou,
Hunan—proudly wearing
her traditional tiger hat.

Kailee Marie Wen (age 12 months),
Zhuzhou, Hunan.

Roscoe James ("R. J.") Xiao
(age 2), Jinchang, Gansu.

"Waiting Children"
by Jan Champoux

We've all heard the adoption process referred to as a "roller coaster." Okay, so if adoption is a roller coaster, then "waiting children" adoption is one of those mega-coasters that dangles you from your seat, spinning you around and upside down, and dropping you down the steepest of inclines at 90 miles an hour. You stagger off and check for a pulse… and then it hits you… what a *rush*!!!

That's the way it struck me anyway; it was an exhilarating ride, but one with many uncertainties at the outset. First we had to get in the right line. Choose the wrong agency and we could miss our child altogether! Then we had to prepare for any unknowns that could pop up around the next bend. Could we handle them? But the scariest part for me was at the top of that first hill… raised up off my seat with my stomach in my throat, attempting to choose our child from a list. How could I ever hope to get it right?

That was almost six years ago, and my head is still spinning. I needn't have worried. Out of all the children, in all of China's orphanages, we were able to find the one little girl who would make our family complete. Our beautiful Emily! I'd love to take credit for being brilliant enough to locate her, but I am really not that smart. Only God and the invisible red thread could have conspired to bring us together. I was just along for the ride.

Sisters—Addie (age 4), Anqing, Anhui; Jessica (age 20);
and Chloe (age 5), Jiaozuo, Henan.

Sisters—Joie Mei (age 4), Guiping, Guangxi;
Jessie Mei (age 4), Changzhou, Jiangsu;
and Danie Mei (age 3), Luzhou, Sichuan.

Just a Child
by Amy Eldridge

I am standing at the playground when a solemn looking boy of about five comes up and tugs on my pant leg. "Hey, lady," he says in a whisper. "Your little boy's arm is missing." He says it with such earnest concern, as if I should start looking for the arm that my son must have dropped along the way. "It's okay," I assure him with a smile. "That's just how he was born and he does just fine with one." I have grown used to the questions and comments, and the much relieved little boy wanders off to play.

When my husband and I first decided to adopt from China, I couldn't wait to bring our child home, but I also had many worries. What if something was "wrong" with the baby? What if she had an unknown "special need"? I wanted a *Healthy* baby with a capital "H," and I would lie in bed at night and worry and worry and then worry some more. Special needs children were as foreign to me as China herself at that time, and I just knew in my heart that it must take a very special family to willingly walk that path. (Where's that halo?) Oh how naive I was, and how very thankful I am that God gently showed me the truth that every child on earth is, first and foremost, just a child.

After adopting my beautiful daughter, Anna, I became involved with charity work in China, and the more time I spent in the orphanages there, the more I fell madly, totally, and passionately in love with those children who had medical needs. I held babies with heart conditions and hugged gorgeous and giggly little girls with Hep B. I rocked baby after baby with cleft lip who would grin at me with their wide smiles and crinkle up their gorgeous eyes. Surely *these* couldn't be the "special needs" that had filled my heart with worry all those years before! These children were amazing, and beautiful, and absolutely perfect in their own way. They opened my heart and filled it with such love.

I will never forget taking a friend to one

orphanage so she could see a school we had opened for children with medical needs and watching her be absolutely enthralled as the kids laughed, ran, and played with such joy at recess. "They are all so beautiful!" she said. "I would adopt any of them in a heartbeat." It was then that I told her that every single one of the beautiful children in front of her was labeled "special needs." She shook her head with disbelief and said, "Every person in the world should have the experience of standing here watching these kids just be kids." I wish that could happen as well, because I know there is so much fear about the term "special needs children" simply because people have never had the chance to meet these wonderful kids. I am living proof of that fact.

In 2006 I was given the honor of bringing home a little boy from China who was on a waiting child list. My son TJ is missing most of his right arm, but he certainly hasn't let that stop him. Within a few weeks of being home, I was already on the phone with poison control telling them that my son had opened a childproof bottle of vitamins and had eaten almost all of them. "Oh that happens all the time," the agent on the other line said. "Trust me that this was quite a feat," I said back, secretly cheering with pride (after I knew he would live) that my two-year-old had managed to crack the safety lid with just one hand.

Now I smile when I think back to praying so hard for "only a healthy baby." TJ is as healthy as can be. He just has to get a little more creative when threading beads or trying to hold two of something. I know he will have to face many comments and stares at times, but I know we will work together to figure out how to respond to people in a way that makes him comfortable. I have already seen that once people are around TJ for five minutes, they don't even remember that he is missing an arm. They only notice his huge smile and even bigger personality.

Today TJ and I played outside with his new red wagon that he loves to pull up and down the sidewalk each day. With his one hand he grasped the handle firmly and off he went. I blinked away tears as I said a prayer of thanks that he is now my son. To me he is perfect just the way he is. I watch him as he plays, and I see no special needs. All I see in front of me is a black-haired boy, a bright blue sky, and a shiny red wagon. TJ drops the handle to turn and wave at me and I am struck once again with how blessed I am to have him in my life. I wave back and shout "I love you, Sweetie!" Satisfied that Mama is near and watching, he once again grabs the handle of his wagon and marches on with determination—a perfectly beautiful little boy with a whole wide world to explore.

Sister
by Helen Edmonds

Two seeds, blown on different winds.
We landed in the same soil, and grow together.
Not my blood, but my heart.
Not my genes, but my friend.
Blossoming side by side,
Entwined with the red thread that binds us.

New sisters—Eleanor Cui (age 3), Shanggao, Jiangxi, and Grace Jie Meng (age 8 months), Gaoming, Guangdong.

TJ (age 2), Shantou, Guangdong.

家庭

Emily (nearly age 4), Jiangxi.

Lulu (age 3), Guilin, Guangxi.

TRYING TIMES IN CHINA
by Darlene Moitoso

I WENT TO CHINA IN OCTOBER OF 2005 TO PICK UP MY LITTLE LULU FROM GUILIN. She was just shy of age three at "Gotcha Day." I had prepared myself for a malnourished toddler with developmental delays, and what I got was a healthy, smart, independent, strong-willed little girl. Oh, and by the way, she hated me.

We ask so much of older children at adoption. We expect them to love us as much as we love them. We expect them to quickly adjust to funny-smelling, odd-looking folks who are so stupid that they don't even understand Chinese. We expect more than what almost any of us could handle ourselves, and yet somehow they adapt. Some children come around in what's known as the magical three days, but for some it is longer—much, much longer—but it almost always happens.

I'm so thankful for having learned so much before I left for China. Thankful for all those who honestly explained their difficulties during their time in China. It truly made all the difference. I knew that what I was going through, and more importantly what Lulu was going through, was normal. The more she grieved, the more I knew that she would be able to love me.

China adoption is not a vacation. It's a hard journey full of transition and adjustment and grief. Yet at the same time it is one of discovery and joy. It is by far the best thing I have ever done in my lifetime. I am most definitely the luckiest woman in the world to have my amazing daughter.

Sisterly Moments
by Tessa Berns (age 5) and Claire Berns (age 3)

"Mama, can I e-a-t c-h-o-k-l-u-t?" five-year-old Tessa discreetly spells. Not to be outdone, her two-year-old sister, Claire, follows with, "Mama, can I h-i-j-k-l-m-n-o-p?"

Tessa's helpful mothering advice, "Maybe Claire doesn't want to get her hair combed. Babies like to do activities, you know."

Claire, explaining the problem, "Mama, Tessa try to have a little privacy. I scream and scream 'Let me in!'"

Tessa, nostalgically, "I wish we were still waiting for Claire to come home from China. That was fun."

Claire's future plans, "When I grow up, I be a big sister. I take care of Tessa, I talk to Tessa, I play with Tessa."

Tessa, explaining the expectations, "Mei-mei, Wo ai ni, but jie-jie doesn't want to see you pulling things off the table."

Tessa, truly perplexed, "Claire, why did you say 'no?' You don't say 'no' to jie-jies."

Claire: "I wish to see a lion dance." Tessa: "I can't make that wish come true for you, sweetie."

Tessa, waking Claire up, "Claire, it's your big sister. I'm happy to see you. I love you."

Sisters—Jade (age 5), Qingyuan, Guangdong, and Maya (age 8), FeiDong, Anhui, with friends and sisters—Tessa (age 5), Qingyuang, Guangdong, and Claire (age 3), Gaoming, Guangdong.

ETCHED ON MY HEART
by David Beck

IT WAS IN JUNE 2005 WHEN I REALLY CAME TO HAVE A DEEPER UNDERSTANDING OF HOW YOUR MOM FELT IN HER ANTICIPATION OF YOU. You see, Lilli, she is a guarded person, who is rather shy on the inside and does not show her emotions to just everyone. It was a simple conversation that is now engraved in my heart forever. We were talking about loving children. I said if you think you love your kids when they are babies, wait until the day they run across the floor, throw their arms around your neck, and tell you that they love you. I told your mommy that she would just melt and there would be nothing that she would not do for you, including laying down her life. With tears in her eyes she turned to me and told me that she would be willing to lay down her life that very moment for you if that was what it would take to get you to your daddy. She told me she had known from when she was a little girl she was supposed to adopt a child and there was one waiting for her.

That moment has crossed my mind so many times this last year. It is so vivid that I remember exactly where we were. The sun was shining on her face and the stillness in the air surrounded us. From that second I knew that your mommy was so in love with you, even though her arms had never held you. She had never heard your cry or your laughter. She had never seen your face or felt your heart beat; yet she was already willing to lay down her life for you. The Bible says, "There is no greater love than to lay down one's life for one's friends." How much more powerful it was for her to be willing to lay down her life for just the thought of you. You see, Lilli, from that very moment I realized that your mother had been pregnant with you for years. Maybe it was not in the traditional way of carrying a baby in a mommy's belly for nine months, but she had carried you in her heart for far longer. She had longed for you to be in her arms. She had battled with a sense of disappointment; yet all of the time down deep knowing God had a special plan which included you, her precious little girl.

I remember her face when she came down the escalator at the airport holding you in her arms. Even though I have seen smiles on her face many times before, I had never seen such pure joy and love until that very moment. Each and every day she grows more and more in love with you. She sits and holds you for hours while you are sleeping and kisses your little lips. She worries frantically when you are a little sick. It bothers her immensely when she thinks she has done something wrong. She carries a great feeling of responsibility for the type of person you will become. She prays for guidance to be the right kind of mother you need. She even runs you around the house with flashcards teaching you colors, numbers, and the alphabet. No matter what happens in your life, how far away from her you travel, you will always have her arms to return to.

Emma Sophia Mingjing
(age 10 months),
Qianjiang, Chongqing.

Above: Ay-La Twylanoelle
(age 1½), Yugan, Jiangxi.

Below: Ky-Le Ayladawn
(age 3½), Yiyang, Hunan.

Abigail Ann ZhiLan (age 2½),
Nanchang, Jiangxi.

Lillian Xiuli (age 2), Lianjiang, Guangdong,
with sister, Meredith Claire (age 6 months), and their dad.

FOUND
by *Julia Trawick*

THIS LITTLE BEAUTY STARING BACK AT ME FROM THE
COMPUTER WAS NOTHING WE HAD TALKED ABOUT
IN OUR REQUEST FOR ANOTHER DAUGHTER. Why
was I sitting there crying like I had lost something,
or found something? I tried calling my husband
and couldn't get an answer on his phone; so I
called a friend of mine. She said, "I think you may
have found your daughter." I felt numb. I knew in
my heart she was right.

Nancy Whitehouse, known as "Lala," with her four granddaughters—
Grace (age 4), Guiping, Guangxi; Jordan (age 1), Xiushan, Chongqing;
Marie (age 1), Xiushan, Chongqing; and Kaili (age 4), Guiping, Guangxi.

A THREAD TO HEAVEN
by Donna Whitehouse

MY FATHER DIED WHEN I WAS 21. Needless to say,
it was a traumatic event for my family. My mother
chose to put her grief into action. About a year
after my dad's death, my mother packed her bags
and headed to China. She had never been before
but just thought it was something she needed to
do. She spent six weeks teaching English at the
Art College in Nanning, Guangxi. It was a life-
changing event for her and for our entire family.

Upon her return, we pored over her pictures and
listened to her stories of China and the wonderful
people she met there. Maybe someday, we thought,
we could go too. Fast forward ten years. Both my
sister and I began the adoption process and, of
course, chose to adopt from China. Mother was
ready to take the trip again. While waiting for our
referrals, we received news that a cousin was also
adopting from China. She was about a year ahead
of us in the process. When she got her referral,
we were so excited! The baby was from Nanning!
What a wonderful coincidence, we thought. She
was actually born in a small town not too far from
Nanning, in Guiping, and had later been moved to
the Nanning SWI.

On October 1, 2001, I received one of the most
important phone calls of my life. I had a daughter!
Her name was Jin Raoling (now Grace), and
she was from… *Guiping*! Unbelievable! I called
my sister, who had gotten her referral for Jin
Zhongling (now Kaili) also from… *Guiping*!
We now had three Guiping girls in our family
and would be meeting our girls for the first time
in Nanning!

When I think about my dad wishing that he
could be with us and his granddaughters, I like to
think that he had a hand in making us a rejoicing
family again. I like to think that maybe somehow,
someway, he pulled my mother to China those
many years ago to somehow prepare us for the
future. I like to think that he looked out and
linked the three babies from Guiping to our family.
I like to think that the red thread goes all the way
to heaven.

Above: Picture drawn by Grace (age 3), Guiping, Guangxi—
after learning that her mommy was going
back to China for a baby sister.

Below: Grace (age 5), with sister,
Jordan (age 2), Xiushan, Chonqing.

The Golden Years
by Carrie Green

JIE JIE'S FACE STOOD OUT ON THE WAITING CHILDREN LIST, AND I PRAYED FOR HIM TO FIND A FAMILY. Our family was complete: Beth, adopted in 2000 at 16 months; Hope, adopted in 2002 at two years; and Matthew, adopted in 2003 at 17 months. In order to adopt Matthew we had to get an age waiver. My husband was 59 and I turned 52 on the day we returned from China with Matthew. We had a beautiful family. My husband retired in January 2005, and we felt so blessed to have been given the opportunity to have three children in our lives, making us a complete family.

I joined Harrah's Waiting Child list so we could encourage families who might consider adopting a cleft-affected child, like our Matthew. I kept watching the list, feeling the tug of Jie Jie's eyes, and mentioned this little guy to my husband so we could both pray for a family for him. In addition to being a six-year-old boy and cleft-affected, Jie Jie had moderate hearing loss in one ear and severe hearing loss in the other. Many children were discussed on the list, but no one seemed to mention Jie Jie.

It was time for the unselected children's files to be returned to China, and I casually mentioned Jie Jie again to my husband. My husband said, "Why don't you ask Harrah's about him and see what the medical says about his hearing loss." I emailed the agency on a Friday night to ask about Jie Jie and about half an hour later got a call from Harrah's asking how serious we were. His file literally was in an envelope ready to be mailed back to CCAA. Sherry had to open the envelope to get the file out in order to share his medical history with us. I looked at my husband and repeated Sherry's question, and he said, "Yes, we're serious!" I must admit that I had concerns about having to learn sign language and that we would have two children the same age, but…

Harrah's was able to receive updated information and called back on Sunday with the wonderful news that Jie Jie—soon to be Sean—was hearing and speaking and living in a foster home; so we began the paperwork *again*.

I was tired of the paperchase after our second adoption and remember thinking how grateful I was that we would never need to do that again, but we did it again, not only once, but twice more! Now we have two eight-year-olds, one six-year-old, and one four-year-old. At ages 55 and 62 we are facing the challenges and joys of parenting in our "golden years."

Siblings—Sean (age 7), Tianjin; Beth (age 7), Honghu, Hubei; Hope (age 6), Hanzhong, Shaanxi; and Matthew (age 4), Datong, Shanxi.

Friends—Emma (age 8) and Marita (age 7), both from Shantou, Guangdong—identifying their place of birth.

John (age 9), with sister, Jasmine (age 6), Guangdong— on the first day of school.

The Boy Who Made Us Complete
by Gail Daras

WE WERE DONE, FINISHED, AND COMPLETE. Our happy family of five had just moved to our dream home. Our family had expanded from three to four in 2003 and then to five in 2004. We finally had a home with enough room for our entire family. It was a Saturday night, and I decided to visit CCAI's waiting children page. Oh, my! I saw the cutest little six-year-old boy and felt an instant connection to him. I went to bed and said nothing to Kirby, my husband. The next morning as we lay in bed, we had one of those quiet moments that do not happen very frequently in our home anymore. I told him, "You have to see this little boy," even though we are done, finished and complete, "because he reminds me of a soccer player on your team last year." Kirby saw the photo, read the short write-up next to his photo, and stunned me by saying, "You have to call that agency!"

He has a round face, sparkling eyes, rosy cheeks, and a happy smile, and he is missing his right forearm. We both agree a child this happy with life in an orphanage would be even more happy sharing his life with a family. Another family was reviewing his file (and I have to admit that I prayed to God for that family to turn his file down). Ten days later Deniece Hess from CCAI called us and asked if we were still interested in Su Xiao Quan. Of course we were. He would be named Sean Richard Quan Daras.

Besides completing the letter of intent that weekend in March 2005, I set out to answer questions on a form called the Special Needs Preliminary Assessment, which CCAI required all parents to do. I came to the question, "Have you identified your local resources and support system for this special needs adoption?" We discovered this to be a difficult task. I searched through my phone book and the Internet for support groups for children like our son but found none in our area.

My feelings of frustration and isolation started

me thinking about creating a Yahoo group just for families who were adopting children with limb differences. I wanted it to be broad and not country specific. We welcomed families who were researching and considering children but felt it important to have families already home who were willing and ready to share their answers. What started out as a few people has grown to a Yahoo group of over 200 families that continues to grow. We talk about issues such as teasing, curious adults and children, school, sports, surgeries, finding doctors, getting your first prosthesis, adaptive tools, medical technology being developed because of the war in Iraq, travel approval, and children still searching for families. We have families with children from China, Korea, Vietnam, Russia, Ukraine, Kazakhstan, Ethiopia, Serbia, Guatemala, Colombia, Poland, and even the good ol' USA.

This group was a tiny seed that grew from my frustration of trying to find support I would need for my son. It has become an asset to families and to agencies alike. To learn more about our group, visit http://groups.yahoo.com/group/AdoptingChildrenWithLimbDifferences.

Sean has been home now for nine months and is doing well in first grade. Nothing slows him down. He ties his shoes and rides his bike. He never makes excuses. This fall he will play his first game of soccer, and I know we will be very proud of him. He shows his love and affection for us daily. We kept one word from Sean's Chinese name, Quan, which means complete. Sean completes us.

Maggie's Poem
by Margaret Jane YunMo Stewart
Written at age 3 years, 11 months

One day there was a girl named Maggie
And she was going to be adopted
And then I love my family who adopted me
And then I love my whole family
And I just love my perfect home
It is so beautiful
And I had my family forever, happily ever after.

MARY GUO LING
by Dawn Simpson

EACH AND EVERY TIME I THINK BACK TO HOW WE WERE GUIDED TO YOU, PRECIOUS MARY GUO LING, I AM AMAZED. Every time I share the pieces of the story, others are amazed. Why did God keep reaching down and guiding us in such miraculous ways? I don't know. Possibly He knew that without His guidance, our family of five just would not find the path that would lead us to you. Maybe there was some other reason that such strong heavenly leading was necessary. What I do know is that you are our daughter every bit as much as if you had been born to us biologically.

Siblings—Sean (age 8), Sucheng, Jiangsu; Lily (age 5), Kuitan City, Xinjiang; Ryan (age 10); and Kirstin (age 9), Ulan, Taraz, Kazkhstan.

TRUE SISTERS
by Chrystal Yaeger

WE HAD JUST BROUGHT OUR YOUNGEST DAUGHTER, ZOE, HOME IN DECEMBER 2004. Since it was Christmas time, we all piled into the car and drove off to a local computer store to check out the sales as our first family outing. I was prepared for the questions I heard two daughters would bring.

"Are they real sisters?" asked the saleswoman. I was ready for this question and responded confidently, "Yes!" I expected that to be the end of her questions, but she persisted. "No, I mean are they true sisters?" I couldn't believe this woman! Yet I felt confident and said, "Yes, they are." "No, are they biological sisters?" I responded, "No, they are not; however, they are real and true sisters in every sense."

True sisters—Aidyn Song (age 4), Yichun, Jiangxi, and Zoe Lynn (age 2), Fuzhou, Jiangxi.

One and one-half years have passed since this incident. I find myself smiling as I think about the question asked. If only that woman could see the way Zoe admires and looks up to her big sister, Aidyn, on a daily basis. If only she could see the way Zoe has to do everything her big sister does. If only she could hear the way they fight over the same doll, cup, or their daddy's attention—she would have no doubt how "real" and "true" these sisters are!

Having had a sister myself, I can already see what the future holds for them. There will be times when Aidyn will not want her little sister tagging along with her. There will be times when Aidyn will be hurting, and only Zoe will know about it. There will be times when they will lean on each other for comfort and times when they will fight. There will be times when they feel as if they have nothing in common, but they will find out later that they do. After all they share the same history. They may have been adopted from two different places, but they both have lived in the same loving home. Their love for each other will be strong. I am confident that love will always carry them through whatever life throws at them. After all love is what makes us family, not biology.

I cannot think of anything truer than that!

New Girl at School
by Ju Ju Cooney

DO YOU KNOW A GIRL WHO WAS ADOPTED FROM CHINA, THEN MOVED TO JAPAN AND LIVED THERE FOR EIGHT YEARS, AND THEN MOVED AGAIN TO HAWAII? Well, now you do. Look around and you will see a girl with long, dark brown hair who just started going to Hokulani school.

Let me tell you about my family. The first thing is: I only have girls in my family—no father and no brother—but, you know, I don't mind not having a father or brother. I'm happy just the way my family is now. I have five members in my family. I have my mother who is American. She has wavy, blondish-brownish hair, and she has greenish eyes and white skin. She loves to teach English and draw art. Then I have my sister who is 14 years old. She is also adopted from China; so she's not my blood relative sister. My sister has short, black hair and brown eyes like mine. She loves to play sports and loves to spend her life on the phone. And then come my pets. They are both girls of course and they fight sometimes, but they don't hurt each other. I got my dog in Japan. My dog's name is Sophie. She likes to go on long walks and loves to run on the beach. She is four years old and is a black Welsh Corgi. Now the other pet is a Siamese cat. I got her here in Hawaii from my mother as a birthday present. Her name is Mia, and she is one year old. If she gets kittens I will call her Mama Mia.

My favorite hobbies are soccer, reading, talking, shopping, and art. But I guess I like reading and art the most. My future goals are to go around the world and be a great cheerleader and to help the Humane Society, and of course to go to college. I think I might even accomplish every one of them, but if I don't get to, then there will be a good reason.

Now you know me pretty well, even though I am a new student at Hokulani school.

Original artwork by Xiu Ju ("Ju Ju") (age 10), Nanjing.

Joshua (age 4); Lia Ruth Qiafu (age 19 months), Loudi, Hunan; and Zachary (age 6)—sharing the fun of family hikes.

Prayer of a Four-year-old Brother
by Joshua Widenhofer

Dear God,

Thanks for giving Lia to our house. I like her crazy hair. I have fun playing with her. I love my sister. Amen.

Best friends—Maiya Irene and Shin Lei (both age 3½), both from Foshan Nanhai, Guangdong.

Happily Ever After... 2006
by Donna Schwartz

A BABY GIRL WAS BORN IN THE COUNTRYSIDE OF FUJIAN PROVINCE. She was born too early and too tiny to people who couldn't take care of a baby, especially such a tiny, frail one. Someone was able to save the baby girl. When they were sure she would live, they placed her in a box and left her at the local gas station. She was found by the orphanage staff and brought to a hospital where she spent the first month of her life.

Later she was taken to an orphanage. The nannies named her Xin Na. Her first year was hard. Her health wasn't good. The nannies worried about her but also had 19 other babies to care for. Na Na was quiet and didn't demand attention. She spent hours in her crib and high chair. Eventually the other babies began walking and babbling. Na Na was quiet and didn't pull herself to a stand. The nannies were concerned about her development. Slowly the babies began to leave the orphanage with adoptive families. Na Na stayed behind.

My husband and I were one of those families adopting a daughter. The week before we left for China, a woman who had met Na Na asked me to check on her. When we arrived at the orphanage, we were greeted at the front entrance by the staff and a friend. With our new daughter, Tessa Mei, securely in our arms, I prepared myself to meet Xin Na. A kind nanny gestured to a little baby sitting on the floor. She was sitting up, but her little legs had no muscle tone. She couldn't walk or stand and everybody was working hard to help her. A nanny bent down and called her name sweetly. This frail baby bumped herself across the floor on her bottom to the nanny. She smiled up at me as I snapped her picture. The orphanage director asked for suggestions for how he could better care for the children. I asked him to please do what he could for Na Na and told him I was sure I could find her an adoptive family.

Back home time flew with everything we had to do with three young girls and an old house. Days were full of children's laughter, diapers, and homework. Often I'd find myself thinking of the little baby with the gypsy eyes and sweet smile. My friend in Gutian wrote that Na Na was going for rehabilitation at a pediatric hospital in another city. She visited Na Na and took pictures of her in her hospital room. The head of pediatrics reported that Na Na was responding wonderfully to the treatment.

Soon I received a picture of Na Na. She looked lovely, like a baby princess, and she was standing! Not long after she could walk and say a few words. I encouraged the orphanage director to submit

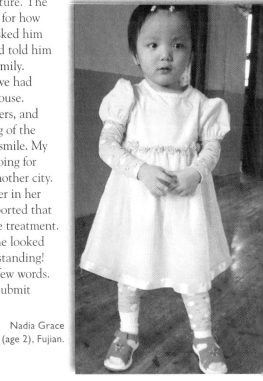

Nadia Grace (age 2), Fujian.

Na Na's file to the China Center for Adoption Affairs so she could be adopted. Adoption professionals in the U.S. requested Na Na be put on their waiting children list.

As adoptive parents continued to meet their babies, Na Na would shyly watch the action. Some brought her clothes or toys. Many contacted me or took pictures of her. We heard, "She's sunshine," "She's talking," "She's going to the local preschool." Somewhere along the way we realized the family we had promised to find her was ours!

As the agencies got lists of waiting children, Na Na was never on them. I contacted everyone I knew, asking them if they had seen Na Na's file. No one had seen her. My monthly inquiries—"Looking for Lin Xin Na, little girl from Fujian"—became routine. Two years from the day we met Xin Na, I received beautiful pictures of her. A confident preschooler was smiling and showing the peace sign! I sent the pictures to an agency that had been advocating for her for over a year. I wanted them to see this beautiful little girl!

One day the phone rang. It was someone from the agency, and I thought she was calling about the pictures. "Isn't she beautiful?" I said. She said that, yes, she was, but that wasn't why she was calling. They received Na Na's file that day! I was blown away by the news and thanked her profusely.

Na Na's story is going to have a "Happily Ever After" ending. No glass slippers or knight on a noble white steed. No kiss from a handsome prince—at least not yet. Her happy ending will be more about the everyday magic that fills a happy childhood… catching fireflies on a warm August night, decorating the Christmas tree and waking up to see what Santa left, Popsicles and Crayola crayons, a birthday party with pink balloons, a warm little bed in her own home surrounded by a family that loves her. We never gave up hope for Na Na even in the darkest times. This is why we have given her the name Nadia, which means "to be hopeful." We never gave up our hope that someday she would come home.

Love at first sight. Siblings—Jacob (age 6) and Hailey WuZhen (age 7 months), Yihuang, Jiangxi.

BROTHER MEETS SISTER
by Erin Lisak

I COULD NEVER IMAGINE THE LOVE THAT IGNITED BETWEEN MY TWO CHILDREN. When Hailey met Jacob in the airport after our return from China, she couldn't take her eyes off of him. She sat on his lap and examined every inch of his face. There is a pretty big age gap between them—six years—so I didn't think they would do much together. I was wrong. I call Hailey "Jacob's shadow." She is right there trying to do everything he does. Hailey looks to Jacob for comfort. He can calm her in the car by just holding her hand. He is very patient when she is messing up his stuff! Hailey's first word was "Jake-Jake." He is the first person she looks for when waking up in the morning. They make an amazing pair.

Real sisters—Lara Jian-Bao (age 1), Gaoyou, Jiangsu, and Cathryn Jiang-Bi (age 4), Lianjiang, Guangdong.

Cameron (age 4), Shantou, Guangdong—looking very handsome.

DOUBLE BLESSINGS
by Karen Rubenstein

WHEN WE BROUGHT HOME OUR SON, CAMERON, HE WAS DIAGNOSED WITH INCOMPLETE CLEFT PALATE, WHICH CAUSES HIS TEETH TO NOT MEET IN THE MIDDLE CORRECTLY. We had issues to deal with regarding his spine and bowel movements. He has two or three more surgeries to go on his hands and feet. But let me add: This little boy can walk, he can run, he can jump, and he can outtalk an army!

He is the brightest spot in my day most of the time. He is lying here beside me as I type. I just looked down at him and smiled, and he said, "Mom, I *like* you!" to which I replied, "Cam, I *like* you too!" Does it get any better than this? I don't think so.

Our adoption of Li Xin was much different than our adoption of Cameron. Li Xin, 4½ years old, had a difficult transition. She grieved for her foster family and did not want one thing to do with me in China. Once we returned to the U.S. and she met her brother Cameron for the first time, the tide began to change. She saw Cameron hugging and kissing me and telling me how much he missed me while I was in China. Slowly but surely she started coming around.

We have only been home one month and I can honestly say this is the sweetest, most loving child I have ever seen. She hugs me constantly, telling me that she loves me. She just started school this week, and she is so happy. I am sure she misses her foster family in China, but her attachment to us grows stronger each day. We are so blessed to have this beautiful Guilin princess in our family.

Happy new sisters— Hannah (age 7) and Ryleigh (age 4), Guilin, Guangxi.

THE LOOK
by Beth Mirabito

OUR DAUGHTER, LYDIA, WAS VERY INDEPENDENT FROM THE VERY START!! We should have known that she could crack, peel, and eat a hard-boiled egg all on her own at just 13 months old, but for some strange reason we didn't. So for two months I cracked, peeled, and cut up ever so small the two hard-boiled eggs Lydia loved for breakfast every morning. Lydia would always give me a puzzled look. I noticed "The Look" every morning about the time I would begin to crack the egg but would ignore it. Then one day I received a foster care report, which stated, "Likes to peel her own hard-boiled eggs." All of a sudden "The Look" made sense. Immediately I grabbed a hard-boiled egg from the refrigerator and gave it to Lydia. She cracked it two times on her little head and smiled at me with the biggest grin as if to say, "Finally!!!" She peeled it and ate it whole. I wonder what else little Miss Independent knows how to do.

Sisters and best of friends—Ocean (age 9); Neela Lin (age 2), Datong, Shanxi; and Reyna Mei (age 3), Loudi, Hunan—posing for an Easter picture with Mommy.

Sisters—Lydia Fu Xiu (age 2) and Hope Li (age 4), both from Hunan.

The Gift
by Brenda Conover

Children are a gift
With love that's never ending
But change with the wind

愛

Siblings—(Clockwise from front) Benjamin (age 7), Maxwell (age 11), Samuel (age 13), and Danielle (age 3), Nanning, Guangxi—at Samuel's Bar Mitzvah.

BIG SISTER
by Adrienne Layne DiMarco (age 17)
Written for a college application essay

I LOOKED OUT MY BEDROOM WINDOW TO A BLACK STRETCH LIMO SITTING IN THE DRIVEWAY. The excitement building up inside of me was more than any eight-year-old could handle. A whirlwind of questions started rushing through my head. Who is going to ride with me? How long is the drive going to be? Where did the limo come from?

Always being the impatient one, I ran down the stairs to where my grandma and little brother were setting up for what was going to be the best party ever. I was even wearing my favorite outfit: jeans, my Titanic shirt with Rose and Jack, and a bright purple hat with the words "I'm the big sister" written in white across the top. My brother had one in blue saying "I'm the big brother," but I knew mine was ten times cooler. After asking when it was time to go more times than I could count, we finally packed up, got in the limo, and began our drive to the airport where I would meet my new baby sister for the first time.

The limo ride was every fourth grader's dream. I had all the soda I could drink, any Disney movie I wanted, and all my best friends riding with me. Pulling up in the long, black, shiny limo made me feel famous. With an entourage of elementary school kids following me, I entered the small, local airport as if I owned the place.

As soon as the automatic doors slid open, I felt short, very short. Everything was so big. I looked around at other families waiting for their loved ones to come off the plane. Were they waiting for a little sister too? I held on tight to the sign my little brother and I had made the night before as my nerves started to get the best of me. My parents promised me I could hold her first, and I was going to make sure they kept their promise. But what if I dropped her? Or what if she didn't like me? Sure she was only a few months old, but the possibility of having a sister that didn't like me was horrifying.

I don't remember how long we waited, but it was too long for this eight-year-old, and I became impatient. I kept quiet though as I watched people exit the plane one by one. And then there she was. Just a bundle in my parents' arms, but I saw her nonetheless. My mom looked tired from the 18-hour plane ride, and my dad was hidden behind baby bags and luggage. I ran up and held the little girl with two hands just like my mom had showed me before she left. Her big, black eyes matched her soft baby hair and stared straight up at me.

Jie-jie means big sister in Mandarin, and that is what I am. My sister is eight years younger than I am and was adopted from China as Wan Jin Tong. Today she is Olivia Rose Jin DiMarco and is nine years old. She plays the piano, dances, and loves soccer. Sometimes we joke about how we look alike, but I love our differences. We respect and honor her culture. We celebrate Chinese New Year to remind her of where she is from. And we burn three sticks of incense on her birthday: one for her mother, one for the lost

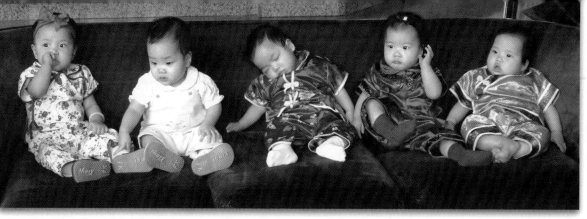

Abigail (age 9 months), Lilly (age 11 months), Maggie (age 9 months), Sydney (age 9 months), and Lydia (age 9 months)—all from Gaozhou, Guangdong, and part of Harrah's AIM travel group.

daughters left behind, and one for her future. We say thank you, or xièxie (pronounced "shie shie"), to China for letting us have Olivia in our lives.

I hate when people try to tell me my sister isn't really part of our family because she looks "different" or that she doesn't share the same blood as the rest of us. We receive emails from other mothers of Chinese girls giving advice on how to tell your daughter she is adopted or different from the rest of the family. My sister is not different from anyone. She likes to put on makeup and paint her nails. She likes to play outside and go swimming. And given the straight black hair and olive skin, I'm pretty sure she knows she doesn't look the same as me and my curly red hair. There is nothing "off" or different about anything she does. We are a family, although we came together in a "different" way from most other families. It took a little longer to complete us, but we are whole. Adoption is just another way of becoming a family. For example, my mother was adopted from Holy Oak, Massachusetts, five years after her older brother was adopted from New York. My two cousins are adopted from California, and one is of Mexican descent. Their new little sister is about to come home from Guatemala, and my father's little cousin was adopted from Russia eight years ago.

I am who I am because of these people in my life. I know who I am and fitting in doesn't matter. Sometimes being out of the ordinary is worthwhile. I don't feel the need to follow the crowd and join the teenage drinking trend because I don't see the point in getting drunk on weekends. I enjoy dressing the way I like, rather than conforming to the skinny jeans and labeled tops, because I am more comfortable that way. My hair is usually messy because I'm usually in a rush, and my political views are clearly stated on the back of my car. I don't mind walking around school with paint on my face; actually I prefer it because it means I've been working on a new creation. I openly discuss the way I feel, and my opinions are my own. Sometimes I seem a little unusual to others. But I'd rather be out of the ordinary than not have my best friend in the world— a little nine-year-old Chinese girl who likes doing her nails and playing with my hair. So when people ask me if we adopted Olivia and then proceed to tell me that adoption means we aren't really related, I just reply "I'm her big sister. Xièxie."

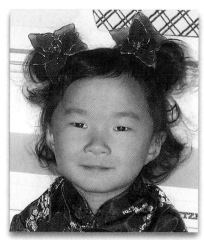

Above: Demetria Sapphire Yong Jiang Dong (age 3), Yongzhou, Hunan.

Left and below: Christalina Jade Yong Yue, adopted with twin sister, Angelina Jasmine Yong Ri, Yongzhou, Hunan (both age 5).

PREPARING MY HEART
by Sheila Archer

MY FRIEND AND I WERE IN THE LOBBY OF THE WHITE SWAN HOTEL IN AUGUST OF 2004 WHEN I SAW A BEAUTIFUL LITTLE ASIAN FACE IN A STROLLER WITH HER PARENTS WALKING BEHIND HER. She looked like she was about three years old, and I was struck by how truly beautiful she was. I felt compelled to approach the family. I stopped them and told them how stunning I thought their daughter was. I shared with them that I was in China with my husband adopting a little girl as well. It was then that they told me that their precious daughter in the stroller was deaf. I said, "Wow!! Please tell me how is everything going." I flooded them with questions about their transition since receiving their daughter. After we had finished our brief conversation, we parted ways and I said to my friend, "That is incredible! I am so thankful that God lays it on people's hearts to adopt precious children like that. But I am so glad that He has not laid that on my heart!!! I could never do that!"

I'm sure that God chuckled at me that day. Little did I know that less than two years later, I would be standing in the same hotel lobby with my new four-year-old son, who is profoundly deaf. Our son has been such a blessing to our entire family. He has such a warm, sweet spirit about him and has touched the hearts of so many people since we have been home. God has a way of slowly preparing our hearts for big miracles.

Megan Claire Xiaowei (age 33 months), Xiaoxian, Anhui, with Mom.

THE OBEDIENCE BABY
by Patti Sheeter

IN FEBRUARY OF 2005, THREE-YEAR-OLD GRACE BEGAN TELLING US THAT THERE WAS A BABY IN CHINA CRYING FOR US. She told us the baby wanted us for her family. One night as I was tucking her into bed, Grace whispered to me, "I know what the baby is named." I asked Grace what the baby's name was. "Obedience!" was her reply. Our children know a Bible song about obedience; so we assumed that was where Grace got the name. From that time on, she began referring to the baby in China as the "Obedience Baby." She would ask us if we could bring the Obedience Baby home, or she would tell us that the Obedience Baby was crying. She wanted us to be her family.

That fall I happened to visit the website for Children's House International, an international adoption agency. Something led me to open one particular child's file and read her biography. My heart stopped when I read the fourth sentence of her report: "She was named *Obedience*" (English translation of her Chinese name, Xiao Wei). She was born on October 20, 2003, in Anhui, China, and had the special need of spina bifida.

After several emails and sending some information about our family to Children's House International, we received a phone call from their China Program Coordinator, Stefani Ellison. She told me that they had reviewed our file and then said, "We'd like to know if you and David would like to be Obedience's family." I started crying right there on the phone and told Stefani

Olivia Tian (age 2), Yichun, Jiangxi.

that I really had to talk to my husband. We had concerns. We went back and forth, but when all was said and done, we felt that we should continue going through whatever doors the Lord opened for us.

On July 10, 2006, we met our Obedience Baby—Megan—for the first time. Over and over again she has shown herself to be a sweet, brave little girl. She is growing so much, in so many ways. We know there are many challenges ahead, both for Megan and our family. She is such a strong and brave little girl to have left the life she had known and come on this great adventure with us. We are simply amazed by her and by God's goodness to us.

We asked Grace how she knew about the Obedience Baby in China. She told us that God whispered it in her ear.

Big brother Jordan (age 12), with Kamryn (age 5), Maonan, Guangdong.

HIS KIDS KEEP HIM YOUNG
by Ken Stevens

SITTING AROUND THE DINNER TABLE WITH TWO-YEAR-OLD MacKENZIE YIN YING CONCENTRATING ON HER FOOD WITH GUSTO (MOST OF THE TIME) AND A CHATTERING SEVEN-YEAR-OLD, KENDRA WEN YU, I know that I am blessed with a family that has an enthusiasm for life and what it has to offer. This is true whether it be the magic of speaking (in one case) or of reading (in the other), or of walking through the woods and learning about nature, or of hugging Mom and Dad. It is true when they are talking on the telephone with their grown sister or singing Chinese children's songs. For such a mom and dad, growing old is not consistent with participation in this active process.

Above: Cadi Wren, Yangzhou, Jiangsu; Callee, Quixi, Jiangxi; and Josi, YiYang, Hunan. Sisters Cadi and Josi spending a beautiful Alaskan summer afternoon with their friend, Callee.

Below: Cadi Wren; Emma, Xiangfan City, Hubei; Josi; and Mia, Dianbai, Guangdong. Sisters Cadi and Josi enjoying a summer reunion with sisters Emma and Mia on the Washington coast.

Sisters—Anna Kate (age 1), Gao'An, Jiangxi, and Kelsey (age 5).
Sisters—Kloe (age 2), Guangdong, and Katelin (age 4), Guangxi.

Natalie Jade HongHu
(age 16 months),
Qianjiang, Chongqing.

NAMING
by Elise Geither

MY HUSBAND IS SLEEPING UPSTAIRS WITH THE BABY ON HIS CHEST. I am downstairs playing with her crayons, trying to make the colors blend, but they won't… when I realize I have never really known my grandmother's real name.

Coming here, to America, Golden Mountain, Streets of Gold, Rivers of Wine, her name was already changed from the-name-I-never-knew to Mimi, nickname Mims.

She had always told us the story of how she had been named after her sister who had died of the coughing. She said she couldn't stand the name, the ghost of the dead girl in the corner of her room at night, in closets, in the pantry eating sweets. My grandmother couldn't hold the name, couldn't tuck it up and under her ribs. It wasn't hers. So somehow she changed it to Mimi— and this name she held. In the market, where she couldn't find potatoes and couldn't speak English enough to ask. In her first home, where she chased out snakes she said the gypsies had left. Over the fire, as she burned all the love letters from her dead husband. Over the lake, behind the house he'd built for her.

My mother named me for a princess who had brothers with wings. This princess knit fabrics from nettles, making peace with the poisoned juices as they slid through her fingers. I'd never be that strong, I thought, to knit with a burning flower.

One day, I asked my mother, "What was Oma's name, her real, real true name?" She paused for a moment, looked at the sky and then back at me. "I think," she said, "it was your name. Yes, it was yours."

I was shocked at first and noticed I was holding my breath. My mother smiled and touched my cheek. She had taken the name, the one full of ghosts and memories and bags of kindling. She had taken that name and with her sore, cricked hands she bent it like a willow, pulled it like pink taffy, and gave it to me. She was strong enough to do this, and then gentle enough to rub my cheek and tickle my back.

My husband is sleeping upstairs with the baby on his chest, the baby I've given a name too long for her small, pixie chin and fuzzy-chick hair, too long for her plump toddling legs. I've given her one name she can hold and one she'll keep from Fuling, China, given because she had been found in the early, frosty morning. And I gave her another name, a name from my mother's favorite movie, to tell her that she can change her name at any time, and I will still know her, find her, sleeping on her father's chest.

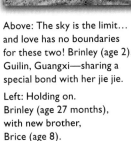

Above: The sky is the limit… and love has no boundaries for these two! Brinley (age 2), Guilin, Guangxi—sharing a special bond with her jie jie.

Left: Holding on. Brinley (age 27 months), with new brother, Brice (age 8).

Jane (age 11 months), Fuling, Chongqing, with brother, Jeffrey (age 10)—meeting for the first time.

LEARNING TO SLEEP
by Nadia Swearingen-Friesen

IN ADOPTING ELIZABETH FROM CHINA, MARK AND I QUICKLY FOUND THAT THE MOST NORMAL PARTS OF ANY GIVEN DAY CAN BECOME DIFFICULT, EVEN MEMORABLE. Learning to help our baby sleep became just such an event for us.

Our baby daughter, having just met us after 11 months in an orphanage, was very aware that she did not know us or have any reason to trust us and felt she had to be awake to remain in control of her young life. Mark and I are experienced parents, but neither of us had ever seen a child fight sleep like Elizabeth did during those first several weeks. We tried everything. We rocked our baby. She fought ferociously against such soothing. We sang to her. She woke up to try to see what we were doing. We held her tightly. She wrestled with such strength that parents and baby were soon exhausted. We tried laying her down and leaving her to her devices. Alone in a crib Elizabeth would twist and turn and flip and bang her arms and legs, all in an extreme effort to keep herself awake. Then the screaming began. We would find ourselves all tired, all awake, with no way to help our beautiful little girl feel safe, know love, or get back to sleep.

A few days after our baby became fully ours, I remember having the rare privilege of watching her sleep. I remember looking at her delicate hands and marveling that she was sleeping in jammies I had bought for her months before I had ever seen her face. As I wondered at the miracle that allowed this beautiful Chinese child to become mine, her brow furrowed, her nose crinkled up, and her mouth opened in a noiseless cry. In the darkness of a Chinese hotel room, my daughter and I cried together for the very first time.

Now many months have gone by, and Elizabeth is settled in her life and family. She plays with her big brothers and watches a bit of Sesame Street and loves to eat pizza. She has well worn tickle spots and favorite clothes. And yet the baby we met in China nearly a year ago is still a baby. A few nights ago, I crept into her room and watched her sleep. I stood in her room for a long time and marveled at the fact that she looked so calm. She stirred a bit then, but she settled back to sleep quickly. And then it happened. In the dim light that fell upon my little one's face, I saw her smile. Oh, she was fully asleep, but what filled her dreams on this night brought happiness to her face. At least for this moment her concerns were eclipsed by some wonderful thought—a happy experience, a hug from a sibling, an unexpected snack, play and laughter, full and free. A sleeping, simple smile. And once again, there were nighttime tears. This time, I cried alone—happy, grateful tears.

Siblings—(Clockwise from lower left) Benjamin (age 6); Josiah (age 2); Noah (age 7); and Elizabeth (age 1), YuanJiang, Hunan.

Adopted
by Joy Saunders Lundberg
www.lundbergcompany.com

"Oh, Mother," the child cried,
Tears flooding precious cheeks,
"They said, 'If you're adopted
Your mother is not your real mother.'"
Then pleading, "Please tell me
The story again."

Nestled in loving arms,
Secure from the hurt
Of unknowing friends,
The words fell from trembling lips
To hungry little ears.
"Oh, child, how I wanted to be
Your birth mother.
I could not.
But I knew you were there,
Somewhere.
We prayed, your Daddy and I,
And God guided us to you.

"There you were,
A beautiful child—my child.
I held you close
And promised to love you,
To teach you,
To keep you from harm,
From distress.
And here I am—
Your birth mother? No.
But your real mother,
Yes."

Brother and sister and best of friends—Taylor (age 4½), Guizhou, and LiAnne (age 2½), Jiangxi.

Bay Area, California friends—(Right) Anna YouLing (age 13), Fuzhou, Fujian, with Triana, in Italy.

Emma (age 11), Zhejiang, Fuyang—fulfilling her lifetime dream of petting a giant panda during a homeland tour of China.

Sisters—Mattea (age 2½), Chenzhou, Hunan, and Quinn (age 4), Shaoyang, Hunan.

A determined and proud Anna (age 7), Yiyang, Hunan, loves to ice skate.

The Colors of Culture
by B. L. Padilla

MY FAMILY WEAVES THREE CULTURES TOGETHER. I am from the United States, my husband is Spanish, and we all became "part Chinese" when we brought our daughter home from China in 2004. For me each of our cultures is like a different set of colored threads, and I'm always asking the question, "How much of each color should we use?"

Often people think that if we are living in Spain and I am from the U.S., our kids are automatically bicultural and bilingual. The truth is, it takes a lot of work to instill a minority culture and language in your kids to a degree that makes it possible for them to move back and forth between two countries and feel totally at home in each one. So every day I am busy selecting different colors from among the many threads these two cultures have to offer us and then trying to weave those into my kids' lives.

The challenge now is to weave in these amazing new Chinese threads. At first I was overwhelmed at the mere idea. Where would they fit? How on earth would we even find time to sandwich one more element into our current design?

I find comfort in remembering I had a simple childhood in a rural area in the USA with virtually no exposure to Spanish language and culture until I went to college. Today I speak fluent Spanish and, thanks to my job, probably know more about contemporary Spain than many Spaniards.

Already the older children are looking forward to traveling to China as a family. They love looking at our albums and glossy picture books and talking about the great and beautiful country their sister comes from. I feel free to explore as much as we can along the way, to weave in as many Chinese threads as we possibly can, but not feel guilty that we can't fit more in. I realize that each of my daughters has her own tapestry to work on, and that I am merely providing a background.

(Front row) Elisa (age 2) and Mei (age 2), Fengcheng, Jiangxi.
(Back row) Natalie (age 7), Mom, Dad, and Adriana (age 10).

Then—Referral photo of Nicole Ren (age 7 months), Lianyungang, Jiangsu.

Now—Nicole Ren (age 2).

Waiting for My Sister
by Monica Davidson

WHEN WE FIRST SAW MY SISTER ON OUR AGENCY'S WAITING CHILDREN LIST, WE THOUGHT, "SHE'S CUTE," BUT I DIDN'T REALLY THINK TOO MUCH OF THIS LITTLE GIRL WITH THE BIRTHMARK. We had been turned down once already, and I was too devastated. We asked anyway and were told she already had a family.

Two months later we got a call, asking if we were still interested. We said yes, but it wasn't until our permission to adopt came from China that she was really *my* sister.

And now, I love her, and I can't believe there was a time when I couldn't see her face. I don't notice the birthmark when I see her pictures now. She's just cute, that's it.

Now she's *my* little sister with the birthmark— and she's never going be just another face in the crowd.

"THEN SINGS MY SOUL"
by Marcia Armstrong

I WAS SITTING IN CHURCH ON SUNDAY. The service was ending with the closing hymn, "How Great Thou Art," before the prayer. While four-year-old Faith began the meeting next to me, it was three-year-old Anna who was sitting on my lap by closing time.

We opened the hymn book, and the congregation started to sing. I am no great singer, preferring to keep my voice inconsequential, even in church where you have an excuse to really belt a song out. But with the weight of Anna on my lap and my hand guiding her little index finger over the words as we sang them, I got to thinking. This child did not spend her nine months of pregnancy listening to my heartbeat, connecting to my voice. She did not hear me sing hymns, or lullabies or pop tunes for that matter. She did not have the opportunity to know me before she saw me, using the timbre of spoken word and song as her guide.

Maybe that is a blessing considering how wobbly my vocal chords can be. Even so it niggled at me halfway through this timeless hymn that Anna and I may have been separated by time and distance in the past but not any longer. We were together now, and she could hear my voice. So I upped the decibels a bit. Then a bit more. Not so much that Eric, who was sitting beside me, could notice a difference, but loud enough that, with my mouth almost touching Anna's ear, I could begin making up for lost time.

New friends at Chinese American Heritage Camp. Lilyanna (age 5), Zhanjiang, Guangdong, with friends, (standing) Sophia (age 7) and Emma (age 5).

The love of sisters. Addison Claire (age 16 months), Gaozhou, Guangdong, and Olivia Grace (age 3½), Korea.

MING'S STORY
by Jim Nobilini

AS MY WIFE AND A GOOD FRIEND SET OUT ON A MISSION TRIP TO A CHINESE ORPHANAGE, I WAS ASKED BY A COWORKER, "WHAT ARE THEY REALLY GOING TO ACCOMPLISH?" My answer was that the trip would probably end up being more of a blessing to her than it would be to the children. Little did I know that God's plan was already being set into action.

You would have to know my wife, Joy, to appreciate her love for infants. Since I was intimately familiar with this aspect of her character, I thought it necessary to be explicit when I told her that adopting an infant was out of the question. We were well beyond that stage with our three biological children, and I was not prepared to restart that phase.

Before we knew it, Joy and the group were in China. On that Saturday morning, Joy called and said, "There is this eight-year-old boy here named Ming who I think would make a great addition to our family." I couldn't help it… I just started laughing. I thought I had been quite clear, but it suddenly occurred to me that I had said "no infants." Silly me, I forgot to include kittens, puppies, and small children.

When she arrived home, Joy set out to research the status of Ming and which agency was representing him here in the States. Following weeks of research with no leads, she gave up. Another week went by and she said to me, "You haven't said anything about Ming. What are you thinking?" So I told her that I had prayed and asked God to provide a sign if this was what He wanted us to do. I was explicit in the details I was looking for: a six-month adoption process and a cap of $15,000. My wife looked at me as if I was crazy. She said, "You cannot test God like that."

Shortly thereafter, my wife found Ming on a "waiting child" list. That was the bonus… you know, the sign that God was giving. Because Ming was a "special needs child," the Chinese government was willing to expedite his adoption with an expected six to eight month timeframe. In addition, two organizations were providing $6,000 in grants, bringing the estimated cost of his adoption down to $14,000. Joy was excited because she knew that she could continue to pursue Ming and dumbfounded that God's sign was so clear.

In the meantime, our best friends had been searching for Xue Lian, Ming's friend, whom they had fallen in love with. About a month into our paperchase, Joy found Xue Lian on a waiting child list. We knew that these two children were meant to stay close to one another.

Eight months later, our family visited China for two weeks to pick up the newest member of our family. Four months after that, our friends went to China to bring home their new daughter. These two previous orphans traveled to the other side of the world to live with their respective families just 15 minutes away from each other. This was the miracle that a simple mission trip accomplished.

Sisters—Abby (age 3), Fuling, Chongqing, and Megan (age 5), Cambodia.

XUE LIAN'S STORY
by Dana Milne

WE FIRST MET XUE LIAN AND MING WHEN OUR FAMILY WENT TO CHINA TO ADOPT OUR DAUGHTER, ELLA, IN APRIL OF 2004. These two children had recently been abandoned, at the age of seven, and my husband and I were able to interact with them in the courtyard of the Fuling Social Welfare Institute. I was not aware at this time that God would work in our lives to return two years later to adopt our daughter, Xue Lian.

I returned to China in the summer of 2005 on a mission trip with our adoption agency. I was stunned when I found out that I would be able to work at the same orphanage where Ella had spent the first ten months of her life. It was a gift to be able to visit the place where my daughter lived her first days. I was also thankful that my dearest friend, Joy, would be coming to China with me and would get to see the country that had transformed my life.

We spent three days working in the orphanage that summer, and I again spent time with the two children we had met the year before. I was not aware that during this time Joy was growing attached to Ming and would soon announce that she wished to adopt him. It was exciting for me to watch as her eyes welled up at the thought of leaving him there.

It was on this return trip that Joy and I made a plan to attempt to adopt both of the children. Her family would adopt Ming, and our family would adopt Xue Lian. We knew it was an incredibly difficult task to adopt a specific child from China, but we also felt that God wanted these children with us, and that He was the only one who could work and make it happen.

It would be only two months after we returned that Joy would learn which agency Ming was listed with and that her family would begin the process to adopt him. At this time we were told that Xue Lian was being adopted, and, although we were sad, we continued to be excited for our friends.

It was two months after Joy's family began paperwork to adopt Ming that we were sent an email that would lead us to Xue Lian once again. The adoption agency, after hearing our story, decided to place her with us. We were excited more than any words could explain and in awe of how incredibly merciful our God would be to keep these two children together.

Joy's family has been home with Ming (Tyler) now since March of 2006, and we were able to bring Xue Lian (Lillie) home four months later. It has been an incredible journey of love, hope, and faith for all of us. We are grateful to have been able to add these two precious gifts to our families and are continually amazed by God's goodness.

On our adoption trip to adopt Tyler (age 9), Fu De Ming, Fuling, we visited the social welfare institute to give Lillie (age 9) some gifts from her waiting family.

Mei Bryn (age 3½), Wuchuan, Guangdong.

Mei Bryn was a Waiting Child with our agency and had a similar heart condition to mine (our red thread). This photo was taken about a year after Mei Bryn had surgery to close a hole in her heart.

THE DAY BEFORE
by Nancy Delpha

Natalie's spine surgery is scheduled for tomorrow, and we met with the surgeon yesterday to discuss his surgical plan for correcting her spine curvature, rib abnormalities, and shoulder blade, as well as the risks involved. Today we are trying to distract ourselves with fun activities, but, every time I look at her sweet face, the tears come, thinking of what she will have to go through the next day. Natalie, at age three, is oblivious to what is weighing so heavily on her dad and me, and she is enjoying herself.

In the afternoon we have pre-op appointments at the hospital, and she willingly consents to giving more blood; "going" in a cup; and being weighed, measured, poked, and prodded one more time. Our last stop is the x-ray department, where she has to have the chest x-ray required for surgery, even though I have lost track of the number of times her little back has been x-rayed and MRIed. We are greeted by a giant of a man, who I am afraid might frighten her simply because of his size. His gentle manner and soft voice quickly put us both at ease, however. Because I had unwittingly dressed her in a zipper dress this morning, she has to change clothes. She slips on a cute little hospital gown decorated in a child's print and poses perfectly for the one last x-ray. Once we are given the okay that the picture is clear, I help her slip out of the gown and put her own clothes back on. As she hands the x-ray tech the gown, she says in her sweet little voice, "Thank you for letting me wear your cute jammies!"

That's my girl, thinking of fashion even at a time like this!

Friends—(Bottom to top) Savannah (age 4), Heather (age 4), Emma Grace (age 4), and Sierra (age 3), ShuCheng, Anhui. Savannah, Heather, and Emma Grace were adopted from Cenxi, Guangxi, in October 2002.

PERFECT TIMING
by Jennefer Welch

DADDY AND I HAD DISCUSSED ADOPTING OUR BABY GIRL FROM CHINA MANY YEARS AGO. Someday we would know when the time was right and we would begin the process. Someday.

Shaylee was born August 1996, and Sophia was born August 2000. Life was great. Although we often spoke of our daughter in China, neither of us knew when or how it would happen.

Fast forward to March 2004. Our small little house held us all perfectly. Shaylee and Sophia were in the backyard playing with their friends, and suddenly it hit me. Daddy came home from work and before he even made it in all the way I said, "It's time for China!"

"Are you serious? Now? Why this instant?"

I explained that Shaylee and Sophia were four years apart and that Sophia would soon be five. Wouldn't we want to keep them all close in age?

"Now? Why now? This tiny little house!"

"We can call Uncle Anthony and have him draw plans for a second story and we can get started on it while we prepare for our baby to come home."

Away we went. The funny thing is that the way Mommy does things, if she wants it done now, it is. Daddy was afraid you might even show up before the weekend was over. For a reason unknown to us, it actually took Mommy and Daddy three weeks to get our initial application signed, notarized, and sent to Holt International, our adoption agency. But when we received our referral for our precious daughter it all made perfect sense.

The night on which we decided it was time was March 26, 2004. The date we finally got our paperwork off to Holt was April 16, 2004. China is 14 hours ahead of us—making it the next day there. Our referral said: Ling Yu E was born March 27, 2004. She was found April 17, 2004.

Given the time differences, the night Mommy got that "feeling" was the same night your birthmother gave birth to you. You were kept healthy and safe until Mommy and Daddy had officially started to head for you.

The guardian angel that sent you to wait for us that day will be forever wound in our family's red thread.

Sydney Frances Yu E (born March 2004), Shangrao, Jiangxi.

Sisters—Maddie (age 5), and Lily (age 1), Kunming, Yunnan.

"WHAT'S THAT?"
by Ruthi Coats

ADDIE HAS A CONDITION CALLED MICROTIA, WHICH MEANS "SMALL EARS." I wrote the following on the day she got her hearing aids.

"Well, without too much ado, Addie got the hearing aid today. A bone-conducting hearing aid on a head band. When it was sitting right we talked softly to her. Her hearing normally is rated moderate to severe loss, but now she could hear us talking in soft voices! I was crying. It was amazing! When we left the building, Addie looked up at Claude and me and said, 'What's that?' Neither of us knew what she was referring to. Then she asked again, and we finally realized that 'that' was birds!"

I still say prayers of thanks that this little girl is mine and that we are connected and she is here. If she would not have come to us and not been adopted, would she have never heard the birds?

Sisters—Kate (age 4), Hanzhong, Shaanxi, and Addie (age 4½), Nanchuan, Chongqing.

Sisters—Emma (age 3), Loudi, Hunan, and Molli (age 7), Yueyang, Hunan.

Sara Madison (age 6), Chongqing.

Forever Family
by Lori Dubbs (December 23, 2000)

Oh my little daughter so strong,
what you must have endured to survive.
I say to you it's ok now,
you can trust me,
I will take care of you.
But you do not believe me,
You don't let me in,
You don't know how.
My heart aches to hold and love you
and have you love me.
When will you let me in?
When will you love me too?
What will it take?
What can I do?
What do you need, my little daughter?
Each smile is a gift,
each laugh a triumph as you struggle to heal.
I admire your strength and courage.
I pray you will learn to love and trust in
   your forever family,
For that is what we pledge to you,
   to be your loving family—forever.

Sisters—Meili (age 6), Shaoyang, Hunan; Xiaomei (age 2½), Kaifeng, Henan; Lianne (age 8), Shijiazhuang, Hebei; Xuli (age 3), Fuling, Chongqing; and Anmei (age 3½), Chenzhou, Hunan—enjoying the beach at the Outerbanks area of North Carolina.

A FAMILY FOR FU BAO
by Karen Clough

WITH GOD ALL THINGS ARE POSSIBLE—EVEN ADOPTING A CHILD WHILE LIVING IN SINGAPORE! A friend emailed me in July with a photo of some little children in an orphanage in Mongolia. My husband, Richard, and I were never able to have children and had never been able to afford adoption. But we felt led to try and adopt one of these little boys, who was three years old. By the end of August we were deep in the paperwork for the home study when we learned that the Mongolian government had written a new law. Suddenly we were too old to adopt the little boy in Mongolia.

For several weeks we prayed and checked out agency websites. We discovered some waiting children and learned about special needs, meanwhile continuing to gather paperwork. The costs of adoption seemed insurmountable and certainly gave us lots to consider.

Richard had just departed for a teacher's conference in Indonesia when I found the IAAP agency's list of special needs children, with many boys needing homes. One boy, Fu Bao, was 13 years old. The listing said he had been waiting for a family for such a long time and this was his last chance to be adopted. The plea was urgent and touched my heart. It didn't matter that he was missing his left forearm but only that he needed a family.

When I looked at his little school picture and saw his big smile, my heart literally skipped a beat! It's hard to understand why this boy hadn't been adopted, but I'm certain that God had been holding him in Liaoning, China, especially for us. A real eyecatcher was that IAAP had already waived their fees, and Love Without Boundaries had granted the orphanage fees. Without their generosity, this story would be different.

My darling husband came home and I gently broke the news of the "treasure" (the meaning of Fu Bao) I had found. He is the practical one with the RHS factor (reluctant husband syndrome); so it took a week for us to be together on this and commit to adopt Fu Bao. Three days later we received new photos. He grew so much over the weekend—from a little boy to a teenager… still with a nice smile!

A month later we've completed the home study and await the final report so we can file paperwork at the U.S. Embassy. We've submitted our Letter of Intent to China for Fu Bao and received back our preapproval. We applied for grants and received an additional $5,000 from Ava's Hope, which will cover many of the costs!

It's an exciting journey, and we look forward to watching it unfold. We're thankful to God for the privilege of soon having a son! Fu Bao's long wait will be over, and he's coming home!

Jesse Bao (age 13), Dandong, Liaoning.

Gracie (age 17 months), Guangchang, Jiangxi.

Xiaomei Yingxin (age 2), Kaifeng, Henan.

Left: Olivia (age 15 months), Changde, Hunan, with Mom.

Below: Friends— Olivia (age 18 months), Changde, Hunan, and Sarah (age 2), Huainan, Anhui.

Linnea
by Michael Bakos (age 10)

Sister
Moon eyes
Annoying, hugging, laughing
My sister from China
Linnea

Left: Mom with Michael (age 6)—at the Great Wall before meeting his new baby sister, Linnea.

Below: Siblings—Caden and Linnea (both age 4), both from Xiamen, Fujian.

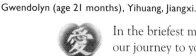

Gwendolyn (age 21 months), Yihuang, Jiangxi.

ANNIVERSARY
by Karen Petty

SIX MONTHS HAVE PASSED. If only the wait to meet you had passed so quickly. It has been six months to the day since we met you and you began inspiring in us unlimited pride and joy. You are our best and most meaningful accomplishment. You didn't arrive amidst pink bows and cheers of waiting family members. Instead, you were brought into a room too small to hold all the families who gathered there and then handed to us by a man whose namesake you carried. You were smaller than we imagined, more beautiful than we could have dreamed, and louder than any other child in the room.

It was sweltering hot, and I mistook your body temperature to be a sign of the caustic end of China's summer heat. I had dreamed for months that time would stand still at that moment, but it passed us by in a blink. In the briefest moment in time, you became our daughter. Just that quickly our journey to you was over. But the journey of you was just beginning.

Tonight I read back over my postings from China. It is the first time I've looked at those words since the days that I wrote them. On the 10th day of our trip, I wrote this:

"Funny how I started this blog to chronicle our journey to Gwen. I guess I didn't realize the real journey is about to begin. Everything about this journey has seemingly been a struggle. Financing this adoption, INS nightmares, run-ins with people who just don't 'get it,' trip logistics, the endless waiting (and waiting) and now… I sit in a hotel room with a sleeping baby and a snoring husband and know that I've waited a long, long time to worry this hard, work this hard, and love this intensely."

I didn't realize at the time how profound those words would really be. Mothering has been the greatest struggle and the greatest triumph of my life to date, as I'm sure it will continue to be. To be a mother is to essentially watch your heart leave your body and watch it flounder and flourish, all on its own, all at the same time.

I thought I knew happiness, and then I saw your very first smile. I thought I knew exuberance, and then I heard you giggle out loud. I thought I knew grief until I watched you cry out in pain. I thought I knew sadness until I saw you grieving. I thought I knew how to mother. I thought I was prepared enough, educated enough, and ready enough. Truth be told, everything I know you have taught me. I breathe in your presence, delight in your accomplishments, revel in your joy, and ache in your pain. To say it in words will never be enough; so my promise to you is to live it as strongly as I can.

Happy anniversary, baby girl. Here's to many more.

Laurel (age 5), Zhuzhou, Hunan—spending time with her friend Huckleberry.

WHAT HAPPENED TO COFFEE?
Excerpt from Travel Journal
by Sheri Marsh

May 22, 2006

As I woke this morning I looked to my left and saw my beautiful daughter watching me from her crib. She had a smile bigger than life itself.

"Good morning, Mom. It's time to get up, change my diaper, make my bottle, feed me, and change my clothes."

What happened to *coffee?* Well, I guess those days are gone! I have decided that I am also the bib for my daughter. *All* of my clothes have some sort of stain on them after each and every meal. Does anyone make mommy bibs??? The other thing I have noticed is that Mommy gets *cold* coffee and *cold* food, trying to inhale bits of my own meal while feeding my daughter. Kyle and I have to shove the food into our mouths and then it is trade-off time. One eats as fast as he or she can, while the other feeds. But you know I wouldn't change any of it for all the tea in China.

Above: Big brother Ryan (age 14),
with Chloe Bao Li (age 2), Qingcheng, Guangdong.

Below: Sisters—Chloe (age 3), Qingcheng, Guangdong; Molly (age 5), Maoming, Guangdong; SaraGrace (age 2), DaTong, Shanxi; and Jillian (age 6), Ganzhou, Jiangxi—having fun with Dad.

Our Waiting Child Story
by Karin Prunty

I SPOTTED OUR DAUGHTER, DANG JIAN CHAO, ON AN AGENCY WAITING CHILDREN LIST ONE DAY. At first I didn't know she was our daughter, but something about her made me keep checking the list to see if she had a family. Finally, after a month or so, I called the agency to ask about her. I was told that a family had her on hold; so I continued to hold her in my heart and wait for their decision.

She was scheduled for heart surgery the following month. The day of the surgery I paced the floors and prayed that she would be all right. Finally someone forwarded a message to me with devastating news. The doctors in China felt that her heart condition was too serious for them to attempt to operate on her. The family who had placed her on hold decided they did not want to pursue her adoption.

I frantically sent emails to Love Without Boundaries, asking if anything could be done and telling them that we wanted to be this little girl's family, no matter what her heart condition was. They emailed back to say that they had already contacted Hope Foster Home about accepting Jian Chao. While at Hope Foster Home, our daughter was able to receive life-saving heart surgery in Singapore, thanks to the efforts of LWB and Dr. Joyce Hill. We are so grateful to them and to the doctor and hospital in Singapore who made it all possible. She is now a spunky, smiley bundle of energy whom we named SaraGrace.

Several months after returning home, I came across a website with pictures of Datong—our daughter's orphanage city. The pictures had been posted by some Americans who were living there. I left a message in the hopes that they would contact me. We were starting another adoption of a child from Datong, and I hoped they could visit him at the orphanage. Two months later I received an email from them. I asked them if they remembered Jian Chao and sent a picture of her. This was their reply:

"You won't even believe this—I'm sitting here at work just crying! My husband and I took five babies, including your SaraGrace, to Hope Foster Home in January! We knew she was the sickest baby and we were all so afraid for her, but our friend, Lily, held Dang Jian Chao and kept her as comfortable as possible on our bumpy, eight-hour ride. Dr. Hill and Hope Foster Home must be the most amazing place in the entire world. We were so sad as we left because we knew we probably wouldn't see the babies again—and today a picture of one of them pops up on my computer!"

There are truly no words to describe our emotions as we read this email from the young couple who had carried our daughter to safety. It is amazing to us that God would put our families together, and we are so grateful to Him for taking such good care of SaraGrace while she waited for her family to come for her. Needless to say we began an email friendship with this couple and hope to meet them later this year when we return to Datong to adopt our son.

Above: Kylie Faye Jing (age 2), Zhangzhou, Fujian.
Below: Jordan Michaeli (age 5), YiYang, Jiangxi.

Sisters—Caroline Elaina MengQiong (age 5), Yunnan, and Catherine Grace FuDie (age 2), Guangxi.

Soar ©May 2005
by Jessica Knudsen for Amelie Rose

With this vibrant new life,
There are endless possibilities.
Like a kite floating on a breeze,
You will soar.

The love of your family
Will give you strong wings;
A jubilant song the heart sings,
You will soar.

As over time we watch you grow,
Surrounded by our boundless love,
Know the joy with which you are thought of,

Amelie Rose Xin (age 20 months), Dongguan, Guangdong.

Zoe YiHui (age 11 months), Beihai, Guangxi.

愛

Bedtime Conversation
by Nancy Delpha

MY HUSBAND IS GONE ON A BUSINESS TRIP, AND I KNOW IF I CAN GET MY TWO LITTLE ONES TO BED AS QUICKLY AS POSSIBLE, I MIGHT BE ABLE TO GET SOME WORK DONE BEFORE I FALL INTO BED MYSELF. Natalie is four years old and Tyler is eight years old, and they are finding every excuse to slow down the process. We are in Tyler's room, deciding who is going to sleep in the top bunk, and Natalie is pointing out to him the two signs that had been carefully made to welcome him home this past summer. One says "Welcome Home, Tyler" in bright red and blue, and one says "We Love You, Tyler" with a big red heart. Natalie had stayed home with Daddy, and big brother Tom had traveled with me to go meet Tyler and bring him home from China. I ask Tyler if he remembers seeing the signs at the airport, and he nods his head and smiles. He says, "Daddy pick me." I respond, "You mean Daddy picked you up at the airport and gave you a hug?"

He shakes his head no. "Ma," he says, "Daddy pick me. Mama pick me. *Pictures!*" Having only been home four months, a discussion like this has never occurred before, but the light begins to come on as I realize the significance of what he is saying. "You're right! Daddy picked you, and Mama picked you. We saw your picture and we knew we wanted you to be in our family!" Beaming from ear to ear, he says, "Yes, Mama, you pick *me!*" I say quietly, holding back the tears, "How do you know that?" Again the huge smile lights up his face, and, pointing his index finger to his temple, he says, "Me just know!"

Daddy's Girl
by Kayla Gute

AFTER 18 LONG MONTHS OF WAITING, BRIAN AND I FINALLY HAD OUR PRECIOUS BABY! She was everything we had hoped and dreamed of and so much more. She was perfect! Except… she would have *nothing* to do with Daddy. She didn't want him in the same room, sitting on the edge of the bed, or even pushing the stroller. She would turn her head from him when he would try to make eye contact. She would wail and scream if he attempted to hold her. It was heartbreaking to watch Brian have his feelings crushed by a tiny little peanut that he loved so much! Of course we had read about this, even read a story of another chided father in the first LWB book "Love's Journey," and thought we had prepared ourselves for this possibility. But the reality of it is, there's no way to mentally prepare for the hopelessness you feel when the one you love more than life itself detests your mere presence. Daddy tried holding her a little every day, but you could just hear the terror in our daughter's voice. Getting ready in the morning, even getting food at a buffet, had become a real chore for Mommy with her Velcro baby.

On one of the last days of our trip, we went to Shamian Island to do some shopping. One of the shopkeepers was having a great time playing with AnLi as she was seated in her stroller. AnLi was completely entertained with her new "friend" while Mommy and Daddy did some last minute shopping. When the young lady tried to get AnLi out of her stroller, sheer panic set in and AnLi started screaming. The first person AnLi saw was Daddy. She reached out her arms for him and practically leapt out of her stroller and into his arms. He took her out of the stroller and comforted her… and Daddy's girl emerged! Now they are inseparable!

AnLi (age 11 months), Hanchuan, Hubei— looking out the hotel window in Guangzhou.

Above: Referral photo of Anderson FuRong.

Below: Anderson FuRong (age 16 months), Xining, Qinghai.

Madyson Eileen (age 4), Datong, Shanxi—holding tight to Daddy's hand while walking through a park on a cold afternoon.

爸

Left: Xiao Lian (age 3), Changsha, Hunan—practicing using chopsticks while eating her favorite noodles.

Below: Friends—Yan Yu and Xiao Lian (both age 3), both from Changsha, Hunan, and Maya Fu Dian (nearly age 3), Hubei—play together weekly.

Our Dynamic Duo
by Jan Champoux

WHEN WE DECIDED TO ADD A FOURTH CHILD TO OUR FAMILY, WE WENT A BIT AGAINST CONVENTION BY ADOPTING A "VIRTUAL TWIN" TO OUR SON JACOB. Eighteen months earlier we had adopted Jake (then six months old) from South Korea, and we felt he would enjoy the company of a sibling near his own age.

I had read that some agencies discourage "twinning" of adopted children, but I also spoke with parents who had actually done this and were happy with the outcome. So in spite of multiple red flags—related to twinning, toddler adoption in general, and adopting a child with special needs—we brought home a sister for Jake, just two months younger in age.

At 23 and 25 months these two could be a handful. And, as expected, there were some hurt feelings at first. Jacob had to learn to share his parents and his toys. Emily had to learn to be part of a family. I had to learn how to read a story with two children on my lap and load them both into car seats without an escape. The first weeks passed, and we all began to settle into a routine.

One morning, about six weeks after Emily came home, I directed the children into Jake's bedroom for playtime. It was nearly 11:00 and I still needed to get the breakfast dishes done! There was nothing in the room but a bed and a tub of stuffed toys; so I figured they couldn't destroy anything. They might even settle down and play nicely. Surprisingly they did just that, and I happily listened to giggling and chattering while I cleaned my kitchen. My husband, Rob, a builder, and his foreman, Rick, came in to go over some blueprints on the kitchen table. I proudly announced that I had just enjoyed 15 uninterrupted minutes to myself!

Then I noticed that the happy noises had stopped. I went to check on the kids. Nobody was there! I knew they couldn't have gotten out of the room and so opened the closet door. There they sat in the dark with a heap of stuffed animals… Emily was buck naked and Jake was still struggling to remove the last of his clothes. They both burst into laughter and made a break for the door.

I caught Jake easily (since his arms were still pinned up around his ears and he couldn't see through his shirt), but Emily squirted out of the closet, out of the room, down the hall, and through the kitchen. She ran several naked laps around the kitchen, past Rob and Rick, laughing and shrieking all the way until I caught her. As we headed back down the hall to retrieve clothing, I heard Rick say, "It's nice to see Emily has come out of her shell."

Since that day Jake and Emily have been filling our lives with havoc and fun, always together and the best of friends.

Sisters—Madison (age 5), Nanning, Guangxi, and Emily (age 4), Xiangyin, Hunan.

In the Eyes of a Child
by Elizabeth Morgan

MY HUSBAND AND I ARE THE PARENTS TO TWO WONDERFUL GIRLS FROM CHINA—NATALIE AND KATHARINE. One night at dinner my husband said that earlier in the day Natalie had been talking about how she and Katharine are "different." Natalie said that, yes, she and Katharine were definitely different than Daddy and Mommy. So we started to talk more about it. I asked Natalie, "So what's different about you and Katharine?"

Natalie thought for a moment and said, "Well, we don't eat salad."

Anya (age 13 months), Xiangyin, Hunan—meeting new sister, Annaliese Chen Le (age 3), Jiande, Zhejiang.

Mary (age 4), Kunshan, Jiangsu, with her big brother, Nathan (age 17).

Sisters—Lucy (age 8), Guangdong, and Juliana (age 6), Jiangsu.

Rhianne XinHua (age 5), Luliang, Shanxi.

HAPPY FOREVER FAMILY DAY
by Mary Reynolds

TWO YEARS AGO TODAY A MIRACLE HAPPENED. In a hot, crowded room in southern China, a woman called out "Reynolds." Two nervous people moved to the front of the chaos. A woman entered the room carrying a beautiful little boy. The boy was wearing black sandals, black and white striped pants, and an orange shirt sent to him in a care package from the other side of the world.

The woman handed the little boy to the nervous mother. The father showed the official paperwork saying that China was giving us the best gift in the world—one of its precious children. The mother kissed the quiet and confused little boy on the cheek. The boy responded by purposefully and deliberately wiping the kiss away. Who knew this was the first clue to a very entertaining little person who would fill our lives with love and laughter?

In the years before our adventure to bring home our son, we never could have imagined traveling to the other side of the world. We never thought that our family would grow in such different and special ways. Our son James came to us through the miracle of medicine. Our son Riley came to us through the miracle of adoption.

My husband commented many, many times over the years about a song that really sums up Riley for him. I agree: "Sometimes I Thank God for Unanswered Prayers." Riley is our answer to our unanswered prayer.

Happy Forever Family Day, Riley! Two years down; a lifetime to go.

THE GREATEST MIRACLE
by Samantha Allen

OUR DAUGHTER, JEZREEL, WAS BORN WITH SEVERE HEART DISEASE, MISSING HALF OF HER HEART AND HAVING SEVERAL OTHER ABNORMALITIES. It was not until after we had chosen her and she was examined at a heart hospital in China that we realized how severe her condition was. She should have had surgery when she was a newborn, and she had been living without sufficient oxygen for three years. The doctors told us it was a miracle that she was still alive and that she needed heart surgery immediately. The procedure was so complex that one of the finest pediatric heart surgeons from Shanghai agreed to come to Wuhan and perform the open-heart surgery. Love Without Boundaries graciously agreed to pay for the surgery.

We waited on pins and needles to hear when the surgery was completed as she would need to spend time on the heart-lung machine and the risk of death was great in her weakened condition. But we knew that God had brought us that far for a purpose, and that was for her to have a new life. She pulled through with flying colors.

Jezreel's second open-heart surgery was completed on Valentine's Day 2006 in the U.S. after her adoption was finalized. The hours ticked by as she was on the heart-lung machine again. Visitors came and went and too much time passed for everything to be going okay. She was in surgery almost ten hours. When the surgeon finally came out, he told us that Jezzie had to be on the lung machine so long that her body was reacting adversely. They had to leave her chest open to leave room for the swelling. So began a month in the cardiac ICU at Medical City Children's of Dallas. When they were able to close her chest, she went from kidney failure to respiratory failure but finally pulled through and was able to go home. She was surrounded by four adoring siblings. More people than we realize helped pray her through.

Because of her illness, Jez could not walk when we got her from China. With great difficulty, in the first few months before her surgery, she learned how to walk. After a month in ICU, she had to learn all over again. Now we are working on Jezreel's speech. It has become apparent that Jezreel's nervous system was severely impacted by her three years without enough oxygen. She is now five years old but has not yet said her first word. However she is obviously a miracle child; so we know more miracles await us. We eagerly look forward to her first "Mama" and "Daddy." There are many things that Jezreel cannot yet do because of her delays, but she sure knows how to love—and that is the greatest miracle of all.

Jezreel with her daddy.

Siblings—Kamryn Corine (age 2), Changsha, Hunan, and Addison (age 10). Pirates of the China seas.

Karlin (age 7), Mother's Love, Guangxi, put this outfit together to wear when we were going to see the musical "Cats."

CHOOSE TO DANCE
Excerpted essay by Paula Flynn

"IS IT HARD?" I have been asked many times regarding my life now as single mother of my beautiful two-year-old daughter, Grace Christine. Possibly the hardest part was the decision to adopt itself. I remember being swayed by concerned friends who thought I was taking on "too much." Of greater importance, I will never forget the moment I decided, at the urging of a friend, to open my heart and follow its yearnings, listen to its whispers, and choose to "dance."

August 30, 2005, was our "Gotcha Day." Our first evening together I gave Grace her first bath! She was trembling and seemed terrified. We were together in the tub, which had been suggested by her pediatrician as a way to expedite bonding. As I was drying her shaking body off, I was singing, dancing, and snapping my fingers to try to calm her down. Suddenly she bore an enormous smile, moved her fingers as if to snap, and made clicking sounds that imitated the snapping sound. Grace, in her way, was saying, "I really like you, Mommy."

In December I took Grace to see "The Nutcracker" and watched as she squealed with delight and clapped her hands at the Sugar Plum Fairy and other beautiful dancers. Later that week she was able to pull herself to stand using the couch! Perhaps the ballet had inspired her. That Christmas season she began feeding herself. These are all miraculous milestones in a biological child, but are indescribable gifts to a mother of a child who is needing to "catch up."

On our first anniversary of our "Gotcha Day," dressed in her traditional Chinese silk pajamas, Grace passed out red cupcakes at daycare and later that night at our "Mommies' Group." Each cupcake was given out with a dimpled smile and a squeal of delight.

My answer to the question, "Is it hard?" is a definitive "yes," always accompanied by a joyous smile. I am forever thankful that I listened to the advice of LeeAnn Womack, who advised that when you get the choice to "sit it out or dance" you should choose to dance. Grace and I have many more dance steps to learn together!

Grace Christine Fu Chang (age 2), Hengyang, Hunan.

LIA
by Danny Hayduk (age 8)

WE WENT ALL THE WAY TO CHINA TO GET LIA. She's like 6,000,000,000,000,000 treasure chests. We've had two birthday parties together. We sort of look alike. We adopted her from China.

Lia fixes our family because now I'm not the youngest, Mom is not the only girl, and Tim is not the only one to still have tonsils. Dad has to carry pink stuff now though.

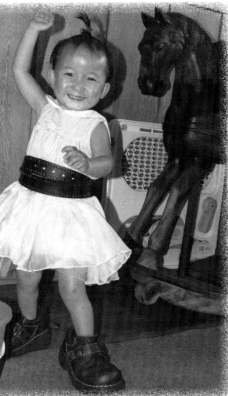

Ting (age 3), Harbin, Heilongjiang. I say just dress up and *dance*!

What Do You Get?
by Susan Sill

What do you get when you adopt a four-year-old boy?

In China you get to:
Try to calm a little boy who is very angry and frightened when he is placed with you
See him interact with those that speak his language
See him struggle with all the changes in his life
Clean him up when he has an accident
Bandage his wound with his first Band-Aid
See the joy on his face when you buy him that toy police car
Find out his potty words and that when he says them you had better get him to the bathroom right then!!
Hold, for the first time, an exhausted sleeping child after a very long flight

When you get home you get to:
See him meet his new four-year-old sister for the first time
See his face when he sees his first bike
Introduce him to your cats
Push him in a swing for his first time
Help him overcome his fear of climbing on the equipment in the park
Take him to his first parade
Introduce him to the Gulf of Mexico and swimming pools
See him start pre-K with a big smile on his face
Calm his fears during a hurricane
See him master walking on a balance beam for the first time
See his first Christmas and all the other holidays
Get the hugs and kisses when he is finally ready to return your love
And with all of that, you get to love him for the rest of your life!

Are They Sisters?
by Kathy Schnulle

"YOUR GIRLS ARE ADORABLE. Are they sisters?" I drag my eyes away from the playground, glancing at the woman standing near me. Distracted, I ask her to repeat herself. "I was wondering if your girls are sisters."

This isn't the first time I have been asked this, and it won't be the last. It seems to be commonly asked of those families who have adopted more than one child. I have lost count of the number of times I have been asked if my daughters are sisters, and when I say yes, people persist with, "No, I mean are they real sisters?"

I think of devoted and protective big sister Emma, whose first thoughts are always of her younger sister. At parties she scoops up piñata treats for Nora, making sure Nora has enough. When shopping I know that Nora will never get lost. Emma will see to that as she never lets Nora out of her sight.

Nora, at three, idolizes her big sister. She is very clear about it and boldly states, "I wanna be like Emma." She watches Emma very closely. If Emma is wearing a skirt, I know what Nora will want to wear that day. If Emma wears boots, I better have a pair for Nora. If Emma falls and bumps her leg, Nora will throw herself on the ground and start crying that she too has hurt her leg.

Recently I walked into our hallway at 6:45 a.m. to find Emma curled up with her blanket, lying on the floor outside Nora's bedroom door. She was waiting patiently for Nora to wake up and play with her.

Just a year and a half apart, Nora and Emma know each other inside and out. They have unspoken agreements between them, such as Emma gets first dibs on anything purple, and Nora gets anything with sea turtles. They go into fits of laughter over the same silly games. If one child gets into mischief, I can bet they both were in on it. They keep close track of each other and don't like to be separated.

My attention is back on the playground. Nora is momentarily out of sight. I see Emma stop running, her eyes scanning the busy playground for Nora's telltale bouncing pigtails. She turns toward me, mouth open, and ready to

Nora Zhong-Ping (age 1½), Chenzhou, Hunan, with sister and best friend, Emma Hao (age 3), Jiande, Zhejiang.

speak but breaks into a grin when she sees my hand already up, pointing out Nora to her. She laughs and yells, "You knew I was looking for Nora!" I smile back at her. I did indeed.

I turn to the woman next to me, smile, and say, "Yes, they are sisters." I don't wait to hear if she is going to add the all too common second question. I am already on my way to join my daughters, who share not only the same parents, but a very real bond of love between them.

Siblings—Ethan (age 4), Shantou, Guangdong; (standing) Taylor (age 9), Nanchang, Jiangxi; Skylar (age 8), Fuzhou, Jiangxi; and Brendan (age 7), Shanghai— at the Fuzhou/Linchuan reunion.

Alaina Brooke JiaCen (nearly age 14 months), Fengcheng, Jiangxi.

爸媽

Parenting
by Vicki Van Nostrand

BEING A MOM TO TEN CHILDREN BRINGS MANY COMMENTS: "HOW DO YOU DO IT?" "God bless you." "You must have so much patience!" Over the past 23 years of being a parent, I have found answers that aren't meant to be cute; they just are the answers. I "do it" some days better than others. Yes, God has blessed me, and, *no*, I don't have all that much patience!

This August I came home with our last child. She is a spitfire, quiet and then loud, and full of fun. She fits into our family like she has been here forever, instead of only three short weeks.

Almost 24 years of parenting, and I am still doing it the way I know best—by the seat of my pants. I love my life and each and every one of my children. Life is good.

AnnaGrace ZhiChang (age 3), Jiangxi; Lia (age 2), Jiangxi; and Aimee FuYu (age 5), Yunnan. Sisters, Anna and Aimee, with best friend, Lia.

Friends and sisters—(Back to front)
Grace (age 5), Wenzhou City, Zhejiang;
Kira (age 3), Taizhou, Jiangsu; Maya (age 3),
Liangping, Chongqing; Analiese (age 3), DeYang, Sichuan.
Grace and Analiese are sisters, as are Kira and Maya.

Elizabeth Catherine SiQi (age 3), Luoyang, Henan.

Love between siblings. Alec (age 10½)
and Zoë (age 16 months), Pingliang City, Gansu.

More Excited than Ever
by Alec Hassurther (age 10)

From a journal entry:

Mom and Lance kept looking for that one special little girl who would become my little sister. At the same time our house was being worked on. They were making your room and the next week laying the wood floor. Then the most exciting thing, a picture of you! I was so excited I didn't know what to say. I couldn't wait to tell everyone! Then the next day we bought you blankets, clothes, and bottles. The only sad part was that you had congenital heart disease, which means you had holes in your heart and would have to have surgery a little while after you got home from China. But I thought that it was not going to be bad and I was right, but it was still going to be sorta bad though and pretty serious. But I knew you would be my sister, no matter what happened. Though I still pray you make it home with all of us. Mom and Lance went to the heart doctor to see how serious it would be. He said it could be worse than it is. Then they asked if you would be able to go camping because we camp almost all the time and he said yes. Then I was more excited than ever!

Precious Zoë
by Michelle Becher

WE WENT TO LOUISVILLE TO MEET WITH A PEDIATRIC CARDIOLOGIST TO GET A MEDICAL OPINION ON A LITTLE GIRL'S CONDITION. During the drive we discussed our fears of what he might say as we knew this little girl was already in our hearts. To our surprise, this wonderful specialist gave us hope and calmed our fears, even when we pressed for a worst case scenario. He made the comment, "Maybe no matter what the outcome, even if she would die, which I don't think will happen, you were meant to be her family and love her during that time."

Without saying a word to each other, we both knew this was our daughter. We called our agency and requested further testing. My husband said if this came through that it would be confirmation from God that we should adopt this child. But by the time we got home we decided to commit to adopting Liang Wan Qiao. When we showed her picture to Alec, our ten-year-old son, and explained her special need, his reply was, "If you don't go get her, who will?" This made our seemingly large decision so simple. We began completing our letter of intent, and that same evening our agency called to inform us that the orphanage had agreed to get another ultrasound—additional confirmation from God.

We met our precious Zoë on June 18, 2006—Father's Day. She is such a delight, and we cannot imagine life without her. We will soon be heading for her open-heart surgery and feel very positive. We know no matter what happens that she is where she is meant to be.

Zoë had successful surgery on September 18, 2006 and is a healthy, happy, smart little girl.

Sarah (nearly age 13 months), Zoë (age 16 months), and Xia (age 12 months), all from Pingliang City, Gansu, with their dads. They joined their new families on Father's Day, June 18, 2006!

MY HEROES
by Dawn Choate

THE PICTURES WERE SPRAWLED ACROSS THE LIVING ROOM FLOOR, AND THE LITTLE FACES STARED UP AT US AS WE SORTED THROUGH THEM TOGETHER. Some smiled sweetly, others looked sad and empty-eyed. Still others struggled to smile from behind faces that were marred from cleft lip and other needs. Joshua, our eldest son, who was eight years old at the time, pointed decisively to one tiny baby boy whose face seemed to have the worst case of cleft lip among the bunch. "That one," he said proudly. "That is the boy I want to sponsor!"

Jordan, our youngest son, continued to drop globs of glue on the back of the photos and carefully lay them down across the large poster board. We were working on a project for his kindergarten class to show the students that he had learned to count to one hundred. He held his marker with great care as he wrote in his best five-year-old handwriting across the top, "100 Kids Who Need a Home." Then Jordan picked up the picture of one little girl who also had a cleft lip, for whom we had said many prayers in the hopes that she would find a home. "Does she have a family yet, Mommy?" I replied, "No, not yet, sweetie." His eyes seemed to fill with so much compassion for such a young boy as he said incredulously, "How could a family not adopt her yet? She is so beautiful!!"

My sons are not saints, and they have dished out their fair share of ugly remarks and unkind behavior. But as soon as we started the process to adopt our first daughter, Hannah, in 2003, a transformation began to take place in their hearts that has slowly, surely changed them. A great interest in other cultures, more compassion for those in need, and a heart to truly make a difference in the world were just some of the unexpected gifts bringing in a child from halfway around the world brought to my sons.

Yet it was their astounding love for their new sister, and for the sister that was to arrive one year later, and their incredible patience in the darkest days of our family's struggle to heal and bond with the girls, that has led me to only one conclusion about my young sons: They are heroes.

So often in adoption the parents are called "saints." The adopted children are lauded as survivors and gifts to their new families. Yet I know that a critical piece of the red thread in our family that tied us to two little girls in China and kept the line from ever breaking was a boy named Joshua and a boy named Jordan. They never signed the papers or stepped on a plane to bring home little girls without families, and yet their fingerprints are all over the red thread tied around those little girls' hearts that pulled them home and knit them to our hearts forever.

Siblings—Hannah AiLi (age 2), Yangdong, Guangdong; Joshua (age 10); Jordan (age 7); and Maggie JieLing (age 3), Duchang, Jiangxi.

No Flower
by Amy Hall

Written for Father's Day, 2004

No flower could be as lovely,
No blossom could be as sweet,
As those little girls,
We traveled so very far to meet.

One has hair like nightfall,
The other is so fair,
Each one is so precious,
A blessing God did share.

Thank you, Lord, for our children.
Grant us wisdom and your grace,
So we can teach our daughters
To know their Father's face.

Silly sisters—Katie (age 5), Jiangmen, Guangdong, and Marci (age 4), Guilin, Guangxi.

OUR JOURNEY TO MADISON
by Martin and Sandra Beecher

OUR FIRST DAUGHTER FROM CHINA, MEAGAN, WAS ADOPTED IN 1996. Back then few children had been adopted from her orphanage. It had many needs, and throughout the following years we tried to help as much as we could. In 2000 we received an email from a charitable organization that included a "wish list" from the orphanage. One item caught our eye: "363 U.S. dollars for 7-year-old girl's club foot surgery." We thought about paying for this child's surgery, but, as you know, sometimes what first comes to you is not the path you end up taking.

When we got the email, we read it from the comfort of our living room—in Okinawa, Japan. After living in Georgia for over 20 years, we had moved halfway around the world. Our family was just getting adjusted to life overseas. The anonymous child in the email kept nagging at us. Would it, we thought, be possible to adopt her? And could we adopt while living in Japan?

There was almost no information locally about adoption. We finally found a Yahoo group for people living in Japan. As we discovered, the process wasn't difficult—just very different. We had to coordinate paperwork between several countries. But that was easy compared to the other part of the equation—actually getting a preidentified adoption approved.

Once the inquiry had been made, the response that came back from China was, "Have you ever heard of polio?" We were taken aback. It was clear to us that this child had needs we had not envisioned. Needs we weren't sure could be handled where we lived. The SWI wasn't sure of her prognosis. Yet, we were drawn to her— so we pleaded with our agency to try and make it happen.

Several months later we were on our way to China for our daughter, who would be named Madison. When we first met her, it was obvious her needs were many. One foot was so contracted she could not wear a shoe. Both hips and one shoulder were dislocated. One knee was frozen in place at a 90-degree angle. Her left wrist was limp. The only limb that worked normally was her right arm and hand. All her teeth were decayed. She weighed only 37 pounds.

Once we got home we found that her needs could not be met in Okinawa. We moved to Germany for two years, where she received several major orthopedic surgeries. Years later we finally have a prognosis for Madison. No, she can't walk, and she uses a wheelchair. She will need several more major surgeries. But her future is very bright.

This summer she competed in the Okinawa Special Olympics and won a gold medal in the wheelchair 50-meter race. She loves school and is doing well. Madison is learning to crochet and just joined the chess club. She is planning for college—she thinks maybe she will be a teacher.

Since we moved back to Okinawa, we've been back to China to adopt another daughter, Michelle. And, by the time you read this, we should be back from China with our newest daughter, who will be named Melody.

We're so glad we took that leap of faith and brought home the girl from the email. Anonymous no more, she shows us daily what courage and determination are all about. Our lives are much better because she is in it.

Madison (age 12), Yihuang, Jiangxi.

New sisters—Grace (age 7), Nanping, Fujian, and Ting Ting (age 4), Fuzhou, Fujian.

HOLES IN OUR HEARTS
by Carol Thompson

IN 1998 I WAS BLESSED BY BECOMING THE MOTHER TO A 14-MONTH-OLD GIRL FROM NANPING, FUJIAN, NAMED YAN XIAO RONG. I named her Grace. In my heart I always wanted two children and planned to adopt again, but time and circumstances made me unsure. One morning, Grace crawled up into my lap and put her arms around me. She said to me "Mommy? Remember when you came to get me in China?" She went on, "You came to get me because you had a hole in your heart and needed it filled, right?" I explained to her that I had indeed had the hole in my heart filled by adopting her and that I loved her beyond words as a result.

Grace took her hand and started gently rubbing it on my cheek and then she put it on my heart. She continued, "Mommy, now we both have holes in our hearts that need filling. I think we need to go to China to get my sissy." Needless to say, my decision was made at that moment.

When I received the file of Isabella, I fell in love first with her name, Ting Ting. I couldn't see much of her pictures as they had been faxed and were quite blurry. She was four years old and lived in Fuzhou, Fujian—the same city I received Grace in. As I sought to learn the meaning of Ting Ting's name, I found out that the translation is "Graceful or Standing Gracefully"; so now I had two Graces. This made me smile. These two children also shared the same birth month and their adoptions were both in May—one day apart.

Ting Ting had been placed into foster care with an amazing family at age three. The foster family loved and nurtured Ting Ting for an entire year to help her to live, trust, and love again. Their incredible gift to Ting Ting was to prepare her to join our family. On the day we met, Ting Ting ran to her new sister, already knowing her name and proudly announcing in Chinese, "This is my sister! This is my sister!" Isabella and Grace have been inseparable ever since, and the holes in all of our hearts have been filled.

Sarah Brooke (age 12 months), Xianyang, Shaanxi, with Dad.

Grace Jing Yi (age 9 months), Yingtan, Jiangxi, with adoring daddy one week after adoption.

Marissa (age 8), Youxian, Hunan.

MARISSA
by Cathy Langguth

OUR JOURNEY TO MARISSA YOU HUI BEGAN WITH A SMALL PHOTO ON OUR AGENCY'S WEBSITE. Something about that sad little face caught my eye. I read about her congenital heart disease and looked at her again. A "waiting child" had not been in our plan. Our plan quickly changed, though, and nine months later we brought our second daughter home from China.

The following weeks were a flurry of doctor visits, tests, good news (her lungs were not damaged), and bad news (she had pulmonary atresia and lead poisoning). Surgery had to wait while Marissa underwent treatment to remove the lead from her blood. Five weeks later she had open-heart surgery, and immediately her lips and fingers became pink!

Marissa has brought so much love and hope to our family. She is soon to start second grade, and her health is good. She is a wonderful big sister to our younger daughter, Natalie, also born in China. We are so happy that she has joined our family and encourage others to consider bringing children with special needs into their homes. You will not be disappointed!

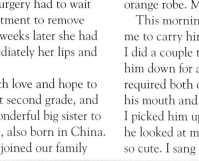

Natalie (age 6), Linchuan/Fuzhou, Jiangxi.

THE HAIRCUT
by MaryBeth Piccirilli

LAST NIGHT I ASKED JIM TO CUT JOSEPH'S HAIR. It was getting too long for him to sport the beloved "hedgehog" look. The girls weren't rubbing his head and calling him "Hedgie" anymore. It needed a trim.

The last time Jim cut Joseph's hair, he must have used the #4 setting because he got halfway through and realized that it was starting to look too short. I came into the bathroom to see a quiet child sitting patiently while Dad cut his hair. When Joseph looked up at me, I got a glimpse of that little boy we had received in October. His haircut was looking like the one he had had in the orphanage again, and I had a sinking feeling. Jim felt so bad about messing up the setting but had no choice but to continue. I left the room to check on one of the girls.

When I came back in the room Jim was done. He brushed Joseph off and put his little eyeglasses back on. Joseph looked up at me. Now he looked more like a Buddhist monk. I pictured him in an orange robe. Maybe it wasn't that bad!

This morning after breakfast Joseph wanted me to carry him around. I had him on my hip as I did a couple things in the kitchen. I had to put him down for a moment to do something which required both of my hands. He had his fingers in his mouth and wanted me to hold him again. So I picked him up and cradled him like a baby and he looked at me and smiled. This kid was just so cute. I sang to him, "Oh my baby, baby, baby. How I love you, love you, love you!" getting louder and rocking him in my arms with each "baby." He giggled with his fingers still in his mouth, loving every second of it. He looked just like my little baby boy with a new haircut.

THIS TRADITION BEGAN AT THE CHINA HOTEL IN GUANGZHOU

Ruby (ages 8 months to 6 years), Chongqing.

Beloved and long-awaited son and brother—Christian HongXi (age 8), Wenzhou, Zhejiang—adopted in October 2006.

Oh Boy!!
by Holly Brooke

HAVING ADOPTED TWO GIRLS FROM CHINA IN 2002 AND 2004, IT SEEMED LOGICAL THAT WHEN WE DECIDED TO GO BACK TO CHINA THAT IT WOULD BE ANOTHER GIRL. Only this time we had our hearts set on adopting an older girl, about five or six years old.

Several times in my search for that older girl, I felt myself drawn to the faces of some of the little boys. I just could not get them out of my head. I began to question myself as to what our motives were for only thinking about adopting another girl, realizing the decision was based on familiarity… girls were our comfort zone. When we took the plunge and submitted a checklist to our agency, at the last minute we added that we would consider a boy, as long as we maintained birth order and he was the youngest of our children.

God obviously had a plan for us, and only a few days later the agency called and caught us off guard. They had a little boy from their last list of waiting children, but his urological condition was not one of the common ones and they had no families that fit their matching profile. I took one look at his photos and knew that he was our new son. Everything just felt right and fell into place about this referral, and in a few days we had accepted him as ours and started the paperchase for the third time. Thoughts of an older girl quickly faded as we fell in love with this new face.

On March 13, 2006, in Kunming, Yunnan, a cute, tanned face peaking out from under a dalmatian hoodie became ours forever. We had not known what was missing in our household, but now we have found it in this little boy. He is charming, happy, laid back, and all boy. The look of pride in my husband's eyes has been an extra reward for me. The possibilities of father and son bonding are endless: Camping, fishing, hunting, and sports are all planned for his future. And I have found that mother and son bonding is just as special as the bond I have with my daughters but in a different way. Because he is a tough boy, he needs me less for the everyday boo-boos, but when he does need me it is something that touches my heart deeply.

Guan Bei Jing was once just a face and a name on a piece of paper, and now Pierce Robert Beijing Brooke is our son. It feels like he has been here forever with us, and we are so grateful that our hearts and minds opened up to the waiting children of China, and especially the waiting boys of China. Our hope is that more people will soon be able to discover the joys that a son brings.

Aubri (age 8), with brother, Andy (age 4), Shenyang, Liaoning.

It's a Boy!
by Karen Bradley

WE ALL KNOW THE FEELING. Dossier submitted, shopping finished, and the wait for "the call" consumes every moment of our day.

I got the call, and a surprise, all at the same time. Months of waiting, buying dresses, dolls and frilly hair bows, a name chosen, and here it was, down to "the moment." The phone rang. It was John Harrah from Harrah Family Services. I will never forget his deep voice as he gave me the news.

"Karen, I have your referral. It's a *boy!*" My heart skipped a beat, and the first thought that came to my mind was, "I have another son." I knew his name in an instant—Kevin—and in spite of all the months of planning and shopping, it was absolutely perfect. Within days the dolls were traded in for Tonka trucks, and the dresses for Levis. Weeks later, when he walked through the hotel room door in Chengdu, I knew he was home.

Recently we celebrated our fifth year as a family. I am forever grateful that Kevin was able to meet face to face with John Harrah, a man who was as thrilled as I was to see a boy join our family.

A Boy From China
by Cheryl Cutting

This was written in honor of our eight-year-old son who is waiting for us in China. So many boys are waiting; it is my daily prayer and mission that they are not forgotten.

I am a boy from China and I am eight years old;
Too long I have been waiting for a family to hold.

I am a boy from China, in my orphanage for years;
I see so many mei meis leaving; why am I still here?

So much talk of China's girls, but we are waiting too;
Can't you see us; don't you hear us calling out for you?

They say I have a special need, and it could take some time,
But my mei mei has a missing hand and her family found her fine.

I am but one of many, a band of brothers, we;
Please tell the world about us—this is our earnest plea.

Boy or girl no matter, both deserve the same:
A home, some love, a family, our birthright to lay claim.

I am a boy from China and I am eight years old;
Too long I have been waiting for a family to hold.

Samantha Yi (age 2), Qujiang, Guangdong.

愛

Before You
by Stephanie Medeiros

Before you, the house was quiet in the evening. We liked that. But now the house is full of giggles, bare feet running on the wood floors, bedtime stories, and proclamations of "I need more kisses." We love that.

Before you, we slept late on weekends. We liked that. But now we hear, "Mommy, come get me," and "Daddy, get up!" You jump on the bed and pull off the covers. We love that.

Before you, Daddy bought BMW t-shirts for himself. He liked that. But now he buys BMW t-shirts for him and you. He loves that.

Before you, it was good old rock 'n roll in the car. We liked that. But now it's "The Hokey Pokey," "I'm a Little Teapot," and "She'll be Coming 'round the Mountain." We love that.

Before you, Mommy watched Star Wars movies a lot. She liked that. But now she watches "Big Bird in China" a lot. She loves that.

Before you, we were always in a hurry—busy, busy, busy. We liked that. But now we take time to look at rainbows and bugs, snowflakes and sunflowers. We love that.

Before you, we were a couple. We liked that. But now we're a family. We really love that.

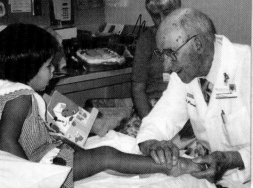

Allison (age 3), Qingxin.

Left: This picture shows the severity of Allison's clubfeet before being treated with the Ponseti Method by Dr. Ponseti himself.

Below: Allison having her foot manipulated by Dr. Ponseti during casting.

Allison (age 4), Qingxin.

Love Anyway
by Stephanie Knipper

EVERY MOTHER HAS DREAMS FOR HER CHILD. Love. Success. A great career. But my dreams are different. What I want, more than anything in this world, is for my daughter to be normal. I want her to walk. To run through the front yard with my son, jumping through the sprinkler, her head thrown back in laughter, her legs strong, and her back straight. I want her to talk. To tell me when she's hungry or tired or wet. And most of all I want to hear her say, "I love you, Mommy." Everything that other mothers take for granted. But normal is the stuff of dreams when you have a child who is mentally retarded.

My husband, Steve, and I first saw Grace on a waiting children list. She had big brown eyes and such a solemn expression; she seemed to be begging for a mommy and daddy. Her special need was listed as a heart condition that had been surgically corrected four days before we saw her picture and developmental delays that she was expected to overcome.

For years we had wanted to adopt from China through the special needs program, but the timing was never right. Now we were in a new house with plenty of room, and our son, Zach, was two years old, and the late nights that come with an infant were over. But most of all, there was this little girl with sad, brown eyes.

So we started the paperwork, and eight months later we were in Nanjing, China, to meet our daughter. When Grace first came to us, she couldn't hold her head up. She had no muscle tone whatsoever. She was more like an infant than a 22-month-old. Her spine was so prominent it jutted out from her back like a string of pearls. She couldn't sit up straight; instead she hunched over until her nose almost touched the floor. Her head was so flat there were points on either side. She had weird hand tics and banged her head into anything. Then there was the rocking. Violent side to side rocking constantly. But most disconcerting of all was her silence. She screamed for three hours the first day and then she was quiet. No laughs. No words. Nothing. She didn't even respond when native speakers called her Chinese name. She just stared past them, locked in her own little world. At the end of her first day with us, I looked at Steve, blinking back tears, and said, "Something is wrong." Gradually, over the next several days, however, Grace began to change. Little things: a smile here, a giggle there. But we noticed, and the fear that had encircled my heart began to fade.

At the end of a very long two weeks, we were ushered into a medical exam room. The doctor frowned and called another

Grace Xinyu (age 2), Taizhou, Nanjing.

doctor. Two of them came in, and now three doctors surrounded Grace. "Ask them what's wrong," Steve told our translator. "What are they saying?" Steve asked.

"They think your daughter is retarded." The word was like a slap in the face.

"What do they mean?" we asked.

"Um, retarded," our guide replied. There was that word again.

"Delayed? Do they mean delayed where she'll catch up?" Steve asked.

The doctor shook his head. Desperation was stamped across Steve's face. Words swirled around me so fast that I couldn't listen. I sat holding Grace as she cried, clinging to me with both hands as if she was determined that no one would pull her away. I held her closer and buried my nose in her thin hair. My heart was in my throat, and all I could think of was this is not what happened in any of the adoption stories I had read on the Internet.

I closed my eyes, thinking of the first time I saw her face on that tiny passport size picture—those big brown eyes and that serious face. I remembered the aching need to hold her as we waited for our travel approval. And I remembered that I loved her. I loved her the first time I saw her picture. I loved her while I waited the eight long months to hold her. And I loved her now, as she sobbed in my arms and doctors told us that she might never catch up. "It doesn't matter," I said loudly so that I could be heard over everyone else. "We love her anyway." Then I kissed her. She was my daughter, no matter what. Our translator translated, and the doctors smiled.

Steve and I still held hope that she was delayed and that we could get her help when we returned home and settled in. Then the doctors' visits began. Far from offering the reassurance I had hoped for, they confirmed my worst fears. Every doctor looked at Grace and fear flooded their eyes. They spoke to us slowly and quietly, as if afraid we would break. "Her head is too small." "Her eyes are too far apart." "Her muscle tone is low." "She is retarded." I didn't even know that word was still used. My world stopped, and I wanted to melt into the floor. But she was my daughter and had been from the moment I saw her picture.

So we started the rounds of therapy. Physical therapy. Speech therapy. Occupational therapy. Developmental intervention. Grace qualified for everything. We had hearing tests, brain scans, genetic work-ups. It has been nine months since that cold December day when we first held Grace, and it has been hard. So hard. Our days are scheduled around her therapy appointments, and she is more like a 13-month-old than a 31-month-old. But she no longer rocks or bangs her head. She smiles freely and laughs when we tickle her. She is walking with the help of braces and even starting to babble in baby talk. Her doctors and therapists are amazed at how far she has come.

And this morning, as she walked through the kitchen holding my son's hands, I thought maybe, just maybe, my dreams aren't impossible. Maybe she will catch up. Maybe she won't. But it doesn't matter. We love her anyway.

Maci (age 10), Yangzhou, Jiangsu.

SYDNEY
by Kathleen de la Paz

OUR YOUNGEST DAUGHTER, SYDNEY YING-YAN, WAS ADOPTED AT ABOUT THREE YEARS OF AGE. Adopting an older child was a bit of a leap of faith for us, but the ease with which she transitioned into our family amazes us to this day. It was as if she was waiting for her family.

Sydney was so comfortable so quickly, in fact, that she made some very memorable comments after being with us for a relatively short time. The first occurred when we were having Friday night's leftovers for Saturday lunch. Sydney looked at her plate, looked at me, and said, "Chinese food, again?"

Around the same time, our entire family was driving in our minivan. We generally would bring snacks and drinks for the little girls in the car. When Sydney asked for her sippy cup, I handed it to her. She shook it, and said, "Why there no ice?"

Yes, it was a very easy transition.

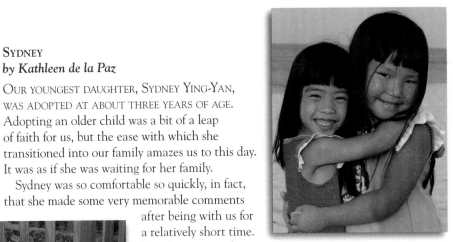

Sydney Ying-Yan, Maonan, Guangdong, with sister, Claire Chun-Mei, Nanping, Fujian (both age 4).

Above: Three days after meeting. Sisters— Hannah (age 22 months), Gaoming, Guangdong, and Sarah Grace (age 31 months), Hengyang, Hunan.

Right: Four months later.

Mikayla (age 3), Loudi, Hunan, with Grandma. Mikayla's great-grandma and grandma share birthdays. Imagine our surprise when we received Mikayla's referral and found that she shared the same birthday.

Door to My Heart
by Stephanie Rodrigues

ONCE UPON A TIME I GOT TO SPEND A WONDERFUL SUMMER IN CHINA, TRYING TO LEARN MANDARIN. The language didn't stick, but another experience did. I got to spend one day at an orphanage outside of Beijing. I had requested this experience from our coordinator because it was my plan to one day adopt an infant Chinese girl, and I wanted to see an orphanage firsthand.

The first room we went to had about 12 newborns in it. I noticed that I happened to share a birthday with one little guy. He was so tiny, just a few weeks old, born while I was in China. My eyes were opened to a whole other possibility: There were boys who needed homes too. He was so precious and lovable, I hardly even noticed his cleft lip. A small door to my heart opened in those few moments.

I reluctantly left the infant room to visit the preschool class. As I went in to the room, a small boy darted out of his seat and rushed to grab my hand. He led me to his small chair and offered me his seat, melting my heart. Next he crawled into my lap and wrapped my arms firmly around him. Yet another door to my heart opened. Now I knew there was a place for a toddler. It didn't seem so scary anymore.

I sometimes get confused when people question our decision to adopt a three-year-old boy with a cleft lip and palate. But then I remember not all of us were lucky enough to have our world turned upside down by the beautiful spirits of two special little boys. I do not know where they are now, but I often think of them when Ty is sitting on my lap and reaches to pull my arm around him.

Ty (age 3), Jiangsu, with Mama—at the White Swan Play Room.

Abigail Kui Yan (age 2½), Zhuzhou, Hunan—enjoying a boat ride on the Illinois River.

Maiya Irene (age 3½), Foshan Nanhai, Guangdong.

Angel Maiya
by Scott and Kristin Novitsky

WE HAD ONE END OF THE RED THREAD SEWN INTO OUR HEARTS during an adoption workshop in late summer of 2000. It would take 1,000 days until we could finally see who was on the other end of the thread.

Less than one year after bringing Maiya to her new home and country, she was diagnosed with a debilitating disease called Rett Syndrome. When Maiya was 18 months old, she began to regress. Within a few weeks the disease had stolen her ability to talk, walk, and use her hands purposefully. She could no longer say Mama or Dada and no longer had the ability to hold and play with her favorite toy. She also began to have seizures, abnormal breathing patterns, and digestive difficulties. Rett Syndrome affects every aspect of her body.

Because girls with Rett Syndrome are unable to talk, they are lovingly referred to as "God's Silent Angels." Our Angel Maiya has now learned to communicate with us with her beautiful eyes. Walking through the door and seeing Maiya's shining smile can brighten up even the saddest of days. And despite the lost dreams we had for Maiya, we have been the most blessed parents in the world to have her with us. Maiya has become our teacher and without a word has led us to the answers to many of life's lessons.

Zoe (age 12 months), Fengcheng, Jiangxi.

Jenna (age 7), Yunmeng, Hubei.

Chloe Xin (born July 2003), Fuling, Chongqing.

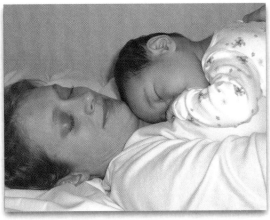

Mimi (age 9 months), Ma'anshan, Anhui, with Mom.

THOSE LITTLE MOMENTS
by Becky Smerdon

I JUST HAD ONE OF THOSE EXQUISITE MOMENTS. Mimi has been part of our lives for less than a month, and I have already long since lost count of the exquisite moments. This one happened at bedtime as Mimi and I snuggled together in her crib. My sweet little girl fights sleep like a warrior in battle; so I crawl into her crib with her to play through the last of her energy and to help her fall asleep. This evening, as I settled in next to her, she turned to face me. Her little fingers traced my cheek, poked at my eyes, and found their way into my nose. As she inched her way closer, she draped her little leg across my waist and pressed her little body tightly to mine. I rested my cheek on her head and listened to her breathing as it deepened and slowed. I should have climbed out as soon as she fell asleep. The house needed cleaning, clothes needed washing. But I wanted to savor that moment; so I stayed and held her a little tighter. My husband, Scott, swears that Mimi falls asleep much later than she actually does. I haven't yet confessed to him that I stay with her long after sleep has overcome her. A friend recently asked me if there was anything that surprised me about becoming a parent and about adopting our daughter. I told her that I had no idea how truly wonderful it would be to have Mimi as part of our lives. If I had known, I would not have survived the wait to bring her home.

TWO FOR ONE?
by Don White

FOLLOWING A MISSION TRIP TO CHINA TO HELP BUILD A PLAYGROUND AT A NEW FOSTER CARE CENTER FOR SPECIAL NEEDS ORPHANS, MY WIFE GRACE AND I MADE THE DECISION TO ADOPT A BABY WITH MEDICAL NEEDS. After the decision was made, Grace came into my office one day and said she thought, at our ages, we should consider adopting two. I have to admit I was a little taken aback, but the salesman in me just rolled with it. Since the paperwork we had was only for one child, I called the agency and inquired about adopting two. The girl chuckled and said, "I'm sorry, Mr. White, but the only way you can adopt two from China is to adopt twins."

I told her twins would work. But she said, "Mr. White, we have been doing this for over eight years. In that time we have had only three sets of twins, and we have never had special needs twins." To which I said, "Sounds like you're due!"

"Mr. White, I do not want you to be disappointed, but the chance of getting twins is extremely remote."

I then said, "Can I ask you how much this is going to cost?"

She said, "It runs about $14,000 to adopt from China."

"So if we do get twins, do we get a two for one discount?"

"No, I'm sorry, Mr. White. If you get two, the fees simply double."

About three days later I received a call from a colleague who said, "Don, I do not know if you know it or not, but you are due a bonus from us."

I said, "That's great. How much are we due?"

"Well, it looks like we owe you $28,300."

I could not stop laughing and said, "Gonzalo, that means we're getting twins!" And from that moment on—even though everyone told us this will hold things up, you are going to be disappointed—everything we did, we did with the expectation that we were getting twins.

It took several months to finish all the paperwork, and on the 20th of August 2004 all of our paperwork was received by the CCAA. We were officially on the list of waiting parents. Now comes the waiting, or so we thought. Just seven days later, on the 27th of August, our agency received its list of special needs children ready to be placed. On the top of the list were Fu Ya Yun and Fu Ya Qiu, one-year-old twin baby girls with repaired cleft lips and palates that still needed to be closed. We called the agency and told them we wanted these girls more than anything else in the world. And on December 11, 2004, less than one year from the time we were first in China building a playground, we drove up to the entrance of Hope Foster Home, walked inside, and saw two little girls sleeping side by side on the playroom floor. They did not know it at the time, but their lives and ours were about to change forever! Sydney Grace Yaqiu and Reagan Elizabeth Yayun are now our beautiful daughters and the greatest blessings of our lives.

Paul Francis Jian (age 2), Nanjing, Jiangsu.

FAMILY OUTINGS
by Pigeon Gibson

WE ARE A MULTI-RACIAL, TRANSCULTURAL, CHRISTIAN FAMILY. It's usually an adventure when we go out as a family. My husband and I, ages 47 and 56, may be mistaken for friends of the family or babysitters, or it is assumed that one or the other of us is married to an Asian. More often than not, I'm mistaken for the grandmother!

Siblings—Paul Francis Jian (age 3) and Frances Paula Xian (age 5), Guangzhou, Guangdong.

Mikey (age 6), Ji Ji (age 5), Nicole (age 5), Nora (age 7), and Emma (age 9)—touring Yu Yuan Gardens in Shanghai as part of Great Wall China Adoption Agency's 10th anniversary reunion held in China.

THE ONE COMMON THREAD
by Margaret McNeill

I ARRIVED IN STYLE, WEARING A BEAUTIFUL HAND-SEWN, RED SILK EMBROIDERED CHINESE JACKET, WITH MATCHING RED EMBROIDERED CORDUROY PANTS AND RED SHOES. It was February of 1964, and I was just an 18-month-old baby, making the trip of my lifetime from my humble beginnings in a Hong Kong orphanage to my home in America.

I had been kindly cared for by the nuns in the orphanage. I was slight in the usual Asian manner but not skinny. I didn't wear a bald ring on the back of my head, a sign of spending too much time lying in a crib; I had been tended to well. But still reality was not kind. I was the youngest baby in the orphanage filled with sad beginnings. I had arrived accompanied by a note from the sisters stating that I was a "good baby" who "loves oranges, bread, and rice." "She is the youngest baby in our orphanage. We call her our little princess." Through fate's push I had now fallen into the arms of a family that had the time, energy, and grace to carry my life forward. For that I would be forever grateful and comforted.

One wonders what made my parents decide to proceed with an international adoption at a time when it wasn't really done. What made Owen and Pat McGowan decide to open their home and their hearts and add one more enormous responsibility to their already full plate? My mother and father were blessed with a richness of spirit. I would be the eighth addition to their big, Irish Catholic family that would soon grow to a family of nine. As a matter of fact, on the same date as my arrival in America, three years later my younger sister would be born.

We lived in the small town of Fall River, southeast of Boston—a city not widely considered sophisticated or rich in ethnic diversity as compared to Boston. Fall River was largely populated by Portuguese and Irish. My father was the Librarian Director of nearby Bridgewater State College, and my mother worked as a writer for the

Catholic diocesan newspaper. She was assigned to write an article encouraging overseas adoption for the Catholic Overseas Adoption Services. It is through this article that my brothers and sisters began lobbying to adopt a baby from China and here I arrived one year later.

Throughout my lifetime, many people have asked me the same question, "So what's it like being adopted?" When people ask me, I don't have to think hard. I tell them that it has been the most amazing experience that has happened in my life. It has been truly life-changing for me, and I continue on about my parents, brothers, and sisters and what they have brought into my life. But that's not what they are really driving at when they pose that question. "Well, no, when did you actually know or realize you were adopted?" "How did you feel?" or "Did your parents tell you when you were little?" I have to laugh. When you are the only Asian looking individual in a family of eight Irish people, it is not like they have to tell you that you are adopted. I grew up knowing I was different, and being different had its privileges as well as some hardships.

My family talked very openly and factually about my adoption. My older sister even recanted her story of how I was orphaned and had been "rescued by two nuns who saw me lying helpless in a basket on a busy road in Hong Kong and swooped down to save me just as a speeding truck was about to crush me to death." While not true, Disney would have loved the script. I do know only what I don't know. As a matter of fact I have infinitesimal information of how and why I was given to the nuns in the orphanage. I can only suppose on what little information I can piece together provided on my birth certificate, baptismal record, and British passport—the only documents that I arrived with. I had no roots, no medical history. What I can gather from the scant information contained in the documents is that I was born in St. Theresa's Hospital and brought to St. Paul's Orphanage by my mother and grandmother some weeks later. At first glance the nuns thought my grandmother was my mother and my mother was my sister because she was so young looking. Such small clues, but at least some information on which to wonder.

As a small child I often wondered about my birthmother. I never asked my parents because I thought it was a very personal matter and kept it to myself. But I did write to Sr. Philippe at St. Paul's Orphanage, a nun I had kept up correspondence with since I could write, and asked her if she had any recollections of my mother. I awaited her response eagerly in hope of some small clue to my past. She said she did not remember anything about my mother at all; perhaps Sr. Philippe was protecting a small child from sad news. I was disappointed but did not dwell on it. I cannot say that I didn't harbor a small void inside of me at the reality of not knowing, but it never interrupted my happiness as a child. Birthdays, although a happy occasion with my family, brought this void to the forefront. It was inwardly a sad time and the only consistent time of year when I would think of my birthmother and wonder if she was thinking of me at that same time each year.

There are in one's lifetime a handful of occurrences that affect the breadth of one's life so greatly that it imparts gratitude of life and your place in it. Usually this is a big event—such as a wedding, a birth, or a death—and it generally occurs later on in one's life, hopefully at which time one has the maturity and perspective to experience that moment in time in its richness or sadness and realize its value. But in my case adoption has been a huge event that has touched my life so enormously.

Sisters—Nora (age 7), Ningdu, Jiangxi, and Ji Ji (age 5), Jianxin, Jiangxi.

Given the young age at which I experienced this, filled with innocence, I was not able to see how profoundly adoption had changed my life both physically and emotionally until several years later. I am now able to realize how this and the luck of my fate in becoming a McGowan family member impacted my being. My parents provided me with unconditional love, allowing me to grow up in the innocence of a child and enabling me to blossom into the person I have become today. The second biggest thing they have given me is security. With this gift and the maturity I have developed through the years, I have come to appreciate the McGowan's choice to adopt me and the tough decision my birthmother had to make in giving me up so as to ultimately give me a better chance in life.

As I button the little red, silk embroidered jacket, I look into my two-year-old daughter Grace's eyes. I had waited a lifetime to one day fit my child in this jacket. This jacket is my treasure, my past, but Grace is now my life, my future. It's hard to believe that she is the only person in this world to whom I am connnected by blood. I have been so fortunate in my life. I have wonderful, loving parents; lots of brothers and sisters who I am close to; many, many friends; and now a fabulous husband and exquisite daughter.

Each story of adoption has its own uniqueness to it, but the one common thread is the love that is born and realized out of it, and that is truly special. For this I will be eternally grateful to my family, the McGowans. But the circle of love and life will not stop here.

It can't stop here just because I have a daughter of my own. My husband, Brian, myself, and Grace look forward to the day when we too, with the help of Lillian and China Adoption With Love, welcome an adopted Chinese baby into our family and home.

Daddy's girl. AnnaClaire (age 9 months), Yifeng, Jiangxi.

Sisters—AnnaClaire (age 9 months), Yifeng, Jiangxi, and Allie (age 2½), Yangxi, Guangdong.

Girls from the San Francisco Bay area visiting the Forbidden City in Beijing in April 2006.

Bette (age 8), Dongyang Zhejiang; Emily (age 11), Shanghai, Jiangsu; Lili (age 11), Sanshui, Guangdong; MeiMei (age 12), Zhuzhou, Hunan; Phoebe (age 5), Chenzhou, Hunan; Abigail (age 12), Changsha, Hunan; Talia (age 12), Jiujiang, Jiangxi; and Claire (age 11), Qingyuan, Guangdong.

Kaitlyn Annamei (age 9½ months), Suichuan, Jiangxi.

A Special Day
by Lori Bowen Tillock

Dear Kaitlyn

Today is a very special day for me. Not only is it our first Mother's Day together, but it is also your first birthday. After all we have both been through as a family, a day could not be filled with more meaning for me.

Twelve weeks ago today your caretaker put you in my arms for the very first time. That was a very important day for our family. I know you weren't so thrilled when you first met us, but you were leaving all that you had ever known. But I know now, just from the love in your eyes, that you are happy to be home.

Our time together in China seems so long ago. You are growing into such a beautiful little girl, full of belly laughs and wet kisses. I love nothing more than to see how happy your big brother, Alex, makes you. When he plays with you, you laugh harder than with anyone else. I know that you and Alex will always have a special bond. He waited a long time for a baby sister, just like we waited a long time for a daughter.

As we mark the milestones today brings, I think about what your next birthdays will be like. Your daddy and I can help you learn and grow so that you can be whatever you want to be in this world. I hope that you will learn how important each and every person is on this earth and that God has a plan for each of us, although we often question what the plan is. Someday you may wonder why you had to leave China, and we will try to help you understand why you were meant to be a part of our family here. Your daddy and I will raise you to embrace your Chinese heritage and celebrate it for that is an important part of who you are.

As I think about all God has blessed us with in bringing you to us, I say a prayer for a woman for whom I know today must be difficult. One year ago today a woman in China, whom we may never know, gave birth to you. While I believe your birthmother and father loved you very much, I know they could not raise you as their own child. I believe that your birthmother's heart broke the day that she had to leave you, and I know that on your first birthday she is saying a prayer that you are safe and happy.

Kaitlyn, I love you with all my heart.

Forever,
Your mother

Above: Torrey Juliana QingYong (age 4), Nanning, Guangxi, with her foster parents.

We visited our younger daughter's SWI in Nanning in 2005 and were able to meet her foster parents during our visit. We were told she was very attached to her foster father. When we got her, she preferred my husband over me the first couple of days, and "Baba" was the first word she spoke at 9 months old.

Below: Kinsey Quinn PingHua (age 6), Nancheng, Jiangxi.

Our daughter Kinsey with the orphanage staff during our visit in 2005. They were showing her the pictures that we had sent of her over the years. They had kept all of them.

Sisters, "Sisters"
by Delia and Tim King

"Hello baby! We're your sisters."
Your puzzled gaze regards the two,
They give you toys; you clutch them tight,
You're two years old and you are wondering
"How on earth am I linked with you?"

Some days later, seated, eating,
At the table in a row,
Proudly watching our three daughters,
"Now we're five!" we say. You look up,
Catch the meaning, thread is clearer,
Happy look, "I'm one of you!"

In the hotel, on the plane home,
Other "sisters" settling too.
Vow to stay in touch back home,
Parents sharing, thread is strengthening,
Meeting up whenever possible.
Four years on we hear you chatting,
Playing games, "Try my shoes on!"
"Sisters," sharing thread of story,
"Sisters," standing in same shoes.

Sisters—Hannah (age 6); Ruth (age 4), Guangdong; and Rebekah (age 11).

Former roommates from Chenzhou, Hunan—Ashlee Xiang and Samantha Ruth YuLiang (both age 3), with Samantha's dad.

BLESSINGS
by Becky Peach

MOST OF US TAKE OUR BLESSINGS FOR GRANTED. Our new daughter has taught us to celebrate even small, everyday occurrences. While in China Lia was overjoyed by bubble baths. As she learned the English words, she exclaimed "bath!"—not just a shower, "warm!"—even better, and "bubbles!"—the best of all. Sitting down for snacks, she arranged the everyday items—chips, banana, and orange slices—into beautiful geometric designs. During her first week home from China, Lia woke up each morning, gazed out the living room windows, and cheered for the sunrise. Simple pleasures: a warm bath, a simple snack, and a sunrise—all good reasons to celebrate and be thankful.

Kai Alois Isaak (age 3), Shantou, Guangdong, with sister, Elise Miriam (age 8).

BUILDING A FAMILY
by Pat Miller

WHEN MY HUSBAND AND I MARRIED, I CHOSE THIS POEM BY KUAN TAO-SHENG FOR OUR WEDDING PROGRAM:

"Take a lump of clay. Wet it. Pat it. Make a statue of you and a statue of me. Then shatter them, clatter them. Add some water, and shape them and mold them—into a statue of you and a statue of me. Then in me, there are bits of you. And in you, there are bits of me. Nothing shall ever keep us apart."

When we decided to adopt many years later, I realized the poem applied not only to marriage but also to building a family. When you get married or adopt children, you promise to love another person forever. You don't love that person because you're related. You become related because you love them. As that love grows and develops, bits and pieces of the people you love become part of you, and vice versa, until you've formed a family whole that's greater than any individual part. My husband and I now have two daughters from China, and they've each added beautiful bits to my life that never would have been there otherwise. They've made me move in new directions and become a fuller person than before. Every day I marvel at their individual talents and gifts that are so unlike mine and yet so perfect for our family. As young as our girls are, they know what makes a family. "A family means you're together," says Sonia, my four-year-old. "A family is people who love each other and would do anything for each other," adds Gwen, my nine-year-old. My husband, daughters, and I began as four people with no apparent connection. To this day we have different interests and personalities. What brought us together, built our family, and keeps us strong are love and the promises we made to keep loving each other. And now? Now it's just like the poem says—nothing will keep us apart.

Sisters—Payton Justus Xiuli (age 4) and Parker Jade Xiuzhe (age 2), both from Xiushui, Jiangxi.

SHOWING AFFECTION
by Nancy Delpha

ONE THING I WAS SURE OF— ADOPTING A SEVEN-YEAR-OLD BOY WOULD DEFINITELY HAVE SURPRISES.

But one that caught me a little off guard was that Tyler did not know how to give or receive affection.

I just assumed that he would have perhaps given and received hugs, maybe even kisses, in his CWI. But as I came to understand, these were quite foreign things to him, as were some of our other customs. I tried to respect his need for personal space and would only pat him or kiss the top of his head good night. But would he ever be able to learn how to give and receive affection? I wondered this often when his little body would stiffen as I got close.

I will never forget how his little hand felt in mine the first time he took it when we were walking in a crowd. I had extended mine a couple of times before, but he had not taken it. So the feel of his little hand, wrapped tightly in mine, was one of the sweetest things I had felt in a long time, exposing a vulnerability he did not often show.

After returning home, Tyler witnessed the affection that my husband and I show our daughter, and he seemed to want to participate. He was still stiff when hugged but would allow us closer than before. The physical contact he made with us was more roughhousing, or goofing around, as if he could make himself comfortable with it if it was just play. But the bedtime routine began to change, as he started wanting to be closer to me when I would lay down with him. It was a big step when he fell asleep on my arm, instead of turning his back to me to drift off.

Shortly after this he began practicing the art of kissing on his own arm or pillow as if trying it out to be sure he knew how to do it! I will never forget the night of my first kiss. He quickly darted in and kissed my cheek, as if to test out my reaction! He giggled and pretended to be asleep. My hopes were restored that this could indeed be quickly learned. One afternoon he caught me completely by surprise, climbing up on my lap and planting a kiss square on my lips. Scrambling down, he cast a glance back at me to see my reaction. I'm sure the big smile on my face said it all!

Now, each night at bedtime, he insists on covering my face with kisses, and as we hug good night he says, "Hold on tight," until we can either one hardly catch our breath. I'm so grateful to be making up for lost time!

家庭

Sisters—Shea Jia (age 2), Shanggao, Jiangxi, and Maeve Chun Li (age 4), Yujiang, Jiangxi—watching the sun set over Lake Michigan.

Best friends forever—Sarina LiPing and Emily (both age 3½), both from Chongqing.

Sisters and friends—Makayla (age 3), Baoji, Shaanxi, and Rachel (age 4), Shanggao, Jiangxi—on a family vacation.

Keira Xingfu (age 3), Xinyu, Jiangxi.

The Second Child
by Pam Moore

I HAVE TWO BEAUTIFUL DAUGHTERS FROM CHINA. My oldest is relatively quiet, looks before she leaps, and thinks about everything way too much. Being that my oldest was so calm and easy-going, I thought that adding a second child to our family would be no problem. No one with more than one child will tell you about the curse of the second child until it is way too late. I believe it is because they don't want to suffer alone.

Enter LuLu, the second child. She came to us in spicy Chongqing. She is full of energy and life. She literally goes at everything full force. She has two volume levels—loud and asleep. She has two speeds—too fast and asleep. Do you see a pattern here? She is the Tasmanian devil that runs through our lives. She is also the sweetest and most affectionate child I have ever known.

She can melt your heart with a smile. And that is good, because she can also be a little monster. She will crawl up on your lap and give you a big hug, followed by "You are my special friend, Mama. I will love you forever." She will then proceed to get up, give you one more kiss, and then dump the bucket of beads that her older sister was playing with all over the floor and just look back and smile.

She will do anything that her older sister is doing and even some things that her older sister is way too sensible to do. Recently at an amusement park, LuLu decided to go on the roller coaster. Her sister said, "No. It is too noisy and too fast!" LuLu responded with, "Not for me!!" She is three years old and feels that she is now grown up; so everyone had better get out of her way.

I wouldn't change anything about this spitfire that has joined our family. I did recently take out accident insurance. I am pretty sure it will pay for itself very quickly. Her next adventures include gymnastics and soccer. I do tell all parents considering a second child that they should spend an afternoon with LuLu. If they believe that they can handle it, I will even write them a recommendation letter.

Cocooned
by Adria Karlsson

"WHAT'RE YOU MAKING? I wanna make one too!" demanded my four-year-old nephew. The "spring scene" we were creating on the large kitchen window of his home already crawled with cutouts. Paper caterpillars, ladybugs, and ants roamed the bottom edge; the sky was filled with flocks of blue jays and robins; and an owl was sleeping comfortably in the trunk of the tree. I watched as the silver blade of my scissors cut through the blank face of the pink construction paper, curving around, pulling out the shape of a wing.

"A butterfly," I replied, cutting in and out for the second lobe.

"How do you make that?" I helped him start his own.

Later I held Nathan up as he taped the bubbly-winged insects onto the window. I hugged him tight, pressing my ear up against his spine and listening to his voice rumble through his back as he talked to me. The steady heartbeat in the background vied for attention and made me think, for about the hundredth time that day, about the new warm body I would meet the next morning. A confused one-year-old; jet-lagged, lost, and newly-named. Talia. How could I begin to put the child in the blurry photo into my own heart next to this warm, breathing body that was her brother? I knew I would. Well, I thought I would. Yes. Well… My thoughts haunted me, my uncertainty blending with the myriad of studies that told me whether or not I could love my new niece. I refused the negativity and sternly told myself to stop being silly. I read Nathan and Elena a story that night, talked to them about their parents coming home the next day, and traded kisses goodnight. They were my family and I loved them. Talia too! My mind reminded me. Oh yeah—Talia too.

A taxi pulled up, the snow blasting across its nose. My sister climbed out of the back and reached in again. I strained my eyes and held tight to Nathan and Elena, who in their excitement were ready to run through the snow in their bare feet. Then I spotted the fuzzy, pink blanket wrapped tightly around a bundle in their mother's arms, which were protecting what it held from the snow. A stranger. A family member. Talia.

As excitement, hugs, and greetings ensued, I hung back to let the nuclear family reconnect. It wasn't until after dinner that I finally got a turn alone with her. I found her playing on the floor and sat down opposite her. I handed her a toy she was reaching for, then gently touched her hands, her soft baby feet, her pudgy calves, and her soft black Chinese hair—so different from my own. Last, as she met my eyes, I let my finger run down the curve of her cheek.

"Butterfly," I whispered, recognizing the curve of the wings and the beauty they framed. She was cocooned in her confusion, in the foreign world around her, but for the first time I saw that a new little girl, a girl that I would love, an amazingly complex and unique individual that I was lucky enough to have as a niece, waited inside. My heart surged and I picked her up and hugged her tight. Here she was at last—Talia! Right in my arms and in my heart, finding that place right next to her brother and sister where she belonged. I looked through the door to the darkened kitchen and saw the window with the moonlight streaming in behind it. A flock of birds and insects framed the crooked letters that were so carefully taped up earlier that day. I whispered into my niece's soft, fuzzy head, "Welcome home, Talia," and it fit just right.

Joy Kathryn Shan Zhen (age 4), Yiyang City, Hunan.

Sisters—Chloe Chun Ni (age 6½), Yulin, Guangxi, and Faline Zi Ai (age 2½), Gaozhou, Guangdong.

OUR DOUBLE HAPPINESS
by Shannon Howard

MY FAMILY: CHLOE CHUN NI, AGE SIX; FALINE ZI AI, AGE TWO AND A HALF; MY WIFE, LINN, AND I. We are like many families except that our children are adopted from China. This and the fact that all of my girls are stunningly beautiful, especially Linn, make us stand out in a crowd. This sometimes begets comments. My favorite is one I heard many times in China as the girls and I were sightseeing. It was always some middle-aged woman who would stop and exclaim, "Lucky baby!" My wife would often try to express her joy at how she was the lucky one. I am not sure if she was successful convincing anyone of that, but it really is the truth. As my wife often says, "We are very blessed."

A couple of years passed before Linn suggested that Chloe should have a sister. I admit I needed some convincing, which Linn did with the deftness of a used car salesman. Linn said, "I want to be a mom again, and besides two will be easier because they will occupy one another." I had some doubt about that, but still there was a kind of logic I could grasp. Then she followed with, "Who will Chloe have when we are gone?" I did not have an answer for that; so I agreed and before we knew it we had daughter number two. Faline was an easy baby. She ate and traveled well. It wasn't until we reached home that she had some difficulty. The first night at home she cried. Not a terrible thing for a baby to cry—normal in fact. But Faline's cry was not normal; it pierced the heart like a sharpened stick. I believe she was mourning. Of what I can only guess. Maybe she only figured out at that moment that she was not going back to the only home she had known. I took Faline into my arms from my exhausted, jet-lagged wife. As Faline and I sat in my chair and rocked that night, we both cried. In my life I have never felt such sadness, and it was breaking my heart. I cried with her and comforted her as best as I was able. Soon she slept, and ever after I was her daddy.

Now my family is complete. We have two happy, healthy, smart, and beautiful little girls—the very definition of double happiness.

Now My Heart Can See
by Suzanne Stuiber

Oh sweet little baby girl
Were you really meant for me?
There was a time I was not sure
But now my heart can see

We got off to such a rocky start
You had a scared and broken heart
A helpless baby without a voice
You lost so much in your short life

How frightened you must have been
To come into my arms that day
Who were these strangers from across the ocean
Coming to take you away

My love for you was not enough
And oh the things I did not know
About what you needed to feel safe
Such a struggle outside my comfort zone

A little baby rejecting my love
This wasn't how it was supposed to be
I cried and prayed for help from above
Please God, show me the way

In my desperate hours, feeling so scared and alone
Tears streaming down my face
Maybe I'm not the right mom for this baby girl
Surely someone must have made a mistake

I finally found help from kind souls
Who taught me what to do
A little baby girl let down her guard
and slowly started to bloom

Little by little you let me into your heart
Trusting me more and more
I know how hard it must be to risk loving again
And I promise not to let you down

Sweet little baby girl, you taught me things I never knew
You've given me so many gifts and
My heart overflows with love for you

We'll find our way one day at a time
And there are sure to be many bumps in the road
But now I see just how perfectly you were meant for me
And I'm the right mom for you

The Miracle of Yi
by Judith Publow

As I spiritually prepared myself for my daughter Hannalee Jia-Yi's upcoming surgery, I was reminded of how I first came to know and love this precious child that God had chosen for us. Yi is from our middle daughter Delaney's orphanage, and she was born with very complex heart defects. I first learned about her prior to her first surgery sponsored by Love Without Boundaries. She was one of five children who was able to have surgery because of the funds raised through LWB's 2004 Born in My Heart Art Auction. Little did I know, as I prayed for this group of children, that one day I would be a mom to one of them.

Yi's condition was so critical and complex that she had to wait for just the right cardiac surgeon to arrive back in Guangzhou to perform her surgery. Following Yi's surgery, Amy Eldridge of LWB posted:

"Well, I believe that God was in the operating room today with baby Yi. Her surgery was so complex and hasn't been done successfully very often. *It went perfectly.* She is doing so well now. Even the doctor who did the surgery is amazed."

Yi's heart condition required a series of three different surgeries to reconfigure her blood flow. Within a month after bringing her home, she had her first cardiology workup at the University of Michigan. It was determined then that she would need to have surgery to repair the shunt in her pulmonary artery that had been placed during her surgery in China. This meant that she would still need three more open-heart surgeries. That surgery was performed in September, and she was in intensive care for a week with many complications. But once again God was with her, and we were finally able to bring her home 12 days after surgery.

In April 2006 we went back to Michigan from our home in central Indiana for her second phase of the repair. Yi would need two separate operations this time—one to address her narrowed pulmonary artery, and then she could go through with her scheduled surgery. Our stay that trip was three weeks long with more complications. We were finally released right before Mother's Day.

That was the best Mother's Day I have ever had as all five of my children were there to celebrate Mother's Day and our homecoming.

We are so thankful that Yi was able to have her first surgery in China through LWB. This enabled her to live long enough to be brought home to America for the advanced medical care that she needed. Without her first surgery she would not have made it this far. I can only say thank you for this gift of life for my daughter.

Hannalee Jia-Yi (age 2½), Shantou, Guangdong—with her White Swan Barbie to be auctioned in the 2006 Born in My Heart Art Auction. She was in the first group of babies to have heart surgeries from the proceeds of the 2004 Heart Auction.

Sisters—Hannalee, Delaney, and Lindsey, with friend, Lucy. Hannalee Jia-Yi (age 2½), Shantou, Guangdong; Delaney Jia-Ke (age 3½), Shantou, Guangdong; Lucy (age 6), Guiping, Guangxi; and Lindsey NianChun (age 6), Pingnan, Guangxi.

Jonathan (age 2½), Kunming, Yunnan.

Jenea Sizhen (age 4), Qingyuan City, Guangdong, with Mommy one day after first meeting each other and after a visit to the SWI.

In Whose Image?
by Sharon MacDonell

I think my sudden obsession with genealogy had something to do with the unanswered questions about my daughter's birth, her parents, her abandonment, her Chinese orphanage—everything about her life before we adopted her.

Much to my husband's dismay, I bought an expensive subscription to an online genealogy website and then spent hours, even all-nighters, trying to find news of my dead relatives. I told my stepmother about this strange new mania, and she sent me my father's family album. The plain red leather binder is full of wonders, packed with computer-generated genealogical charts that trace MacDonells back to the 18th century. There are photos of smooth-cheeked, smirking children, long dead of old age; joyous letters from my grandmother to her sister; and brittle, fibrous newspaper clippings about my Grandfather Frank. My favorite photo is of Catherine, my grandmother. It's the mid-1930s. She's sitting on a wing-backed chair surrounded by my four aunts, whose girlish features resemble various parts of me and my sisters—a familiar nose here, a chin like mine there. I look at my father's family album and feel the thrill of belonging to a lineage of colorful ghosts who clearly gifted me my hair color, my squinting right eye, my short stature, and my love of writing. It's all there in those pages.

I compare this book filled with my family's history to the frustration I felt working on my daughter's life book. The book was intended to reveal the story of Patti's early months. The problem was, we knew virtually nothing—just the basic facts. She was born in China, and her biological parents decided not to raise her for reasons we will never know. She came to us with two things—pink pajamas, three sizes too big, and her Chinese name, Xiao Yi. We stored the pajamas away and took her Chinese name, chosen by the orphanage director, as her middle name. It graces the first page of her life book, which has more about Chinese history and her hometown's landmarks than personal data. She looks at it happily today, but certainly someday she will realize how little information is actually there.

Over the years my interest in genealogy has waned as I'm far more interested in my descendant now. Now, in addition to the life book, we also have a dozen photo albums and at least 20 videotapes of her mad childhood adventures.

We have a cute picture of Patti, wearing a tiny aqua-colored bikini, kneeling beside her first kiddy pool. There's another in which she's sitting on my lap in the dentist chair while I have my teeth cleaned. She's so curious she's leaning forward to peer into my mouth. A favorite family photo shows Patti sitting on her daddy's lap. Both of them smile as if they share a sly secret. In most of the shots with Mom, Dad, grandparents, and friends, Patti's smile prompts dimples from her silky cheeks— dimples we didn't see until she gave us a shy grin on our second day together in China.

It is our true hope that these joyous albums will cheer her far more than the prescribed life book will sadden her. But we understand that to be whole herself, Patti will have to celebrate the beauty of her entire life—the happy one we've all built together, as well as the mysterious other life that, for reasons unknown, was left unfinished.

Angel (age 2½), Guangxi, Guilin— with her proud daddy at a daddy/daughter dance.

Eden Zuliang (age 2), Qingyuan, Guangdong— at the 2006 Chinese New Year parade.

For Angel (Tian Shi)
by Howard and Diana Minto

On celestial wings
As you first arrived
You entered our hearts
And fulfilled our lives

Your new life is beginning
Hear our voices sing
Our lives adorned in miracles
That only Angel brings

We wish you love and happiness
Good things as life unfolds
For you are truly heaven sent
Our blessing to behold

With love,
Your "Forever" Mama and Daddy

Nicole Liu-Lu (age 3½), Wenzhou, Zhejiang— adopted at age 27 months.

Lara Elisabeth Meng Na (age 16 months), ChangDe, Hunan.

"Home"
by Tina Ocheltree

This has become Kai's favorite word. He says it often and gets very excited when we are out and hit the familiar main road that leads to our street. He says it gleefully after getting into the car when we have been somewhere. He says it first thing in the morning when inventorying our family. "Cam?" "He's at school." "Ben?" "He's at school too." "Baba?" "Baba's at work," I say. Then he will say very happily, "Kai *home!*"

It has been incredible to watch him make sense of this new world we have put him in. To become familiar with the people, places, and routines of his new life. And this recent constant declaration of "home" seemed to be much more than just a comment about his physical location. He seemed to be feeling something very deep and something most of us experience as infants, too young to verbalize or even think about consciously.

So I decided to look up the word "home" and see what Webster thought about all the meanings of this word. I think I found the one Kai is describing: "Adv. 3. To the center or heart of a matter; closely; directly; deeply."

Ah, there's no place like home!

Kai Hui (age 3), Baoding, Hebei, with Mom and Dad.

Left: Carli Jie-Miao (age 3), Gaoming, Guangdong, with big brother, Jack (age 10)—at FCC-NY's Chinese Culture Day 2006, where she performed a Chinese dance with her class.

Below: Carli (age 3).

GETTING A SISTER
by Angela Shomler (age 10)

HI. MY NAME IS ANGELA, AND I HAVE BEEN AN ONLY CHILD FOR TEN YEARS. Being an only child means I have no one to play with except for my neighbors when they are home. I have lots of friends, but I think nothing would be better than having a sister.

During the past ten years, my mom and dad have been talking about getting another child. Well, in 2002, China changed the rules on adopting. We didn't know this until 2006, in June. My parents found out when they talked to my friend's parents, who adopted from China two to four years ago. About two weeks after they started the paperwork, they told me.

Getting a sister is really exciting. Now, I can't wait until I go to China to get her. I think we will have a lot of fun together.

I can't wait to go to China to get my sister. Her name is going to be Danielle. Yes, Danielle—a very pretty, sophisticated, and awesome name. I think it might fit her. I feel that being a big sister will be a big job. I have to watch over her and even maybe babysit her. I will also have to teach her and help her when she is sad and help her with her homework.

THE JOYS OF BEING AN OLD DAD
by Bruce Sherman

LIFE TAKES US ON SOME UNEXPECTED TWISTS AND TURNS. Okay, let's be honest—life is nothing but unexpected twists and turns. In my younger days I never would have guessed that—at age 50 and with a son in college—I would be a retired, stay-at-home dad to three indescribably magical girls: Maisie, Carly, and Lainey (ages six, four, and two, respectively). One of the great joys I have come to treasure is being home to witness those fleeting moments that can only be fully appreciated firsthand.

Carly is quite the conversationalist. In fact she is a chatterbox extraordinaire. She can and will talk to anyone about anything; silence is simply not an option. Oprah, watch out!

Maisie and Carly are best friends and constant companions. Their conversations are non-stop—with Carly doing 90% of the talking, 100% of the time. One day Maisie was out running errands with my wife, Alyson. During Maisie's absence, Carly was feeling deprived of peer communication. Lainey, at the tender age of two, is not yet a wonderful conversationalist. Carly tried and tried to engage Lainey. Mostly Lainey responded by not responding at all, instead focusing all of her attention on the brightly colored Duplo blocks before her.

Carly—out of sheer desperation—started "interviewing" Lainey. Carly asked Lainey what she wanted to be when she grew up. Not surprisingly, Lainey did not answer. Carly decided to try specifics: "Do you want to be a vet?"

Lainey replied: "Yes!"

"Do you want to be a ballerina?"

"Yes!"

"Do you want to be a *cowgirl*?"

Lainey replied: "Mooooooo!"

As you might imagine, many of our girls' utterances are true treasures—no doting dad syndrome here!

Recently, Maisie treated us to a recitation of the Pledge of Allegiance, which she had just learned in kindergarten. She smiled from ear to ear as she began: "I pledge allegiance to the flag of the United States of America…"

Alyson and I beamed as Maisie stood erect with her hand over her heart, "…and to the republic…"

Our hearts burst with pride. "…for which it stands."

We found it difficult to contain ourselves as she continued: "…one Asian under God."

I have never quite believed in the cliche that we are not getting older but, rather, we are getting better. Well, I for one may just be getting older, but life—thanks to Alyson and our girls—has never been better. And I thank God for life's unexpected twists and turns.

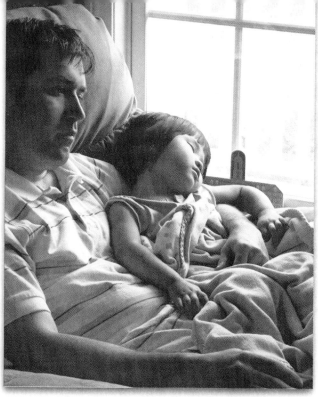

Willow Xijun (age 26 months), Feixi, Anhui—relaxing with Dad and her favorite blanket.

Katie Lin (age 2), Jiangxi—helping Daddy at work.

Olivia Ren (age 1), Yiyang, Hunan, with Dad and Mom.

Olivia Ren (age 2½).

Adrianna Min (age 19 months), Tonggu, Jiangxi.

THE YIN AND YANG OF LIFE
by Melanie Mannos

NOVEMBER 10, 2004, WAS A DAY THAT CHANGED OUR LIVES IN MORE WAYS THAN ONE. That morning I got "the" call from our agency. "You're a mommy" were the first words I heard! It was the day for which we had waited for so very long. We had been referred a precious, healthy baby girl, 11 months old, from Yiyang, Hunan. We were elated! Shortly after I received another call—this time from my mother to tell me that my father had been taken to the emergency room after a fall. Later that evening I would find out he had terminal lung cancer. Suddenly the best day of my life was now the worst. As I struggled with my roller coaster of emotions, I tried to find the meaning of it all.

I thought about the opposing forces which the Chinese believe bring balance to life. The Yin, which represents sadness and the darkness of life, and the Yang, the happy and brighter element, are believed to be present in our everyday lives. One cannot exist without the other. We cannot experience the joy of new life without the sorrow of death. Exactly four weeks later, as we waited to travel to China, my dear father passed away. I was heartbroken, knowing that he would never hold Olivia in his own arms. No one had been more supportive and excited about this adoption. Dad was constantly talking about his sweet "China Doll" and had even written a letter to her... something we will always cherish. Even more so I was sick to think that Olivia would never know her "Papa."

On the 4th of January 2005, our whole world changed when a beautiful little girl with big eyes and an even bigger smile was placed into our arms. She was certainly apprehensive at first, but within hours it seemed as if we had always been together. The translation of Olivia's Chinese name, Ke Ren, had the meaning, "We hope she brings joy and happiness to others." The name fit her perfectly as this child brought more joy and happiness into our lives than we could ever have imagined. She came home to us when we needed her most. With her contagious smile and her big dimples, she turned our sorrow into complete joy. I knew immediately she was a special gift from God. Olivia was our Yang—our ray of sunshine.

Almost two years have passed since my father left us. We miss him terribly, but I know he is with us, and I'm certain Olivia can feel his love. She often talks about her papa in heaven. At age 2½ I'm not sure she knows exactly what that means, but someday she'll understand. I want her to know how much he loved her. And I suspect he knows that she loves him too. This summer we released a balloon into the sky. As we watched it gracefully float higher and higher, Olivia told me she was sending it to Papa in heaven "to make him happy." The miracle of adoption has touched our family deeply and taught us many valuable life lessons. Among them we have learned that behind every cloud, no matter how dark, there is always sunshine, there is always hope.

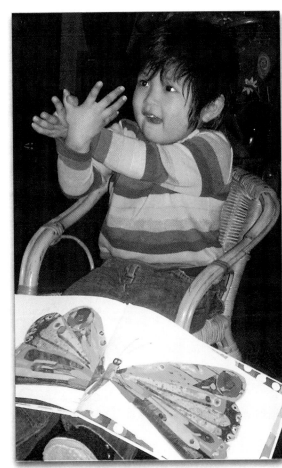

Le Dan (age 3½), Shantou, Guangdong— learning sign language.

My Sister Lili
by Rebecca Victoria Orton (age 10)

My dear sweet sister,
I love her so much,
The soft skin on her face
Is lovely to touch.

My dear sweet sister,
I love the smell,
Of her sweet black hair on her head,
Especially when she's ready for bed.

My dear sweet sister,
I love the way she tries to talk,
And the funny way she tries to walk.

My dear sweet sister,
I love her so much,
She's all I ever wanted.

For Lili Grace Yang Min Orton,
I'll love you forever.

Loving sisters—Rebecca (age 10) and Lili (age 3), Yangjiang, Guangdong.

Twin sisters—Allison Shen Ao and Samantha Ying Ao (age 4), Lu'An, Anhui—throwing the first pitch at a Chicago Cubs baseball game. Pictured with their parents.

SPECIAL NEEDS MEANS SPECIAL LOVE
by Stefani Ellison

WHEN WE APPLIED TO ADOPT OUR FIRST TWO DAUGHTERS FROM CHINA IN 1995 AND 1996, WE WERE REQUIRED BY LAW TO ADOPT A CHILD WHO HAD SPECIAL NEEDS. I can't imagine what our lives would be like today if China had not enforced the then special needs provision in the law. China now allows all eligible families to apply for the adoption of healthy children but will expedite processing for families adopting children with special needs so that these children can get to their families as quickly as possible.

My second daughter, Taisha, was described to us as profoundly deaf and mute when we got her referral on December 4, 1996. Her travel approval came to us at four minutes after midnight on Christmas morning, and her life has continued to be a wonderful present for us.

When we arrived in Wuhan in Hubei Province and met her for the first time on January 13, 1997, we found a child who had suffered terrible and long-term ear infections. Infection had worked its way out her cheekbone and had erupted through her cheek. Her left ear lobe was torn from her head. She also had shigella, giardia, and asceris (long intestinal roundworms), but nonetheless she also had a healthy soul. She was almost 30 months old.

Taisha had eyes that took in all the details of her world. She had trust that we were going to love her and care for her. She had a heart full of love to share with us. She had the determination and grit to survive losing her family and entering a social welfare institution at 25 months of age and the bravery to attach herself to new parents and risk being hurt again. She has taught her mother true heroic courage.

Most of all Taisha teaches everyone around her joy. Anyone who knows her can see that this child understands joy. She doesn't watch her life; she lives it. She has a delightful, contagious laugh. People can't help but join in when they hear the chortling begin. I will never forget my daughter's

eyes when she went on her first amusement ride. Her face melted into joyous wonder and then came that marvelous giggle! I'm sure that part of it is her personality, but maybe it has been from Taisha's trials that she has learned to reach out and enjoy the moment. Is it these same trials that taught her unbelievable compassion and kindness? She brings me tissue when I cry and does everything a child can think of to soothe a fretting baby. She is most attentive to people's bumps and bruises, always ready with comforting kisses.

She had surgery to "implant" two complete eardrums, had another surgery to take out her tonsils and adenoids, and has made tremendous progress in her ability to hear and speak. She cannot use hearing aids due to her recurring ear infections. As she finally learned to talk, we found that she has a significant stutter. We will deal with these problems that are just part of Taisha, and it will be okay no matter how big or small they turn out to be. One day, as I picked her up from school, three teachers came to say good-bye and sneak hugs and kisses from her. They all told me that Tai had stolen their hearts. One teacher's comment will always stay with me. She said, "How were you so incredibly lucky to be given this child?" At the time of her referral, many people didn't think we had been so lucky. We were matched with an "older" baby and one that really did have true special needs. They thought we were crazy to accept. Indeed we are still crazy—crazy in love.

Tai has always been drawn to people who need help, and she is never afraid to offer hers. I am the China Coordinator for Children's House International, and when Taisha was nearly seven years old, I was able to take her and her sister Shayna with me on a business visit with the CCAA. While we were in Beijing, we were also able to visit the Great Wall. Tai has always had a deep desire to stand on the Great Wall of China. She has drawn pictures of that moment for years. The day we were at the Great Wall is one I will always remember as Taisha stood tall on those ancient bricks—not only

in body but also in tremendous spirit. We took our usual photos at different strategic points, and, as it was so hot, we decided to take a break and enjoy some cold drinks. We sat under the canopies of tables graced by umbrellas. There Tai saw an elderly woman collecting plastic bottles for recycling. Tai was most interested in what she was doing and asked me a myriad of questions. "Why is she doing that? Why does she need money? Why can't she come live with us, because we have plenty of room and money?" She got up from her seat and started going from garbage can to garbage can, table to table, collecting plastic bottles. With her arms full, she approached the old woman and delivered them all to her. Classic Tai.

Later we went back to our bus, and, as we readied to board, we saw an old man resting on his cane next to the bus. He also had a bag and stick for collecting trash. We got on and walked back to our seats. Tai kept looking out the window at the man and asked, "Does he need money too?" With a nod of my head, she reached into her purse and took out all her money. I gave her some from mine as well, and she bounded off the bus, handing over to him her currency. By the time Tai had returned to her seat, the old man had hobbled to our window. He gave a wave and a smile. That moment became an Ellison treasure, and he became Tai's new friend.

At the Forbidden City, Tai was full of concerns once again as our guide explained about the emperor and life at the palace years ago. Tai was indignant that in each room there was only one chair and that chair was only for the emperor. "That's not fair. He should have a chair for all the people to sit down, not just for him. I'll go tell him to get some more chairs." She was completely undone when the guide tried to explain that there were also servants at the palace. It just wasn't right that people would have to work at the palace if they didn't want to! After days of these kinds of experiences, our guide gave these parting words to Tai as we left Beijing, "Taisha, I have never met another person like you. I know that you will make the world a place of better equality.

For the first time, you make me wish I could have a second child with the hope she would be kind and curious just like you."

A couple of days later, we realized a dream and were able to visit Tai's city and, more excitedly, her social welfare institution. At the time of Tai's adoption, we were allowed to visit neither. We met with the director and head caregivers and were told they would like to let us visit with the other children there. They took us to the 12- to 24-month old children's room first. There were two "aunties" and about 20 children. Some babies sat in wooden chairs, each playing with a toy while others were on the floor trying out their newfound mobility. Tai tugged at my hand and asked, "Where are all their mommies?" Every day of her life with our family I have worked helping families unite with their Chinese children, and we've talked openly, almost daily, about her life in China. But I don't think it was until that moment that she began to understand just what an orphanage really was. I replied, "They don't have mommies, Tai. That is my job. I need to help find their mommies and daddies." Later that night at dinner, out of the blue, Tai stated, "I got it, Mom. Now I got it. You don't have to explain it to me anymore. Now I know why you are working hard in your office. I won't bug you. I'll let you work. You need to find more mommies."

I am not afraid of the special needs issue anymore. In fact we went on to adopt five more children with special needs and are awaiting approval to travel to adopt our sixth "extra special" child. I am especially drawn to the children in the Waiting Children Program. Each one is deserving of their own forever family. I pray that all the children can find families, but also that someone will consider the children with special needs, for I know that with the hardships come heartwarming blessings. What a child may lack in body, they can make up in soul. These are my feelings because of my own personal experience. In my life I was the one with the special need, and my child was the one that filled it. How was I so incredibly lucky to be given this child?

Jayme (age 4), Fuling, Chongqing.

Quinn Xingyue (age 4), Jiangxi.

Siblings—(Back row) Audree (age 2); Emilee Reneé MuDan (age 4), Yueyang City, Hunan; Seth (age 11); and Gracee Carroll XiaoBei (age 3), Huaibei, Anhui. (Seated) Caleb (age 13) and William Roy FuYaNan (age 3), Jiaozuo, Henan.

Abigail Mae-Xiao (age 9 months), Gaozhou, Guangdong, with her proud daddy.

Phoebe (age 2), Shangrao, Jiangxi. Phoebe's heart was healed through surgery before coming home to Texas.

Hannah (age 2), Dianbai, Guangdong.

SWEET DREAMS
by Micheline Moorhouse

AS A YOUNG GIRL I DREAMED OF ADOPTING A DAUGHTER FROM CHINA. My husband shared this dream. Sometimes our sweetest dreams cannot compare to our real life blessings.

After giving birth to two sons, my husband and I decided to put our dream into action and began the process of adopting. We submitted our dossier in September of 2003. As we waited for our referral, I was drawn to various waiting children lists. There were so many beautiful faces. How would we know if one was meant to be our child? I came across the file of a little girl who was only six weeks younger than our youngest son. Her special need was spina bifida. That was a scary need for me, but my curiosity got the best of me and I decided to view her picture. Instantly a smile came over my face and my heart melted. As I intently read her medical file, I was encouraged to see that she had begun taking her first steps. I had the misconception that all children with spina bifida were paralyzed and in wheelchairs.

After much prayer and discussion, we decided to pursue the adoption of little ChaoYing, whom we named Melanie Joy. Melanie came home in May of 2004 and had major surgery in November of the same year. She is a joy and blessing. Our family was complete with three beautiful children, or so we thought.

In October of 2004, just weeks before Melanie's surgery, I was casually looking at waiting children lists. I came across another beautiful little girl with spina bifida and got that familiar smile on my face and warm feeling in my heart. I found out weeks later that not only did she have the same need as Melanie, but she was from the same orphanage as well. The red threads were too strong to deny.

We were worried about the timing. We had only been home with Melanie for six months. How would this affect her? Was this the best decision for our family? With God's leading we decided to pursue Men Hai's adoption in December of 2004. We named her Bella.

Melanie and Bella are the best of friends. Days after coming home from China, we realized how much they meant to one another when they snuggled up in bed together. Bella was having a difficult time sleeping and cried a great deal in the middle of the night. We decided to let her sleep with her sister. She slept like an angel in her big sister's arms and no longer wakes crying. These sisters are inseparable and are each other's biggest fans.

As I watch our daughters run, dance, jump, and climb up the stairs of the bus, I think of what their lives may have been like if they had never gotten the surgeries they needed. Then I think of our lives without them. I shudder to think of it. Never in our most wonderful dreams would we ever have imagined two daughters as special as our girls. What an honor it is to be called their mommy and daddy.

愛

Li Anna Li (age 4), Hengyang, Hunan— on a trip to China to adopt her new sister, Taozi.

LI LI
by Judith Peckenpaugh

LI LI IS THE DAUGHTER WHO STOLE OUR HEARTS. We were planning to adopt a non-special needs infant when we casually viewed three-year-old Li Li's photo on a waiting children list at our agency's office. She jumped off the page and made us pay attention to her. We argued with our hearts. We weren't planning on adopting an older child. Plus we already had a name picked out for an infant! In addition we already had a three-year-old bio daughter and worried about sibling rivalry. This little girl had some unknown issues; we weren't sure we were prepared for that. But by the next day we knew that we were going to be her parents. We were hooked. We couldn't get her off our minds.

We had our dossier revised for a special needs adoption and were soon on our way. I won't pretend that our first reactions were pure joy; it was more like shock. Li Li had more serious issues than what we prepared ourselves to see. It turned out that she had had a stroke or brain bleed and was affected with cerebral palsy. While it was scary at first, we soon realized that she was much more capable than we first imagined. With exercise, therapy, minor surgeries, and lots of love, she is doing wonderfully! She's the most loving and sweetest daughter one could ask for. The sibling rivalry is a non-issue; they are best friends. Li Li runs, jumps, climbs, and hops now. She's beginning to read and can do simple math. She's about to enter first grade and is loved by her classmates and teachers. But most of all, Li Li has a family who adores her and cheers her on all the way!

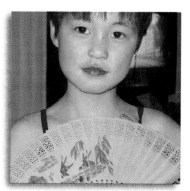

Taozi (age 7), MaAnshan, Anhui— shortly after her adoption.

Kaylie (age 3), Hungmei, Hubei.

Ana Wallis Han (age 2), Dongguan— with repaired cleft lip and palate.

A LETTER TO MY DAUGHTER
by Judith Peckenpaugh

Taozi, my little firecracker of a daughter—you were supposed to be "Brianna Wei Tao!" But, no, you told us right away that your name was "Taozi"! You made us say it over and over until we said it right—and continued to correct us for days when we still couldn't say it with the correct accent. I think you finally gave up on us and settled for our version of "Taozi."

When we traveled to China to get you, you were seven years old and the year was 2005. We only knew of you through your photograph; we thought, and still think, you are so beautiful. We had a vision of your personality in our minds. We imagined what you were like. We couldn't wait to meet you!

You were a huge surprise to us when we got to know you. You're so much more interesting than we could have imagined. You are so full of life and so sharp and witty. You were so patient with us when we couldn't understand you! We are still in awe of you that you could learn English so quickly!

You've endured more than any nine-year-old child should have to. To know the love of a family in China, to learn to live with strangers at an orphanage, and then to have to travel to a foreign country where the people didn't even speak your language—wow, you are amazing! You've endured two open-heart surgeries—one in China and then one in the U.S. You've had more dental work than any child I know, and, still, you smile and forgive me for putting you through all this.

Thank you for your love, your hugs, and your patience. I've never parented a child like you, Taozi. I have to remind myself of where you've been and what you've seen to try to understand what's inside of you, to try to help you sort it out when you don't know yourself what's going on. We're growing up together.

I am sure of one thing, baby—I love you all the way up to God's spiked hair!

Mom

Kelly (age 3), with friends Lillie, Mira, and Julia, all from Maoming, Guangdong.

Sisters at last. Marinne Minqian (age 2½), Huishui, Guizhou, and Karelle Fumei (age 8 months), Datian, Fuzhou.

Left: Ryan (age 4), Shantou, Guangdong.
Drawing (below) by Ryan (age 5).

This Child of Mine
by Lori Dubbs (January 29, 2000)

For Lianne

I see her first smile in the morning,
I kiss her goodnight.

I hear her laughter,
and dry her tears.

I feel her joy and her pain,
and hug and hold her to calm her fears.

I sleep near her at night
when she is sick.

I share with her the wonder of books and music,
and the world around us.

I watch her learn,
explore and grow.

I hold her tiny hand in mine,
and marvel at the love and trust in her eyes.

I learn from her about life,
and the depth of a mother's love for her child.

I thank Him for this most precious gift.

I love her more than mere words can express,
and treasure the bond between us.

For I am her mother,
this child of mine.

Lia LiJun (age 2½), Hanchuan, Hubei.

Lianne ZiMing (age 6), Shijiazhuang, Hebei.

Ian ("Jing Jing") (age 3),
Taishan, Guangdong.

REFLECTIONS IN AUTUMN
by Melissa House

CRINKLE, CRINKLE, CRUNCH. The leaves chatter beneath our feet, my big Nikes and her little pink boots. A sea of color floats past on a breeze.

As the sunlight streams downward, I catch a glimpse of auburn sparkle where the sun has kissed her ebony tresses, and she giggles while watching the squirrels running past in their haste.

Such simple pleasures, and yet they are so easy to miss. I wonder if she ever had a yard as big as this in China, where you pay to walk through parks and gardens, where people live in cities teeming with traffic and noise and smog. Where the young sprouts and old hardwoods stand together in the whirlwind—big, kind old people's hearts filled with longing for the old ways and a simpler time; bright, energetic youth filled with longing for TVs and CDs and MTV on primetime.

A diverse and changing future spinning out of focus, caught in a storm, and little girls and boys and families scattered like the leaves, not knowing where they will go or if they will ever return, and wondering, "What will become of all the little seeds?"

The winds of change bring such memories, our lives like a looking glass, a reflection of autumn in all its glory as they mirror the dandelions' last aerial swim. Just as the maple and the oak and the sycamore tumble down and form new roots, so has my girl gone through many seasons in this short year in America—severing old ties, forging new bonds, feeling scattered in the wind, and coming up gasping for air and clinging to life.

She is my own now, and I am in awe as we walk hand in hand, giggling.

I am in awe of her survival. No, not survival. I am in awe at the way she has flourished and blossomed. She has learned a new language, become addicted to new foods, and taught me that trust is a delicate tightrope walk. She has made new friends, started school, and mastered sarcasm and practical jokes. She has shown me that I didn't really know anything about struggle but that a 2½-year-old can figure it out pretty darn fast.

She has convinced me that no one is ever lost to a destiny out of their control; they just haven't learned how to master the destiny they are given.

She smiles at me, so innocently, and I'm pulled back into peace with her contented sigh.

Crinkle, crinkle, crunch. The rainbows fall from the tree.

"Hey, Mommy, can we have a picnic lunch? Out here, on the big green lawn?"

Out here where there is freedom for the birds, and the squirrels, and for me.

Friends and "soul sisters"—Elizabeth and Christi (both age 6), both from Yangjiang, Guangdong.

Sisters—Soraya (age 2), Cenxi, Guangxi, and Yanina (age 5), Fuling, Chongqing.

Siblings—Benji (age 7), Beijing, and Sara (age 4), Urumqi, Xinjiang.

GIRL AYAP
by Lisa Perry

WE STARTED THE PROCESS TO ADOPT OUR FIRST CHINA BLESSING IN APRIL 2003. From the beginning, I couldn't imagine adopting any child other than a baby girl, as young as possible. My thinking went like this: "Why would anyone even request anyone different with so many healthy baby girls available?" I don't think I even realized there were boys available at the time or even that "waiting children" lists existed. All I knew was that I wanted a baby girl. Why? I guess because God had already blessed me with two biological sons. I wanted a baby because I didn't want to miss all of the "firsts" and because it just seemed easier.

On April 9, 2004, my birthday, we got the referral call that we had been waiting for. She was a beautiful, healthy 11-month-old baby girl. I must admit that at the time I wished she were younger. This may sound silly, but I actually grieved for the months we had missed. We missed some of her big "firsts" (first steps, first birthday, first words), which I really didn't want to do. On "Gotcha Day" I was actually a little envious of the other parents in our group. Our daughter was the biggest baby; she could walk and didn't seem to be delayed at all. Don't get me wrong, I was so thankful to have a very healthy little girl, *but* I also wanted a baby and not a toddler. I remember that my husband kept saying how beautiful she was, and of course I agreed. But inside I kept thinking, "I was just handed a baby girl who looks more like a two-year-old boy." The shock and those feelings quickly wore off, and by day three I was totally in love with my precious, not so little, baby girl. And today I believe she is the smartest, most beautiful three-year-old little girl on the planet. She lights up my life daily.

The day we visited my daughter's orphanage was a life-changing day for me. I had seen pictures of the rows of babies in their cribs, but I wasn't prepared for all that I experienced that day, nor for the way my heart and feelings would be transformed as I saw the older children in the orphanage. Why again did I *need* a baby? My heart was forever changed. I got back on the bus that day and honestly felt like I was leaving someone behind. I held my 13-month-old toddler so tightly on the three-hour bus ride back to our hotel and thanked God the entire trip back for leading the way.

About eight months after we arrived home with Lilyan, I became aware of a 2½-year-old girl on an agency's waiting children list. She was from the same orphanage that our Lilyan was from, the one that had changed my life. She was the little one my heart was telling me that I had left behind that day. She was one of the last little ones left on this agency's list. I took one look at her picture and thought she was perfect, beautiful, and definitely meant to be my daughter. I couldn't believe how much God had changed my heart and opened my eyes in those last several months. I didn't care how big she was or how much I had missed. All I knew was that she needed me. And most of all I needed her. Lorelle was just over three years old when we brought her home. She bonded quickly to us and us to her. She's my hero! She's strong and brave, beautiful inside and out, and the perfect big sister to Lilyan.

We are now in the thick of the paper chase to bring home a 4½-year-old son from China. He's an adorable little guy whose file was just about to be sent back to China when we found him. We can't wait to bring him home!

I am proof that your heart can change. If you would have asked me three years ago, I wouldn't have guessed in a million years that I would have any desire to adopt a child other than "a girl, as young as possible." How wrong I was. There are some very special kids out there who are not babies but who need us to open our hearts to them. Most of all they need to be loved.

Sisters and best friends—Lorelle Yan (age 4) and Lilyan Xiao Min (age 3), both from Yangjiang, Guangdong.

Best friends—Nichole (age 2), Xiajiang, Jiangxi, and Grace (age 3), Bengbu, Anhui.

ALL THINGS GREAT AND SMALL
by Coni Gann

OUR NEWEST DAUGHTER, JALI WEN, WAS ADOPTED AT 33 MONTHS OF AGE. We realized that children often attach to objects such as clothing, washcloths, or a special teddy bear for comfort and security and were aware that this need could often last for long periods of time. When we got home and comfortable in our own world again, we began to forget some of these lessons; however Jali had an amazing ability to remind us of what was important.

Jali became very attached to her shoes. She loves shoes (as does her mom) and had several pairs of shoes in different styles and colors. She wasn't comfortable with her prized shoes being out of her sight; so they stayed piled (not so neatly) under the end table in the living room.

About six weeks after we got home, we spent a quiet evening at home with the children. We watched Jali play on the ottoman in our living room. On this particular night she had taken her shoes out from under the table and lined them up neatly across one side of the ottoman. She turned them around and moved them to the other side and then lined them up again. Gradually she became quiet and eventually just stood there and looked at them for 30 seconds or so. Then one by one she kissed each little shoe and returned to moving them around to the other side again.

Jali had always had to share her possessions. Now she had her own shoes. And no one has ever loved her shoes more than Jali! And no one could love Jali more than we do!

Sisters—Elizabeth (age 5) and Katelyn (age 6), both from Guangdong.

Best friends together again. Jali (age 3) and Raines (age 2), both from Kunshan, Jiangsu.

Addie (age 4), Nachuan, Chongqing, and Kate (age 3),
Hangzhong, Shaanxi—having fun with Dad.

OUR JOURNEY TO TAO YING
by *Ruthi Coats*

HAVING ADOPTED TWO GIRLS WITH MICROTIA—
A DEFECT OF THE EAR—MY HUSBAND, CLAUDE, AND
I BELONG TO SEVERAL ADOPTION SUPPORT GROUPS
where members often advocate for "special
needs" children to be adopted. In February of
this year I was checking my emails and noticed
one that said, "Five-year-old girl needs family" in
the subject line. I opened the message to read that
the agency was searching for a family for this child
with microtia and could we please advocate for her
adoption. I said my prayers for her and hit send to
forward her information on to others, hoping her
forever family would find her.

Later that day, Claude came and stood by me
and asked if I had seen the email about the five-
year-old. "Yep," I said. He asked if I had asked for
her file. "Nope," I said. He said, "You can't, can
you?" I just shook my head. "You know we don't
ask for a child's file unless we know we are looking
at it to make sure that the child is ours."

Claude went to put the girls down for a nap and
came back very quiet. Then he said, "I feel that we
are supposed to ask for this child's file—to make
sure we are to either advocate for her adoption
or to see if she is ours." So I sent a message to
the agency, Villa Hope, and asked if we could be
considered to see her file. We told them about
our experience with adoption and microtia. They
responded immediately with her information, and,
when we opened her file, we both knew that Tao
Ying was ours.

Claude's comment was "She is beautiful." What
I noticed were her hands. She was holding a girl's
hand in comfort and smiling at another little girl.
I saw her as a big sister to our girls and a little
sister to the boys. And so we are expecting again.

I know that God knows every child's parent,
and I really do feel that He has guided us in
these adoptions… and raising three little girls
from China.

Sisters—Kate Jia Xin (age 4½),
Hangzhong, Shaanxi,
and Addie Min Lan (age 5),
Nanchuan, Chongqing.

Audrey (age 2), Xiushan Miao and Tujia, Chongqing,
with brother, Lucas (age 4).

Ella Li She (age 20 months), Hengdong, Hunan,
with big brother, Ryan (age 13), and big sister, Chelsea (age 16).

Becca (age 2), Guangdong.

Siblings—Max Fan, Shantou, Guangdong, and Eva Qiong Hua, Changsha, Hunan (both age 2).

Emma Lei Pei (age 3), Yiyang, Hunan.

HALF CHINESE
by Cyndie Dobson

MY SON ALEX, 11, CAME HOME FROM SCHOOL TODAY. He slapped his books angrily on the counter and then started to cry. I was surprised at the emotional outburst. "What happened?"

"My teacher and I had a fight."

This had never happened before, and my mind questioned what would have provoked such a confrontation. "What was the fight over?"

"I told her I was half Chinese, but she said I wasn't!"

I looked at my sweet, blond-haired, green-eyed son and tenderly said, "But, Alex, you're not half Chinese; you are Caucasian."

"But Mom, our family eats Chinese food more than American food. We all speak some Chinese, and you and Dad speak a lot. We always celebrate Chinese New Year, wontons are our family's favorite food, and now we have Becca. Becca *is* from China, and she *is* Chinese. She's our sister; so that makes our family half Chinese!"

Alex's teacher, like most people, only saw the outside. But Alex is also adopted, and he knows that a family's identity goes beyond skin color or eye shape or genetics. It's how we think and feel and love that makes us who we are as a family. He knew what his teacher didn't—that somehow our love for and embracing of Chinese culture, as well as having a Chinese sister in our family, does indeed, make us part Chinese. Alex, you are right. Our family *is* half Chinese and proud of it!

THEIR RED THREAD IS A LITTLE LESS TANGLED
by Teresa Orem Werner

ON JANUARY 20, 2005, I SAW A PHOTO OF A LITTLE GIRL THAT MADE MY HEART PRACTICALLY LEAP OUT OF MY CHEST. "It couldn't be! *No way!*" was all that could come out of my mouth. I could not believe how much this little girl looked like my own daughter. I slid back in my chair, took another breath, and then leaned in for a closer look. "No way!!!" It was not my daughter, but it sure looked like her. "Could it be? What are the odds," I said again in my head.

I decided to contact her family. I did not know where this discovery was going to lead, but if I did not at least make contact with her family, I felt I might someday regret it.

I soon discovered that this little girl was a year older than our daughter. They were both from the same social welfare institute in Changsha, Hunan. They were found only blocks away from each other. Over the next few months PingPing's mother and I exchanged many photos, video, and phone conversations. We soon discovered that our daughters had a lot in common, sharing many of the same habits, mannerisms, and developmental milestones. The girls talked on the phone and were able to communicate through web cams we set up for them. Their interactions were amazing, and they truly enjoyed their "chat" times. We knew if our hunches were correct that this was going to impact them for the rest of their lives. We did not take this decision lightly. We researched DNA testing and decided to move forward with this route.

On April 1, 2005, XiaoLi and PingPing's red thread became a little less tangled. We discovered that our daughters are birthsisters. A couple months later PingPing and her mother boarded a plane for the West Coast for our first visit. The girls had a wonderful time together. We found ourselves comparing their feet, fingers, toes, ears, etc. I remember sitting in the living room watching them play together and thinking that I never would have guessed a year before that I would be in my living room watching my daughter play with her birthsister.

Discovering and meeting Natalie's birthsister brings a whole new meaning to the red thread belief for our two families.

Lily Xin Hao Min (age 2), Qinzhou, Guangxi, with her parents.

GOD'S PLAN FOR ME
by Kara Siert (age 10)

I CAN'T REALLY REMEMBER A TIME WHEN I WASN'T WITH MY FAMILY, BUT I KNOW THERE WAS BECAUSE I'VE WATCHED MY ADOPTION VIDEO MANY TIMES. I was screaming at the top of my lungs when I was handed to my parents for the first time at the age of 11 months. I must have been really scared to have been taken away from my foster parents, who took good care of me for five months. We have kept in touch with them, and I hope to go back to China someday when I'm older to see them again and also to see China.

I am very grateful for all the people who cared for me while I was in China: the ladies at Mother's Love orphanage, my foster parents, and all those who helped in the adoption process. I know it took a lot of effort from many people to make my family possible. I know God had His hand upon me, taking care of me and knowing the plan for my life from the very beginning. Sometimes I wonder about the person who found me by the river and took me to a safe place when I was so helpless and could've easily died.

I'm thankful to have been adopted into a Christian family from the United States. God has been an important part of my life. I have loving parents who care for me and have many opportunities I may have missed out on in China. My parents homeschool me, and it has given me the time to develop my writing skills. When I was living with my foster parents, in the Chinese tradition of celebrating first birthdays, they presented me with a tray of objects to see which ones I would choose. The object I chose was supposed to signify my future. They said all I wanted was a pen. I think that is neat because I have always loved to write ever since I was old enough to hold a pencil.

My dad is in the U.S. Air Force, and when we moved to England a year ago, at the age of 9½, I began to have pain in the upper part of my right arm. I tried to ignore the pain because I was afraid I'd have to go to the doctor, and my memory of doctors was getting shots. But before long the pain got so bad that my parents had to take me to the clinic to get my arm checked. It was a shock to find out I had a huge tumor growing in there. I didn't realize how serious it was until later when my parents talked to me about it. They were really worried. Seven weeks later we got the results of a biopsy and found out I had bone cancer.

God must have known way back when I was a baby that I would get this cancer and that I needed my family to take care of me. Having God in my life has helped me deal with the cancer and the treatment. My parents have been honest with me about it from the beginning, letting me know that I could have lost my arm; that I could even die. They encouraged me, though that, because of my faith in Christ, my home is really in heaven. They would be very, very sad, but I would be very happy with Jesus if He took me to heaven.

Abbey Zhuo Grace (age 13 months), Chongqing, with Mom and Dad.

Charlotte Jiao (age 5), Kunming, Yunnan.

Kara (age 10), Nanning, Guangxi— holding her published book, "Tales of Cunburra and Other Stories."

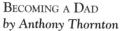

Mary Catherine Fu Hui Ying (age 3), Fuling, Chongqing.

BECOMING A DAD
by Anthony Thornton

Excerpted from an article that first appeared in the Daily Oklahoman

DON'T LET ANYONE FOOL YOU. Adoption ain't easy.

For adoptions from China, requirements include autobiographies written by each prospective parent, a social worker's home study, criminal background check, medical reports, and enough government forms to fill an accordion file. In our case, most of the work fell on my wife Gayle's shoulders.

And then there's the waiting.

Several times last year, our faith was tested. What child would be chosen for us? Would we grow to love her? What if she came with medical problems that her orphanage didn't know about?

The most serious test came in November 2004, when a paperwork glitch from six months earlier delayed the selection of a child. Though our dossier had been submitted the previous May with those from five other families, we wouldn't be traveling with that group or receive a child from their children's orphanage.

Since college 20 years earlier, I had hoped and prayed to be a dad. It was the one thing I felt competent to do. But for a variety of reasons, it had never worked out. Now I feared that by some cruel twist of fate, we would be given a child other than the one God intended.

Looking back, of course, that notion seems silly. What held us together for the next month were stories from other couples who had experienced similar delays. Each told us that as soon as we saw our daughter's photo in the referral package, we would wonder how we could have doubted.

For us, that day was December 16th. Certain that our referral wouldn't arrive until after the holidays, we took a quick vacation to Santa Fe, New Mexico. After driving back into cell phone range from a day of skiing, we found seven messages on Gayle's phone. Each was from someone trying to convey the news: Our referral was here.

We rushed to the Santa Fe library and connected to an email that contained Yu Zhuo's photos and medical history. Our euphoria wasn't shared by the librarian who kept telling us to be quiet, even after we explained, "That's our daughter!"

That moment it hit me: I was about to become a father.

Just two months later, my wife and I met our daughter for the very first time. She was the most beautiful thing I had ever seen. Sure, every new father says the same thing when his eyes first gaze upon his daughter. But she was no newborn, and this was no hospital delivery room. This wasn't even my country.

This was a third-floor orphanage lobby half a world away and packed with one-year-old girls. Among them was one who looked nothing like me or my wife and whose name neither of us could pronounce, bawling in the most terrifying moment of her young life, as a nanny in a red jogging suit handed her to us.

Still, she epitomized her given name. Zhuo, in Mandarin, means "outstanding" or "excellent." To these biased Okies who had traveled 7,700 miles for her, she was exactly that.

And suddenly she was ours. I can tell you with pure sincerity that my daughter, Abbey, still remains the most beautiful thing this new father has ever seen. Occasionally people—a couple of them not even relatives—say the same about her.

Since I can take no genetic credit for this, I politely agree.

Kira (age 2), Changsha, Hunan—playing "styling salon" with Mom.

Emilee Elizabeth (age 3), Guiping, Guangxi.

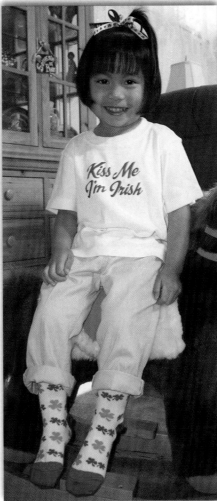

Alexander Liang (age 2), Pingliang, Gansu, and Abbey Zhuo Grace (age 3), Chongqing, with Mom and Dad.

Friends—Megumi (age 1½), Chenzhou, Hunan, and sisters, Lilia Hua (age 22 months), Zhejiang, Hunan, and Talia YuPing (age 3), Nanfeng, Jiangxi.

Watching You Become A Father
by Noriko Lovasz

I distinctly remember the day you asked me to spend
   forever with you
Only half hearing you, I remember uttering the words,
   "Huh?" and "Yes!"
Then all the fun of planning our special day and honeymoon
We would invite only our closest friends and family to share
   in our special day
While others would send their good wishes by mail
All the parties and fun we had, celebrating our special union
For someone who gets bored easily,
   I wasn't sure how long it would be good
It has been good for over eight years now,
   truly a remarkable union
Our love grows deeper over the years, our friendship too
And then came that amazing day
We traveled halfway around the world to reach her
She would finally make our family complete
The daughter we always dreamed of
We would name her "blessing"
Because that is what she is

When I look at the two of you together
My heart is filled with joy
Whether you are walking down the street
Her little hand wrapped around your index finger
Or whether she is sitting next to you on the couch
Watching TV with you and asking for Elmo
The day I married you, I looked at you and couldn't believe
   the love I felt for you
But watching you with Megumi makes me realize that
   I love you even more now

My Cherished Heirloom
by Stacy Lawson

WHEN I WAS YOUNG, 18, AND LOOKING FOR SOMETHING TO DO THAT SUMMER, BESIDES WORK, I DECIDED TO USE MY EARNINGS TO BUY A ROCKING CHAIR. It had to be special, very comfortable, and attractive. I hoped that it would become a family heirloom, that I would rock my children to sleep in it, that it would be a treasured piece for years to come.

I found an unfinished rocker and spent a month or more meticulously sanding, staining, and polishing the rocker. From there it went with me everywhere: to dorm rooms, my first apartment, and every apartment or rented room thereafter.

When I was poor in graduate school and sold my furniture, I kept the rocker. When I got married and moved to my first house, I brought the still comfortable rocker. When we decided to adopt, I put the rocker in the baby's room. Late at night my husband would smile as he watched me rock and imagine holding our baby while waiting for our referral.

When the baby turned into a toddler at referral, I kept the rocker in the room, hoping it would be of some use. When I tried to hold our new daughter in the rocker, she would fight, hit me in the face, and squirm out of my arms. It wasn't at all what I had pictured. My husband tried to use the rocker but had the same experience—holding a baby girl that was fighting tooth and nail not to be held.

As time went on our daughter started to be willing to sit in the rocker for 30 seconds without a fight. I thought about taking the rocker out of the room, as the room is small and it didn't seem to be doing us much good. I put off taking the rocker out for a few days; it was somewhere for me to sit while our daughter played.

On our daughter's second birthday, my mother said our daughter showed her the rocking chair and told her the rocker was very special. I was shocked. Since then our daughter has asked to "rock a baby" every day. It took me a while to realize that didn't mean rocking the baby doll in the new cradle she got for her birthday; it meant *she* wanted to sit with *me* in my rocking chair. Now she sits quietly, holding on, not fighting, pointing to the carved leaves and wheat in the wood of the rocker.

Last night she woke up in the middle of the night and asked to "rock a baby." When we rocked she fell back to sleep in my arms. She's a little bigger than I imagined, and it has taken a while, but the moment was still sweet.

My rocking chair may yet become the cherished heirloom I had hoped it would be.

Sisters—Kirsten Nicole-Lin (age 5), Wuchuan, Guangdong, and Emily Elyse AiJie (age 3), Zhanjiang, Guangdong.

Friends—Anna Makenzie Linghua (age 8), Kunming, Yunnan; Amy Lianne Hai (age 7), Xiangtan, Hunan; and Anna Olivia (age 5), Shantou, Guangdong—preparing to perform for the Chinese New Year.

Two Gifts from God
by Rhonda Steczkowski

MY HUSBAND AND I HAD THREE SONS AND DECIDED IN SEPTEMBER 1998 THAT WE WANTED TO COMPLETE OUR FAMILY BY ADOPTING A DAUGHTER FROM CHINA. We completed our paperwork in December and sent it to China. We decided to name our daughter Meredith. Our boys prayed daily for her that she was being loved and hugged. On New Year's Eve we received the letter telling us that our dossier had been registered on Christmas Day. What a great Christmas gift!

On July 2, 1999, we received the most wonderful phone call telling us we had a daughter. We learned we had named our daughter three days before her birth, and that the day she was born we received the letter saying our paperwork had been registered in China. We knew from these events that God had a plan from the beginning for us to be a family and that the red thread connected us to our daughter. In August 1999 we traveled to Nanchang, China, to meet our daughter, Meredith MaoYe.

Nearly five years later we were given another gift from God. We were not seeking another adoption at the time but had not ruled it out. I had an overwhelming feeling one day in April 2004 to visit the Rainbow Kids website. I saw a little girl whose eyes spoke to me. When I opened her picture, I felt an instant connection to her. My husband and I contacted the agency that was placing her and found out that she was being considered by other families. A week later I contacted them again and was told that she was probably not going to be adoptable. She had a hemangioma on her face, and the other families had been given some scary medical opinions and had all decided to turn her down. The lady at the agency wanted to offer me another child to consider. However I explained to her that we had not been looking to adopt but felt a connection to this child. She said, "I don't think she is going

to be adopted. I am going to send her back through the system, and she will not be able to be adopted." I begged her to let us consider her, and she finally gave in and said she would overnight her information. She told me that we needed to seek medical opinions and make a decision quickly.

Meanwhile my husband and I began researching hemangiomas to learn as much as we could. We happened upon the Vascular Birthmark Foundation, which answered a lot of questions and referred us to a doctor close to our home who specialized in these conditions. The next day the video arrived. I was about to show the video to a friend when the phone rang. It was the lady from the agency. She had received a call from the founder of the Vascular Birthmark Foundation, who had seen the picture and taken it to a national specialist in hemangiomas. He said, "That little girl is fine; she will need a couple of laser treatments." The lady at the agency was so excited to tell me because she wanted the girl to be adopted. We met with a local specialist, who confirmed the other doctor's diagnosis. This convinced us that she was meant to be our daughter and that God was working it all out. After this meeting we called the agency and told them we wanted to move forward with the adoption.

In December 2004 we traveled to Hefei, China, to meet our new daughter, MacKenzi Xia Fang. She had her first of two laser treatments a month later. Our local doctor was a gift from God to help our daughter with her hemangioma. We know that both of our daughters were meant to be part of our family and that God put everything in place to make it happen.

MaryBeth LinYao (age 3½), Xiaonan, Hubei.

媽爸

Elizabeth Rose (age 3), Gaozhou, Guangdong, with Dad in lion mask.

Chosen One
by Cami Schaubroeck

A mother looking at her babe
And marveling at her charms.
My daughter, yes, my firstborn child
Was placed into my arms.

The minute that I saw her face,
The instant we locked eyes,
I knew she was my *chosen one*;
A gift, forever mine.

And then another daughter came.
Would my heart now be torn?
I wanted so to love her too,
My child, my second born.

But when I heard her laughter
And saw her silly ways,
I knew she was my *chosen one*,
Forever mine to praise.

And then one day I fell in love
With a child I had never met;
A tiny stranger far away
I could not hold, and yet…

God in His great compassion
Reached down upon her bed
And laid a special blessing
Upon her silken head.

He said, "You are a *chosen one*."
I have such plans for you.
Your mom and dad are waiting,
And you have some sisters too.

And so my precious daughters,
So different, yet so loved,
Remember, you are *chosen ones*;
My gifts from God above.

JACK'S STORY
by Reese Williams

Our family had wondered how Jack, age five, would adjust to having his new one-year-old sister, Olivia, in the family. His parents, grandmother, and aunt had been preparing him all along during the extended adoption process and all hoped for an easy transition from being an only child to being a big brother. From the moment they arrived back from China with his new sister, Jack seemed to accept his new role after a short adjustment period. Just how short a time this took was confirmed last week at the playground. After a summer's worth of bonding, the transition to brother and sister came to the final step. While visiting their grandmother, the two were playing at the neighborhood playground with other children. After a while one of the other children asked Jack the obvious question: "Is Olivia Chinese?"

Without missing a beat, Jack replied with all straightforward candor, "No, she's my sister." The process of forming a family is now complete.

Sisters—Meredith MaoYe (age 7), Jian, Jiangxi, and MacKenzi Xia Fang (age 4), Hefei, Anhui.

Anna Rose (age 2), DianJiang, Chongqing, and
Kayla Ann (age 3), Loudi, Hunan—reading with Daddy.

Gwion (age 3) and Ceinwen Jiannan (age 18 months),
Nanfeng, Jiangxi, with Mammy.

BLESSED
by Lori Grysen

IT WASN'T AN EASY DECISION. After all we were "coasting" with our older kids. Life was getting easier, right? I spent many sleepless nights, scared to death, wondering how I was going to give up my independence. How was I going to be able to work? How could we do this financially? What happens if her heart condition is worse than we know and she doesn't live? At 2:00 a.m. those thoughts are very heavy. Nevertheless God gave us our answer through many undeniable events, and with peace we decided to pursue the adoption of Yun Xiao Yue, whom we named Sophia Lin.

Months later I still wake some mornings wondering, "What would I do today if Sophie wasn't here?" I think of the things that occupied my time while my kids were in school. Lunches with friends, shopping, work, and quiet time at home. I did enjoy those things, but they don't compare with the blessings of spending time with our daughter.

I have found that the things that I thought I would miss are not important in the scheme of life. Instead of Panera bread, it's McDonald's for "fries, Mama." Instead of relaxing evenings after dinner, it's playing on the family room floor. Sippie cups, diaper bags, a potty chair, and car seat are part of our lives again. But, as seasoned parents, we know from experience that these phases fly by way too fast. Before we know it, she will be going to kindergarten.

While we were considering a special needs adoption, a good friend told us, "We believe that God puts before us opportunities, and we need to explore them before we dismiss them based on human thought." I can't imagine our family now without our daughter. I am honored that God chose our family to raise and love Sophie. People say she is "blessed" to have been welcomed here in our family and country. We believe that it is our family that has been blessed.

Siblings—MeiXing ("Mei Mei") (age 3), Youyang, Sichuan;
Koji (age 6); and Shei Lan ("Lala") (age 2), Yuanling, Hunan.

I Am Lian
by Julie Flynn Coleman

I am Lian
Love me if you can
I am Lian

You are my baby
Let me rock you
No need to do it yourself… Mama's here
My love will dry your tear

I am Lian
Love me if you can
I am one

You are my baby
Let me feed you
Together we can explore
Love will unlock your door

I am two
I am Lian
You are *my* mam?

You are still my baby
Let me dress you
Why do you cause such furor?
Will my love do… or do you need more?

Lian (age 5½), Loudi, Hunan.

I am three
I am Lian
Where is *my* mam?

You are our daughter
Your muqin's and mine
Let me bathe you
We will play baby... but our eyes won't meet
Feeling secure in our love is still such a feat

I am four
I am Lian
I *love* my mam.

You are my daughter
Let me guide you
Why are you so oppositional?
Well hear this, "My love is unconditional!"

I am Lian
I am five
I want to stay alive

You are my girl
Let me baby you
You tell me you can't remember it...
You're afraid to grow more...
Don't worry our love WILL endure.

I am *your* mam
I love you *my* Lian.

Molly Suzanne Kai (age 10),
Zhanjiang, Guangdong.

Sisters—Rachel (age 11 months), Guiping, Guangxi,
and Julia (age 3).

Right: Kiana (age 7),
Yueyang, Hunan.

Below: Sisters—Joy (age 3), Ningdu, Jiangxi,
and Grace (age 4), Shantou, Guangdong.

SUCH A JOY!
by Angela Palmer
Blog Entry,
April 3, 2006

Rachel is doing beautifully here at home, and everyone has pretty much settled back into the regular routine. After just a few days of getting adjusted to the time difference, she is now sleeping through the night. She is crawling everywhere and can stand up on her own. We have to really keep an eye on her since she is so mobile and seems to be especially drawn to anything that she shouldn't have!

She is such a happy girl and rarely cries, usually only when she falls during one of her climbing expeditions. Her eyes sparkle with life and intelligence, and she lights up whenever she sees one of her family members (or the cat, which she loves). She loves rough-housing with her brothers, and following her sister around. She babbles and giggles, and moves to music. She still loves her thumb!

She had her studio pictures done on Friday and was a great little model. I can't wait to get the pictures back. She has her first doctor's appointment tomorrow. Today she is going to visit Harrison's classroom. He is so proud of his new sister and wants to show her off to all of his friends.

We are all so much in love with our little sweetie. We love to rub her fuzzy little head and tickle her tummy to make her giggle. We love her slobbery kisses and the way she lays her head against our cheeks. She is such a joy to us, and I can only hope that we bring the same joy to her.

Three peas in a pod. Siblings—Myka Kei Keyi (age 2½),
Changsha, Hunan; Maxwell Jai Hailin (age 2½), Changsha, Hunan;
and Meisi Li Hui (age 4½), Guiyang, Guizhou.

Twins—Alexandra and
Charlotte (age 5), Shanghai.

LUKE'S NEW BIKE
by Lori Melton

OUR OTHER CHILDREN WERE RIDING THEIR BIKES WHILE LUKE, AGE EIGHT AND HOME FROM CHINA FOR JUST THREE WEEKS, WAS LEFT TO RIDE A 14-YEAR-OLD BIG WHEEL THAT LOST ITS SEAT LONG AGO. We decided it was time for that boy to get his first bike. We made the trek to Toys R Us and found a bike that was the right size. I took it off the rack and had Luke push it back toward the front. He shyly and awkwardly maneuvered it to the front of the store.

Most of the time Luke seems like just a normal kid. Most of the time there are no reminders of his beginnings in life. But as he carefully pushed that bike through the aisles, barely able to steer it and avoid tripping over it at the same time, he seemed so small and so vulnerable, needing someone to take care of him and to love him.

I asked Scott if he thought Luke realized the bike was for him. Scott thought he did; I wasn't so sure. Luke doesn't assume anything, doesn't take anything for granted. Scott told him "Luke's bike." I patted the seat and said "Hong Yong's. Hong Yong's bike."

Luke has a look that we do not see often. It's a modified soldier/survivor look. We only see it at times when his heart rate must be high. His eyes get big and he doesn't blink. He gets very still, yet is not stiff like when he is in full soldier/survivor mode. His face also appears to change color, if that's possible. He almost looks like a different kid. This is the look that came over him. I think he was trying to decide if he was understanding us correctly. He pointed to himself and said "Hong Yong?" "Yes!" we replied "Hong Yong's bike." He took a deep breath and said very slowly "Sank you, Mama. Sank you, Baba." It was very obvious he was trying very, very hard to enunciate his words the very best he could. It was very obvious he was touched and grateful and totally surprised. It was a moment that I won't soon forget, and I hope I never do—that look, the great care he took to thank us, the strong emotions he was obviously feeling.

This is why we adopted an older child. *This* is what we yearned to do. We wanted to share the many blessings the Lord has given us with a child who might otherwise never experience them.

Siblings—(Front row) Meili (age 3), Gaoyou, Jiangsu; Breanne (age 6); and Raegen (age 4), Loudi, Hunan. (Back row) Luke (age 9), Yangquan, Shanxi; Rachel (age 17); and Jake (age 8).

Snow princesses and sisters—
Ciara Xiaoqing (age 3), Gutian, Fujian, and
Molly Mei-Xing (age 5), Yueyang, Hunan.

MEILI'S STORY
by Lori Melton

HER REFERRAL PICTURE SHOWED A SWEET-FACED, UNSMILING INFANT. Her medical reports said her right arm wouldn't raise, her right hand grip was weak, and she had a small ASD and a VSD of almost an inch. We knew almost immediately that she was to be our next daughter. We decided we would name her Meili.

After receiving our initial approval from the CCAA to be her parents, we sent announcements to family and friends with her picture. Jake, our first-grader, took one to school to share with his class. I noticed it on the bulletin board each time I visited the classroom. What I didn't realize was that Mrs. Dot VanderPol and her first-graders at Rockford Christian School prayed for Meili each day. I learned later from other parents that some of their children prayed for Meili each evening and on weekends as well.

Before we traveled we received an update that said the social welfare institute considered Meili to be in serious but stable condition. They said it was obvious she wasn't getting enough oxygen and asked us to hurry for her. Because of the size of her VSD and the update we received, the cardiologist allowed us to schedule her open-heart surgery before we traveled. It was to take place just two weeks after she arrived home.

When we traveled to China in February 2004, we weren't sure what Meili's condition would be. But instead of a blue, sickly baby, we met a round little girl who showed no indications of her medical condition. Her arm movements were a little jerky, but we attributed that to the new-found freedom of movement she gained after we removed the multiple layers of clothing she was wearing. She had difficulty sitting unsupported, but I think that was also because of the removal of her accustomed layers. We were worried that crying would make her heart condition apparent, but, the few times she cried, there was no indication she was not getting sufficient oxygen. We soon

forgot she was a 17-month-old who would soon have open-heart surgery. We quickly fell totally, madly, and forever in love with Gao Fu Fan, who would forever be our Meili.

One week after arriving home, we traveled to the University of Michigan C. S. Mott Children's Hospital for her pre-op appointment. Tests were run, her cardiologist examined her, and we were escorted into a consult room. When the doctor came to talk to us, he told us that her ASD was healed. This didn't surprise us as many small ASDs heal on their own. He went on to tell us that her VSD was one-third of the size it was in China and, because of its position on the heart wall near the tricuspid valve, the valve was helping to regulate the blood flow. Although a one-third inch hole is still large, the relative size of the hole was small. She did not need surgery at this time!

The first thing I did when we arrived home was to call Mrs. VanderPol. I asked her if I could bring Meili to her class the next day. I held my miracle baby in my arms in front of that first-grade class and thanked them for their prayers. I relayed our good news and then told them to look at Meili and to remember her face. I encouraged them to remember her and to never forget the amazing power of prayer. Mrs. VanderPol then had those little first-graders gather around us and they prayed for us one last time.

Mrs. Dot VanderPol retired this year. She told me that Meili's story is one of her favorite memories from her almost 40 years of teaching. It's a story I will tell Meili over and over throughout her life.

Siblings—Katie (age 20), holding Melanie (age 5), Jiangxi; Emilee (age 6), Hunan; Eric (age 14); and Peter (age 17).

Family photo taken two weeks after arriving home.
(Back row) Mom, Sarah Kathryn (age 12), and Dad.
(Front row) Jon Cole (age 3), Samuel (age 3), Pingjiang, Hunan, and Elizabeth (age 5).

I Am the One
by Fang Fang Wu Lee (age 13)

I am the one who knows me.
I am the one who breaks the silence, the one who
    filters out the right words to say.
I am the one who is fearless in front of everybody;
Yet I am the one who is extremely self-conscious.
    Sometimes so self-conscious am I that I can
    spend hours deciding my outfit for the new day.
I am the one who loves to shop. I am the one who
    shops everywhere—Maine, Beijing, Tokyo—
    you name it.
I am the one who loves talking to people of any age.
I am the one who is constantly there to help, to
    lend a helping hand. When I grow up, I want to
    be the one who gives America a better name

China. That is my country. I am a daughter of China.
I am the one who was brought, not taken, from a
    province known as Yunnan.
I am the one who is unsure of her heritage.
I am the one who always answers, "I don't know
    where they are."
I am the one who would do anything to get them,
    my birth parents, back.
I am the one who appreciates my life now. A life in
    the orphanage was a life without hope.
I am the one who kept my first language, a gift that
    most adoptees don't have.
I am the one who takes frequent journeys back
    home to China. I go everywhere.
I am the one with a loving family.
I am the one whom they drive crazy sometimes,
    but for the most part,
I am the one who loves them all dearly.

I am the one who strives for the best, and only
    the best.
I am the one whose classmates are sometimes
    jealous of; they don't understand the difference
    between perfection and high standards.
I am the one who people call a "goody-goody."
Sometimes I am the one who is misunderstood
    and disliked.
I am the one who works hard because I choose to.
I am the one who knows me.

Above: Vivienne Zhen Ling (age 4), Nanning, Guangxi.

Below: Augustine Xu XuDong (age 2), Xuzhou, Jiangsu.

Alyssa Weilin (age 13 months), Qingyuan, Guangdong.

MY MOTHER
by Ya Li

Written in Chinese approximately one month after returning home from China and translated for a school assignment to write an essay: "The Most Important Person in Life."

FATHER AND MOTHER ARE THE GREATEST AND THE MOST HOLY CAREER IN THE WORLD. The children who have father and mother must be the happiest children in the world. No matter they are poor or rich, the parents are always ready giving all their love to their children, no matter whether the children are their own or adopted.

I have a great mother. She adopted my sister, my brother, and me from China. Even though three of the children are not her biological children, she gives all her love to these three Chinese children.

My mother is very beautiful. She has brown hair and bright, meaningful eyes. She has a big, high nose. She is very tall and slim. My mother takes very good care of me in daily life. I have been eating the Chinese food since I came to America because my mother worries I am not used to the food here. At night I feel scared, and my mother sleeps with me. Whatever I want, my mother always buys for me. Sometimes I feel I am asking too much. But my mother always understands and comforts me all the time. When I saw some white hairs coming out from my mother's beautiful hair, I feel very sad because she works too much for us. So in the daily life I wish I could do something to make my mother happy and try my best to help her.

The Chinese food my mother makes is very tasty. I like it very much. Sometimes we also have Western food. I am fully grateful to my mother. Here in America I can really enjoy Mother's love, which I have never had in my life. I love my mother and love her big heart.

Alexa Lan (age 4), Huazhou, Guangdong.

Ya Li Liu Louise (age 14), Xuzhou, Jiangsu.

Siblings—Skyler ("Sky") Xiaohe (age 2½), Zhuzhou, Hunan; Quinn Qiuyi (age 9 months), Dingyuan, Anhui; and Kyle (age 7).

PRAYER OF A BIG BROTHER
by Laura Sundvall

"DEAR LORD, PLEASE BRING ME A BABY SISTER," WOULD BEGIN THREE-YEAR-OLD KYLE'S NIGHTLY PRAYERS. We had never mentioned adoption to Kyle. He just wanted a sister. Not knowing where to begin the adoption journey, we got on the web and began to search. Twenty-one months later, on Father's Day of 2002, we received eight-month-old Sky Xiaohe, a bundle of energy, from Zhuzhou, Hunan.

Sky brought the true meaning of pink and princess to life. She has boundless energy and a joy for life that rubs off on all who meet her. We have no doubt that her dreams of being a prima ballerina will in fact come true.

"I want a brother! I have a sister, and now I'd like a brother!"

We had decided to adopt again as soon as the one year rule was up. Kyle did not know this; he just knew in his heart he wanted a brother. "Dear Lord, please bring me a brother." We explained to Kyle that again we would request a girl or boy, but it will likely be a sister. "I want a brother but if I get a sister again, I will call her Flower." "Why Flower?" I asked. "Because she will be as beautiful as a flower," he said.

In May of 2004 we received Kyle's Flower from Dingyuan, Anhui. Kyle was bummed at first that Quinn Qiuyi was not a boy and cried when we did not name her Flower, but shortly after her adoption, Kyle told us he was *so happy* she was not a boy because he wouldn't have his sister. Quinn was different than Sky. We witnessed a nine-month-old

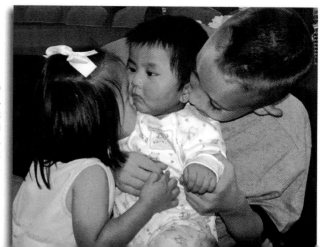

Brothers—Kade Jiabin (age 6½), Shantou, Guangdong, and Kyle (age 8½).

Emalie Quinn (age 4), Fuzhou, Jiangxi.

baby who was shut down emotionally and had leg issues. But through a lot of love, nurturing, and therapy, a little baby who had a rough start now rules the roost! The legs we worried would never be fully well can now run faster than her older sister! The little girl who was emotionally shut down is now full of mischief and a hoot to all who meet her. She stomps around in princess shoes but gets more excited about Bob the Builder and hammers on the tool aisle at Home Depot. Kyle and Quinn are the closest of the siblings. He didn't get a brother or a Flower, but he got Quinn.

My heart for another boy was not fulfilled, and my husband still wanted another child. We beat Kyle to the prayers and surprised him on his eighth birthday with news that he was getting a brother! The grin couldn't have been bigger. Prayers for a brother changed to, "Lord, please keep my brother safe until we get him." Kyle made his third trip to China in four years to get his long awaited brother. Kade Jiabin, from Shantou, Guangdong, joined our family in June 2005 at age 6½. Adopting an older child is a whole different experience, but Kyle has demonstrated the true meaning of compassion, patience, unconditional love, and nurturing.

Our family cherishes Kyle's true heart for adoption. He has willingly shared his parents' attention and love, emptied his piggybank when hearing about Quinn's orphanage's needs, sat through Sky's dance classes, and shown endless patience and had fun with his younger brother, Kade. We are truly a family formed through prayer—the prayer of a big brother.

EXPECTING "TWINS"
by Jason and Araminta Montague

WE MAILED ELLEN'S OFFICIAL ADOPTION DOSSIER PAPERS ON JANUARY 5, 2005. Two months later we found out we were expecting as well. Since our decision to adopt had always been based on a desire to adopt and not out of necessity, the natural thing to do was to go ahead with our adoption, and so we did.

When our son, George, was ten months old, we left him home with his "Nana" and headed to China. When they placed Ellen Mei Lou in our arms, we knew that our family was now complete. What did we ever do without her?

With George and Ellen both almost two years old, we jokingly refer to them as "the twins." When they hug one another or when Ellen rubs George's back because he is crying, we melt all over again. If we could do it all over, we wouldn't change a thing!

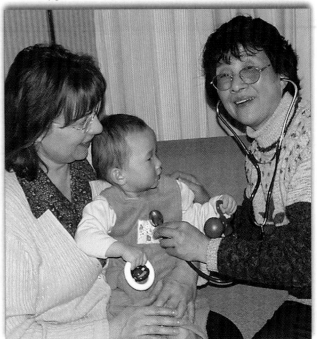

Lauren (age 15 months), Wuxue, Hubei, with Chinese pediatrician.

Ellen Mei Lou (age 2), Loudi, Hunan, with her grandfather.

During the process of adopting Ellen, we found out Araminta's father has Alzheimer's disease. However he understood what we were doing and told anyone he could about this new, wonderful little girl coming to our family. A few months later, he lost his ability to speak and barely recognized us. This past June (2006), we visited my father at his new nursing home. As Ellen ran around the corner, we heard her calling, "Papa! Papa!" There was her papa, standing in the hallway, smiling at her and reaching out his arms. We like to think that even with the best part of his mind gone, he just knew she was his.

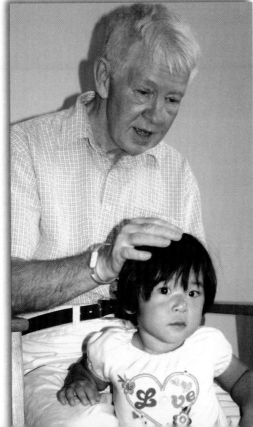

Faith (age 3), Anqing, Anhui.

ELEVEN YEARS AGO
by Kim Breuer

ON OCTOBER 4, 1994, I AWOKE AT 3 A.M. I sat up in bed. It had just hit me, while sound asleep, that we had just submitted our application to Holt that day for an adoption in China. What was I thinking of gallivanting off to the other side of the world to do something like that?? In those days an American adopting in China was not very common as the program was new. Originally we had thought to adopt from Korea, but it was not possible then for those of us living in North Dakota. Holt had suggested China to us. We agreed, and our paperwork was sent off. Now, in the darkness of night, I was questioning myself.

Referrals came in really fast back then. We were at the 11 week point when our social worker called and said, "Kim, I have a referral for you." The baby was about 3½ months old. As I was trying to reach my husband to break the news, it suddenly occurred to me she was born on the day our dossier had left for Holt!

Our social worker overnighted the information to us, and we were somewhat troubled the next day to get photos of a very weak, very sick, very thin baby. Her medical reports said she was not in the best health, but it didn't matter; she was our daughter, and we were going to go bring her home.

My husband was in the Air Force at the time, and shortly after the referral came in, he left for a 90+ day tour of duty in the Middle East. Luckily my mom stayed with two of our children, and my 12-year-old son and I flew to Hong Kong. I had never been out of the country before; so this was a real experience.

The next few days were a whirlwind—meeting our travel group, orientation, flying into Jiangxi… After arriving at the hotel, I'll never forget my son, Stephen, rushing into the room shouting, "The babies are here!" The next thing I knew, they were placing Emilee in my arms. That was the start of our adventure with this amazing child. Shortly after she came home, our other son told us it was almost like Emilee had always been with us. Then he said, "And she's not adopted, she's my sister." Those sibling bonds grew rapidly.

Today, as we look at our 5'4", 11-year-old daughter, we marvel at how she has grown. She is an amazing child, who will soon start sixth grade. We are so proud of the young lady she's becoming. She can repair things. She rearranges furniture to the point of my wondering, "Now why didn't I think of that first?" She plans and cooks complete meals on her own. She loves to go shopping with me and out on mile walks. Her dad can teach her to do all sorts of technical things.

We frequently think of what a perfect job the CCAA did nearly 11 years ago when they matched Chen Yu-Nan with our family. What an adventure the past 11 years have been since she came into our lives in Jiangxi! We never envisioned what she would become or how much she would mean to our family. Our family truly changed that day and for the better. We thank the Lord daily for the unique privilege of being Emilee's mom and dad.

Kailee (age 2½), Guiping, Guangxi—
picking apples with Daddy.

Emilee (age 11½),
Nanchang, with Dad.

A SPECIAL CONNECTION
by Jenifer Steger-Parker

"ARE THEY TWINS?" In the weeks and months after we arrived home from China in July 2006, this question came from everyone. Our family—with our three-year-old son Garrett, 12-month-old son Noah, and eight-month-old daughter Kaitlyn—stood out wherever we went. At first we answered cheerfully, explaining that Noah and Kaitlyn were four months apart in age. Soon, though, the question became an annoyance. Could anyone really believe they were twins? Aside from being the same size, they looked nothing alike. And yet the question kept coming.

The first month was hard. Garrett loved being the big brother and adored his new sister. Unfortunately his baby brother and sister did not appear to feel quite the same way about the new arrangement. Noah had been the baby of the house for the last 12 months, and he was not interested in sharing his parents, his space, or his toys with Kaitlyn. Kaitlyn, on the other hand, had Mommy and Daddy's full-time attention for weeks in China, and she was equally uninterested in sharing us now that we were back in the U.S. Both insisted on being carried everywhere—at the same time. Both wanted to sit on Mommy's lap or hear a story—at the same time—and *not* together. Our days were spent taking long walks in the double stroller, one of the few activities that we could do together that seemed to make everyone happy.

And then something happened. After about six weeks, uncontrollable laughter was heard coming from the nursery at naptime. Noah and Kaitlyn were standing in their cribs facing each other, mimicking each other, and laughing hysterically about it. Noah would jump up and down, and Kaitlyn would jump up and down. Noah would fall down, and then Kaitlyn would fall down. Giggle, giggle.

Are they twins? Right around that time, Noah and Kaitlyn became best friends. They sat next to each other at the dinner table and shared their

food. When Mommy would say "No, Noah, you can't have any more pasta until you eat some green beans," Kaitlyn would calmly hand him some of her pasta. "Ya-Ya" and "Kaitie" (their names for each other) chase the kitties around the house, dance to music together, and wake us up in the morning by singing "E-I-E-I-O" at the top of their little lungs. They are partners in crime, pushing us to our limits with their antics and mischievous grins.

Are they twins? In addition to all their silly moments that make us laugh, there are also moments that melt our hearts. Ever since the day they discovered the framed photos of each of the children in our bedroom, they have developed a daily routine where they pick up each other's photo and carry it around. On Kaitlyn's first day of day care, Noah took her under his wing. The teachers reported that as long as she could see Noah, she was happy. When we took Noah out of town for the weekend without his sister, he yelled "Oh no, Kaitie!" as we were backing out of the driveway and then burst into tears when we told him that she was not coming on the trip.

Are they twins? As I watch them playing a rambunctious game of hockey with Garrett and their daddy, I wonder how they would answer that question. They did not share a womb, but they share a connection that is undeniable.

A. J. (age 5 months), adopted domestically, with brother, Adrian Wen Kai (age 2), YiWu, Zhejiang.

Jillian (age 8), Zhaoqing, Guangdong.

Bread Crumbs
by Ohilda Bombardier

WE STARTED OUR ADOPTION PROCESS ALMOST THREE YEARS AGO, TRYING TO ADOPT KAI, A BEAUTIFUL, HEALTHY LITTLE BOY FROM EASTERN EUROPE. Two weeks before we were to leave, the country shut down to international adoption. We were completely heartbroken. After picking up the pieces of our hearts, we took a leap of faith and switched to China. We fell in love with an adorable little girl on our agency's waiting children list. We knew for sure that God would grant us that child; yet we got the call from our agency that we were *not* chosen to be her family. My husband and I decided that we would remain on the non-special needs path and that a special needs child was not meant for us. We were so very discouraged.

Months later, toward the end of our wait for a referral, our agency received a new waiting children list. My husband and I agreed to look at it together, one last time. I secretly asked God that if our child was on that list to please give me a sign. I told Him that He knew I totally trusted Him, but that I needed something—a bread crumb—to assure me.

Scott and I sat in front of the computer. The first picture came up, then the second, the third, and so forth. I was desperately looking for "*the sign.*" Midway through the list, I asked Scott if he was drawn to any children, and he said, "Not really." We were approaching the end, and I was getting very discouraged. He opened up a picture and I froze. I saw the name Kai—the same name of the little boy we lost from Eastern Europe.

Half a second later Scott said, "Oh my God! Look! *That's a sign!*" His eyes were like saucers. "I haven't seen one of those in 30 years!" Huh???

I thought he was talking about the name. He said, "Felix, the cat! I had that toy when I was a little boy! I loved it!!" I then said, "Scott, look at his *name!*" We both started crying. Then we scrolled down. His birth date was Scott's birthday—May 27th—*and* on his birthday in 2004, we received the original Kai's referral! On the day we were getting our referral from Eastern Europe, this little boy was born. As we read through the information, we noticed that on October 9, 2004, his paperwork was approved for international adoption by the CCAA—the same day we were told that the Republic of Belarus had shut down. Scott looked at me and said, "*This is our son!*"

God not only gave us a bread crumb, He gave us a loaf! On April 3, 2006, Kai was placed in my arms, and I felt such joy! It was a very long journey for us, but I would do it again in a heartbeat. Our hearts were changed from wanting a very young, healthy baby to an older child with special needs. I am ever so grateful to God for that wait because otherwise we wouldn't have our precious Kai.

Kenneth ("Shuai") (age 5), Shanghai.

Raegan Jean (age 2), Guangdong.

Siblings—Garrett (age 4), Noah (age 22 months), and Kaitlyn (age 18 months), Xiushan, Chongqing.

Sisters—Mirielle JinShiLing (age 3½), Guiping, Guangxi Zhuang, and Maelynna LiQing (age 2), Gejiu, Yunnan.

SEEING INNER BEAUTY
by Donna Klinger

I STOOD ON MY NEXT DOOR NEIGHBOR'S BACK PORCH, CHATTING WITH AN OLDER CHINESE COUPLE WHILE WATCHING MY THEN FOUR-YEAR-OLD DAUGHTER PLAY IN THE BACKYARD. After exchanging pleasantries about how we knew the party hosts, the woman turned to me and said, "Your daughter is as beautiful inside as she is outside. She is so joyful, and you can tell that all the other kids want to play with her." I have automatically thanked hundreds, if not thousands, of people for their comments on Emma's beauty, but this time my gratitude was genuine, and I beamed. This woman got it. She understood that it is inner beauty that matters. This conversation occurred four years ago, and I can still replay the scene in my head.

REACHING THE SIX MONTH MILESTONE (GIVE OR TAKE A MONTH!)
by Sheri Moreau

I WAS WARNED ON THE E-LISTS UNCOUNTABLE TIMES DURING THE WAIT FOR MAELYNNA THAT THE FIRST SIX MONTHS HOME WITH HER WOULD BE THE HARDEST. Adjusting from single-with-one to single-with-two would certainly take *at least* that long. Thus I felt prepared and even stoically braced for the worst, whilst hoping secretly for a second easy transition—lightning can strike twice, can't it?!

Mirielle, my oldest daughter, is of course no angel, but Miri truly is a wonderful child: loving, easy, accommodating, brave, bright, and beautiful—altogether utterly delightful, with only a very few exasperating quirks. Maelynna, on the other hand, was a handful, right from the get-go. She too is bright, affectionate, very smart, equally beautiful… but from the first she was prone to *loud, screaming temper tantrums* multiple times a day. Maely was initially very anxiously attached and would not let me out of her sight. She loathed the car seat; our ten minute drive to and from day care became a horror. There were times I felt as if I were in jail, because leaving the house just wasn't an option to be undertaken lightly. I watched in shock as I morphed into a Mommy Who Yells—something I didn't like one little bit and have worked darn hard to rectify.

I kept telling myself things would get better after we had been home six months—everyone said so. But our six month anniversary came and went, and while things had indeed vastly improved, I still found myself questioning where was the sheer *joy* I had felt from the first as simply Miri's Mommy??? Believe me, I was worried!! Then one Sunday, when Maely had been home six months and 12 days, the promise came true. We had had a great weekend: gymnastics, shopping, a visit to the pet store to admire the critters, a long stint on the county playground. We had had friends with children of a similar age over to visit. We took a long walk and chased butterflies with nets. We had a first-ever viewing of "Mary Poppins"—entailing much singing and dancing about the family room—and all in all had shared a whole lot of laughter, giggling, tickling, and assorted shenanigans.

After putting the girls to bed that evening, I stood outside their doors and told them softly that I was going outside to move the car into the garage, but "Mommy would be right back." I proceeded to do same, then futzed about in the garage for a few minutes, then came back in the house and softly called up the stairs: "Good night, my sweet girls. I love you!!"

And my daughters' calls came wafting back from above: "Good night, Mommy, I love you!!" "G'ni' Mommy, wuv you!"

I just stood there stock still for a moment… then walked quietly down the hall to the kitchen with a full heart and tears in my eyes. At that moment, suddenly, softly, and totally unexpectedly—because miracles happen that way—for the very first time since we became a family of three, I knew I was, once again utterly, completely, and unequivocally able to call myself: "World's Happiest Mommy."

Mom with daughters—(Clockwise from upper left) Bethany (age 9), Anqing, Anhui; Elisabeth (age 7), Wuchuan, Guangdong; Sarah (age 2), Bengbu, Anhui; and Rachel (age 3), Longquan, Zhejiang.

(Clockwise from top) Sisters—Ellie (age 9), Qidong, Hunan; Mimi (age 5), Fuling, Chongqing; YuYu (age 6), Nanning, Guangxi; and Nora (age 5), Guilin, Guangxi.

Sisters—Eden (age 8), Changshu, Jiangsu; Sarah (age 6), Shantou, Guangdong; Maria (age 9), Jiujiang, Jiangxi; and Laurelin (age 12), Nanning, Guangxi.

BEING CHINESE
by Maria Haas (age 9)

I THINK IT ROCKS TO BE CHINESE BECAUSE PEOPLE THINK THAT I CAN SPEAK A LOT OF CHINESE, BUT I CAN'T. Sometimes I want to be like my aunt, who speaks two languages: Chinese and English.

I don't like being one of the only Chinese kids in my school because other kids say, "Americans rock but Chinese people don't." I don't say anything because I don't want to fight.

I am glad I have sisters who are Chinese. I would have doubts if I was the only Chinese person in my family. My sisters are 12, eight, and six, and I am nine.

An Mei (age 2), Yugan, Jiangxi, with Mummy.

BEING ADOPTED IS NO BIG DEAL
by Laurelin Haas (age 12)

BEING ADOPTED IS NO BIG DEAL. I have grown up knowing that I am different from other kids, but most of the time I forget that I am Chinese because no one ever treats me differently. If I don't act different, then I won't get treated differently. Of course there has to be some prejudice and stereotyping. You can't stop that.

I only have one friend at my school who is Chinese, and last time I checked, being Asian didn't bother her either. None of my other sisters have friends in their school who are Chinese either, but that doesn't bother them. In fact, my youngest sister, Sarah, is the most popular kid in her class.

At my middle school I didn't face any special treatment from other students because I was Chinese other than a couple questions. A lot of the kids didn't even know that I was adopted by the end of the year, and when I told them, they didn't treat me any differently.

I have been back to China twice—once when I was four, and once when I was five; so I don't really remember anything. I would love to go again, but now that we have four kids in the family, we may have to make two trips back to visit all of our hometowns.

Basically I'm just a normal American kid. I love to read and bike and watch T.V., and I've got some great friends. Just because I'm Chinese doesn't make me any different than anybody else. In fact I'm special in another way that most of the people I know aren't— because I'm Chinese.

Siblings—Kim (age 8), Guangdong; Corey (age 5), Hubei; Alia (age 3), Shaanxi; and Eli (age 3), Jiangsu.

Siblings—Sean (age 5), Fuzhou, Jiangxi; (in blue dress) Charlotte (age 3), Fuling, Chongqing; and Leah (age 5), Yangdong, Guangdong, with Mom.

Adopting as an Older, Single Parent
by Barbara Rappaport

THROUGH MY 20S, 30S, AND 40S I LIVED AND CRIED THROUGH NUMEROUS MISCARRIAGES, ALWAYS… ALWAYS… ALWAYS WANTING TO BE A MOTHER. I spent my entire 41st year crying every time I saw a commercial with babies or saw a mom holding a child's hand while walking down the street. Six months before I turned 49, I finally decided to fill out the adoption application that I had been holding onto for five years. Five years of looking at it, switching it from file to file, moving it from one place to another. On that day I actually mailed it to my agency.

That night I wrote in my journal how I was taking the biggest step of my life to adopt as a single mother who was almost 49. Oh, my God, what was I thinking? I then proceeded to have the biggest anxiety attack of my life. That night when I told an older Chinese woman in my neighborhood about my plans, she told me that she felt that my daughter had already been born in China and was waiting for me to bring her home.

Months later when I turned 50, two pieces of mail arrived in my mailbox. There they were together: my INS approval and my invitation to join AARP. Was this a good sign or a bad sign? Could I actually raise a child at my age? Would I have the strength or energy to keep up with her? My single and married friends in New York City either had no children or their children were already having their own children.

But then in August of 2000 I received my referral for a stunning 15-month-old girl from Shantou. It seems like I stood forever staring at that amazing little face in the tiny referral photo. This is my daughter? This *is* my daughter! I was overcome with emotion. I was now responsible for this precious life, half a world away.

Right before I traveled to bring Anna home, all of my fears resurfaced, and I questioned my ability to be a mom. I cried to my own mother that I couldn't do it, that I was making a mistake, that I had to cancel everything, that I was so afraid. But I got on that plane. The moment that Anna was put in my arms, even though she was screaming bloody murder, I knew that I was put on this earth to be this little girl's mommy. Forever.

Anna has filled a place in my heart that I never knew existed. She's my best friend. We learn from each other every day. She has made me young (don't tell my knees), and over the last six years she has given me a new and wonderful life. I love her more than anything on this earth. Now if I can only keep up with her dreams of being a rock star!

Cousins—Emma (age 4), Henan; Quinn (age 4), Jiangxi; Rami (age 2), Hunan; and Analise (age 7).

My Sister
by Emma Fuzhong Klinger (age 8)

The first day I saw my sister,
She frowned, she cried,
She even smiled for the first time.
After that, we took a bath.
She poured and I dumped cups of water.
We wiggled and giggled.
We were happy.

Cara (age 3), Hangzhou, Zhejiang—
giggling with her new sister, Emma (age 7), Longyan, Fujian.

Cost of taking my then 7-year-old daughter, Emma, along to adopt her 3-year-old sister, Cara: $1,088. Value: priceless. Cara may not have been ready to call me Mama for several days (that name belonged to her foster mom), but she was ready to claim Emma as her sister immediately. Within an hour of meeting, they giggled as they played. That night, they took a bath together, and the laughter reverberated off the bathroom walls. Cara's transition to our family was made so much easier by having her jie jie in China, and Emma had the priceless opportunity to witness the process that I had gone through to bring her home more than six years earlier.

How Do You Do It? Or…
It Takes A Village
by Donna Laurie

I AM A SINGLE MOTHER WITH FOUR CHILDREN. As long as I can remember, people have been saying things like, "How do you do it?" or "I don't know how you do it." When I announced that I was adding a fourth child to my family, I noticed a change in what people were saying to me. I began to hear, "I couldn't do what you do." At first I brushed that off. Of course anyone could do what I do. I am not superwoman, and there are a lot tougher things in this world than being a single mother to four. I am not so special, and I am not a perfect mother. I even tried to convince the people in my life that they too could open their homes to a child without a family.

But one day, after hearing those words again, "I could never do what you do," I stopped and really thought about why so many people feel that way, while I can't imagine not having added three Chinese daughters to the family that once consisted of just my son and me. It occurred to me that maybe it was true; maybe everyone can't do what I have done. In that moment I saw a bigger picture than I had seen before. It wasn't that I was so special, capable, or unusual. And it wasn't that my friends, family, and coworkers were any less so. It was because we all have a different purpose, a different role to play, a different piece to contribute. Because it really does take a village. It takes a friend who watches one of my daughters at soccer practice while I take the other one to a soccer field on the other side of town, and another who takes my children overnight so I can go on a business trip. It takes someone to run to day care when I am running late and someone to take three little girls shopping for Mom's birthday present. It takes grandparents who love every grandchild with all their hearts, regardless of how much or how little the family resemblance. It takes an uncle who takes a little boy to Cub Scout camp while I stay home with his baby sisters. It takes

Mom with Kristen (age 3), Fenyi, Jiangxi; Lindsey (age 7), Jiaozuo, Henan; and Marissa (age 9), Yangzhou, Jiangsu.

the stay-at-home mom who says that it's no trouble to take my kids to gymnastics and Girl Scouts when she takes her own children. It takes coworkers who never complain because I leave at 5:07 instead of well after 6:00, and it takes a boss who understands that a child's surgery comes before a business plan. And it takes a son who loves his sisters so completely that when asked if just one more is one too many replied, "It's not about me."

So now I see why everyone can't do what I do, but I hope that the people in my life understand that without their encouragement, their help, and their support, I could never do what I do either. So if you are someone who could "never do what I do," then look around because someone nearby needs you to be part of his or her village.

Siblings—Anna (age 3), Tam Key, Quang Nam, Vietnam; Alex (age 2), Xianyang, Shaanxi; and Amanda (age 5), Yixing, Jiangsu—enjoying a day with Mom at the Botanical Gardens in Singapore.

Journey to TianTian— Adopting a Six-Year-Old
by Donna Laurie

We met TianTian yesterday, and all has gone very well. She is a sweet and lively little girl. She has been well prepared for us and came to us willingly, although a bit shyly. She wouldn't speak, despite lots of encouragement and prodding. But, once everyone left our room, she opened up like a flower and was saying our names and pointing to everyone in the photo album we sent. She mimics extremely well and has awesome retention. She and her new big sister, Marissa, hit it off over coloring books and Silly Putty and DVDs. By evening they were being very silly together, laughing and tickling, and TianTian babbled at us in Chinese. She seems okay with the fact that we don't understand her.

Her English is coming along. Just words right now, but she is a little parrot. Some things she definitely understands; others she is just repeating. She loves calling "MomMee." I wrote *Lindsay* on her little erasable board, and before I could say anything she told me "Lindsay." We don't use this name right now, but she clearly knows it and understands that it means her. She can count in Mandarin and English too.

She has stuck to me like glue since yesterday morning. We spent time outside playing with friends, but she never showed any interest in staying with them over me. At bedtime she got her pajamas without a minute's hesitation, although I would have been fine if she returned to her own bed for the night. She and Marissa duked it out a bit overnight. TianTian fell out of bed once, and Marissa finally conceded and put a comforter on the floor just before dawn. Tonight should be even more fun. We are definitely looking forward to the king-size bed at the White Swan in Guangzhou!

Sisters—Christie (age 5), Ningxia, and Katie (age 6), Jiangsu.

Ryan (age 15) and Marissa (age 7), Yangzhou, Jiangsu, with new sister, Kristen Laurie (age 13 months), Fenyi, Jiangxi.

Sofia ZiTian (age 7), Xinhui, Guangdong—
New Year's Day in San Francisco.

Sofia running for a piece of her 7th birthday cake.

ELEPHANT SNOT, OR THE CHALLENGES OF AN OLDER CHILD ADOPTION
by Marji Hanson

OH, GOOD HECK! Our guide, Matthew, says it is perfectly normal and Chinese children are raised this way, but that still doesn't make it easy to take Nora's smart mouth. When asked if she wanted anything to drink at dinner, she said no. She always says no to everything. I think no is her first line of defense in a world gone crazy for her. When Matthew said something about misdialing a phone number, she called him a "fool pig face." Matthew says learning to talk tough is the Chinese way.

This morning Nora and YuYu were playing with a blanket spread on the floor. I looked up as Nora was trying to get YuYu to move, but since she doesn't know English, she was just hurting YuYu instead. I had to get stern, "*Ting! Bu yao na yang*"—"stop, you can't do that!" We instantly went from giggly play to big tears and loud wailing of "*Mama, Mama, Mama*"—and she did *not* mean me.

Later today we went to the Nanning Zoo with YuYu's foster parents. We arrived at the zoo in time for the morning variety show in the amphitheater. Before the show starts the audience is invited to feed elephants sweet potato chunks. As the elephants got closer to the edge of the arena, it became pretty chaotic. One cheeky fellow started reaching too far into the crowd, and Nora started to scramble and panic. I had to quickly get between that over-reaching trunk and my kid and pretty much got a full load of elephant snot all down the back of me. Matthew called me "hero mother," high praise in Chinese culture. However I was just glad that the laundry man was coming today. Oh, totally gross!

I know after four days with my new daughter, this entry should be more about Nora, but she's simply not letting me know what she's about. She is *loud* and exuberant when I'm not involved or she doesn't think I'm watching, she has a smart mouth, and she is very, very pretty, but that's all she will let me see so far. Add the language barrier to her dislike and distrust of me and we're still very much strangers.

Some people say that they've never considered adoption because they couldn't love someone else's child. When I hear something like that, I am overwhelmed with frustration. I immediately fell in love with Ellie and Mimi, my two daughters who were adopted as babies. I fell in love with YuYu, adopted at 4½ years of age, more gradually. Over time I have grown to love her every bit as truly, madly, and deeply as I love my first two. These are my children. I would without hesitation throw myself between them and any deadly, speeding object, e.g., bullets, trains, buses. As I type this I am looking at Nora sleeping next to YuYu, and I know I'm not there for her yet. Oh yeah, sure, I'd take a bus for her too, but out of obligation instead of love. But, to my credit, I did take a big stripe of elephant snot down my back for her on our fourth day together; so I know I'll get there for her too and hope the feeling will become mutual.

Sisters—Bailee (age 9), Yangchun, Guangdong;
Callee (age 4), Sanshui, Guangdong; Sammie (age 9),
Yangchun, Guangdong; and Maizie (age 4), Xiajiang, Jiangxi.

Brenna Meng-Jiao (age 5), Chenzhou, Hunan, with Mom.

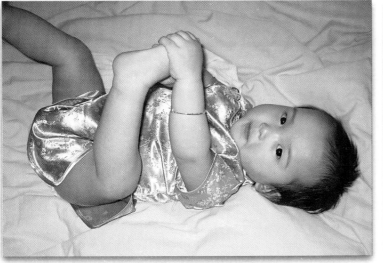

Kambry Hope (age 11 months),
XiuShan, Chongqing.

Kayden Faith (age 3),
Guigang City, Guangxi.

Siblings—Noah Xiang (age 2), Dingyuan, Anhui, and Mia XueQin (age 3), Changde, Hunan.

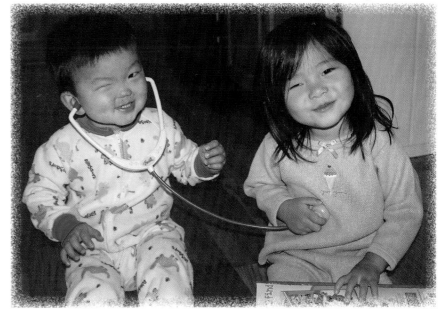

(Back row) Dad, Kuyler (age 18), and Kolton (age 11).
(Front row) Kayden Faith (age 3), Kenzie (age 10), Mom, and Kambry Hope (age 1).

Mia MeiLi (age 4½) and Meisi Jade (age 3), with their brother, Aaron (age 18).

Countries Participating in International Adoption

Taizhou, Jiangsu "sisters" and now friends in Canada— Kelly Yue-Lin (age 29 months) and Olivia Hui Hui (age 28 months)— receiving their Canadian citizenship certificates on Canada Day, July 1, 2005.

Alyssa (age 3), Yongzhou City, Hunan.

Canada

Sisters—Jane Min Ru (age 4), Baoji, Shaanxi, and Lana Rose JiaHuan (age 2), Ningdu, Jiangxi.

Maxwell (age 7), with sister, Eva Xu Lu Bo (age 2), Anqing, Anhui—with Acadian flags while on vacation in Cape Breton Island, Nova Scotia.

OUR CHINESE/CANADIAN GIRL
by Theresa Martin

DAVID AND I ARE THE HAPPY PARENTS OF A CHINESE/CANADIAN LITTLE GIRL, AND WE ARE RAISING HER TO BE PROUD OF BOTH CULTURES. When we adopted Kelly Yue-Lin Xiang in January 2004, at age 11 months, we promised that we would teach her about the customs and traditions of China and Canada. Finding the right balance between these cultures is one of our most important challenges.

Back in 2004 I couldn't wait for the last piece of adoption paperwork to finally be completed because the paper trail seemed endless. However, while waiting for Kelly's Canadian citizenship papers to come, I realized that soon her last connection to China would be gone.

Kelly still had her passport as Tai Xiang Yue, but soon she would no longer be a Chinese citizen. She would be like thousands of other girls and boys—cherished and loved by their new families but unable to keep their Chinese citizenship once officially welcomed into their new country. This is the bittersweet reality of Chinese adoptions.

Having Kelly learn about life in Canada has been so much fun. Our photo albums are full of wonderful pictures: Kelly's first steps, her birthdays, wearing rabbit ears at Easter, dressing up for Halloween night, going to swimming lessons, meeting Santa Claus, and opening presents at Christmas. And there are also cute photographs of ordinary days at home.

Finding meaningful ways to connect Kelly to her Chinese heritage would take much more thought. In April 2004 Kelly was baptized as a Catholic, wearing a red silk dress from China. It was a fitting way to honor Kelly's heritage by having her wear red, the color of celebration in China. The pictures turned out beautifully, and I hope someday Kelly will be very proud of the decision we made.

We have celebrated Chinese New Year, tried moon cakes, and decorated our home with items purchased in China. Because Kelly's birthday is so close to Chinese New Year, we have a new tradition where Kelly wears a silk outfit for her family party.

We have all learned new Mandarin phrases by watching Kelly's language videos. We have a growing book collection about Chinese adoptions, and we regularly look at our photo albums from our trip. On our Forever Family Day, we give Kelly a special gift from China. We hope that she will treasure these items and look forward to receiving a new surprise each year.

Kelly was officially welcomed as a new Canadian on Canada Day, 2005, at age 28 months. She wore a red and white dress and enjoyed waving her Canadian flag during the ceremony. Dave and I felt proud of how well Kelly has adjusted to her new life with us.

There will be new challenges along the way as we help Kelly understand her past, enjoy life now, and prepare for her future, but hopefully she will always be proud of her Chinese/Canadian heritage.

Jade Xiaoqing
(age 12 months),
Nanning, Guangxi,
with her brother Jarrah (age 6).

Australia

IN 2000, WESTERN AUSTRALIAN FAMILIES ADOPTED THE FIRST TWO CHILDREN FROM CHINA. Since then the number of adoptions has continually increased. According to the Australian Institute of Health and Welfare (AIHW), nationwide, between 2000 to 2001, there were 15 children adopted from China (one male and 14 females). Between 2001 to 2002 there were 39 children, in 2002 to 2003 there were 46 children, and from 2003 to 2004 there were 112 children adopted from China.

The child's visa to enter Australia is issued in Shanghai.

Australians go through the process in the following order: Inquiry, Education Program, Application, Assessment, Approval.

Jarrah (age 10); Jane Zhangyi (age 4), Gao'An City, Jiangxi;
Jade Xiaoqing (age 5), Nanning, Guangxi; and Mark (age 9). Siblings Jarrah and Jade are Australian-American citizens, and siblings Jane and Mark are Canadian citizens.

Julia (age 8), Fogang, Guangdong, with friend Ella (age 5), Hepu, Guangxi.

Mei Xiao Bin
(age 23 months),
Changsha, Hunan.

Xiaolan Molly Shi (age 9), Fogang, Guangdong.

Above and below:
Nina Cai (age 4),
Huizhou, Guangdong.

New Zealand

Ville Kang (age 4½), Shantou, Guangdong.

Sweden

Ellen (age 2½), Loudi, Hunan—on the famous Dala horse of Sweden.

(Fourth from left, seated) Ada Min (age 3), Nanchang, with children dressed up as Mallorquin farmers at Saint Anthony parade in Spain.

Spain

Susana Yi Qin, Yiyang, Hunan— in typical Spanish dress.

Irish Inter-country Adoption
by Rosemary Walshe

Our intercountry adoption journey started when we completed the initial application forms sent to us by the H.S.E. Southeastern Region in March 2002. These forms, one for each of us, included lengthy and required clearances, medical reports, referee details, as well as answers to a comprehensive list of questions relating specifically to our desire to adopt. Upon completion of the initial paperwork, we were told that it would probably be a year or thereabouts before we heard back with a date for a required pre-adoption course.

True to form, about a year later, the long awaited letter arrived, giving us details of the pre-adoption course. We finally felt that we were starting on our journey. The course was completed over an intensive three-day period—one day a week for three weeks. The first day was both interesting and daunting, and we went home with our heads spinning and our eyes very much opened. We were given homework to complete in an accompanying workbook, which covered numerous adoption related issues. It was great to meet other couples who were on the same journey as ourselves. Some of them seemed to have a great knowledge of the whole process and had already decided on their country of choice. We, on the other hand, were very much undecided and had at that stage only spoken to one other couple who had adopted from Romania. During the three days of the course, we listened to talks by other couples who had been through the whole adoption process, as well as viewed adoption videos, worked in breakout groups, and listened to talks by the social workers who made us realize that our journey ahead would not be easy. By the third day we were starting to feel a little more confident and relaxed in the knowledge that the majority of the other couples had experienced similar concerns to ourselves. This helped keep us focused and sustained over the past four plus years.

After completing the course, we were able to set up an initial meeting with our social worker. Due to a variety of factors, including receiving counseling (as was typically recommended by social workers), an extra year was added to the process. Eventually the social worker's report was presented to the committee just over three years from when we had set out on the journey.

We shortly received the good news that the committee deemed us as suitable to adopt, which paved the way for us to begin in earnest on preparing our dossier for China. The "to do" list looked pretty daunting to say the least, but we worked our way down the list, being careful to do everything correctly so our application with the CCAA would not be jeopardized. Finally, following notarization, we made the trip to Dublin to get our letter of authentication from the Supreme Court, our stamp of approval from the Department of Foreign Affairs, and our letter from the Chinese Embassy. Our dossier was then sent to the Adoption Board to double-check that everything was in order and to forward it to the CCAA. Our log-in date was September 30th. Since then we have been waiting patiently, and sometimes not so patiently, for news of our referral. It looks like our wait will be around 14 months long, requiring us to renew some of our documents. We have started to buy a few bits and pieces in anticipation of the arrival of our referral.

It has been a long and emotional journey for us both, and people wonder how we have kept positive for so long. Our family and friends, some of whom have been with us from the start, keep asking us if we have any news. We knew it wouldn't be an easy journey and that there would be pitfalls along the way, but thankfully we have overcome each of them so far. When we do get the referral call and make our journey to meet our new daughter, it will have been all worthwhile.

Eilidh Fu Yi (age 3), Desheng, Guangxi.

Scotland

Irish rugby supporters. Siblings—David (age 9); Meisha Ya Qian (age 3), Xinhua, Hunan; and Jake (age 12).

Ireland

Fleur (age 3), Loudi, Hunan.

Belgium

PANDA CLUB
by Sadie Carroll, Anne Wilson, and Sara Lavery

IN THE SPRING OF 2006, THREE FRIENDS WHO HAD RECENTLY ADOPTED BABIES FROM THE PEOPLE'S REPUBLIC OF CHINA WERE CONTEMPLATING THE QUESTION, "HOW DO WE MAINTAIN OUR DAUGHTER'S LINKS WITH THEIR BIRTH CULTURE?" We all attend the local CACH Summer and Winter parties and the Chinese New Year celebrations, but this did not seem sufficient to give our girls knowledge of Chinese culture and a sense of pride in their cultural heritage.

We devised a wish list: First, we wanted the girls to have a peer group of other children adopted from China. Second, we wanted them to have the opportunity to learn Mandarin, make Chinese crafts, and celebrate Chinese festivals. Third, we felt it would be useful for adoptive parents and those just starting the process to be able to meet regularly and support each other. In order to fulfil these wishes, we felt we needed either a good Chinese fairy with a magic wand or had to be proactive and do something ourselves. In the absence of a good fairy, but with the support of other adoptive and adopting families in Central Scotland, we started the Central Scotland Chinese Adoption Support Group and a Chinese playgroup, which we call Panda Club.

Panda Club now meets once a month in Stirling. Around nine families attend each month, with ten Panda Club members between the ages of 20 months and six years. The meetings last about two hours and include a welcome to the children from "Xiong Mao," our Panda bear glove puppet, and an opening song sung in Mandarin. Then one of the parents will introduce the festival for that month (we always manage to find one!), before our lao shi, or teacher, teaches 30 to 45 minutes of "fun Mandarin." After snack time we have a Chinese craft, which is usually linked to that month's festival, and we finish with either another song or a Chinese story. Some of the highlights of our festival celebrations have been making paper dragon boats and racing them across a paddling pool and performing a puppet show of the story of Chang E and Hou Yi for the Moon Festival. A new development has been organizing separate language lessons for the adults, so that we can encourage the girls' efforts to learn Mandarin.

The meetings are fun and sociable. Parents and parents-to-be are able to share information and support each other through the ups and downs of inter-country adoption. We are very happy that our wishes have come true. In the future we hope to positively raise the profile of inter-country adoption in Central Scotland and that the Panda Club continues to thrive.

Finland

As of 2004, 461 children were adopted from China to Finland. Adoptions are processed by the Finnish Board of Inter-Country Adoptions Affairs.

Sisters—Ma Ling (age 5), Nanning, Guangxi, and My Ping (age 9), Qingyuan, Guangdong.

Sisters—Amanda Jun (age 4), Yiyang, Hunan, and Johanna Rigmor (age 2), XiuShui, Jiangxi.

Friends—Catarina Annabelle Fuhong (born July 2001), Changting, Fujian, and Johanne Zhangjia (born June 2002), Gao, Jiangxi.

Norway

There are three approved adoption agencies in Norway. One-fourth of the children adopted in Norway are from China.

On average an adoptive family in Norway can expect to wait three to six months for their social report to be completed and then another three to four months to finalize their application with an agency.

Icelandic Adoption
by Ólöf R Ámundadóttir

The Icelandic Adoption Society (IAS) was founded in 1978 by adoptive parents as a voluntary nonprofit organization. In January 1988 the Society opened an office in Reykjavík. IAS is the only organization working in the field of international adoptions in Iceland. It is authorized by the Ministry of Justice to assist residents of Iceland to adopt children from abroad.

The IAS takes responsibility for compulsory parent preparation courses, the preparation of the adoption dossiers, sending dossiers abroad, and assisting the family in planning the trip to meet and bring home the adopted child. Records are kept of every child and his or her family, and follow-up reports are sent to the child's country of birth. The organization also hosts several social meetings, such as annual Christmas parties, weekend trips, and bi-monthly meetings for children and their families. The IAS issues a newsletter and has published educational brochures.

The IAS works with a number of countries. The largest group of children in Iceland is adopted from India. Other countries of origin in addition to China are Sri Lanka, Indonesia, Colombia, and Guatemala, to name a few. The first group of children adopted from China came home in May 2002. Since then 94 girls and one boy have been adopted from the provinces of Guangdong, Hubei, Hunan, Chongquing, Jiangxi, and Guangxi.

The process after the application is sent to IAS until Advance Approval is issued takes about four to eight months. During that time a social worker does a home study of the applicants and their families. After the Advance Approval is received, the dossier is translated into English, and adoption dossiers for a group of families are sent together to China. In 2005, Icelandic families adopted 35 children from China. Adoption of children from China with special needs began in 2006.

Sigrún Meng (age 20 months)—
an Icelandic girl from Guangxi.

Dressed in traditional Icelandic sweaters—Sara Rós Lin (age 10 months), Árný Thelma (age 23 months), Guðrún Edda Min (age 16 months), Margrét Lin (age 11 months), Alfa Magdalena (age 23 months), and Annalei Róslín Hai (age 16 months), all from Guangxi.

Iceland

Ásgerður Jing (age 3), Hubei, with her grandmother on Jing's baptism day on June 17, 2005, Icelandic National Day.

The first group of Icelandic girls adopted from China. Þórdís (mother of Hildur Björg), Hildur Björg, Jóhanna Lan, Ragnhildur, Sunna Líf Zan, Áslaug Rún, Sunna Lind, Líney Rut, Ninna (age 2, little sister of Liney Rut) and Stella Tong. All the girls except Ninna are age 5 and from Guangdong.

Sisters—Xanne Fu Shen (age 2), Cenxi, Guangxi, and QiQi Xiao Hua (age 5), Yangdong, Guangdong.

Xiu Mei (age 3½), Wuchuan, Guangdong.

Netherlands

Sisters—Xia Lu (age 9), Jingmen, Hubei, and Yue (age 6), Bengbu, Anhui.

Ying Xin Louise (nearly age 2), Wenzhou, Zhejiang, with her mother.

ADOPTION FROM THE NETHERLANDS
by Karen Visser

WE ARE KAREN AND PEPIJN AND LIVE IN THE NETHERLANDS WITH OUR BIOLOGICAL SON, CASPER (BORN 2002), AND OUR ADOPTED DAUGHTER, YING XIN (BORN 2004). When Casper was only nine months old, we started the paperwork for the adoption of a foreign child. When I tried to get pregnant with Casper, we already discussed the alternatives if it would not go as smoothly as we planned. We both agreed that we did not want to pursue all medical options. Obviously you can only cross that bridge (or not) when you really get there. Adoption, to us, seemed a chance to combine our desire for a second child with the opportunity to help a child somewhere in the world—a child with less chances than our own son already had. Since we knew it takes about four to five years in our country from the first form to "touch down" on the airport with your child, we started sooner than we would have done with a second biological child. In the end it would take us about three years. The main reason for a shorter

period was our choice to adopt a child with a special need.

We started to read about the possibilities, the Dutch agencies available, and the choices we had to make. China was one of the few countries we could adopt from as a great number of countries prefer parents who are unable to conceive a child or parents with a specific religious profile. Very early on it became clear for us that we wanted to adopt a child with a special need. As we explained it to our family and friends: "If we adopt, why open the door just a little bit and let only 'perfect' children in?"

In our country you cannot browse through files; the match between parents and child is made by the agency, and they do not consult you beforehand—apart from determining what your boundaries are regarding the special needs. Then there are age limits. Dutch law does not allow an age difference of more than 40 years between the child and the youngest parent. The maximum age for adoption is 46. Our agency also has a policy that the age difference with the other child in the family has to be at least two years, thus resulting in a "natural" order of children. We waited anxiously.

In September 2005 we got the referral of Ying Xin from Wenzhou, Zhejiang, China. She is 21 months younger than our son. Her special need is Poland's Syndrome. (This means she has a left arm that stops just below the elbow and a small left hand with only two fingers.) We were the happiest parents ever! Gotcha Day was on February 20, 2006. She was a reserved, wary child who did not cry when given to us but looked at us as if we were from Mars—which we were, if you think about it. Nine months later she is a funny and sweet girl with a great sense of humor and increasing self-confidence. She is a picky eater, talks more and more in her new language, and loves conspiring with her older brother where to hide best so as to scare Mommy. We enjoy having her around every day and can't imagine our family life without her.

Sally (nearly age 6), Qi Dong, Hunan.

Denmark

Esther (nearly age 4), Wuchuan, Guangdong.

France

United Kingdom

Lily (age 4), Dingyuan, Anhui, with siblings—LiZhi (age 2), Bengbu, Anhui, and MeiXi (age 4), Dingyuan, Anhui.

Singapore

By agreement between the Chinese and Singapore governments, effective from April 2004, all Singaporeans seeking to adopt Chinese children must apply to the CCAA through two authorized agencies— Fei Yue Community Services and Touch Community Services.

Sisters—Sarah (age 2), Youxian, Hunan, and Kate (age 3½), ZhuZhou, Hunan.

Elizabeth LiHan
(age 11 months),
Hanchuan, Hubei.

United States

China Moms Maryland friends celebrating July 4th.
(Front row) Emma Fuzhong (age 6), Longyan, Fujian; Elisabeth Liu (age 5), Chongqing;
Molly Mei-Li (age 4), YiYang, Hunan; and Amy Yingtong (age 3), Wuzhou, Guangxi.
(Back row) Liah (age 7) Yangchun, Guangdong; Jamie Lin Jiang Hua (age 7),
Zhenjiang, Jiangsu; and Sarah FuRui (age 7), Longyan, Fujian.

Sisters—Ginny (age 5), Yangchun, Guangdong,
and Rebecca (age 3), Nanchang, Jiangxi.

Siblings—Miriam (age 3), Chongqing; Carl (age 7);
Bethany (age 6), Yangchun, Guangdong; and Christian (age 9).

Savannah (age 3), Yangchun, Guangdong, with Mom.

Close friends—
Lily Fu Hui Hua and
Mary FuHui Ying
(both age 3),
both from Fuling—
celebrating July 4th.

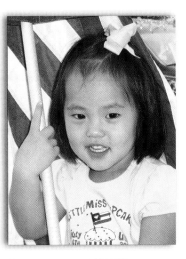

Happy 4th of July.
Madeline Susan YuWei
(nearly age 3),
Chengdu, Sichuan.

Claire Gabrielle Mei
(age 20 months),
Chenzhou, Hunan.

Ella (age 2), YiYang, Jiangxi.

On the day that Ella was in the United States
for the same number of days as she had been in China
(Half-Life Day), a flag was flown in her honor over
the U.S. Capitol. Pictured here is Ella with that flag.

Lianne (age 2),
Shijiazhuang,
Hebei.

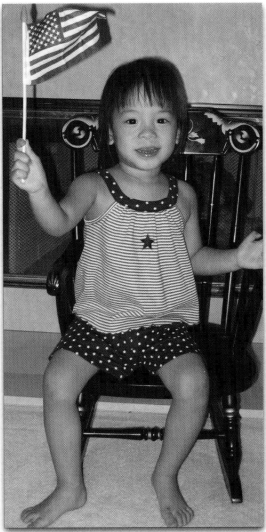

Ashley (age 30 months), Yangjiang, Guangdong—
proud to be an American!

Cherishing the Tapestry

There is an old analogy that compares our lives to that of a tapestry.
From the back all one sees are random and chaotic threads and knots.
There seems to be no rhyme nor reason to the imperfect order.

Chloe ZhiHong (age 3),
Changsha, Hunan.

Madeline Jade (age 8),
Chongqing, Sichuan.

Chunfan Ziran (age 6),
Huainan, Anhui.

Faith (age 3),
Shangrao, Jiangxi.

Lianne Marie (age 8),
Jingdezhen, Jiangxi.

Molly (age 1½),
Beihai City, Guangxi.

But when one steps to the front, suddenly the realization comes that every stitch and every knot is important, and that they all fit together to form one magnificent picture.

In international adoption there are hundreds of stitches and knots along the way. We rejoice that we can share in our children's new lives and yet mourn what we know they have lost. We study and celebrate Chinese culture, we honor birthparents and caregivers, we find ways to give back to those who still wait. And yet we often find ourselves struggling to find the answers to our children's very real and honest questions. We join adoption groups, make online friends, and begin to understand both the challenges and joys of being multi-racial families.

So many stitches, so many knots, as two cultures combine into one unique creation. When we step to the front of the tapestry of adoption, we do indeed see wonder. We look at the complex design and see a magnificent picture that reflects unconditional love, commitment, and the strong and beautiful bonds of family.

Adopting from China is an incredible journey. We begin by clinging tightly to that single red thread and then watch in wonder as the fabric of our family is woven together. We realize that the beauty of these unique tapestries will impact generations to come. Our children's stories will be passed down to their children and their grandchildren, creating a cherished heirloom to celebrate and honor forever.

Matthew Wayland (age 12), Chuzhou, Anhui, with his new family at the Summer Palace in Beijing.
(Left to right) Matthew, Brian (age 13), Mom, (standing in front of Mom) Ally (age 7), Nicole (age 15), Robyn (age 11), Dad, and Grandma.

ONE HUNDRED WISHES
by Maresa Fitzhenry

ONE OF THE THINGS WE LEARNED WHEN WE STARTED OUR ADOPTION PROCESS WAS THAT THERE ARE YAHOO GROUPS FOR EACH MONTH OF DOSSIERS SENT TO CHINA (DTC). We joined and have now made lots of friends from all over the world. In the group we have exchanged lots of stories—some funny, some sad. We learn a lot from each other and help each other out wherever possible. There was a postcard swap, with each containing a wish for the children we will hopefully someday adopt. There is also a birthday card swap for all the mums and dads. Now the group is currently organizing the second 100 good wishes quilt swap.

We were really excited when we heard the May 2006 DTC Group was organizing the quilt swap as we had heard lots about it from others and even had a book about it. The 100 good wishes quilt, or Bai Jia Bei, is a tradition in some parts of China. It is the custom to invite 100 people to contribute a single square. The squares are then sewn into a quilt containing the luck, energy, and good wishes of all who contributed to it. So far we have received over 45 squares and wishes for our quilt. We are hoping that by the end of the year we will have our 100 wishes so we can start putting the quilt together! It is hard to pick out our favorite wishes, but here is a selection that we have received so far:

Is maith an scáthán súil charad
A friend's eye is a good mirror
Maireann croí éadrom i bhfad
A light heart lives long.

BAI JIA BEI
by Becky Neustadt

WE ARE WORKING ON CREATING A "100 GOOD WISHES QUILT" FOR OUR DAUGHTER, CARLI. There is a tradition in the northern part of China to make a Bai Jia Bei, or 100 Good Wishes Quilt, to welcome and celebrate a new life. It is custom to invite 100 people to contribute a single square patch of cloth along with a "good wish" note. The 100 patches are sewn together into a quilt that contains the luck, energy, and good wishes from all the families and friends who contributed a piece of fabric and a wish. The wishes are collected and placed in an album for the child to read and to know how widely and deeply he or she is cherished. The quilt is then passed down from generation to generation. We want Carli to know how much she is loved by her family and friends and how we will always celebrate her being a part of our family.

(Back) Dad and Andrew (age 18). (Front) Emily (age 15); Nathan (age 9); Grace (age 21 months), Taihe, Jiangxi; and Mom.

We didn't give you the gift of life,
But in our hearts we know.
The love we feel is deep and real,
As if it had been so.
For us to have each other
Is like a dream come true!
No, we didn't give you
The gift of life,
Life gave us the gift of you.
Author Unknown

One last road to travel
One last way to go
One more day forever
Just to let you know
The wait is finally over
The journey now is through
And now this comes to let you know
Dreams really do come true.
Author Unknown

An Irish Prayer
May God give you…
For every storm, a rainbow,
For every tear, a smile,
For every care, a promise,
And a blessing in each trial.
For every problem life sends,
A faithful friend to share.
For every sigh, a sweet song,
And an answer for each prayer.

A Wish for a Friend
Wishing you a rainbow
For sunlight after showers—
Miles and miles of Irish smiles
For golden happy hours—
Shamrocks at your doorway
For luck and laughter too,
And a host of friends that never ends
Each day your whole life through!

RETURNING
by Amelia Mowery

WHEN WE RECEIVED THE REFERRAL FOR OUR SECOND DAUGHTER, ELIZABETH, WE WERE THRILLED TO DISCOVER THAT SHE SHARED OUR OLDER DAUGHTER'S FIRST HOME IN FULING. During the two years since we first held Kathryn, we had the opportunity to know other families who had also adopted from Fuling through a parent group and website. We had a feeling of having "been there and done that" as far as our travel expectations and felt very comfortable as we prepared for our trip.

What I couldn't prepare myself for was my reaction as we walked through the gates of the orphanage for the second time. There was a flood of emotion as memories of our first moments of parenthood washed over me, and then they were pushed out of the way by the excitement of meeting our new daughter. We were greeted by the director with a warm hug, as if we were old friends, but we felt the anxious anticipation of the new life we were getting ready to begin.

The whole day had been completely surreal, and I couldn't help but feel like I was watching it all happen from the outside. I was brought back to reality in the instant that I saw my baby girl brought into the room. Everything else went away, and all I saw was my sweet Elizabeth.

Keli Zhan Yin (age 3½), Nanning, Guangxi, with new sister, Mali FuMa (age 4), Shaoguan, Guangdong— on Mali's adoption day.

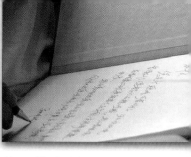

Above: The Suzhou, Jiangsu, orphanage director wrote a note inside a book to Anna to read when she grows up. Photo taken by Anna's brother, Christian.

Left: Sisters—Faith (age 3), Qinzhou, Guangxi, and Anna (age 3), Suzhou, Jiangsu—beginning to bond. Anna had been home for three days.

GIFTS TO SHARE
by Lisa Kaden, Executive Director, *Sending Our Love: Destination China*

IF YOU HAVE BEEN GIVEN A GIFT, IS IT BETTER TO HOLD IT CLOSE, HIDDEN FROM THE WORLD? Or to hold it out at arm's length, for all the world to see?

We are all gifted with special talents in a wide variety of arenas. The key is tapping into your gifts and seeking out how to utilize them. It is important to keep in mind that no gift is worthless or lesser in value than another. If we all possessed the same talents and skills, we could have a million heart surgeons and no hospitals for them to work in. "Giving back" to our children's birth country involves taking a closer look at our own interests and hobbies—at least that is what I told my older daughters after we returned home from our first adoption trip in 2003. They were looking for a way to help make a difference in the lives of the children we left behind and were feeling inadequate because they were merely children themselves. At the ages of ten and seven, they discovered that their passion for China and their love of art could be combined to create something really wonderful—a fundraising charity. They now share their love for China, spread the message of adoption, and impact the lives of beautiful children every time they sit down to sketch and paint. As Sending Our Love: Destination China develops, they are not only discovering the joy of giving and helping those in need but also are challenging themselves to move outside of their own comfort zones to spread their message of love. We aren't trained to perform miracles in an operating room, or powerful in the business world with "connections" to raise large sums of money. We are just a family in Wisconsin giving a little of ourselves. We all have gifts to share; remember that none is too small. You are valuable and have something of value to offer the world. Just stretch out your arms… and share.

"You may not be able to give every child the world, but to one child you may *be* the world."

Above: Ella (age 3), YiYang, Jiangxi—
celebrating her third birthday.

Below: Original artwork by Ella (age 3).
Ella often talks about her four moms:
her birthmother, her foster mother,
her mom (*me*!), and her godmother.
She told me that she drew me as
the only mom with a smile because
I am the only one who gets
to be with her every day!

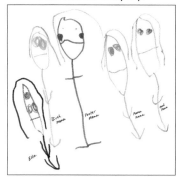

Siblings—Tallon (age 6)
and Chloe ZhiHong (age 3),
Changsha, Hunan.

Tea Time
by Norene Adams

MY DAUGHTERS, QUITE BY ACCIDENT, CREATED A WONDERFUL TRADITION FOR OUR FAMILY. Several years ago at an orphanage reunion for my oldest daughter, Marita, we were given a bag of tea from her hometown. Since the actual name of the tea was written in Chinese, we just referred to it as "Shantou tea."

Having Shantou tea became a regular part of our celebrations. We would have Shantou tea for Thanksgiving and Christmas dinner; to ring in the New Year; and to celebrate Chinese New Year, adoption day, and birthdays.

One day my youngest daughter, Ella, then age two, said that she wanted Shantou tea with dinner. "Is today a special occasion?" I asked. She responded, "Yes. I was not crabby at all today!" Now that *is* a special occasion! So as I was making the tea she informed me that we had to use "special" cups. I asked her which cups she had in mind, and she pointed to the china cabinet where my grandmother's china is stored. I had not used this china in many years, but upon her insistence I brought it out on that day.

It was a moment that will remain with me forever as I watched my daughters celebrate this very special occasion with tea from their homeland in tea cups from their great-grandmother. Ella is named after my grandmother, and I have to wonder if she might have whispered this idea to Ella that day to celebrate the extraordinary within the ordinary. She would have embraced this tradition, and I love that she is a part of it.

We now celebrate all of our important moments: getting an "A" on a spelling test, becoming potty-trained, participating in dance recitals, losing a tooth, going to the first day of school and the last day of school—and, of course, not being crabby all day—with a cup of Shantou tea in Great-grandma's tea cups.

Emily Qian, with Mom on Easter Sunday.

Sisters! Mia (age 4), Jingxi, Guangxi,
and Ellie (age 2), Hengyang, Hunan.

A Snapshot in Time
by Chantal Cagle and Karen Eikenberry

IT IS NOT OFTEN THAT A PHOTOGRAPH PROVIDES A GLIMPSE INTO BOTH THE PAST AND THE FUTURE. But for two families a chance sending of a disposable camera ahead to the orphanage did just that. For single mom Chantal Cagle, adopting her third daughter from China, the photographs provided a treasured look into the life her daughter lived before she arrived home. For Steve and Karen Eikenberry, the photographs showed them the daughter they didn't know they were waiting for.

It all started out with a handful of orphanage photographs. In almost every photo of Alia there was another little girl as well. The little girl seemed so prominent in Alia's photographs, and Alia was so animated when she saw her friend's face. Her mom wanted to put a name to the face and preserve another tiny bit of her daughter's past.

While Chantal was in the process of corresponding with the orphanage and volunteers that worked there, the Cagles and the Eikenberrys were enjoying a Sunday dinner together, looking through newly adopted Alia's photographs. All were struck by the evident bond that these two girls seemed to have had during their time in the orphanage.

The Eikenberrys had also adopted from China and were happily settled into parenthood of one child. So what was it that drew them to consider, out of the blue, the adoption of another child—an older waiting child? Alia's friend's special need was a birthmark on her face. Her paperwork had been sent to the CCAA, and she had a preliminary referral to a family in Europe. For some reason they didn't proceed with the adoption. Karen couldn't believe a child would be left behind for such a minor need.

The search was on now—not to just put a name to a photograph, but to bring a little girl home to her forever family and to reunite orphanage friends. Anyone who has ever tried to find a child in an orphanage from a glimpse of a random snapshot can tell you the odds are almost impossible. Yet those who have dealt with red threads can also tell you the impossible happens when it is meant to be. The first break came when a volunteer at the orphanage emailed Chantal to let her know the paperwork for the little girl, Chun Yu, known as Katie by the Western volunteers, was being sent to a U.S. adoption agency, but she had no way of finding out which agency. Chantal began contacting everyone she could think of who had insight into the waiting children program, trying to figure out where Katie's paperwork might be. Karen contacted many agencies but with little luck at first. Then an email came from one of the agencies a few weeks later. The little girl, Chun Yu, was on another agency's list.

It wasn't until the Eikenberrys were in China visiting Alia's and Katie's orphanage that they learned that Katie had two previous adoptions fall through. The orphanage director had decided not to submit her paperwork a third time to CCAA but changed his mind when he heard the story of a family who was waiting to bring her home. Just a few weeks shy of Alia's first Gotcha Day, Katie came home to her forever family and friend, Alia. Now two photo albums are tucked away to someday provide a glimpse into two little girls' pasts.

Above: Angela, Tian, Maliah, ShenHua, Lydia, and Shayna (all age 9 except Lydia, age 8½), all from Jiangxi—meeting at Lake Tahoe to rekindle and build friendships.

Below: Makena (age 6), Fuzhou, Jiangxi, and Maliah (age 8), Xinyu, Jiangxi, with new sister, Mierra (age 3), Fenyi, Jiangxi.

RAISING "OUR" DAUGHTER
by Julie Elkes

MY ONLY THOUGHT WHEN WE RECEIVED OUR DAUGHTER WAS THAT SHE WAS BEAUTIFUL—A PRECIOUS GIFT FROM GOD. I loved her so much at that moment, and my only thought of her Chinese parents was how sad they would not be able to see her grow up, or know what a beautiful child they had, or get to see her accomplishments. I cried for them, knowing there was so much they would miss in her life.

Today I think more and more about the Chinese parents who made the decision to leave their daughter in a public place so that she could be found. Whether they know their daughter is adopted or not, I feel now it is our responsibility to her parents, as well as to our daughter, that we raise her with the good intentions and expectations I think her Chinese parents would have had for her: that she be educated, that she be given opportunities to discover her abilities, and that she be loved for who she is—a wonderfully sweet-natured, smart, funny, and loving child who has so much potential for her life.

I also think that we should honor her Chinese parents by teaching her about China and its language, customs, holidays, history, art, and culture. We want her to be proud of who she is and where she came from.

My hopes are that someday these children, if they so desire, will be able to find a way to meet their Chinese parents. If our daughter someday wants to know who her Chinese parents are, I don't believe it means we will be loved less as her adoptive parents. I understand the inclination to want to know who you are… and part of that answer will come from her Chinese parents.

Referral photo of Kenzie (age 15 months), Changsha, Hunan.

And last, I would give anything to say to them "thank you." Thank you for giving her life and, in doing so, enriching the world for her presence. Thank you because your decision gave us the joy and blessing of being her parents. And I'd share with them all the pictures, video, and milestones they had missed—so they would know how much this beautiful child is loved.

A happier and stylish Kenzie (age 3). What a change from her referral picture! She is by every definition happy, outgoing, and fun-loving.

VISITING TAIZHOU
by Nora Tai-Xiu Groves (age 11)

THIS SUMMER I WENT TO CHINA!! China is so beautiful. I didn't know it was going to be so pretty and so much fun to tour. This is what I wrote in my diary:

> Dear Diary,
> This trip is going to be so so so exciting. I'm expecting people to look at me or actually come up and talk to me. And I'm expecting to have the funnest time of my life!!!!!! I can't wait to see my orphanage. I can't believe I'm going to see it. I want to see if any of the helpers remember me or if they're still there. I'm going with my cousin Sarah and my mom, Martha. Well, bye for now.

While on the trip I got to visit where I had lived as a baby. It was so interesting to see my orphanage, the Taizhou Social Welfare Institution. We looked through our adoption files and then toured two rooms filled with babies. A woman came over to me and called me by my Chinese name, Tai Xiu. It turned out that she had been one of my caregivers when I was in the orphanage until my mom adopted me in 1994. My mom, by coincidence, had brought a picture of the same woman holding me in the Nanjing hotel where my mom met me. My mom cried when she saw the caregiver and showed her the picture.

After we toured the baby rooms, we headed to a restaurant for a banquet with the orphanage staff. On the way the vans pulled over, and the orphanage doctor told us that we were across the street from the "finding location for Tai Xiu." (I'm not even sure that was the right place!) He told us we could not get out of the van but could take a picture through the van window. The place is now a park, but he told us that when I was found there, it was a grassland. Then we drove by the finding locations for the other three girls. After the banquet we toured a memorial to Mei Lanfang, a famous Beijing opera star who grew up in Taizhou. (Hu Jintao, China's president, also grew up in Taizhou.)

I liked visiting the orphanage a lot. I communicated with the babies. It was fun. It brought up feelings, wondering what I must have felt like when I was there. As for Taizhou, it felt like home. I wish I could be there right now.

Siblings—Mary and Luke—celebrating the Chinese New Year with friends—Natalie and Lily.
Mary Catherine Fu Hui Ying (age 3), Fuling, Chongqing; Natalie Zihui (age 3), Gaozhou, Guangdong; Luke (age 6); and Lily Fu HuiHua (age 3), Fuling, Chongqing.

Grace (age 6), Changsha, Hunan— enjoying herself at an adoption agency picnic.

NEW YEAR'S CELEBRATION
by Joy C. Lenz

THE SOUND OF DRUMMING IS EVERYWHERE, POUNDING IN MY EARS AND PULSING THROUGH MY BODY. The lion dancers are leaping around in front of me, swaying and bowing and blinking their long-lashed eyes. Little girls scream in delight and half fear, jumping back when the lions come near. My husband is holding our 12-month-old, Katherine, who is watching the commotion with a huge grin on her face. She screams with excitement and claps her hands. I want to freeze the whole scene and watch it again in slow motion. It is our first Chinese New Year.

We have gathered this evening in a church gymnasium to celebrate a holiday for the sake of our daughters. There are about 200 people here tonight at this Families with Children from China gathering. We all have, or will soon have, daughters or sons from the People's Republic of China. Nearly all of the adults here are Caucasian. We are Kansans, from the heart of the Midwest. Most of us barely knew that a lunar new year existed until we made the adoption journey. All of us were changed by the trip to China and what we encountered there. We want our children to be proud of their birth country and its long and beautiful history; so we have created tonight. We have embraced Chinese New Year and made it our own, imperfect though it may be.

Katherine is too young to join in the making of a glorious dragon, fashioned out of crepe paper and streamers, but she eagerly watches as dozens of children climb underneath it and join the dancing lions in a parade around the room. All of the kids are wearing Chinese silk clothes. As they flit about the gym, they look like shiny rainbow-colored butterflies. Katherine is wearing silk too—the red tunic and pants embroidered with peonies that she wore on her first birthday. On her feet are red squeaky shoes, bought in Guangzhou, and she is wearing tiny bracelets of red thread and pearls. She is resplendent in all her finery.

After the dancing we eat Chinese food catered from a local restaurant. It's not quite the same as the food we all ate in our children's birth country, but we slurp noodles and eat bits of pork and remember other delicacies. Katherine is fascinated by the shiny red decorations strung along the walls—lanterns, good luck calligraphy, red thread knots. Someone has made paper roosters to decorate the tables, welcoming in this Year of the Rooster. Later I learn that each family brings what decorations they have collected and adds them to the pile. With everyone's contributions, the room is transformed.

Several adults walk around passing out "lucky" red envelopes. Katherine receives one embossed with peaches and rosy-cheeked children. Inside is a one-dollar bill. She waves the envelope around, happy with her new prize. I look around at the tables scattered across the room. These are people who listened and prayed for us during the endless waiting time. They have also rejoiced with us as Katherine has joined our lives. The families that went before us are showing the way to the future, and tonight, home only three months, Steve and I have found ourselves listening and encouraging families still waiting. It's a wonderful web of support.

It's hard to believe that only two years ago, I never knew events like this existed. I am so glad to have been a part of this loud, bright, glorious holiday. As we leave into the wintry night, I wave and shout, "Gung hay fat choy!" and start dreaming about next year. What will it be like to welcome in the Year of the Dog?

Siblings—Elena (age 4); Talia (age 2), XianYang, Shaanxi; and Nathan (age 6).

WHO ADOPTED WHO?
by Joe Hampton
Proudly adopted by Joy XiuYang
and Hope XiaHong

YOU DON'T PLAY FAIR. You didn't follow the script.

I was supposed to be the hero. Your Knight in Shining Armor (that's me) was supposed to ride in, rescue the Infant Orphan (that's you), and whisk her away to safety.

But then you smiled. And your eyes twinkled with delight. And, oh, those dimples!

That's all it took.

Your magic wand of a smile instantaneously transformed a cynical, burned-out, worn-slick geezer into a new creature—completely and utterly captivated by the spell you cast so innocently.

Thank you, little one, for adopting me. You are my hero.

Wynter (age 4), Huainan, Anhui—at the Festival of World Cultures in Dublin, Ireland.

Siblings—Molly Qingting (age 6), Nanning, Guangxi; Stephen Karl Zhishang (age 8), Nanning, Guangxi; and Meili Joy (age 9½), Liuzhou, Guangxi.

DEAR CHINA MOTHER
by Laura Mitchell (Xin), (age 7)

May 25, 2005

Dear Mother in China,

I love you, and I wish I could live with you and be with you. I like it in America. It is fun. I am six right now. I like to play sports. I am doing t-ball right now. I am going to do summer camp and I will do karate and do arts and crafts and do Vacation Bible School and choir camp. We will go to the pool too. In the winter I will be playing basketball. I have two brothers and one sister. My brother James, he likes to wrestle with me. He sometimes doesn't get hurt. I like books. I like Magic Tree House books.

Sometimes my dad takes me to his work and sometimes I get a Happy Meal at McDonald's. We have Shrek music. All the kids like to dance around. I run and I wrestle with James. My sister doesn't like when we wrestle. She always gets hurt. Shrek music makes us happy. We have other music that we dance to. But it is not the best as the Shrek music.

I have one brother and one sister from China. My sister is the Year of the Dragon and my brother is the Year of the Horse. And I am the Year of the Tiger! My mom, my other brother, and my dad are the Year of the Sheep.

There are five people moving in our neighborhood. And my teacher lives near me. And my friend Ryan, who is in my class, lives near me too. I have lots of friends in the neighborhood.

Do you have a son? Do you have a daughter? Do you know God? Do you have a husband? Are you poor or not?

I have no cavities right now. I might get some when I get older. I'm not sure.

I have a Grandma and a Grandpa. And I have a Nana and a Pop Pop.

I am sad because I cannot talk to you with my voice. I'm happy because I can at least write a letter and tell you what is happening in my life.

I sleep with my sister, and our bedroom walls are purple. Sometimes we don't get along very well. Mostly we do. The best part about school is recess and snack, science, math, and language.

Love,
Xin

Above: Pingnan, Guangxi red thread sisters—
Sage (age 11 months) and Jenna (age 16 months).

Below: The red thread has wound from Pingnan, Guangxi to North Carolina. Jenna (age 5) and Sage (age 4) get together a few times per year.

Margaret Lin Chen (age 1), Xiaonan, Xiaogan, Hubei, with her daddy. Photo taken on Margaret's first birthday, which also happened to be the day she was first placed in our arms.

JOURNEY TO HEPU
by Aileen Berry

EVEN AT 9 A.M. THE DAY WAS STEAMY—THE TEMPERATURE MOVING INESCAPABLY TOWARDS 30 DEGREES C. It would go even higher during the day—almost to 40—with the humidity staying above 80 percent until after 6 p.m. But inside the air-conditioned van, we were reasonably comfortable.

Ella and Shay were in the rear of the bus, enjoying the sort of freedom that comes with no seat belts. The rest of us had our hearts in our mouths at first, but the girls sat (or slept) quietly for much of the trip.

Initially they bobbed around on the back seat, watching the traffic behind us. Not long into our trip, our driver stopped to queue for petrol. Hawkers, spotting the Westerners on board, clamoured at the sides of the bus, offering us fresh peaches, lychees, and bananas. The hawkers and attendants alike were fascinated to see two small Chinese girls with obvious Westerners.

The journey south to Hepu was very comfortable on wide, uncrowded highways and with lots of toll roads. Our guide, Roger, told us that the price of the tolls kept people off the highways unless they had good reason to spend the money.

The countryside that surrounds the freeway is lush and green, punctuated by small villages of run-down buildings, occasional shacks, and the odd highway stretching out underneath a road bridge. We were fascinated by the large plantations of eucalyptus that lined many parts of the road—very thin and sickly looking and planted sometimes only half a meter apart. They may have been new plantings, or they might not have established themselves in the local soil, but they seemed a far cry from the strong spreading trees we see along our roadsides in Australia.

As we drew closer to Hepu, we began to see much more farming activity, with large banana plantations and intensive cropping on almost every piece of arable land. Small, bent women in coolie hats pushed heavy carts or carried large dirty bundles. They looked old, tired, toothless, and weather-beaten. They all appeared to be in their 70s, but, given their hard lives, could be decades younger.

Off the highway (some three hours after we set out) we passed through small, terribly poor towns with locals working at the front of their businesses and their homes behind. I saw one man splitting logs for a huge pile, while a girl no more than seven played on the dirt road beside him.

Traveling further from Nanning, we left the cars and motor scooters behind, and the method of transport changed to bicycles and clapped-out trucks. Our driver took us to the main street of Lianzhou, a town in Hepu County, to the gates of the middle school. There we were to meet our local guide, who would lead us to see the Hepu Children's Welfare Institute.

Our guide drove a small, modern, silver-grey van similar to the one used by the CWI to ferry babies and children from Hepu to Nanning to meet their new parents. We learned later that the CWI didn't own a van when Ella and the other girls were transferred to Mother's Love, and the staff had to borrow one to make the trip. Our guide was pleased to meet my Hepu pearl and her Qinzhou friend. We all jumped back into our cars and traveled just five minutes to the CWI.

As we drove toward the Institute, I saw the cyclone wire gates of the CWI, and my eyes filled with tears as I realized the enormity of what I was seeing. It was at the foot of those gates that Ella, only hours old, had been left by someone who clearly knew what business was conducted in the building beyond.

Ella Rose Xiao Jun (nearly age 4), Hepu, Guangxi, with Mom.

Referral photo, Anhui Province.

Red Thread to My Soul
by Donna Sadowsky

China
You are the Red Thread to my soul
Beautiful country that opened my eyes
    and my heart
The ties I feel to you are so strong
You gave me my daughter
It is impossible to put into words,
    the love I feel for
My daughter of China, daughter of mine

Beautiful Bao Zi
You have completed our family
You have made my life whole
We are tied, you and I
Together to a country far across the ocean
Together to a woman we may never meet
    but love just the same
Forever bonded because of you,
Beautiful Child
My daughter of China, daughter of mine

At "My Daughter's" School
by Teri Watson-Tracy

MY DAUGHTER WAS FOUND IN FRONT OF A TEACHERS' COLLEGE WHEN SHE WAS JUST THREE DAYS OLD. I have always wondered if her birthparents were perhaps too poor to dream of sending their child to college someday, and so they chose this location hoping that whoever found her would know they dreamed of the best for her.

Last year, when she was nine years old, we traveled back to her city, and she said she wanted to visit the school. I asked her over and over again if she was sure, and she said, "Yes," with a determined jut of her chin. I have learned not to argue with that "look," and so that is how we found ourselves standing in front of the gate of the school—a red-haired mom with her black-haired daughter—and how we found ourselves surrounded by curious college students who wanted to try out their English.

My daughter has always had a strength about her that goes well beyond her years, and, when they asked why we were there, she simply told them the truth. She explained that nine years earlier *someone* had decided to leave her in a basket at the gate, and that she had returned just to stand on the spot.

The crowd grew as she explained that she now lived in the United States, in California, and that she loved playing soccer. She answered questions about her cat and her three older brothers, and about whether she liked being back in China. Many more people watched as we photographed the spot and as we held hands together for a few moments, just thinking.

As we finally turned to leave, I watched as the crowd began hurrying away to tell their friends and family what they had just seen. I knew exactly what was being said: "A local girl has returned; she is safe and living in America." I imagined it being told over and over again. As I watched them quickly head off, I could only wonder if the news would reach whoever it was who had left her that day. Was that even a possibility? I grasped the hand of my daughter tighter thinking that maybe, just maybe, our visit would bring peace not only to my daughter, but to her family in China as well.

Darah Bao Zi (age 14 months), Wuzhou, Guangxi, with her new brothers, Jared (age 10) and Jason (age 13), and parents.

Ville Kang (age 4), Shantou, Guangdong.

Kathleen Jiatong (age 5), Pingnan, Guangxi.

Simone Hope Xu (nearly age 3), Shangrao, Jiangxi, with her cousin, Sara Anne (nearly age 2).

WHO'S THE LUCKY ONE?
by Devin Smith

PEOPLE TELL ME ALL OF THE TIME WHAT A LUCKY LITTLE GIRL YOU ARE. In all reality I am the lucky one! You gave me back my life. You gave me a reason to get up in the morning. You have put joy back in my life. After you came into my life, I realized it was you I have waited for. In every way you are my daughter. I may not have given birth to you, but truly you were born in my heart. Thank you for coming into my life. I thank your birthparents for bringing you to life. It is with God's graces we have become a family.

With all my love for always!
Mom

"Fu sisters" and their siblings. (On couch) Rachel Renee Xiu Tian (age 6), Jinjiang, Fujian; Bethany Hua Wen (age 4), Shenyang, Liaoning; Hannah Qing Yu (age 5), Nanning, Guangxi; Angelica Rose (age 9), Fuzhou, Jiangxi; Autumn Jade (age 4), Wuhan, Hubei; Stephanie Susan Xiao Zhen (age 9), Fuzhou, Jiangxi; and Samantha Grace Ye Ping (age 9), Fuzhou, Jiangxi. (On floor) Grace Fu Youjuan (age 9), Fuzhou, Jiangxi.

MEETING RELATIVES
Excerpted essay by Jane Soo Hoo

WHEN WE ADOPTED JENNIFER IN 1995, WE DIDN'T TELL ANY FAMILY UNTIL RIGHT BEFORE WE LEFT FOR CHINA. I am Chinese. My parents both came from Kaiping and had enough time to contact my mom's older sister (86 at the time) and younger brother (in his 60s) to let them know that we were coming. We made arrangements through our facilitator to meet them the day after we received our daughter at the White Swan Hotel in Guangzhou. My Chinese had disintegrated over the years, and I was unable to communicate with them. So we asked our facilitator if Martin, his China assistant, could accompany us to translate. My uncle had hired a car to take us back to their place, but when it was apparent that communication would be a problem and Martin couldn't be away from his duties for long, we went out to lunch at a nearby restaurant. Much as we tried, we couldn't understand each other. At one point, Uncle said, "Oh, she's speaking the village dialect"—I guess a very basic version of Chinese. I don't know what we spoke at home when we were younger, but, as my sisters and I all left home for college, we forgot a lot since we spoke it less and less.

I recently learned that Kaiping is in the same area as Jennifer's orphanage in Jiangmen. She met a friend at camp this summer, also from Jiangmen, and they said that they must be cousins since they look so much alike. So perhaps we're all related closer than you might think.

HOLDING ON BY A RED THREAD
by Pam Robinson

FOR THOSE OF US WHO WAIT TO REACH OUR CHILDREN IN CHINA, THE RED THREAD OF CONNECTION SEEMS SLENDER AND PRECARIOUS. When my husband, Jim, and I prepared our dossier, we were filled with anticipation. As the months dragged by afterward, our hope almost unraveled. Then it came—it finally came—the phone call to announce our match.

On Mother's Day 1998, 19-month-old Meilan (meaning "pretty flower") Hong, aka Jessica Meilan Robinson, was brought sleeping to our hotel room in Nanchang, China, and placed in my arms. As my husband and I remained speechless in wonder of our daughter, I laid her carefully in the crib. I wanted to wake her right away and see the world through her eyes, but motherly love taught me patience—until 3:00 a.m. It seems to me Jessica awakened on her own; my husband says I woke her.

Her dark brown eyes blinked curiously at the sight of Jim and me. Since she didn't cry we assumed she approved of us. In the days that followed Jessica reassured us that we were indeed a family come together forever. The red thread was stronger than my imagination had ever conceived.

On day two she reached for us. She laughed for us on day three when my husband blew on her belly as she reached for the sky and kicked her heels. On day four she "talked" as the two of us looked down from our hotel window at the busy street below. By the time we reached Guangzhou again for our return to the States, our family was tightly knit together.

A friend and I often talk about the great mystics in all cultures. Many of them believe our souls have existed from the beginning with God. More importantly, God never forces our souls into any choices—including the choice of our parents. If we allow ourselves to consider this idea, we come to understand our Chinese children have wanted to touch the lives of two sets of parents. It further incites our compassion for the Chinese mother, heart aching, who shares such a short, spiritual contract with her child. Under the most difficult of circumstances, she willed to set her child free to live in safety and comfort. Compared to the Chinese mother's choice, the adoptive parents' choice is easy. We should remember the Chinese mother's selflessness and honor her always. It is a selflessness inherited by her child, so willing to trust, with abandon, souls from halfway around the globe.

Thank God, my husband and I held faithfully our end of the red thread. Our connection with our daughter is, ultimately, a miraculous mystery, filled with awe and gratitude.

Sisters—Tessa (age 9), Dongyang; Maisie (age 8), Nanchang; and Lily (age 5), Bengbu— posing with statues in Guangzhou.

CHINESE LESSONS
by Linda Mitchell

I'VE KNOWN FOR YEARS THAT I WOULD NEED TO FIND A WAY FOR MY ELDEST DAUGHTER TO LEARN CHINESE. Since her adoption in 2000 at the age of 15 months, she has maintained a personal connection to China beyond my understanding. As a toddler in the grocery store, she'd wriggle in her seat to make eye contact with Asians and would say "ku," the Mandarin word for cry, when she heard other babies cry in the store.

At the age of three we "played" adoption with a tiny set of glass animals kept in a glass box on her dresser. By her rules she was "China" and I was "Mommy" asking for a baby to love. I had to make a long list of promises to feed the baby cookies and ice cream and provide "mama lovey" before being allowed to take the tiny animal home.

However by the age of five my daughter's feelings about China had changed. There was a sadness that I couldn't figure out. After spending some time talking to our social worker, I understood that my daughter was grieving her loss of connection to her birth country. It was time to connect her to China through language and culture… but how?

I knew of a large multi-cultural church near our home; so I asked them for assistance in locating someone to help us learn Chinese. Within 48 hours a woman named Alice responded to my plea. She was from China, spoke Mandarin, and lived nearby. Perfect! We arranged for her to visit us, and she arrived at our door on a November afternoon with a smile and a willingness to teach us right in our home.

We began by learning our names, numbers, and how to read and pronounce pin yin. We made colorful flashcards, played vocabulary games, and navigated helpful websites Alice shared with us. Our lessons always included conversations about life in China and the U.S. Alice and her husband taught us how to make dumplings for the lunar New Year, and we eagerly swapped culinary knowledge by explaining confusing ingredients for American cooking such as "salad dressing." My younger children began to pick up words from our lessons and use them.

When Alice made a trip to China, we arranged to continue our lessons by email and web cam. But when the Internet connections didn't work, we missed each other. We realized we had moved beyond teacher and students; we were now friends. When Alice returned, our lessons extended into visits to restaurants and field trips in our area.

In the process of learning the Chinese language, I realized that we've not only been learning about China, we've also been sharing with our new friend what we love about our own home. This sharing has done more than soothe the sadness in my daughter's heart. It has given her a reason to be proud of her roots in both countries, and it has knitted a lifelong friendship between two families.

Valerie (age 12 months), Huanggang City, Hubei.

Valerie is my special girl. She came to us crying and afraid. I am sure she felt alone in her new life with us even though she had our love. It took some time for her to adjust to all the changes, but now she is happy with her mommy, daddy, and big sister. She has overcome a lot. She is special in my heart because of all the struggles she has had. I love her with all my heart. Love, Daddy

Madeline (nearly age 3), Kunming, Yunnan.

Madeline is the sunlight in my day. When I see her smile, she just melts my heart. She is always full of joy and happiness. I can only try to put into words all the things she is to me. I love her with all my heart. Love, Daddy

THE PERFECT DRESS
by Cassie Epperson-Jones

MY DAUGHTER HAS THE MOST PERFECT DRESS. It's mostly purple with pink, gold, and blue accents. The top part is a traditional style Chinese blouse with knots for buttons that take me way too long to fasten. With its high collar and fanciful pattern, there is no doubt that it is made in China.

The skirt on the other hand is like that of a ballerina. It is whimsical and fun—the kind of skirt that little girls love using for dress up. It is all American.

To see her in this dress takes my breath away. And it breaks my heart.

The dress is a beautiful metaphor for her life. She was made in China, a land rich in beauty and ripe with complexity. She comes from a country whose history goes back thousands of years. Artistry and poverty coexist, creating some truly magnificent objects that become commonplace. The needs of the family are emphasized over those of the individual members. Honor, duty, and face are words whose depths cannot be explored on paper. She has a bittersweet history, left to be found at a week old, cared for in an orphanage full of love but lacking in material goods, adopted by strangers who would become Mommy and Daddy.

Her future holds the bright promise of the American dream. She has been showered with love and whatever anyone thought that she was lacking by those who loved her just by looking at a picture. It is quite likely that she now has more clothes just for her than the orphanage has for all of its babies. She has a beautiful room of her own filled with wonderful toys. She will have access to nutrition, education, and opportunity in ways that would not have been available to her in China. Most importantly she is loved and cherished. She will grow up with freedom and responsibility.

Despite everything that she has gained, there will always be something she has lost. Her birthparents, her homeland, and the Chinese culture will be just out of reach for her. While we may be able to teach

her the language, it is not the same as being immersed in it. While we may be able to celebrate her heritage and cultural holidays, it is not the same thing as living it. While we will always be her mommy and daddy, we will never replace those who gave her life and a chance at something other.

She is a citizen of two nations. She will carry the marks of both countries that claim her. In her facial features and coloring, she will always be Chinese. Growing up in America will alter her to some extent. The nutrition may give her face a fuller look and her skin a different quality than those raised in China. At times she may long to be surrounded by faces that look more similar to hers. When she has the chance to return to China, she may feel that everything is unfamiliar. She may never feel quite at home.

So I look at my beautiful daughter in her perfect dress, and I am humbled. She has an amazing life ahead of her. We bought her dress in Guangzhou when we adopted her. It is a city that caters to the adoption community, and little baby Chinese girls are seen carried by American families all over Shamian Island.

She was such a tiny thing when we got her that none of the clothes were small enough to fit. We bought the tiniest dress we could find. It was not until two months later, at Chinese New Year, that she was big enough to wear the dress. This too has metaphorical significance—she did not become Americanized overnight (American, yes). We did not become family instantly. It is something that, like the dress, needed growing time (and growing pains).

While I will never fully understand her point of view, this I know: I too am a citizen of two nations. I am American—at home in my world, sometimes more than others. But I am also a child of God. I will not be truly at home until I am in heaven. I understand the bittersweet feeling of longing for what seems just out of reach. By His grace I will grow into my life the way that my beautiful daughter has grown into her dress.

Annelise LiChen (nearly age 13 months), Hengdong, Hunan—wearing "the perfect dress" for Chinese New Year.

Sisters—Mia MeiLi (age 4½), Guangchang, Jiangxi Province, and Meisi Jade (age 3), Zhangzhou, Fujian.

The Family of Adoption
by Joyce Maguire Pavao

You cannot change the truth,
These are your children,
 but they came from somewhere else.
And they are the children of those places
 and of those people as well.

Help them to know about their past
 and about their present.
Help them to know that they are from
 extended families, that they have only
 one parent or set of parents, but they
 have more mothers and fathers.
They have grandmothers, godmothers,
 birth mothers, mother countries,
 mother earth.
They have grandfathers, godfathers,
 birth fathers, and fatherlands.
They have family by birth and by adoption.
They have family by choice and by chance.

Childhood is short;
They are our children to raise;
 they are our children to love;
 and then they are citizens of the world.
What we do to them creates the world
 that we live in.
Give them life.
Give them their truth.
Give them love.
Give them all they came with,
Give them all that they grow with.

Your children do not belong to you,
But they belong with you.
You cannot keep them from what is theirs,
 but you can keep loving them.
You do not own your children,
 but they are your own.

Xinli Yunchen (age 3), Shanghai.

Sophie Lu
(age 21 months),
Sichuan.

Lana Hui Hope
(age 2½),
Guixi, Jiangxi.

Sisters—Zoey Zi Ting (age 3½), Gaozhou, Guangdong;
Amaya YiQin (age 5), Changzhou, Jiangsu;
and Tess Yilu (age 1½), Shanggao, Jiangxi.

FLOATING ON A CLOUD
by Carrie Culp

BEFORE WE ADOPTED OUR DAUGHTER, I HAD NEVER FLOWN ON AN AIRPLANE AND WAS A BIT APPREHENSIVE. Here is part of a journal entry from our first night together. "I have gone from feeling 'flying is fun,' to 'flying is enjoyable in small doses,' to 'will we ever walk on the ground again,' to 'will we ever touch the ground again from this cloud we are floating on since meeting you!'"

Now, after two years filled with sweet "I love yous," precious smiles, and the beautiful melody of your laughter, we have yet to "touch down" from the cloud we are still floating on! Thank you, God, for Lana Hui Hope, and her sister that we've yet to meet. God bless all the daughters and sons from China—those who are already home and those still on their journeys!

A reunion between Marita Joy (age 7)
and Emma Xue-Jia (age 8),
both from Shantou, Guangdong.

LASTING TIES
by Sue Golabek

WHAT BETTER WAY TO FORM A BOND THAN BEING IN A ROOM WITH A GROUP OF PEOPLE WHO, LIKE YOU, ARE MEETING THEIR CHILDREN FOR THE FIRST TIME? For all three adoptions I can recall in vivid detail the rooms where the families were situated and the general reaction of each child as she acclimated to a new family. Add to that traveling, in goodness and in bad, for an intense two-week period, and you have the makings of lifelong friendships. People from all walks of life who, under normal circumstances would not cross paths, spend virtually every waking moment together and turn quickly into friends. Our favorite gatherings are those with past travel mates.

I utilized a local agency for Amaya and Zoey's adoptions. Because the agency conducted monthly waiting parents' meetings, we had the wonderful opportunity to make new acquaintances a year before traveling. Consequently my Amaya, age five, is best friends with a little girl of a couple who have become my best friends. Despite the hundred miles separating these Changzhou, Jiangsu, girls, they see each other frequently. Each visit seems like a continuation of the last. The front of their refrigerator is home to a timeline—dozens of photographs depicting the growth of two hugging, giggly girls. We also keep in close contact with another lovely family from Amaya's travel group who lives ten miles away. It's not an uncommon site to see our five girls, all adopted from China, snuggled together in one oversized chair. Each year we join them in attending a Chinese culture day—a four-hour drive but certainly worth the trip.

Likewise my Zoey, age four, becomes so excited when she sees her Gaozhou, Guangdong, buddy. I recently watched them reading books and playing with dolls on a bed and flashed back to three years ago when the two of them sat side by side, too young to interact, on a bed in the White Swan. They may not see each other very often, but when they do the connection is instantaneous. They look alike, and Zoey is convinced that all the photos hanging in her friend's home are really of her.

For Tess's adoption the facilitating agency was not local. We have our travel group ties but of a different nature. What a delight it is to see an email waiting in my inbox from one of the families, spanning four states and one country away. I linger over and save attached photos. Whenever I answer the phone and hear a voice I first heard in Shanggao, Jiangxi, a smile spreads across my face. I can't wait for our girls to reunite.

A very special bond from China lies at the basis of all these friendships—friendships we deeply cherish and vow to maintain.

Beyond Your Tears
(for my daughter's birthmother)
by Shana Rosengarten

I imagine you kissed
her sweet face so round
And gently placed her
where she would be found

I imagine your heartache
your pain and your tears
I wish I could show you
and soften your fears

I'd show you a girl
with hope in her eyes
A girl who loves stories
and sweet lullabies

A girl who laughs freely
and loves to play
A girl who sings sweetly
and dances all day

A girl with a future
So funny and smart
A girl who loves music
and reading and art

A girl who I hope
has your courage one day
I know it took courage
to love and walk away

Her beautiful smile
I wish you could see
She looks like you
and laughs like me

DARLING DAUGHTER
by Deana Groves

FUNNY, I NEVER KNEW
HOW MUCH I COULD
LOVE AND MISS SOMEONE
I'VE NEVER MET until
I started the journey
to you.

So imagine her laughter
Imagine her touch
I wish I could show you
she's loved so much

Remember her face
Remember that kiss
And when you cry,
remember this

Beyond your tears
Beyond your pain
Sometimes the sun
shines through the rain

And I know that she'll ask me
about you one day
I'll tell her you loved her
and wished she could stay

I'll help her remember
and imagine you too
when she starts to wonder
and dream about you

We'll look at the moon
I'll give her a kiss
and when she cries,
I'll tell her this

Beyond your tears
Beyond your pain
Sometimes the sun
shines through the rain

Siblings—Shannon (age 11); James (age 5), BeiHai, Guangxi;
and Emma (age 7), Hohhot, Inner Mongolia.

Siblings—Joshua (age 9); Sarah (age 2), Xinzhou District, Shangrao, Jiangxi;
and Caleb (age 6).

RETURNING FOR A SISTER, RETURNING TO VISIT
by Sharon Manuel

ALMOST SIX YEARS AFTER ADOPTING 11-MONTH-OLD KENDRA WENYU, WE
RETURNED TO CHINA TO ADOPT 14-MONTH-OLD MACKENZIE YINYING. Kendra
loved seeing her homeland, especially places she had read or heard about or
seen in the "Mulan" movie. While in Beijing we climbed part of the Great
Wall, saw the Forbidden City, had lunch in a hutong, and visited a number
of other special places. It was a lot of fun to try out our Mandarin. Our years
of weekend language and culture classes were paying off even more than we
had expected.

We flew to Hunan, had a quick dinner and sleep, and were up early the next
morning to board the bus to the Changsha Civil Affairs Office. A few minutes
after getting there, MacKenzie YinYing was placed in my arms—the second
of the two best moments in my life. My new daughter, whom I'd carried in my
heart for weeks, was coming home. Kendra Wenyu now had a little sister. Ken
and I had a new daughter. MacKenzie did not look back or cry once in the
first few hours we had her. She just seemed to be taking it all in.

In the final leg of our journey we got to make a brief return visit to
Kendra Wenyu's social welfare institute. Kendra is from a city just about an
hour outside of Guangzhou; so it was an easy trip for us. It was strange, but
wonderful, to be riding once again from the White Swan down the highway
to Kendra's city. We met with the woman who was the director when Kendra
Wenyu was there and who has since retired. She in turn facilitated a gift
we made to the social welfare institute. I was delighted to see the affection
Madame Huang had for Kendra and that Kendra expressed to Madame
Huang. The visit to the orphanage itself was very moving. We got to see
the baby room, which we had not seen before. The current director and his
staff were very kind to us and clearly loved the children. One sign of their
continued interest in the children was that several walls were covered with
snapshots that adoptive parents had sent back over the years. There were
some of Kendra and the other three girls adopted at the same time. Later
we went out for a
banquet-type lunch
with the director and
several staff members.
Kendra Wenyu still
talks about that return
visit, and I know we
will make a longer
return trip in a few
years when MacKenzie
is a bit older.

Sisters—Abbie (age 2),
Xiaoxian, Anhui,
and Ashlyn (age 5),
Guilin, Guangxi.

Because We Don't Fit In Anymore
by Stefani Ellison

THERE IS A REASON THAT WE CALL THIS AN ADOPTION JOURNEY. It's because it is a process and there is actually no end. Yes, the adoption is completed, but its effects last a lifetime. Your mind is changed, your heart is changed, and you are no longer the person you were when you began.

So when you come home and you feel you don't fit in, you are right. You don't. No longer can you sit through pointless social gatherings. You become glassy-eyed at the long-spirited conversation your neighbors have about whose dog upset the trash can like it really matters. "Things," and the chasing, collecting, and maintaining of those "things," lose their glitter when you think of the sparkle that could be put on the face of a child for mere donated pennies or some of your time tying blankets for bitter cold toes.

You lose patience with those who cannot understand the urgency of the task before you—that children are crying, children are dying. And the world keeps on shopping. Spending billions of dollars on things—things that don't matter.

When you look into the eyes of a child in the orphanage you visit, your own eyes never see the world the same again. Most of the world doesn't get it. To those who do, we must stick together because otherwise it's a lonely place. For those of us who continually hear in the back of our minds the crying of the children left behind, we cannot rest because we cannot forget. There is no silence. Our friends, our families, our spouses may not understand, and we ourselves may not understand why we cannot make the crying stop or make the urgency end. So we do what we can do. We give what we can give. And often, we join in the crying.

Sisters—Leah An (age 7), Shaoyang, Hunan, and Julie Lin (age 9), Linchuan/Fuzhou, Jiangxi.

Sisters—Annika (age 2), Ningdu, Jiangxi, and Cayanna (age 4), Shu, Anhui— with friend, Lan (age 4), Guangzhou, Guangdong.

Red Thread Reflections
by Ginger M. Holland

I still remember staring at those huge, silver
   metal doors.
Butterflies started fluttering in my tummy.
Am I really ready to become a mummy?
As I hold you for the first time will you shriek and cry?
Will it be hard to tell your favorite nanny good-bye?
Will I know how to make your fears go away?
Can you be patient with me when I try to make
   your bottle just a certain way?
These thoughts flooded my mind,
As the sun's rays glinted and shined
On the metal doors before me.
Bringing me back to the sign that read
"Jiangxi Province Center of Adoption Service"
   overhead.
Now all I could think about was you being inside.
Someone came and unlocked the door—our guide.
I walked up some steps in a daze and almost numb.
Walking down the hall, I saw some
Ladies holding babies wandering about.
I was so close to you now, no doubt.
I was finally breathing the same air as you too.
We were led to a room to wait with ado.
With rosewood benches and red lanterns
   hanging above,
I knew this was the room where we'd fall in love.
I had stared into your eyes to know you.
Your referral photo showed a baby girl who
Was a little bit chubby with lots of black hair.
Your bottom lip was pulled in like you were
   sucking on it without care.
You were looking straight ahead with a longing,
   searching gaze.
I was snapped back to reality when I heard that
   famous phrase:
"Family #1 (that was us), you may come up
   to get your baby."
At first glance, you looked different, and I thought
   just maybe
This isn't really the same little girl.

I handed you a set of plastic keys and the SWI director
   helped you curl
Your tiny fingers around them to hold.
All that hair I was expecting was not as much to
   behold.
The bald patch on the back of your head
Was probably due to the grass mats you slept on in
   your bed.
And what happened to the chubbiness I thought
   I'd see?
I think it was because they had you dressed in layers
   of three.
All I had to do was look into those eyes of yours,
To know the red thread legend does indeed exist
   and endures.
And how does one explain your calmness when they
   first handed you to me?
Especially after I was told you were so picky
As to allow only one nanny to care for you.
Or how about your name we chose—Holly—
   before we even knew
You'd have a December date of birth.
Some things we are just unable to explain
   here on Earth.
But however it happened that day,
Between the CCAA matching us and the red thread,
   we must say,
"Dear Daughter, you make our hearts burst
   with love."
And every time I look up to the moon above,
I hope your birthparents are looking too,
And can sense you're safe and happy through
   and through.
I say "thank you" to them for giving you life,
Making the decision in storm and strife.
The red thread says we'll always be connected
   to them as well.
I thought, our journey together as a family
   has just begun.
The red thread has bound us together and can never
   come undone.

A Grandfather Celebrates
by Annabel Golden

When we went to China to complete our
second adoption, my parents accompanied us.
My father, an extremely proud granddad, turned
65 years while there and celebrated his birthday
in Shanghai. China was a country which my
father thought he would never visit in his lifetime.
He really wanted to visit the country of his
granddaughters' birth and wanted to experience
a little bit of their birth culture. The red thread
led him there and has given him cause for
celebration every day. He is showered with love
from his Irish/Chinese grandchildren. Following
our red thread has taken us from our normal life
to an extraordinary one, brimming with love and
adventures.

Mother's Day Reflections
by Andrea Nissley

Just over a year ago a beautiful little girl looked at me with eyes full
of sadness and shrouded in fear. As she tentatively said, "Mama," time
stood still. My heart got caught in my throat and tears threatened to spill
from my eyes. For the first time that word referred to me.

As I stood on the brink of motherhood, questions threatened to overwhelm
me. How could I be a mother to this precious little stranger who was about to
lose the only life she knew? Should I touch her? Would she scream if I tried to
hold her? How long would it take for her to love me?

A year has passed. That timid little stranger is my beautiful daughter,
Leisha. Joy shines in her eyes. She loves to jump, to sing, to laugh and to
talk. She loves with abandon, freely giving hugs and kisses to those special
people in her world. Now I talk to her, smother her with hugs and kisses, and
hold her close to my heart. I put Band-Aids on her scratches and bows in her
hair. I read books to her and try to answer her endless questions. We play
outside together on sunny days. We throw her big purple ball, swing, and blow
bubbles and dandelion heads. We sing and dance when the music is loud and
sit quietly on the rocking chair at the end of the day to talk and pray. She
wants to be just like me. I am her mama.

Being a mother can be difficult at times, leaving me exhausted and at my
wits' end. However being a mom also reminds me to slow down and enjoy the
moment, to relax and laugh out loud, to take time for tickle wars and make-
believe coffee and ice cream. It increases my confidence because every day
two little eyes look up at me with
complete admiration and trust.

Today, on Mother's Day, my
heart is bursting with gratitude
that I have been chosen to be
Leisha's mama. A twinge of
sadness is there too because I
know there are countless children
around the world who do not
have a mother to celebrate on this
special day. In my mind is the face
of a beautiful Chinese girl who
does not know what the love of a
mother is like. My heart aches to
hold her close.

Today, on Mother's Day, I will
cherish my daughter. And next year,
on Mother's Day, I will be the proud
mama to *two* beautiful girls.

Rachel Grace Li (age 9 months), Guiping, Guangxi—smiling at her daddy while touring Tiananmen Square.

SPECIAL TREASURES
by Terry Priestap

MY WIFE, JEAN, AND I ARE THE GRANDPARENTS OF 18 GRANDCHILDREN, 12 OF WHOM ARE ADOPTED. We have five special little treasures from China—Jillian, Molly, Chloe, SaraGrace, and Jordan. Recently our daughter Karin and our son-in-law Jeff came back from Guatemala with Jacob, another treasure! We honestly thought when Karin and Jeff adopted Jillian that she would be the last one! Little did we know that their house, hearts, and faith would continue to expand with each new special little treasure. There is no doubt God has been at work! They also have two very special boys (young men now) from Oklahoma.

Each little girl "sparkles." It is just hard to imagine our lives without them. I call them the "cheering section!" Little SaraGrace had a serious heart problem and was listless. Through Love Without Boundaries she had successful heart surgery and now is the most energetic of the bunch! She loves to dance and sing. It is a delight to hear her sing "Jesus Loves Me." Chloe has a foot with some missing toes, but let me assure you it does not slow her down! She is so bright that we wonder what her future will be. Molly is so sweet and wraps herself around everyone's hearts. She knows right where the jelly beans are in my den! She is my little "buddy." Jillian, the oldest, is so articulate and bubbly! When these four are all in motion, it truly is the "cheering section." Jordan and Jacob have balanced the gender number out with their sweet ways.

FROM TRAGEDY BLOOMS A FAMILY
by Shannon Duvall

ON SEPTEMBER 11, 2001, MY HUSBAND WAS IN HIS OFFICE AT THE PENTAGON. We had just moved back to the United States after living in Europe for six years. He was the new guy in the office, excited about a new job and the new challenges that awaited him, while I sat at home unpacking boxes. The morning changed quickly for all of us. It was the longest day of my life. When I could no longer take the news, I sat on my doorstep and watched the commuters struggle up a path from the Metro station. I knew I would see my 6'4" husband any minute now! I waited for hours; he finally showed up at around 4 p.m. It was the longest day of his life too. Remarkably it was the most beautiful day you can imagine outside, the sun shining brightly as a nation reeled.

After many years of marriage we had reached a point in our lives where we were content with having just each other. On that day something inside me said I wanted more. I slowly began to research adoption, finally approaching my husband about adopting from China. To my surprise he said, "Let's look into it." That was all the encouragement I needed!

What a difference a few years can make. On March 9, 2004, a beautiful little girl entered our lives, changing us forever again. Often I have asked myself, "What was I thinking?" I'm so unprepared to be a mother! In China it dawned on us that we didn't know a single nursery rhyme or more than the first few lines of any children's song! While in China we were treated to a trip to an elementary school. The children sang "Five Little Monkeys" to us in English—we sang that song for the rest of the trip!

As a childless couple my husband and I dined out often. Would that change? Would we be able to sit in a coffee shop and watch the world go by ever again? Well we still don't know any nursery rhymes. Carly's favorite song is the Rolling Stone's "Wild Horses," and she can play a mean air guitar! Her first question upon rising on a weekend morning is, "Are we going to Starbucks?" and she would rather eat out than eat my cooking! What a perfect fit!

She amazes us every day. We just sit and stare at her, making eye contact with each other, knowing that she is what we had been waiting for all those years.

Carly Elise Yu Min (age 3½), Sanshui, Guangdong.

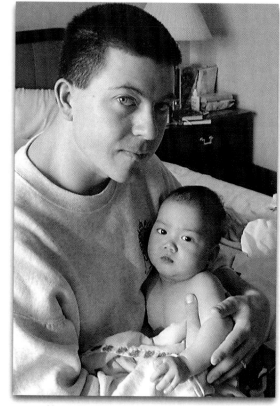

Above: Kati Mei Xiaokai (born January 2001), Wuchuan, Guangdong, with Baba.

Below: Kati Mei Xiaokai (age 5).

Maya Grace
(age 2), Hunan.

Giving Back
by Alisa Mandler

In October 2005 LiLi and I were invited to travel to China with a friend who is a Chinese National and whose brother is the Minister of Culture in Beijing. We stayed with our friend, Chun, and her family in Beijing and were given tours by her brother to Beijing's main tourist sites, as well as some local sites.

We were very fortunate to have been given the opportunity to tour the CCAA, which culminated with the post-adoption room where we were invited in to look at our family

Sydney Alexandra LiLi (age 35 months),
Yangdong, Guangdong.

photos. We were received very warmly and shown all of the rooms where the staff was very busy working.

We also spent a week in Xian where we had an opportunity to tour the Xian Handicapped Children Rehabilitation and Training Center. Before going there we bought three big bags of toys. During our tour we distributed them to all the kids. LiLi enjoyed playing with the other kids so much and giving them toys. She felt so rewarded from the whole experience.

I was so impressed with the cleanliness of the center. In fact we were required to wear shoe covers during our tour. The nannies were very warm and loving. They showed us that they take photos of the kids throughout their stay at the orphanage and document their milestones so there is a nice book to give to future adoptive families.

The impact this trip had on LiLi is amazing. She still recognizes the landmarks if she sees a poster of the Temple of Heaven. She really enjoyed the Terra Cotta Soldiers and knows they were in Xian versus Beijing. She loved climbing the Great Wall and still talks about it. But the thing that she talks about the most is the orphanage in Xian.

After arriving home from China, she took all of her stuffed animals and made her own big building where she is the nanny and she takes care of them. They are all under our dining room table. Every morning she adopts two babies and takes them for the day. At night she tucks all of her babies in.

A week ago she came to me and wanted to start fundraising to collect money for the babies and kids in Xian at the building there. She said since she could not take care of them, she wanted to raise money so the nannies could.

We are in the process of trying to have a fundraiser at a restaurant, and at this time LiLi has raised almost $100. All this from a three-year-old!

Olivia's Lullaby
by Ashlee Cook
Submitted by Stacy Cantwell

Rock-a-bye, rock-a-bye,
Sleep in sweet peace,
My precious angel.

With eyes that aren't mine,
Lips that aren't mine,
Blood that isn't mine,
I love you.

I didn't hold you before your birth,
I didn't know your self inside of me
I didn't watch you burst into the world
But I love you.

Your cries sounded across an ocean
Resounding in my dreams
An angel without a guardian,
I loved you.

Trusting the Father that adopted me,
I flew across the ocean with prayers for wings.
Your little hands reached up to hold me,
And I loved you.

Oh, my precious angel,
Little gift from heaven,
Rock-a-bye, rock-a-bye.

As I hold you in my arms,
Suddenly blessed with an angel,
You grant me a baby smile.
I love you.

How deep does this love go?
I've yet to find its end.
I will be your protection and comfort and mother.
I love you.

Rock-a-bye, rock-a-bye,
Sleep here, within my embrace.
Sweet, dear, precious angel.
Rock-a-bye, rock-a-bye.

Olivia Faith
(age 4), Hunan.

Oliver (age 2), Fuling, Chongqing.

A Blessing in Pink
by Briana Melom

SEVERAL YEARS AGO I VISITED A LITTLE SHOP IN THE COASTAL CITY OF ST. AUGUSTINE, FLORIDA, where I fell in love with a beautiful pink tie-dyed dress. It was hand-painted with bamboo and a Chinese character on the front. I didn't have much money, and I hemmed and hawed about whether to buy it until my friend said, "If you don't buy the dress, I'm going to buy it for you." I've worn it so many times the paint is beginning to fade but hadn't worn it in over a year since my husband and I began the process of adopting from China.

Our son, Oliver Fu Ai Hao, came home from Fuling, China, in December of 2005. Yesterday, when I put on my old pink dress, my jaw dropped. Of all the—what is it, something like 3,000?—Chinese characters in the world, do you know which one is on my old pink dress? The Fu "blessing" character, which is the first of our son's three names.

Tears began to well in my eyes as I realized my son's name was literally written across my heart years before he was conceived. He is the joy of our days, and we are utterly, profoundly connected to one another. Our sweet Fu is a blessing indeed.

A Blossoming Friendship
by Teresa Orem Werner

THE SEED FOR THIS BLOSSOMING FRIENDSHIP WAS PLANTED A FEW MONTHS BEFORE THESE GIRLS WERE EVEN BORN. It all started with a simple dinner invitation. A friend of my husband asked us if we would come over to talk with the family about our experiences with adoption. I was excited to go. I love to talk about how wonderful it has been to build our family through adoption. Little did we know that our dinner with the Hansons would be the catalyst for starting our third adoption.

It was time to add a little girl to our lives. Our sons were very excited to hear that they were going to be big brothers to a new little sister. Over the next few months, the Hanson family quickly became some of our closest friends. They were a few weeks ahead of us in the process. Brenda and I often spoke of how wonderful it was going to be to have our girls growing up together and commented, "Wouldn't that be amazing if they were from the same orphanage?" News of their approval from USCIS came. I realized that since we were still a few weeks out for our approval that our girls would most likely not be from the same orphanage. At first I was saddened that we would not travel together and share the experience of receiving our daughters with our friends. I soon realized that our girls would still be close and that we could still be a part of the Hanson's journey; it just would not be firsthand.

Well, the Hansons had a different plan. They called WACAP and had their paperwork put on hold until ours caught up to theirs. I was so excited when Brenda called to tell me what they had done. I could not believe the news she was sharing. Less than two weeks later our approval arrived from USCIS. All of our paperwork was sent together in April 2003. We spent the next ten months planning for our trip and sharing the ups and downs of the adoption process. On February 19, 2004, Barry and Brenda Hanson picked us up at 8:10 in the morning for an hour's drive to Seattle. I could not believe that we were getting ready to board our flight to China—a flight that would forever unite us with our daughters.

In the end our daughters did not come from the same orphanage. They did however come from the same province. That is not what is important. What is important and truly special is that we got to share our journey to our forever families with our amazing friends. Friends like this don't just happen; they happen for a reason. Our daughters were destined to grow up together, and we are so truly thankful for our friendship.

Kai (age 4), Tianjin—so excited to meet his baba.

Happy new sisters—Sophie (age 3), Feixi, Anhui, and Holly (age 2), Shangrao, Jiangxi.

Both from the Hunan Province— friends Natalie and Brianna (both age 3).

Jiujiang, Jiangxi girls— Lily and Peyton (both age 4).

Sisters—Brianna Liang (age 4), Dianjiang, Chongqing; Corban Huiyan (age 1), Chenzhou, Hunan; and Abigail Qianhui (age 6), Anqing, Anhui.

Emma Charlotte (age 2), Nanning, Guangxi.

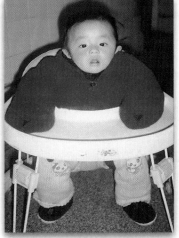

Cao Yu Cai, soon to be Peyton (about age 10 months), Jiujiang, Jiangxi. A week before meeting her new mom.

Tate (age 3); Sawyer (age 6); and Sofia ("Ning Ning") (age 2), Datong, Shanxi, with their great-grandma.

TOGETHER AGAIN
by Marilyn Blumenstein

I REMEMBER THE MOMENT YOU WERE PUT IN MY ARMS. You were crying your heart out, leaving the comfort of your caregiver and being placed in a strange woman's arms. At 17 months you were more aware of strangers than the other babies. I will never forget the kiss your caregiver placed on the back of your head with tears streaming down her face, and then she disappeared. I wondered if I would ever see this woman again. I often watched you playing and wished she could see you. How proud she would be.

I made a promise to you that some day we would visit your first home to experience the wonders of that special place. At eight years old, given the opportunity to participate in a summer camp in China, you returned to your homeland with much excitement and confidence.

It tugged at my heart when you left me to visit your new friends' homes overnight in Shanghai; yet I was so happy for you. I can still hear your excitement when you share your stories. The Chinese people opened up their hearts to you and shared their pride in their culture.

As I planned our return visit to your orphanage, my mind kept returning to your caregiver. Could I dare dream that we would see her again? When the golden gates of the Maoming Welfare Institute opened, so many caregivers came running; they were so excited to see you. They took turns tweaking your cheeks. The more you giggled, the more they tweaked! I thought, "What could be better?" Then in the excitement it happened—they pointed to your caregiver's picture in your life book I had brought. Soon she stood in front of us. When the three of us hugged, I felt a completion and contentment. We were together again, sharing the joy of your life.

Kate Goldie Marie (age 8), Maoming, Guangdong— reuniting with her orphanage caregiver.

Elijah James Le (age 3), Guangzhou, Guangdong.

Sisters—Jaiden (age 5) and Jali (age 33 months), both from Kunshan, Jiangsu, with sisters—
Megan (age 23 months) and Mia (age 5), both from Zhanjiang, Guangdong.

MY XIAMEN SISTERS
by Mei Ling Messner (age 10)

THE DAY HAD FINALLY COME. We were all meeting up again. I was getting to see all of my Xiamen sisters. All eight of us were adopted on the same day, at the same time in Xiamen, China. We see each other about every three years now. Last time I saw all of the girls was when I was five. I saw two of the girls since then—Krissie and Cassie. Well, anyway, the day had finally come.

My family was hosting the reunion this time here in Arizona. My mom and I had been planning this for a while. We made special name tags and passports. We added leather ties to the cowboy hats we bought for everybody. All of the families met at the Doubletree Resort. We were all a little shy but happy to see each other. That night we talked about memories about when we were little at the restaurant, and we had tons of fun. Before I knew it dinner was over and we went back to the hotel for a "dive in" movie and to bed. The first day was so much fun. I couldn't wait for the next few days to arrive. We visited the Chinese Cultural Center the next day and went to the Science Museum. We made scrapbooks about ourselves and even had a big birthday party for all of us. Our cupcake cake was in the shape of a cactus and there were eight cactus flowers on it. We all exchanged birthday gifts and played games. We even played a Xiamen trivia game to learn more about our birthplace. Some of the stuff we did over the following days was go to the Grand Canyon, Meteor Crater, Flagstaff, and Sedona, and so much more. We ate real Navajo tacos on the Navajo reservation.

The days went by so quickly. Soon each family said their good-byes and departed. It was sad, but we were going to see each other in another two or three years. Soon it was our turn to leave. We said our good-byes and rode home. I was glad that our parents had decided to let us know the people we were adopted with. I hope when we grow old that we will stay in touch and always remember each other. I know I will remember each one of my Xiamen sisters. I will never forget them.

MEA'S STORY ON RETURNING
by Mea Rose FuDeJi Campbell (age 4)

Our family returned to China in October of 2006, and we visited the Fuling orphanage so our daughter, Mea, could visit her careworkers. We were able to have lunch with her primary careworker, Chen, and two others. This is Mea's essay.

I GOT A BIG BEAR FROM THE HOTEL. I liked the breakfast. I could say Ji Dan (chicken egg in Mandarin) and ask for my egg. I liked when Chen sat next to me at lunch. I love to go to China and I wish I could go back and I love my baby sister and I can't wait to go and get her and she will be my baby sister forever and ever.

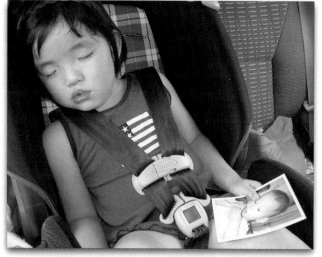

Alea YunCai (age 3), Jiangyin—holding photo of her little brother,
Isaac HuanHuan (age 1) of the same orphanage.

KiLee JiaYun (age 4), Guangdong.

Above: Kevin (age 6), ZhaoQing, Guangdong. Nothing will hold this boy back!

Left: Mei Ling (age 10), Xiamen, Fujian— caught in the act of throwing water on her brother.

The Evolving Tapestry
by Kyle Messner

WHEN I ADOPTED MEI LING IN 1996, I KNEW THAT MY LIFE WAS GOING TO CHANGE. As a single mom with no family nearby, the initial changes were a bit overwhelming. My life centered on my child and her needs. I lost a few of my single friends who just weren't up for my new lifestyle, but many others came forward and helped me through those rough days. Little did I know the changes and the enriching relationships were just beginning.

As Mei Ling's health needs changed, and I got more adept at motherhood, my life changed in other ways. I helped start a Families with Chinese Children chapter in the mountains of North Carolina where we lived. We became a part of the local Chinese community. Mei Ling wound up with Ah-yi Cindy and Kai Ma (Chinese godmother) clucking over her. She even got to dance with the Hong Kong Ballet when they were in town. We were included in many of the celebrations that our Chinese friends held, and we included them in our family and FCC celebrations.

Meanwhile our world grew bigger with our Internet connections. Through Yahoo groups I connected with other families who had adopted from the same orphanage, kept contact with our travel group, and even met Jie, a woman who was from Xiamen. During the Cultural Revolution she lived near Mei Ling's finding place. As Mei Ling got older she wrote to Jie and developed a friendship with her. Jie even took Mei Ling's pictures to the village in TongAn to show people the local girl who is now in America. She also took pictures of the village and sent them to my daughter.

And then came Kevin. In 2004, Mei Ling and I decided it was time to grow our family to include a little boy. Again the Internet broadened our lives. Through the waiting children listserv, we learned about special needs and faced our fears. On the ZhaoQing list we met people who had known my son since he was a baby and others who were able to take updated pictures. When we went to bring him home, we met some of the university students who volunteered at the orphanage, and they gave us precious baby pictures of him. They took us to the orphanage and showed us around ZhaoQing. They told us of Yao Laoshi, the preschool teacher who loved my son, and made sure we met her. We have managed to keep up many of those friendships.

And the changes continue, but now the changes are not so overwhelming. Our lives are so enriched and fulfilling. My passion for helping children in China has pushed me to advocate and help children find homes. My children and I help raise money for several organizations that help orphans in China. We attend happy reunions of Mei Ling's travel group. Living now in Phoenix, we are involved in the big FCC and do things with the Chinese community. The changes continue, and the initial red thread that bound us together is now developing into a rich tapestry.

"Twin" cousins—Zachary (age 4), Russia, and Kevin (age 6), ZhaoQing, Guangdong. Kevin and Zachary think that they are twins.

They Didn't Know
by Kyle Messner

CHINESE NEW YEAR WAS APPROACHING. Kevin's kindergarten teacher told me that I could come in and share with his class. A friend offered to loan me a lion dance costume to use for the presentation. I was really excited because this particular year I had a ton of decorations complete with confetti poppers.

I told Kevin that we could teach his class about Chinese New Year and do the lion dance. He quietly said okay. Well, three mornings later, I was driving Kevin to school when I heard a small voice coming from the back seat. "Mom, you can't bring that stuff in to school." "Why not?" I asked. "Well, I only told Jacob [his best friend]. I didn't tell the other kids." I asked him what he had only told Jacob, and his answer nearly made me pull over. "I didn't tell the other kids that I am Chinese." Needless to say, my 10-year-old daughter, Mei Ling, started to chortle. I quickly gave her an evil eye look to not say anything, but of course she blurted out, "Kevin, they already know we are Chinese." Kevin got a shocked look on his face and then said, "Okay, which one of you two told?"

Above: Katrina Mei Bao (age 10), YiWu, Zhejiang.

Below: Kelsey Mei Li Dan (age 5½), Hepu, Guangxi.

Julianna Claire (age 3), Gaoyou, Jiangsu—
enjoying her first sledding experience in deep snow.

Nicole Liu-Lu (age 4),
Wenzhou, Zhejiang.

BRINGING ELLA HOME
by Marita Adams (age 7½)

WHEN I WAS 4½ YEARS OLD I WENT WITH MY MOM AND MY UNCLE TO CHINA TO BRING HOME MY BABY SISTER, ELLA. I was happy thinking that I would have a sister to play and laugh with. We took an airplane and were on it for a very long time. In China we went to the Great Wall. My mom only made it a little way up, but my uncle and I walked almost all the way to the top. I remember that the most. I liked seeing the Chinese people in China. They looked like me. I wore a card around my neck that explained why I was in China. It was written in Chinese. Everyone was very nice to me. They asked me where I was born. I told them Shantou. They told me that smart people came from Shantou. Sometimes they gave me a hug. Sometimes they gave me presents, like a bracelet. They were happy that I was visiting China. I was happy to be there too. It was fun to meet Ella. I made her laugh. I remember that my uncle carried Ella as we walked around China. We took lots of pictures in China. We ate good food. It was very spicy. My mom says that someday we will go back to China. Just to visit. It will be fun to go back. I will show Ella our China.

Friends—Maleah (age 2), Ruijin, Jiangxi, and Sarah (age 4), Yiyang, Hunan—helping with a garage sale fundraiser to benefit orphaned children.

Above: Mia Kennedy (age 14 months), Qianjiang, Chongqing.

Left: Mia Kennedy (age 10 months), meeting her new family.

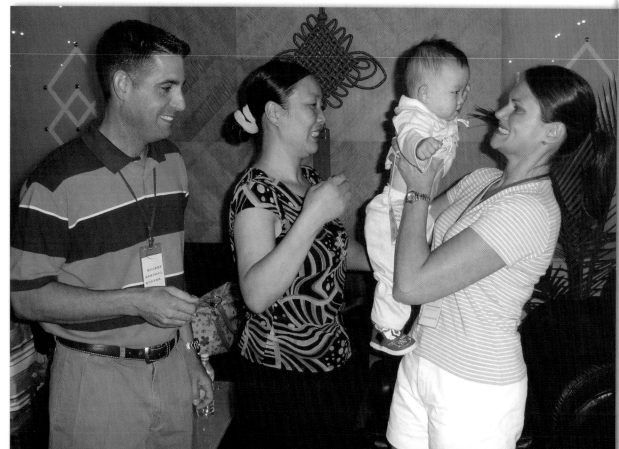

Lela (age 19 months), Shaoguan, Guangdong, with Papa.

THE TAPESTRY
by Jennifer Wilson-Pines

WHEN I THINK ABOUT THE RED THREAD BINDING MY DAUGHTER AND ME TOGETHER, NOTHING OBVIOUS LEAPS TO MIND—no matching birth dates, amazing coincidences, or such. It's more a deeply woven tapestry, with tiny reflections and secret vistas peeking out unexpectedly, small knots, hastily darned holes, elegant embroidery, and a slender scarlet thread, sometimes almost invisible, winding through.

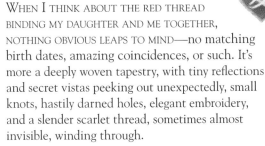

Kailei QiongXiu (age 11 months), Hengyang, Hunan.

Above: Grace Pei Pei (age 2½), Yangdong, Yangjiang, Guangdong.

Left: Siblings—Sam (age 13), Noah (age 10), Margaret (age 9), and Grace Pei Pei (age 18 months).

FAMILY REUNION
by Deborah Mann

IT IS ANOTHER GATHERING OF OUR 11 FAMILIES. As I look around, I count 22 children, not including grown children; not so amazing really unless you know that 14 of them were born in China. Although all of these families live in the same community, four years ago I didn't know any of them. We met because we were individually inspired to make an important choice in our lives—we chose to adopt from China.

Since meeting we have endured one another's long waits to referrals, played together, prayed together, shared parenting experiences, supported each other through crises, and, most importantly, become a family. A family brought together by a choice and held tight by the profound understanding of what these 14 children represent: that half a world away 14 women were conceiving and bearing the children we call "ours" at the same time we were deciding and preparing to adopt. The power of this is often lost on those who have not experienced it, but it is no small thing to us.

It is a miracle really. Our hearts thrill daily with the opportunity to love these children, and we catch our breath in awe of the miracle, or series of miracles, that have brought us together with them. We are humbled by the perfect timing and events involved—in our individual lives, our children's birthmothers' lives, even the disappointment and delay brought on by SARS—in getting us to this day. A complex web of circumstances has been spun through which the Hand of God directed all involved in delivering these children we have been given to love. Some call that miracle "the red thread," but for us the red thread is God weaving Himself into all our lives for good.

Once a month or more our special family comes together so our children can play and the adults can catch up. At one of our outings this spring, a camping trip to a local hot springs, the pool manager looked up at our group and asked, "Is this a family reunion?" We just looked at each other and smiled as we proudly responded, "Yes!"

Revisiting a Christmas Rhyme
by Christine Archer-Davison

'Twas the night before Christmas and all through the house
Something was different, for me and my spouse

We waited all year, and at times it was tough
But the wait was all worth it, more than enough

The room was all done with such love and such care
In hopes that our baby soon would be there

Never again would our house be the same
For there's a new addition who we've given our name

She comes from afar, near a land by the ocean
Where life was not easy, some say a commotion

Her birthparents made the only choice that they could
Their decision is quite often misunderstood

It took them great strength and a whole lot of love
A gift to us all from someone above

Our family was blessed to be "the one"
To raise this little girl for we loved her a ton

She has dark brown eyes and small little ears
And her beautiful smile brings us great cheer

She dances around both our home and our hearts
We hardly remember being apart

Our love for this girl could never be stronger
She comes to us now, we are lonely no longer

The love that we have transcends earth, moon, and stars
And it will grow even more, for she is finally ours

Ian Thomas Dong (age 5),
Urumqui, Xinjiang.

I was paperchasing for a second NSN daughter in February 2003 when I kept being drawn back to my agency's Waiting Child list and a listing for the most beautiful boy with albinism. The day I saw the words, "My file will be returned soon to the CCAA," my heart hit the floor, and I realized I needed to bring him home. Three years later, he has been in our family more than half his life. He is a beautiful, challenging child, who humbles me daily as a parent. I call parenting him "my life's lesson."

JiaNan Jin (nearly age 6),
Shantou, Guangdong.

CRICKET CULTURE
by Charlotte Halsema Ottinger

I HAVE ALWAYS TAUGHT MY CHILDREN THAT WE ARE A CHINESE AMERICAN FAMILY, NOT JUST A FAMILY WITH A CHINESE CHILD. We learn about Chinese culture together as a family. So when we made plans to return to China for a visit to my daughter's hometown, I sought ways to make it a meaningful experience for my biological son who had not yet been to China. I wanted him to bring back some experience or knowledge that would connect him to China as well.

Tapping into what all five-year-old boys love—bugs—we set about investigating what I refer to as China's cricket culture. We read articles on how crickets are kept as pets in China because of the lovely music they make by rubbing their wings together. We learned about the different types of decorative cricket cages made from such things as carved bone, cloisonne, and even gourds. We also discovered that crickets are thought to bring good luck. By the time our family arrived in China, my son was on a mission that was purely his own: finding cricket cages. He left with two very unique examples and a certain expertise that would carry him through the first grade.

What started with an article about crickets in "China for Children" magazine grew into a young boy's career on the lecture circuit. My son put together a presentation about China's cricket culture, complete with a growing cricket cage collection, a diagram of a cricket, and examples of real crickets encased in acrylic molds. His program concluded with a reading of the Chinese folktale "The Cricket's Cage." My son's presentation was in hot demand during Chinese New Year and again in the spring. He wore his brocade jacket while he proudly shared part of his family's Chinese American culture with several elementary school classes, local college classes, and a Brownie troop. My son's exploration into the world of China's cricket culture gave him an opportunity to make his own personal connection to China.

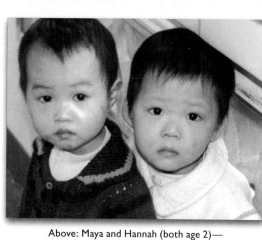

Above: Maya and Hannah (both age 2)—
Liangping, Chongqing, cribmates.

Hannah and Maya were cribmates as newborn babies in the Liangping SWI. They grew up and became best friends. Across the ocean, their mommies-to-be were also building a friendship, unaware that their daughters even knew one another. It was a wonderful surprise to learn that they were so connected, and we could not wait for an opportunity to reunite them.

Below: Hannah and Maya (both age 3)—
reunited at home in the U.S.

Brady (age 2), Shantou, Guangdong—
home for one month.

FRIENDS FOREVER!
by Karen Maunu

THEY WERE THREE OF MANY CHILDREN ON THE VIDEOTAPE I WATCHED. I just had met another family who had also just come home with their two-year-old daughter. We met sitting across tables at a restaurant. Our new daughters were just a few months apart in age, we both had older biological children, and we didn't live that far from one another. We were soon getting together to let our daughters play as we got to know each other better. It was on one of these play dates that my new friend first played her adoption video for me. On the video was the baby room at her daughter's orphanage with about 20 children, ages six to 18 months.

Little did I know that my daughter was on that video. After we had been home about six months with our first daughter, we decided to start the adoption process again. We couldn't wait to bring another daughter into our family. My friend told me about her agency, which was trying to place a few children with special needs. These children were from the same orphanage that her first daughter was from. One of the little girls was a child that they had fallen in love with on their first adoption trip. Another one of these little girls was to be our daughter, one of the toddlers from the videotape. Soon we had our paperwork in, and we were both waiting for our new daughters to come home. The time went so slow, as it always does, but finally our referrals came, and we were both ready to travel to China.

Because of the timing of the referrals, our family decided to travel right away, while my friend and her family decided to wait a few weeks for their older children to be in school. As sad as I was to not be traveling together, I knew that we both made the right decisions for our families. Our new daughter was a delight, and we all quickly fell in love with her outgoing, sunny spirit. On one of our last days in our daughter's town, we were able to visit her orphanage. We had so much fun playing with all of my daughter's little friends, many of them from the original videotape that I had watched over a year before. One of the little girls would not let me put her down. I held her and my new daughter much of the time we were playing with all of the toddlers. This sweet and special little girl was another child I remembered from the videotape, but I didn't know if she would be adopted. I knew I had to go home and advocate for this little girl; I had fallen in love with her too.

Not too long after we were home, my friend and her family traveled to China to adopt their daughter. I told her to be sure to give this special little girl a big hug and take a lot of pictures of her. She was able to take pictures of many of the children, especially this little girl. While she was in China we found out that this little girl was on a waiting child list with an agency and was placed immediately. We frantically searched for this child's new parents. We were so surprised to learn that she was placed with a family 20 miles from where both of us lived. This was amazing, because the agency was on the other side of the U.S. from where we lived. In addition this family also had older biological children and many things in common with our families.

We were all at the airport when this third little friend arrived home. You can imagine the look on her face when she saw our two girls—she was shocked! We have had so much fun keeping these three little girls connected along with all of the rest of their siblings. The play dates have continued, even though it is harder with all of the girls in school now. They still have a close bond and know that their "sisters" are nearby. I love that they will have this special relationship and will always remember my first time watching these three little girls on the videotape.

Friends—Olivia (age 4), Yin Chuan, Ning Xia; Nicole (age 4), Wenzhou, Zhejiang; Tiana (age 6), Xi'An, Shaanxi; and Averi (age 2), Cangwu, Guangxi.

Sisters—Steffie (age 3), Chenzhou, Hunan, and Annie (age 5), Cenxi, Guangxi.

Friends—Sarah (age 3) Fengcheng, Jiangxi; Hannah (age 3) Fencheng, Jiangxi; AnnieLynn (age 1) Ji'An, Jiangxi; and Madelyn (age 2) Yongzhou, Hunan— sharing a sweet treat on a hot day.

The Eight Girls of Change
by Lily Cooper (age 10), July 21, 2006

RECENTLY I RETURNED FROM A REUNION IN ARIZONA THAT CONSISTED OF MY SEVEN XIAMEN SISTERS AND THEIR FAMILIES. Our families have gotten together every five years to celebrate the special bond between us. The bond is made special by friendship and joyfulness. We are sisters because in 1996 all eight of us joined our forever families at the same time and in the same place. When the big moment came, our parents were shedding tears of joy and laughing with pride at the eight babies. They were so proud, and here is a possible reason for them to be even more proud.

After our reunion, when I returned home to Wisconsin, I was looking at videos in a movie store and saw a new movie release, "Eight Below." It is a story about courage and the power of strength when a group stays together. This gave me a few ideas. Is our group as special and as close knit as the famous dogs in the movie? If we are together hooked by some invisible bond, can we survive much better than if we were apart? I also wondered if we could love each other as much as the dogs did. Dogs are supposed to be loyal, trustworthy, loving, and much, much more. Can we eight girls make a difference in the world by having those characteristics and working together, rather than alone? Can we be stronger if we pull together and cooperate for a better world? These questions are some questions that need not be answered but just mulled over and taken seriously. Eight different girls, eight different dogs; yet together the dogs survived, and the tie between them was so strong that the fiercest warrior, Hate, could not break it.

If we, the eight girls, could do something astounding, I would think it would be that we unite the world with friendship. The planet Earth needs love, not hate. If we were to all love one another, there would be no barriers between races, no tense words, and no shells between family members. There would be only a magical, bonding, combining force connecting people from around the world. There wouldn't be any need for fear, for every criminal and terrorist would be turned into a loving person. Think of the possibilities of love.

家庭

Abby (age 2), Guangdong.

My Promise
by Eileen Lynch

My promise to love and cherish is not one but many.

For I must
Be courageous and love you always.

I must also
Give you the courage to trust in that love.

I must
Honor, respect, and take part in your heritage.

I must also
Give you reason to honor and take part in mine.

I must
Believe in you.

I must also
Help you believe in yourself.

That is my promise. It is not one but many.

Above: Guiping Sisters reunited. Julia, Julia, Maya, Claire, Myah, Ella, Emma, Anna, Kailee, and Carly (all age 29 months).

Right: Fifteen months earlier. (Back row) Kailee, Julia, Claire, Julia, Carly, Anna, and Ella. (Front row) Maya, Myah, and Emma (all age 14 months).

Clara Ruth Huan (nearly age 2), Xinhui, Jiangmen City, Guangdong.

Sisters—Sophia (age 34 months) and Julia (age 27 months), Guiping, Guangxi—waiting for Dad to come home.

FOREVER GUIPING SISTERS
by Jill Biehl

TEN LITTLE GIRLS IN GUIPING, CHINA—WAITING, WAITING FOR THEIR FOREVER FAMILIES. Ten families from four states—waiting to find their daughters. Like many other families we had joined online groups to learn more about China, how to prepare for our trip, to prepare our families for the transition that would be coming and, of course, to meet others in the same process.

On January 31, 2005, we received the call about our daughters. Soon we would be traveling to Guiping to get them. We were so excited to meet the other families traveling. We had become friends but hadn't yet met each other. We talked every day about our daughters and our upcoming trip. We couldn't believe we would be getting our daughters soon. We prepared for our trip and coordinated our flights so that we could all finally meet in Hong Kong. We shared that very special day that forever changed us all.

The day we met our Guiping daughters, never did I expect our experience to be as beautiful as it was. That day I thought I was just gaining a daughter. But really I was gaining a family. The connection we felt for our daughters blended into the connection we had for each other. We knew that our daughters were connected as Guiping Sisters. We grew so close over the course of our wait that we knew without a doubt that after returning home we wanted to visit, see how the girls had changed, and keep our connection alive.

Labor Day means many different things to people, but to these ten families it means a Guiping Reunion. When our last reunion ended, we were anxious to begin planning the next one. We hope that these reunions will help our daughters see the love we have for them, for the families we traveled with, and for our love of China. We can only hope that our daughters will see the friendships of their mothers and fathers and develop their own close friendships. Although Jin Yan Run, Jin Yan Hong, Jin Yan Qiu, Jin Yan Zhuo, Jin Yan Fen, Jin Yan Wei, Jin Yan Kang, Jin Yan Fei, Jin Yan Yi, and Jin Yan Jiang are now Ella, Julia, Emma, Carly, Claire, Kailee, Julia, Maya, Anna, and Myah, they will always and forever be Guiping Sisters.

Henry JunJie (age 2), Baoji City, Shanxi.

Mia Biying (age 4½), Changsha, Hunan.

ONLINE FRIENDS
by Robin Meeker

WHEN YOU ADOPT FROM CHINA YOU TRULY BECOME PART OF A VERY UNIQUE COMMUNITY OF PEOPLE, THE VAST MAJORITY OF WHOM ARE HOOKED TOGETHER ON AT LEAST ONE YAHOO GROUP. There are orphanage email groups so that parents with children from the same orphanage can learn more information and keep their kids connected. There are Yahoo groups for those who adopt waiting children and for those who are single or older or adopting boys. The biggest Yahoo group of all is Adoptive Parents China (APC), which at last count had over 15,000 members who love to debate every issue out there about adoption—from using the family bed for bonding to the best type of baby carrier to buy to whether people in small towns should be allowed to adopt transracially. Each and every day thousands upon thousands of email messages wing themselves around the world dealing with the subject of adoption.

I know this because I am the member of no less than 40 online groups, and I am the first to admit I am addicted! I wake up an hour before my kids do so that I can log on and keep up-to-date with everything going on in the adoption world. I am on a list to discuss agencies, a list to discuss attachment, and a list to discuss adopting an older child. There are others to discuss taking my child back during the Olympics and more for my DTC groups. I joke with my family that when I added up all the groups I am on, I think I have about 20,000 online friends. My husband joked that our church could never hold that many people in the event of demise; so he hopes I can have an online funeral someday.

Honestly I love my email groups because the people truly understand how wonderful adoption is. No matter how many debates we get into, the ultimate truth is we *all* love our kids. If you aren't a member of an online adoption group, you should join one! The friendships that you will make will bless your life.

A Generous Man
by Scott Ocheltree

I haven't always been a huge fan of Jackie Chan. I enjoyed his movies and found his martial arts skills amazing, and I was impressed by the physical stunts he performs in his films. Other than that I didn't really know much about him. Then on one of our family's most memorable days we were touched by Mr. Chan.

September 18th was the Chinese Moon Festival, and our youngest son Kai's "Gotcha Day." We received Kai into our family at the Baoding Social Welfare Institute, which functions mainly as a nursing home for seniors but also provides care for approximately 70 children. The building where the children lived was showing its age and becoming overcrowded.

One of the first things the directors told us as we toured the facility was how excited they were about a new building for the children, which had been donated by Jackie Chan. They were very proud of the large, beautiful structure which was nearly completed, and we were impressed as well.

After we returned home I began to wonder about this gift from Jackie Chan. Curious as to what his connection to Baoding was, I looked at his website and discovered that this building was a small piece of the amazing charitable works of Mr. Chan. I was impressed by the scope of work his foundation does. Having visited this facility and seen the children whose lives would be affected by his gift, I was moved to thank Mr. Chan. These are children who had been Kai's friends, and it was comforting to know the quality of their lives was being improved.

Through his website I sent an email to Mr. Chan telling him our story. The next day we received a message from the site's webmaster saying that Jackie was touched by our story and asked if they could share it on the website. I was impressed that we had heard back at all, let alone so quickly. I wrote again saying we'd be happy to have Kai's story on the website. A few days later a little story about Kai, complete with pictures, appeared there. We were excited to see this, and even more pleased when Kai received an autographed photo of Mr. Chan.

Our adoption experience led to an unusual connection, and a few months later an even more amazing connection bloomed out of this. We received another email from the webmaster saying that a family from Tennessee, who had adopted a little boy from the same social welfare institute, had contacted her asking her to pass their information on to us. We contacted the family of Nate, a little boy almost the same age as Kai. When we saw his picture we recognized him immediately because Nate and Kai were together in many of the photos that we had from the orphanage. Although we lived across the country from one another, and we adopted through different agencies, our families were able to connect—thanks to a gift from Jackie Chan.

Siblings—Tony, Jiaozou, Henan, and Lorallan, Changshu, Jiangsu (both age 4). Only three days' difference in age and the best of friends.

Jackie Chan.

Our Connection with China
by Ned and Tessa Hill, proud parents of Lia Rose Yang Hill

Our connection with China was forged on Mother's Day, 1999—just over a month before our dear Lia was born, as it turns out. While a mother and father in China worried over their soon-to-be born child and the incredibly difficult decision they faced, her parents-to-be began a joyful journey that would bring us closer to a country on the other side of the world. We say our connection was "forged" on Mother's Day that year because the connection actually began years earlier—when my wife, as a little girl, felt God place this connection in her heart. Years later, as we contemplated growing our family, discussing and debating whether or not to have a third child, God's whisper suddenly rose above all else and proclaimed: "Go get your daughter in China!"

I have to admit, up until we began considering adopting a child from China, I hadn't given much thought to the country. I knew the basics: a bit of its history, some key cultural elements, and its political situation. But this was all on an intellectual level. Now I was going to have a real and tangible connection—on a very emotional level. I needed to know more about China… for my own sake and for my daughter's sake! I needed to feel a connection with the people and the country so I could lay the foundation for a deep, heart-to-heart connection with my little girl.

Through all the drudgery of adoption paperwork, we began the process of enlightenment—books on Chinese culture, on travel, on the people. We met other adoptive parents and heard their stories— and met their little girls. Oh, how they melted our hearts! Of course all (or at least most) young children can have that effect. But these were little Chinese girls, with their beautiful, black silky hair, their fun personalities, and their spunky spirits. They were my link to China and to my daughter— and, oh, how I longed for my little Lia.

Josie Lin and Reese (both age 3½), both from Xinyu, Jiangxi, with their dads.

After the months of waiting, we finally began our travels—a trip that promised to be another important step of truly understanding the world of our daughter. We arrived in China a week before our travel group came together—using the opportunity to play tourist. But this time also served to personalize much of what we had read and heard. Seeing the historic Chinese sites, such as the Great Wall and the Forbidden City, certainly allowed us to relate their grandness and significance in a personal way to Lia. But even more profound, we ate dinner in a Beijing hutong—away from the tourist areas and in the middle of "real" urban China. We saw how the people live and we experienced their warm hospitality. That was a special night.

Our time in China also gave us some keen insight into the spirit that fills our daughter. We saw determination and perseverance in the people. We saw hard work and ingenuity. And we also saw love and compassion. In short we saw the heart of a proud people—the same heart that we see every day in our little girl.

We can't wait to take Lia and our other children to China. I am hopeful that she will recognize something familiar and comfortable about the place where she was born—familiar to her regardless of the fact that she spent only 14 months there. It will be fun seeing her make the connection, and realizing that China is a proud part of who she is as a person—and a very proud part of who we are as a family.

For all the little girls from China
by Penny Callan Partridge

Whenever I see one
I know there will someday be
this incredible sorority
of women brought here
as babies from China.

And their Great Wall
will always go all the
way through them to
split what happened in China/
what's happened here.

But they will help each other
over this wall all their lives
until those walls at their
centers are merely their
strong and flexible spines.

Maybe on the basis of
collective cultural hybrid
strength which they'll
find many ways to cultivate
(the strength of their stories!)

these women of the world's
first international
female diaspora
will inherit the earth.
And do something good with it.

Brynn Xuan (age 20 months),
Gao'An, Jiangxi.

Emma and Kaitlyn
(both born September 11, 2005),
YangXi, Guangdong, spent their
first nine months together.

Emma Paige (about age 12 months), YangXi, Guangdong.

AND THE TWO BECAME ONE
by Lorelei Kay

I WAS TEN YEARS OLD WHEN I TOLD MY BEST FRIEND THAT I WAS GOING TO ADOPT A LITTLE GIRL FROM CHINA ONE DAY. I didn't know much about China politically, but I knew that they had strong family ties. I knew that they had honor and integrity. It was the commitment and dedication to one another that intrigued me.

Twenty-one years later I received a picture of a beautiful little girl. My heart's desire was coming to pass. As my husband and I walked the streets of Guangzhou, I saw the love, hard work, and unity of the community. I felt like I was home. I cannot begin to fathom the pain that was felt so that I could be so richly blessed. However, I do know that it wasn't only a family that was united—but two nations became one.

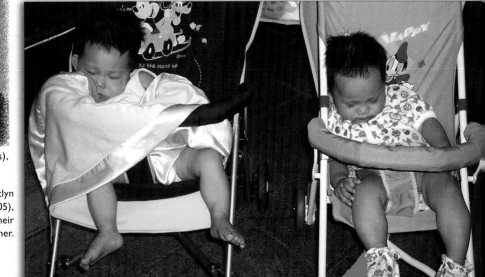

Molly (about age 14 months), Beihai City, Guangxi,
Molly was hiding behind my legs but kept peeking out to say hello.

MOLLY'S BIRTHMOTHER
Excerpted essay by Anna Salvage

NEVER COULD I HAVE EVER IMAGINED HOW MUCH I WOULD LOVE GUO RUO CHEN (NOW KNOWN AS MOLLY). She is the most amazing child, so full of joy and so smart and loving! I hope she will always know how much I love her and how much I wanted her. The wait for my referral was extremely difficult. It was so emotional, so much more than I had expected. There were lots of tears and sleepless nights. I wondered would I ever get a referral, would China close its doors to single mothers, did my dossier get lost? Was my baby cold, hungry, safe? Was there someone who soothed her when she cried? Most days I felt like the wait was too much to bear and wanted to give up. But now I have Molly. All that pain is just a memory for me, but not for her birthmother. I cannot even imagine how difficult it must have been for her birthmother to give her up. I am so thankful that she left Molly to be found in a public, highly visible place. I didn't realize how much I would think about Molly's birthmother. But I think of her every day and wish that I could let her know how much I love Molly and how well she is doing. But most of all, I want to say thank you, even though those words are not enough. It breaks my heart that I cannot express my gratitude to her and reassure her that Molly is very loved! I often get told that Molly is lucky, but I am the lucky one and I am thankful every day.

Dear Birthmother (or I'll Always Wonder)
by Karen Ellard

For 10 days you held her.
For 10 days you kept her safe and warm.
I wonder what you did during your time together. Who knew?
Did you make a choice or bend to forces beyond your control?

Did you wonder what would become of her?
Wonder because she is a girl? An orphan?
Wonder because of a medical condition?
I will always wonder what you thought and know that I'll never know.

Did you worry about what her future held?
A waiting child in a sea of children
Did you kiss her 12 toes, loving her?
Worrying that she would spend her days alone?

Did you hope against hope that she would find a home?
Someone to accept and love your daughter
Know that I kissed those 12 little toes
And sobbed when we "fixed" them.

Would it ease your pain to know that I hold her every night?
Your baby, my baby, our baby
Know that she is happy, safe, and loved.
Above all she is cherished.

Nothing can erase your sorrow, but…
Would it ease your pain to know that she is loved?

That baby that you had to leave with such uncertainty is home.

Brother and sisters together forever.
Morgan (age 12); Kelsey (age 13 months), Cangwu, Guangxi; and Daniel (age 14).

SHOPPING IN CHINA
by Marcia Armstrong

I DID SO MUCH SHOPPING AT HELEN'S STORE WHEN WE WERE IN GUANGZHOU IN FEBRUARY 2005 THAT SHE RECOGNIZED ME WHEN I RETURNED THERE RECENTLY. Me! Out of all the Americans she had seen in the 18 months since we were last in China! Back then she and I did a lot of haggling over the things I wanted to buy, and we both came away happy.

My forte is haggle. I thought I was the best at it until that night when I watched a master at work. I had already done my haggling with Helen and settled on a price for all my stuff when my travel mate sat down in front of a table full of shoes and baby clothes she wanted for her 16-month-old daughter. The shop girl started at one price and my friend started way lower than that, but she ended up getting most everything she wanted for her price. Wow! Watching her was like a high school graduate watching someone who has five Ph.Ds. I want a Ph.D. in haggle too!

We were in Helen's store for at least an hour when my daughter, Anna, woke up. She sat in the stroller, then got out to play with the toys in the shop, and proceeded to rearrange all the hair barrettes. Soon Anna started fidgeting. You know the kind of fidgeting I'm talking about. When asked she said she had to go to the bathroom. I told Helen, but she didn't want me to leave yet because I hadn't spent enough money. Helen got Anna interested in stringing beads for a bracelet that she said she was making as a gift to me. Anna strung beads for at least 20 minutes and then came to me, grabbed my hand, and led me to the door. I told Helen that Anna really had to go to the bathroom this time. Really. I started to leave, but Helen wanted me to buy the mother-of-pearl necklace with the sterling silver chain. She went to the back of the store and brought out a little red bucket. She took Anna behind a curtain and, well, you can guess what happened next. How's that for customer service? I really do like that necklace.

Siblings—Sam (age 16); Emma Xiao Jing (age 3), Yulin, Shaanxi; and Maggie (age 13).

Born to shop. Nora ZhangLiang (age 31 months), Zhuzhou, Hunan.

FATHERHOOD FEELINGS
by Andrew Woodhall

As a man blessed with a wonderful wife and daughter, I cannot imagine being happier than or as contented as I am today. I recall experiencing this feeling firsthand for the first time back in October 2004 when Fallon Reece Xiu Wei sat in my arms and stared at me, without so much as a blink or a sound. The bond I had heard so much about—I felt it, I understood it, and most of all I loved it!!

It is very hard to put into words the emotional bond and ties that develop between a parent and a child. That moment you hold your child in your arms, it clicks. The realization of the months and, at times, years of thoughts, worries, and feelings sits in your arms, and you truly realize at that point what you have. The feelings you thought were there were none other than a glimpse or taste of what was to come. For no matter how much you imagine, the truth is, the reality of actually holding your child has no real resemblance to those feelings you conjured up in the time leading up to this moment. The moment of reality makes the strongest muscle bow, the driest eye tearful, and certainly in my case the most vocal of us speechless.

A man has his defined roles in life or, at times, so he thinks. For a child who relies so heavily on your love, care, and attention, you are willing to do anything, in any way, to cater to his or her needs. Some say there is no greater challenge or rewarding vocation than that of rearing a child. This I believe wholeheartedly for I cannot imagine any other emotion powerful enough to wash away any distress, frustration, or anger of the day than that of what a child offers. Their mere presence or action, which might appear outwardly so small, is at times so meaningful and appreciated; it is a power like no other.

I never thought I would experience these feelings or emotions as I had no inkling they were possible. I had no idea they existed within me.

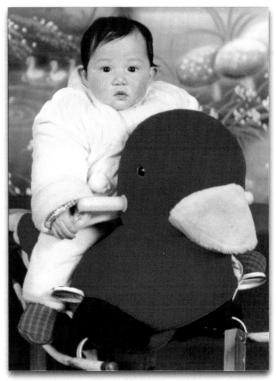

Above: Eleanor ("Ellie") ZhaoMan (about age 6 months), Yuanling, Hunan.

Below: Eleanor ("Ellie") ZhaoMan (age 3).

To a Very Special Woman in China
by Kim Beagle

You will never know how grateful I am to you. Even though we will never meet, I feel forever bonded to you. You have given me the most incredible gift of all—my precious daughter, Kaylee.

She is stunningly beautiful. I often find myself just staring at her, marveling at her perfect skin and gazing into her deep black almond-shaped eyes… wondering what you look like and what she'll look like when she's older.

I long to tell you that your daughter is safe and happy and very, very loved. She has brought endless joy to our lives and to the lives of everyone who knows her. She is outgoing, smart, kind, and so full of life. You would be so proud of her if you could see her today.

There are many questions I have that I will never have answers to. What I do know is that you took incredible risks so that your daughter could have a brighter future. I will always be grateful for that heart-wrenching decision you made. I can't imagine how painful it was to walk away, leaving your three-day-old baby in front of that school. I mourn for you often, and certainly every January 31st. I can't help but wonder if you're reliving that moment over and over in your mind and wondering what happened to that tiny baby girl. I wish there was some way for me to tell you that she's halfway around the world in America laughing and giggling, taking gymnastics and swimming lessons, having tea parties with her little sister, and sitting in her bed having "princess parties" with her stuffed animals when everyone thinks she's taking a nap. I wish you could hear her giggle as she acts out the story of the "Three Little Pigs," or watch her lead us all in a marching band parade around the couch, or listen to her sing her heart out into her pretend microphone. Above all I just wish you could know that she is safe and happy… and so very loved.

It saddens me deeply that you and I will never meet. I would love to be able to hold you tightly and tell you, with tears in my eyes, that your daughter means everything to me. I could not possibly love her any more, not if I had given birth to her myself. I never imagined that I could love someone this much, and I never imagined my heart could be so full. I don't know how to thank someone for such an incredible gift.

Deep down, even though it contradicts everything I know to be true, I'm still holding out hope that one day we will be able to find you.

With deepest gratitude,
Kim Beagle

Above: Sisters—Lauren (age 16 months), ChangDe, Hunan, and Molly (age 4), Maoming, Guangdong—meeting Nana.

Right: Molly XiaoLu (age 7), Maoming, Guangdong—in costume for the traditional Chinese Molihua (jasmine flower) folk dance.

Sophie Mei You Zhi (age 12 months), Chenzhou, Hunan—receiving a "Sophie sandwich kiss" in the courtroom just after our adoption was finalized.

Our Chinese Brownie Troop
by Charlotte Halsema Ottinger

THE EARLY SCHOOL YEARS CAN BE A VULNERABLE TIME FOR CHILDREN WHO ARE ADOPTED. This is when they begin to be confronted with questions from their peers while they also try to understand their own personal stories. We want our children to learn about, and feel proud of, their Chinese heritage while comfortably growing into "All-American" kids. As a result of conversations about these issues, fellow adoptive mom Chris Jacobson and I decided to form a Brownie troop to give our daughters an opportunity to develop friendships with girls whose backgrounds were similar, while participating in a very American tradition—Girl Scouts—with a unique emphasis on Chinese culture!

Our troop is different in that we are a city-wide troop and have 30 members. Our meetings focus on traditional Girl Scout activities and goals while infusing projects and information related to China. For example, when working on the "Special Languages" patch, we invited a deaf woman to speak to our group using an interpreter. Then the girls learned about the differences between how deaf people live in China versus the United States. With this new knowledge the troop decided to sponsor a deaf Chinese orphaned child in school for a year.

Whenever possible we invite Chinese Americans to help with our programs, such as our Mother-Daughter Chinese Tea. During this meeting the girls learned about tea cultivation and were shown aspects of a traditional Chinese tea ceremony. They also learned about YiXing teapots and were able to see several examples. Each girl had an opportunity to "show and tell" her own favorite teapot, make a pot of tea, and enjoy a variety of Chinese snacks, all while earning a "Tea Party" fun patch. In addition to American Brownie patches, the girls will be earning patches such as "Chinese Festivals" and "Calligraphy" from the Hong Kong Girl Guides, part of the International Girl Scout network.

Thanks in part to a grant from Our Chinese Daughters Foundation, our first year concluded with a trip to Chicago's Chinatown where we had a luncheon speaker discuss Chinese dining etiquette. Following lunch they participated in special programs at the Chinese American Museum of Chicago. The girls also took part in a photo journalism project with specific photo assignments in Chinatown to record their visit and to stimulate conversation about their experience. Each girl completed a scrapbook that they were proud to share with friends upon returning to school in the fall.

Although some of the concepts presented to the girls have been more involved than can be fully understood through one program—such as our hands-on activities with the abacus at the Chinese American Museum—our intent is to expose the girls to Chinese culture. Mastering many of the skills and understanding traditions is a process that will require years of involvement in the Chinese American community and "layers" of instruction. Our girls seem to be more aware of their heritage. "I have certainly noticed that my daughter, Lia, seems more interested in and aware of her roots," said co-leader Chris Jacobson.

"Big sister" Sherri Geng (age 19), with Kayla (age 9), Yiwu, Zhejiang.

Big Sis
by Kayla Robbins (age 9)

WHEN I WAS EIGHT YEARS OLD I MET SHERRI GENG. I tried two programs to find a big sis, but I didn't like them. Then I tried another one and found that I had a very nice, generous, and sweet sister. So we kept on doing fun things together like kite making, walks, going to restaurants, museums, movies, and a lot of fun stuff together. I like having a big sister because it's a person you can look up to as a role model or ask them anything you want, and I'd bet they would have a good answer because they'd been through all of that stuff I'm dealing with now.

Chinese Brownie troop in Indianapolis, Indiana. (Back row) Julia, Gracie, Josi, Mikaylin, Sarah, Lin, and Maggie. (Middle row) Ellie, Leah, Kate, Emily, Eliza, Ginger, and Olivia. (Front row) Katelyn, KaiLian, Grace, Abigail, Emily, Vivianne, Cara Marie, and SarahMei.

John Liang, (age 4), Hefei, Anhui.

Sisters—Abrienna Liying (age 10), Nanping, Fujian; Lucy Alexandra Jialian (age 5), Lianyungang, Jiangsu; and Annalizi Kristine (age 10), Nanping, Fujiang.

PRECIOUS FRIENDSHIP
by Amy Eldridge

SOME OF THE BIGGEST BLESSINGS I HAVE RECEIVED IN ADOPTING FROM CHINA AND THEN SUBSEQUENTLY WORKING THERE ARE THE DEAR FRIENDS I HAVE MADE ON MY TRAVELS. In one city I visit frequently, I met a young bellboy named Ao. He was 18, and he was fascinated that a white woman would come all the way to China to work in an orphanage. In this particular town, there are only 12 foreigners who live in the entire city; so my presence never went without notice. We struck up a conversation one day, and he asked me *so* many questions about my life, my children, America. Every time I would come into the hotel he would run over to speak with me, and he would call out, "Hello, Mrs. Amy Eldridge!" when I walked through the lobby.

On my next few trips we became better and better friends, and I always looked forward to seeing him. In early 2004 he was promoted to bell captain. He was so proud of his new uniform and continued to brighten my days when I would come back and forth to the hotel, usually at very late hours. During our cleft trip, he was so very kind to me. He knew I was working 18 hour days, and he would send up fresh fruit for me. I didn't get a chance to see him very much on that trip, but I would still occasionally hear, "Hello, Mrs. Amy Eldridge!" as I came and went.

On my next visit, he came running up to me in the lobby with a bag he had saved for me for six months. Inside were surgical scrubs that our team had worn back in May. He had folded them all up and placed them in the back office, just waiting for the day that "Mrs. Amy Eldridge" would come back to claim them. The first thing I noticed on this trip was that he had on a sport coat. He proudly told me that he was the new night manager of the hotel. At age 20! His English was becoming better and better, and he told me that he was teaching himself by using an English dictionary for long hours at a time. One night I brought back some of the teenagers from the orphanage for a quick visit,

and he had them all in giggles as he escorted them to the elevator and then bowed and waved us in. He said, "And these girls are?" And I smiled and said, "My very good friends." He then gave a deeper bow and said, "Then warmest welcome to you ladies," which had the girls in an absolute titter.

A few days before I left on one trip, I realized how very much I looked forward to seeing this young man who always has a smile on his face and who always welcomes me back in such a warm way. So I went out shopping for him, and I found a beautiful blue and silver pen that was simple, but elegant. I could just imagine Ao using it in his work. It was not expensive… not at all… but I had fun shopping for him. When I arrived I immediately noticed that he had on a full suit, and he came hurrying over to do a full turn so I could take in his uniform. He then proudly presented me with his business card which said "Assistant Manager." I did a pretty Oklahoman thing and gave out a "Woohoo!!!," which made everyone in the lobby turn to see us.

During my few days in the area, there were several times that Ao came to find me to talk, and suddenly I realized that he always asked about *my* work, and I had not asked about his. So I asked him to tell me his life story. He explained that he was from way far north, in a place I wouldn't know. I smiled and said, "Try me." He said he was from Dalian, in a small town called Siping. When I said "I know that town; there is an orphanage there," he couldn't believe it. He did not know there was an orphanage in his hometown. He told me the town was very, very poor. Ao told me that his father had died when he was very young, and that his family was always struggling to survive. His mom did not have good health, and so, at the age of 16, before he could finish his schooling, he decided he had to become a man and set out to find work to support his mother. He told me that there was just no possible way for him to go to college; so he quit school knowing he had to find work. When he was just 16, he said good-bye to his mom and got on a train, not really knowing where he was going.

He rode on the train for 53 hours straight and then got off in the southern part of China. For six months he tried to find work, and finally, *finally*, he was hired at the local hotel as a bellboy. He said he worked as hard as he could to send money to his mother. And then after two years he became bell captain, and then night manager, and now assistant manager. I told him that his mother must be so very proud of him, and he smiled and said she was. I told him I was proud of him too!

The last night I was there, I asked him to come up to my room because I had a gift for him. He was speechless and said he could not accept. But I just smiled and told him that it was such a small gift and so he had to take it. Upstairs in the lobby I gave him the small box with the blue and silver pen. I told him again, "Really, it is such a small gift, but I had so much fun thinking of you and buying it for you." And then Ao—this young 20-year-old who had lived the last four years on his own—told me he had no gift for me in return. But then he said, "Perhaps you would accept a story as my gift?" He then apologized if his English wasn't perfect and proceeded to tell me an old Chinese tale from Dalian.

He told me the story of a simple peasant and a very kind emperor who did great things for the people of China. The peasant wanted to give the emperor a gift, but he had no money at all to do so. One day the man saw a beautiful golden bird, and he wanted to give it to the emperor so badly; so he worked and worked and worked trying to catch it. One day he succeeded, and he held on to the golden bird with all his might. The man started the long journey to the emperor, and he walked and walked and walked, under the hot sun and over mountains, all the while cradling the beautiful golden bird, knowing that he would have a fitting gift for the king. Right before he got to the emperor's home, he was so weak from walking that he relaxed his grip on the bird and it flew away. The man jumped and tried to catch the bird, but he was only able to grasp one golden tail feather.

Saddened, he headed to the emperor and got in line with others bringing gifts. The people around him all laughed at his gift. "What sort of gift is that for a king?" they asked.

Finally it was the peasant's turn, and he humbly went up to the emperor with his single feather. He told the king, "I had wanted to bring you a golden bird like the sun, but the bird escaped. And so I bring you a gift that is not grand, but very small. But please, kind king, know that this simple gift carries with it all of my love, and I give it to you with all of my heart." By then Ao was standing in the hallway with tears streaming down his face. He said, "Mrs. Amy Eldridge, I give you this story with my whole heart because you were the very first friend I felt I had in this city."

Somehow I managed to get back inside my room before crying. The next day he was at the manager's desk, smiling his regular huge smile, saying, "Hello, Mrs. Amy Eldridge!," and he took his new pen from his suit coat pocket and waved it at me. It was very hard to say good-bye to him this time because I did not know how long it would be before our paths would cross again. I will miss seeing him.

I absolutely treasure the friendships I have with people in China. I think the beauty of forming friendships between people of other countries is that when you sit and talk one-on-one, you realize that no matter what our differences might be on the outside, we are the same on the inside. We all have hopes and dreams, and we all want the best for our families. We enjoy laughing, and friendship, and sharing stories. I have met so many wonderful people in China—dozens and dozens of people like Ao, who live with so little and yet who live with such kindness and grace that it brings tears to my eyes. I will never forget Ao's story because he gave it with his whole heart. It has nothing to do with how much a gift costs, does it? It has everything to do with your heart. You cannot measure the worth of something given with such sincere kindness, and he showed me once again that friendship is truly one of the greatest gifts of all.

Siblings—Natalie Louyuan (age 5), Xi'An, Sha'anxi, and Tyler Jiaqing (age 8), Wenzhou, Zhejiang.

Christina (age 5½), Nanning, Guangxi—posing in Guilin with performers dressed in the attire of her Zhuang minority group.

(Left to right) Savannah, Alice, Emma Grace, Heather, Lily (all age 4 or nearly age 4), all from Cenxi, Guangxi, and Sierra (age 2), Shucheng, Anhui, with their "Cenxi family." Yearly we rent a vacation home. We spend months planning and looking forward to our "Cenxi family" vacations.

Siblings—Jackson (age 4), Yangzhou, Jiangsu; Bethany (age 2); and Anna Lei (age 4), Yongfeng, Jiangxi.

A SINGULAR ENCOUNTER
by Anthony Thornton

DURING OUR TWO-WEEK STAY IN CHINA WHILE ADOPTING 13-MONTH-OLD ABBEY ZHUO GRACE, WE ENCOUNTERED THE TYPICAL STARES, MOSTLY QUIZZICAL BUT GOOD-NATURED. Once in Abbey's native Chongqing, we attracted a crowd so large that I lost sight of my wife and daughter amid the circle of people surrounding them. Like most other Americans adopting from China, we also encountered the occasional chiding from locals concerned about the slightest amount of skin showing on our new daughter's limbs, even in 80 degree weather.

On the 13-hour flight from Beijing to Chicago, the longest leg of the grueling journey home we all experience, our new family was lucky enough to have the middle row of seats virtually to ourselves. This was a godsend for we quickly learned that Abbey's orphanage director wasn't kidding when referring to her as "active." She had no interest in sitting still for ten minutes, much less 13 hours. During one of the many times I tried to keep my squirming daughter from kicking the man sitting in front of us, I glanced to my right and noticed an older Chinese woman watching us. We made eye contact; she smiled and slowly nodded for several seconds. No words were spoken. None were needed. In that moment this woman was conveying her acceptance, her approval, her fond wishes for our new family.

Through several experiences during our stay, we developed a fondness for China, and especially for her people. But no single encounter is as indelibly imprinted for me as the one that occurred at 40,000 feet.

MY CHINA! OUR CHINA!
by Ed Childs

EIGHT WEEKS AFTER RECEIVING OUR REFERRAL FOR CATE, WE WERE IN THE AIR AND ON OUR WAY TO OUR DAUGHTERS' BIRTH COUNTRY. Big sister Cara had a window seat and conducted a non-stop monologue about her sister to anyone who was within earshot on the plane. As we prepared to land in Beijing, my thoughts raced to the more practical matter of whether Cara would be frightened when the plane landed. I told her that the plane might make some loud noises as it kissed the ground. Thump. Thump. Thump. The wheels of the plane made contact with the runway. Cara yelled out a loud "Wheeeeeee!" as if she had just been on a 15-minute amusement ride instead of a 15-hour international flight. I raised the window shade so she could look out at the runway. Cara excitedly clapped her hands. "My China! Dada! Mama! I'm in *my* China! We are here!" That level of enthusiasm is hard to ignore, no matter what language you speak. The back of the plane erupted in laughter and applause.

Cara Lin Xin (age 4), Xiaonan, Hubei, and her parents with referral photo of Cate (about age 5 months), Fengcheng, Jiangxi.

We spent five days in Beijing and each day began with similar greetings from Cara. She would salute the tour bus daily. "Hello, bus." "Good morning, China!" Seeing the city through her eyes made us realize that this was going to be a very different trip. Routine events for adults are anything but that for young toddlers. While we were excited by our visits to the Summer Palace, hutongs, temples, and the Great Wall, Cara was most enthralled with the street billboards and food wrappers. "Mama! Dada! Look here. *That's* Chinese!" "Mama! Dada! I'm in *my* China!" The Chinese were both curious and extremely friendly to our daughter. Cara would say over and over, "These are my friends! My *bestest* friends!"

Then the big day arrived. We walked into the conference room at the Gloria Hotel in Nanchang, and we immediately recognized our sweet baby, Cate. She was sitting on the top of the conference table playing with a book we had sent her a few weeks before. When an employee of the orphanage motioned Cara over, we lifted her up on the table, and she quickly scrambled to sit in front of Cate. Cara turned to us and said, "That's my sister!" She then turned all of her undivided attention to Cate. In wonderment Cara touched Cate's hands and then, as if to reassure, gently stroked Cate's exposed bare feet. It was the most incredible moment to witness this exchange between these two beauties of China whose lives would now become forever linked.

Cara turned to the nearby orphanage workers, who were now looking intently at the Chinese baby and the Chinese toddler. Cara smiled and pointed to Cate. "My China. My sister." While they did not understand the words, they knew the genuine sentiment being expressed. The women broke out into big smiles.

My wife and I looked at each other and knew that our China travels had come full circle. We had been waiting a lifetime for "Our Girls," but in that moment we realized that our daughters' birth country would now and forever be "Our China."

Pei Xiang (age 2), Fuzhou, Jiangxi.

Abby (age 2½), Fengcheng, Jiangxi.

A Letter for Xiang Xiang
by Belinda Cooley and Simon Deacon

***Our precious Pei Xiang,
we write this letter to say thank you.***

Thank you for being our daughter.
Thank you for showing us how to love unconditionally.
Thank you for teaching us patience and understanding.
Thank you for making every day special.
Thank you for your cuddles and kisses.
Thank you for your strength and determination.
Thank you for filling our home with laughter and joy.

Left: Cate Xue He (age 9 months), Fengcheng, Jiangxi.

Below: Forever friends—Lillian and Cara (both age 3), Xiaonan, Hubei. The girls' families live in the same small town and were surprised when they received their referrals at the same time to learn that their daughters were from the same orphanage.

Above: Mom and Kate (age 12 months), Yuanling, Hunan, finally meet.

Right: Kate (age 16 months)— all dressed up.

SWEET EMBRACES
by Marcella Nicotera

ONCE AGAIN IT IS 2 A.M. AND I HEAR YOUR CRY. I am awake and ready as I run to your room to see why. As usual I find you in your crib, your arms opened wide ready for my strong embrace. I hold you close as you snuggle in my arms.

What woke you up tonight, my sweet princess? Is it your teeth? Does your tummy hurt? Did you have a bad dream? Or are you just checking to see if I am still here?

As we sit in the rocking chair and I sing our lullaby, you wrap your arms around my neck and whisper, "Mommy." Oh, Kyara, you will never know how much we love you—we are your forever family.

As Dad peeks in the doorway moments later, I hear your soft breath as you fall asleep knowing that all is well once again. I will cherish these nights, my sweet angel from heaven, as I know soon they will be a distant memory as we watch you grow up so fast.

Kyara Fu Ai Li (age 2), Fuling, Sichuan.

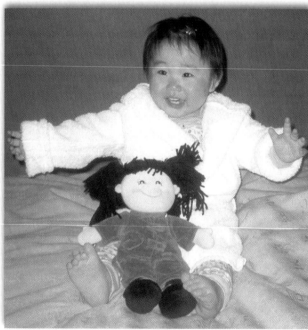

Brother and sister.
Above: Jack (age 3),
Shantou, Guangdong.

Left: Lily (age 3),
Shantou, Guangdong.

Sisters—Xuedan (age 7),
Shantou, Guangdong,
and Jing-Mei (age 6),
Huaibei, Anhui.

给来自中国的女儿们

迈克 马哈西

来自中国的女儿们 -
你们中我相识寥寥无几
你们中多数我素不相逢
我却深爱着你们每一个

我的心在为你们呼唤
呼唤你们将会被拥抱
呼唤你们将会被养育
呼唤你们将会被热爱

我的心为你们渴望
渴望你们会去拥抱
渴望你们会去养育
渴望你们会去热爱

我的心为你们去搜寻探索
愿你们会拥有你们的世界
愿你们会温暖你们的世界
愿你们会保佑我们的世界

愿你们有勇气和希望
为你们，来自中国的女儿们
永保你们的温柔和优雅
去改变你们的世界，我的世界

啊，来自中国的女儿们
旴用你们的爱来改变我们的世界
记住，我永远和你们同在 -
现在，明天，永远！

To the Daughters of China
by Mike Mahathy (2005)

Daughters of China—
Some of you I know,
Most of you I do not.
All of you I adore.

My Heart cries for you
That you will be held;
That you will be nurtured;
That you will be loved.

My Heart yearns for you
That you will hold;
That you will nurture;
That you will love.

My Heart looks to you
That you will claim your world;
That you will warm your world;
That you will bless *our* world.

Please have courage and hope.
For you, the daughters of China,
Hold the tenderness and grace
To change *your* world, *my* world.

Oh, daughters of China,
Please change *our* world with your love;
And do know I am with you—
Now, tomorrow, always.

Susanna XueZhu (age 10½),
Zhenghe, Fujian,
now lives in Helsinki, Finland.

Anna Olivia (age 8), Shantou, Guangdong.

NEW CONNECTIONS
by Kyle Messner

ADOPTION OPENS UP A WHOLE NEW WORLD FOR EVERYONE INVOLVED. Lives become fuller, filled with new people and relationships. Children are united with their forever families, and families are transformed as the newest members are woven into their world. As the changes occur, threads are added to the tapestry and it grows. Communities are formed: Families with Children from China, adoptive family organizations, orphanage listservs, special needs Yahoo groups, individual travel groups, agencies that offer continuing support, volunteer organizations that unite to make life better for those left in the orphanages—the list goes on and on. New friendships blossom and grow as people meet together for cultural activities and talk online and offer support. Strangers reach out to others in amazing acts of kindness. Travel groups meet for joyful reunions as families strengthen the ties their children have with each other. People who were previously strangers become aunts and uncles to each other's children. Identities change further as families become part of the larger Chinese American community. New holidays and customs are celebrated. New knowledge is gained, and "guangxi" is developed. Ordinary lives are transformed into extraordinary ones as the new connections weave and interconnect.

HEATHER RETURNS
Dictated to Mama by Heather Joy FuHeng Brogan Gealey (aka Xiao Jie Er, "Little Miss") (age 5 years, 15 days)

I LIKED CHINA BECAUSE I COULD SEE MY NANNIES. A lot came to my hotel. They were happy and laughed a lot because they loved me. I was a baby a long time ago. They said I was beautiful and naughty. They said I loved only one of them and made all the rest sad because they loved me. They called me Xiao Jie Er. I was beautiful and spoiled. Only one nanny could hold me or sleep with me. I loved her. She is beautiful—very, very beautiful. They said which one is favorite. I hugged my favorite. She was so happy I remembered. I remember love.

Everyone loved me. They gave me a green toy bunny. He is funny when he sings. He has funny red eyes. I love him because my nannies gave him to me. They love me. His name is General Fu. I am going back to China. In China I am Hengheng. I have a *lot* of names.

Heather (age 4), Cenxi, Guangxi,
with caregivers and orphange officials.

Sisters—Ava (age 15 months), Xuwen, Guangdong;
Rebecca (age 4), Nanchang, Jiangxi;
and Ginny (age 6), Yangchun, Guangdong.

ADVOCATES FOR ADOPTION
by Janet Jin

I STARTED WORKING AT A SMALL NONPROFIT ADOPTION AGENCY LOCATED IN BEAUTIFUL HAWAII IN 1999 AS A MANDARIN CHINESE TEACHER. Eventually I took the job as the director of the Waiting Child Program in 2004. It was the kind of the job that requires putting in a lot of heart.

Finding homes for the first group of waiting children was a disaster. I had five wonderful children on the waiting list, but since I didn't have the knowledge and support network then, I could only find a loving home for one child with a congenital heart condition. The rest of the children's files were all sent back to CCAA. That experience almost broke my heart and made me want to quit my job. I still often take out the pictures of those four children and wonder how they are doing now.

Kyle Messner, one of the wonderful advocates for these waiting children, learned that I only found a home for one child and emailed me back, saying she would help me find homes for all the children in my next group. When I read her email, I thought that was very nice of her to encourage me, but honestly I wondered how that could be possible. We all know families that adopt waiting children belong to a very small, special group, and there are so many waiting children out there.

The miracle did happen! It was around the beginning of 2005. Some parents who adopted waiting children began support groups on the Internet. The speed of how these groups grew was just amazing. Kyle, Donna Schwartz, another strong advocate, and one of my clients, Susan Arritt, formed a voluntary support network to help find homes for all five children in my second group. I was so moved by these women's enthusiasm and love for these waiting children. The effort and time that they put in was as if they were trying to find a good home for themselves! All five children found homes!

While I have the waiting children's files for three months, it feels like I am destined to be their temporary mom. These three months are stressful and emotional, but it also helps me connect to and work with a lot of wonderful loving people. The most rewarding moment of my job is finding homes for every one of the waiting children, knowing that they came home safely and will grow up to be healthy, strong, and happy. I always feel so blessed to be a part of the process, and this process has shown me that miracles do happen, as long as we put in a lot of love and prayer for these waiting children.

Sarah (age 2),
Xinzhou, Shangrao,
Jiangxi.

Woven
by Fang Fang Wu Lee and Hanni Beyer Lee

I am what I am
Such a wonder to me
A child of China
The trip of a lifetime
Soft as tofu
Sweet as new rain
From the Miao tribe;
I knew you were different
when you showed me your pierced ears
One of 56 treasures of China
That's you, Fangyi
I am you
You are her
You have woven me and
made my threads
I watch a tapestry unfold
of someone I have never met
and yet, know intimately
Every grain of rice
that goes into my body
is proof
of your hard laboring
But what was her labor?
Farming?
What did she plant?
Were you not also her labor?
I am me
I watch you constantly
With each note
That I pluck on my gu-zheng,
An ancient sound of heaven
I remember everyone
who was there
Raising me
to be what I am now
There are many of us, I know
Sometimes I wonder if we are too many?
We who love you so
It took a village
to raise me
Your villages are widening circles now

I am a proof
of her
This is the sweetest and saddest truth
I speak the language
of the Great Wall
Bilingual Butterfly, you are
And the dialect of the
sweet taste
of lychees
I always know how much
you miss Yunnan
from your writing
I am you and
You are me
I wonder about this—
so you feel this too?
Even though
I wasn't born
From you
And yet, I swear I can see
What a baby named Xiaofang
Might have looked like
The most beautiful baby ever born...
I was born from
Your soul
Is this why then, that my soul
Is so touched in your presence?
And you are
Still my Mama
I am—and
You are my—can I say it?—
my baby.
My blueberry in Maine,
My searching poet,
My dark chocolate treat,
My first daughter
And always
will be
Always.
I am you
and you are me
Mother and daughter
My greatest wish fulfilled.

Anna LiWen (age 2),
Shantou, Guangdong.

REMEMBERING LILLI'S BIRTHMOM
by Tyla Gilchrist

I LOVE TO CELEBRATE MOTHER'S DAY. For so many years I wanted to be a mom, and I feel so blessed to have my children. I am blessed to be a mom both by birth and by adoption. My children are each so very special to me.

But how can Mother's Day go by without remembering the amazing, brave woman that carried Lilli in her womb and got her to safety despite the risks? In fact, how can any day go by? I think of her always.

I wish somehow she could know that Lilli is safe and loved and happy. I wish she could somehow know how much her sacrifice means to us. I wish she could somehow know that she too is family to us and how much we love her.

Each Mother's Day I buy a pink balloon. Lilli and I sit together in the grass and talk about her birthmother. We pray together for her to know that Lilli is happy and that her birthmother finds peace with the difficult choice she had to make. We release the balloon so it can carry our thoughts, prayers, and thanksgiving to her in China. We will always remember.

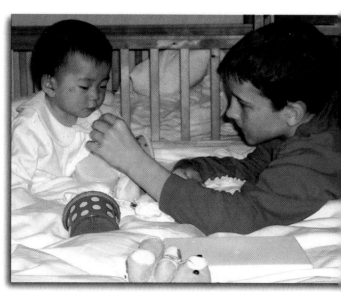

Above: Lillian Li (age 13 months), Yongzhou, Hunan, with big brother, Ben (age 12).

Below: Sisters—Lillian Li (age 3), Yongzhou, Hunan, and Audrey Lina (age 13 months), JinChang, Gansu.

Christmas family photo. (Back) Austin (age 9). (Front) Amber (age 8), sitting by Dad; Savannah (age 6), sitting by Mom; and Ava (age 11 months), Qianjiang, Chongqing.

FALLING IN LOVE... WITH CHINA
by Kristen Fitzgerald

WHEN YOUR DAD AND I MADE THE DECISION TO ADOPT A BABY FROM CHINA, THE THING THAT WORRIED ME MOST WAS THE TRAVEL. I hated to fly, and that flight was so long! But by the time we received your referral and saw your chubby little face, I just couldn't wait to go and meet you!

I knew right away that I would be falling in love with you. What I didn't count on was falling in love with China! The sights, the food, the warm and friendly people—what a wonderful place! Most of all, you, our beautiful daughter, were once a small part of China. And China will always be a part of you. We can't wait to go back and explore with you the amazing country where you were born.

Sophie Lulu JingXiao (age 29 months), Guilin, Guangxi, with sister, Isabelle YangTing (age 24 months), Huai'An, Jiangsu.

Maci Gail Kong (age 2), Nanjing, Jiangsu—being held by Mom. These women surrounded me after we received our new daughter last October, saying in English to us "thank you, thank you" for giving one of their Chinese daughters an opportunity to have a life full of love, happiness, and a forever family. In turn we tried to thank them for allowing us to love one of their daughters.

BRINGING CHINESE CULTURE INTO YOUR HOME
by Jane Peters, Ph.D.

WHEN OUR DAUGHTER CAME HOME FROM CHINA, WE RECOGNIZED THAT AS TWO AMERICANS WE DID NOT KNOW MUCH ABOUT CHINA. We could befriend Chinese Americans, visit China, read books, participate in Families with Children from China (FCC) and local Chinatown events, and eat Chinese food. We have done each of these and more, and each has been important in giving our daughter a connection to China. But we wanted to give her more—a connection to people she might know in the future and a way to understand China from others her own age.

When our daughter was age seven, we read about a program to host high school students from Asia for three weeks while they studied English. We called, met with a social worker who screens families and introduces the program, and decided it was worth a try. We had to transport the student to a specific location each morning so she could meet with her group and go to the school where she was studying English. There were opportunities to meet other families and do some events with the students. The first student improved her English but was never really comfortable talking with us, the adults; yet she spent hours with our daughter.

When the student left, we were a bit disappointed because we did not think that we would have contact with her again. But it had been a good enough experience that we decided to do it the next summer as well. The second student was one of those students that everyone dreams of—warm, open, and excited to learn English, eat American food, and try anything that we suggested. At the end of his three-week stay, we were sad and cried to see him go and knew we would stay in touch. Two years later we did, in fact, visit his family in Taiwan. Then, a year later, his family visited us. The student, now attending college, spent the summer with us this past year. Soon we will leave on our second trip to visit him and his family in Taiwan for Lunar New Year.

We hosted one more summer student and then decided to host a student for the academic year. We learned of a program through another FCC family and applied. Our school district has a defined process for exchange students, and the sponsoring organization must be approved by the district before the process can begin. We helped the organization get the necessary information and began the process.

Our first student came from Hong Kong. We selected her by reviewing applications online from all the students this organization had accepted. We were looking for a student from a Chinese culture whose interests and personality seemed to match our daughter's. We are now hosting our second full-year student and plan to do so again next year. The mother of our current student is contemplating visiting us for the last week her daughter is with us.

There are many benefits to having a foreign exchange student—especially a teenager when your own daughter is a pre-teen. Our daughter is an only child. Having another child around is teaching her to share and to respect another person's space and needs. Most of the students we have had were very responsible, offered to help in the kitchen during mealtimes, and have kept their living space tidy. These behaviors set a good example for our daughter as she becomes a teenager.

The exchange students really want to learn English. They have all studied hard—clearly a cultural expectation for them—and this also provides a good role model for our daughter.

Through the students our daughter gets to learn a bit of what Chinese culture is like for teenagers. We have Chinese pop music in our home, we learn how to make Chinese food, and we teach the exchange students how to cook American food. Our daughter learned how to use instant messaging from these teenagers, and she is seeing them use it responsibly to communicate with their friends and families.

Additionally our family is learning about Chinese culture by talking to these teenagers and learning about how decisions are made in their homes, by going to their countries and meeting their families, and by inviting their families into our home.

We feel our daughter is gaining "sisters" and "brothers" throughout the Chinese world. She will always be much more American than Chinese, but Chinese culture will not be foreign to her. She has a standing invitation to spend a summer in Taiwan with her "brother's" family when she is a teenager, and we hope she does.

Sara Elizabeth (age 3), Changsha, Hunan, with sister Emily Grace (age 2), Qiandongnan, Guizhou.

Siblings—Erin (age 3½), Guangdong; Jack (age 7½); and Kate (age 18 months), Xinjiang.

Ellie Jane Ru Cao (age 10), Jiujiang, Jiangxi—enjoying a Chinese dinner with her family and an exchange student and his family.

Sisters—Tiana (age 5), Shaanxi, and Averi (age 2), Guangxi.

ONE YEAR AGO TODAY
Excerpted letter by Helen Lamsam

WOW! I have been thinking that and saying that word many times during the last few days. It's hard to believe where we were at this time last year and how far we have come since that day.

This day marked the end of a very long journey and the beginning of our family. A child who did not have a family became a daughter, granddaughter, niece, cousin, and friend. Little did she know all the people who were already loving her and waiting for her at home.

Instead of a pregnancy we had months of paperwork and waiting. We then hopped on a plane and flew around the world to a country that was as different as is possible. This place had sights and sounds I could never have imagined, and yet I felt very much at home. The people were beautiful, kind, and giving.

In that minute when the nanny handed me a little girl and told her in Chinese that I was her mama, a husband and wife longing to be a mommy and daddy, and a girl needing to be a daughter, were united… finally and forever. Those first moments were so precious and exciting and followed by days of happy times. We embraced every moment of the rest of our trip and enjoyed every new thing we learned about our dear little girl. We found that she laughed easily and loved to have fun and was truly a *perfect fit* for our family.

Bethany (age 9), Anqing, Anhui, with Ms. Xu, the current SWI director, and Mr. Zhu, the previous SWI director.

Mia (age 3), Maoming, Guangdong.

TWO HOMES
by Bethany Woods (age 9)

WE'VE BEEN BACK TO VISIT MY ORPHANAGE TWICE SINCE I WAS ADOPTED. I've never gotten so much attention before in my life (except from my family). My orphanage staff took us to lunch, and it was a nice surprise that the former director was able to join us.

China was my first home, but it will always be my second home as well. I feel like I have two places I belong.

Photo by Mary Armstrong.

Lauren YiZhen (age 21 months), Chenzhou, Hunan.

Cousins—Helena (about age 4) and Madeline (age 5), Chongqing, Sichuan.

Friends—Mei Mei, Zhuzhou, Hunan, and Abigail, Changsha, Hunan (both age 12)—at Abigail's finding location.

RETAIL THERAPY
by Peggy Lee Scott

I TRAVELED BACK TO CHANGSHA WITH MY DAUGHTER, ABBY, AND SOME FRIENDS FROM OUR TRAVEL GROUP, HOWARD AND MEI MEI. Howard is a widower; Mei Mei's mom died when she was very young, and her maternal grandfather had died more recently. Despite her many losses, she and Abby are both very glass half-full girls, and they adore each other's company. We stayed in the same hotel we stayed in 12 years earlier. It was the perfect metaphor for how much China has changed—now featuring an executive tower, an indoor swimming pool, and a sub-floor goldfish pond in the lobby, which you walk over on a little bridge. It was all very chi-chi, and the girls were ecstatic.

Abby was unsure about returning to visit the orphanage where she was from and wanted to know why I would want to go back there. I replied, "The best thing that ever happened to me in my whole life happened there: adopting *you*." Besides I wanted to find out how many older kids still resided there so we could take them out to dinner and buy them new clothes. She stopped dead in her tracks. "You mean…" she sputtered. "You mean we can go shopping?" When I said yes, she asked, "Can we buy them whatever they want?" I said sure, within a budget. We'd figure out what we could afford and see how much that would buy; and in China it would buy quite a lot. So that was it—retail therapy was Abby's path through her uncertainty.

In Changsha we found the Apollo store and the orphanage. There the older kids showed us their dorms, which were kind of fun—crowded, but filled with posters, desks, books, and clothes. It didn't feel lonely at all. The kids have clearly become family to each other, and at dinner they sat on each other's laps, played tricks on each other, and laughed their heads off at a garish TV show that was playing above the dinner table. They practiced their English with Abby and Mei Mei, who, while clearly outnumbered, were included in the hubbub. It all seemed so darn normal.

The next day we went to Mei Mei's orphanage in Zhuzhou. This time we were the support team, taking photos and staying in the background. It felt fine to be out of the limelight for awhile. That afternoon we visited the Buddhist temple in Changsha and then, somewhat to my surprise, our guide mentioned that we were not far from Abby's finding site. "Did we want to go there?" she asked. This was something I certainly should have discussed with Abby, but somehow it had gotten lost in the shuffle of other events. Abby and Mei Mei both perked up. "Whoa, that would be cool!" she enthused; so off we went.

It took some searching, but the third police station we visited was the charm. It houses the campus police for the Changsha Medical School. The police station was closed for the day, but Abby stood next to the sign in the courtyard for a photo, a large smile lighting up her face. She and Mei Mei wandered through a glade of trees, delighting in the beauty and quiet of such a place, smack dab in the middle of this bustling provincial capital. It is difficult to describe exactly how we felt. Somehow the sheer beauty and quiet of the place felt loving and caring, and brought a kind of peace to our souls. Abby was not left-to-be-found until she was two months old, and we all felt this place confirmed how deeply she was cared for. As a tiny baby others remarked that "someone had really loved her," and they didn't mean me. Of course we cannot really know what happened to our children before we knew them, but I have always known in my heart that the beginning of this child's life was spent in loving arms, and the finding location seemed to confirm this.

On the way home Abby was in quite a funk. I gave her a penny for her thoughts and asked if she could tell me why she was so blue. "Back to school, back to sports, back to where everybody doesn't look like me," she answered glumly. Then she threw her arms around me. "Mom, I love China so much. When can we go back?"

Shaoyang "sisters"—Chloe, Claire, and Jaden (all age 4).

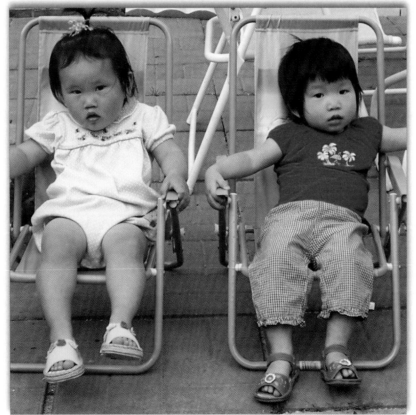

Cousins—Lulea and Sarah (both age 2), both from Huainan, Anhui.
Lulea and Sarah shared their Forever Family Day a month before this photo was taken.

Samantha Zhen-Yi, Gutian, Fujian. Our precious daughter on the red couch at the White Swan Hotel in May 2005.

When Love Takes You In
by Steven Curtis Chapman

I know you've heard the stories
But they all sound too good to be true
You've heard about a place called home
But there doesn't seem to be one for you
So one more night you cry yourself to sleep
And drift off to a distant dream

Where love takes you in and everything changes
A miracle starts with the beat of a heart
When love takes you home and says you belong here
The loneliness ends and a new life begins
When love takes you in

And somewhere while you're sleeping
Someone else is dreaming too
Counting down the days until
They hold you close and say I love you
And like the rain that falls into the sea
In a moment what has been is lost in what will be

When love takes you in everything changes
A miracle starts with the beat of a heart
And this love will never let you go
There is nothing that could ever
cause this love to lose its hold

When love takes you in everything changes
A miracle starts with the beat of a heart
When love takes you home and says you belong here
The loneliness ends and a new life begins
When love takes you in it takes you in for good
When love takes you in

Anna (age 7), Shantou, Guangdong, with Mama Zhang.

This photo was taken the day Anna had to say good-bye to
Mama Zhang, the woman who cared for her in the orphanage.
They exchanged red thread necklaces, one with a lock
and one with a key. They are wearing them in this photo.

Siblings—Ciana Mei-Lin (age 7), Yangchun, Guangdong,
and Kai Kamron (age 3), Changchun, Jilin.

MAMA ZHANG
by Anna Eldridge (age 7)

I WAS NERVOUS BEFORE MY FIRST TRIP BACK TO CHINA. I was going to get my baby brother, and I was afraid he wouldn't like me. The plane ride was fun. I got to watch DVDs on the plane and listened to music. My big sister was so tired she slept on the floor of the plane!

In Beijing my legs got tired on the Great Wall. It was so crowded and everyone had hair like me, which was pretty cool. We saw acrobats, and I saw ten girls ride on one bike.

Then it was time to go to where I was born. I was thinking a lot about the aunties who took care of me and if they would remember me. I was nervous they wouldn't recognize me. I liked meeting my aunties the best. My whole life my mom had told me about Mama Zhang. I knew Mama Zhang worked in the orphanage. She loved me when I was a baby. I had pictures of her, but I didn't think I remembered her. I was just a baby when I left China. My mom said it was okay to be nervous, and I was shy when I first saw her. She came to my hotel even though it was really late at night. I was in my pajamas, and she gave me a kiss on my cheek the second we met. I was sad I didn't know Chinese because I wanted to talk to her. I thought Mama Zhang was so beautiful.

When we went to the orphanage I got to see many babies with cleft lips. They made feel sad because I wish they had their surgeries. I even got to feed a baby. My mom took me to the room I lived in, and I saw my blue crib. The aunty told me I used to have a favorite doll. I felt really comfortable there in that room. There was a baby in my old crib, but that was okay.

That night I got to meet all the teenager girls in the orphanage who lived there when I was there. They all remembered me. They laughed and called me "A Han." It was really fun to meet them. We ate hot pot. It was sad for me to say good-bye. I did not want to say good-bye to Mama Zhang. I still feel sad when I think of her. I remember now that I loved her. She gave me a special gift. She gave me her diary from when I lived in the orphanage and she wrote about me every day; so I got to read about myself as a baby. I gave her a necklace with a lock on it, and I kept the necklace with the key. I cried when I said good-bye to her. We did a huge hug. I like knowing there is someone who loves me in China. I wish I could see her again. I miss her and my mom says that is okay.

I am glad I went to see the country where I was born. I was excited to be in China. I got to try new foods and see new things. I am proud to be from China. I think I am the luckiest one in my family—to be from China and America too.

The love of a mother.
Above: Sarah Hope (age 12 months), Fengcheng, Jiangxi.
Below: Anna Brooke (age 13 months), Hefei, Anhui.

Chinese New Year baby.
Abigail-Jean ChunXing
(age 9 months),
Dianbai, Guangdong.

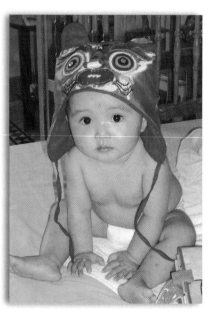

MADE TO LOVE
by Kitty Larochelle

EACH AND EVERY DAY I MARVEL AT THE BEAUTIFUL GIRL LOOKING BACK AT ME. We may have been separated by an ocean for a while, but we look alike, act alike, and love alike. Every day I remind Karina that God made her for us to love.

That makes her smile… and me too.

Rachel (age 9), Shanggao, Jiangxi, with her best friend, "K.C."

Above: Sisters—Chloe Jiaoling (age 5), Guangxi; Kya Mingzhou (age 3), Hunan; and Lyssa Xuying (age 1), Jiangxi. Soon a new brother, also from Jiangxi, will be joining his sisters.

Right: Friends—Chloe Jiaoling and Cora Isabella (both age 5½), both from Guangxi.

Julianna Grace Nianhong (age 1), Anqing City, Anhui.

KEEPING HER NAME
Excerpted essay by Madeline O'Neal

ON OCTOBER 13, 2004, LATE AT NIGHT, I POSTED ON APC THAT, "WE ARE PLANNING ON KEEPING OUR BABY'S CHINESE NAME IN HER FULL NAME." At that same time, it was the next day in China—October 14, 2004— my daughter's birthday.

My reason for keeping her Chinese given name as part of her full name has much to do with my work in genealogy and family history. When my father died, one of the ways I was able to handle my pain and grief was through the research I did that constantly had me thinking and mulling over the information I had on my father and that side of my family. Every little piece of information I found—down to where they lived, his siblings, their jobs, the ways they died—was truly like being tapped on the shoulder by one of them as if they were right there with me saying, "See, look at this. This was my life. This was how I was important to the world. This was who I was. This is how you came to be."

My child in China will also have those connections. Even though she may never be able to know a lot of the details, I pray that she will eventually be able to gain some of that information somehow. She will carry the genetics of her family in China. She will have those little quirks, gestures, and ways of being alive that will be "like her birthmother" or "like her birthfather," even though we won't know exactly what they are. Her name and each of these pieces of information will be a part of her history and legacy.

My New Life
by Wang Jiaoli
Submitted by Marjanne Laeven

WHEN I WAS 11, I WAS SENT TO THE JINGMEN ORPHANAGE WITH MY SISTER, JUNLI. Then I started my new life. There were so many children here. I also had a good time. The times flies, and it is time to go to the university for me. It should be a good news for me and the staff, but the great tuition is a hard problem. Then the Karregat-Laeven family helped me with my tuition and living expenses. We get in touch with each other by sending email and photos. It is a happy time for me to receive and reply the letters. I call them mother, father, and sisters. They give me an intact family. I am always feeling the great love from the family. They usually watch the China weather report and ask me to take care of myself. Especially on the Children's Day I received the best presents—some beautiful flowers from my family, although it can't be my festival. But I knew why. In my parents' eyes I am a child forever. They are studying Chinese. They say we can get in touch with each other very well if they can speak Chinese. I was so moved and knew love without boundaries truly. Now I must say that maybe I am an unlucky girl, but I can say proudly I am also a God's favorite because I have a family who loves me so much. Mother, father, and sisters, thank you! I will study hard and pay back your love.

Love from your daughter, Jiaoli

Jiaoli (age 21), Jingmen, Hubei—
holding her grandmother who took care of her and her sister.

Six-year-old orphaned child with cousins and grandmother on day of appointment
with GGEF to determine her eligibility for a subsidized education.

Day at the zoo.
Lilly Resa YueLu (age 2),
Kaifeng, Henan.

Hope for the Future
by Marji Hanson

LET ME TELL YOU ABOUT OUR FIELD TRIP ON FRIDAY MORNING. Our guide, Matthew Xu, is the site coordinator for Girls Global Education Fund (GGEF). His job title doesn't really begin to describe what he does for GGEF. There is no universal education in China; all families must pay to send their children to school. In 1996 Robin Bernard, an adoptive parent, founded GGEF, a U.S. nonprofit agency, created to send underprivileged and orphaned girls, who might otherwise not receive an education, to school. With Matthew's help GGEF launched its pilot program in Guangxi Province in 1997. It is GGEF's goal to break the poverty cycle, to give these girls both a future and a childhood. GGEF has grown slowly but steadily.

So Friday morning we went with Matthew and his assistant to a village about 45 minutes outside of Nanning. As the city fell away, we went further into the beautiful countryside.

We were on a really nice new two-lane highway for most of the trip until we pulled to the side to pick up Mr. Tong. Mr. Tong is one of many local people who keep their ears open to learn about girls who could qualify for GGEF support. Mr. Tong directed the driver to pull off on a fairly good dirt road. We drove for a few more miles until the road got not so good and soon saw the local teacher waving at us from the side of the road. The teacher was very happy to see us, but his only English was "Long live Chairman Mao." We got out to walk and the teacher led us the rest of the way—about a half mile to some modest homes on a little rise. We were invited into the first home. It had an open fire pit in the middle of the room, a sick dog sitting in its own urine at the back of the room, a dirt floor, and a well. This is where the little six-year-old girl we were to meet and interview lived with her paternal grandmother. Her father was killed four years previously in a car accident, and her mother disappeared two years after that. She looked like she may not have smiled since.

I made the pledge to sponsor this sad little girl through school for as many years as she wanted to attend. She would have to walk 1½ hours each way to elementary school and then go off to board at middle school when in the fourth grade. I hoped to be a part of making a better future for her.

We left her village and drove back into FuLi, the town where the middle school is located. We went there to meet four girls sponsored by GGEF. The little kids were frightened and wanted nothing to do with me until I took a photo and showed them their faces on the digital screen. I was swarmed by beautiful kids trying their hardest to see their own faces on the screen. After each photo I turned the camera, and they would crowd close and cheer in unison. I met the four GGEF girls who live at the school, often with less than one Yuan a week for food, living on rice and cabbage, owning one change of clothes, walking many miles back and forth from home on the weekends, and left completely in charge of themselves at such a young age. I told them how impressed I was that they could live away at school and take charge of feeding, dressing, bathing, and studying on their own. I gave them my heartfelt best wishes for their bright futures and stood amazed at the ripple one concerned, involved, and creative adoptive parent can make in this big global pond.

Luke (age 6) and Christina (age 5½), Nanning, Guangxi, with new friends in Suzhou on International Children's Day.

Children at orphanage enjoying the view.

School children in FuLi, Guangxi—crowding to see themselves in the digital camera screen.

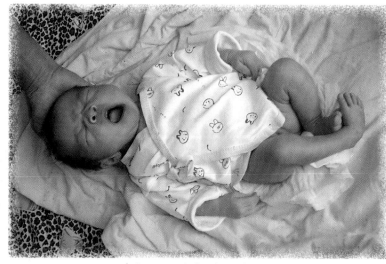

A tiny new arrival at the orphanage.

One of the beautiful children benefiting from foster care in China.

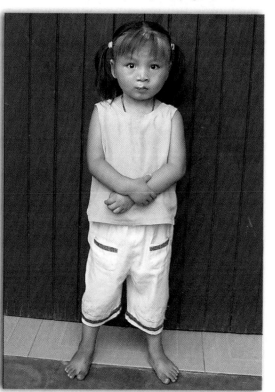

Friends for life. Jimmy (age 18 months), Zhangye; Annie (age 3), HuaiHua, Hunan; Marie (age 5), Fuling; Taylor (age 5), Fuling; Kathryn (age 5), Fuling; Elizabeth (age 3), Fuling; and Olivia (age 3), Fuling. Marie, Taylor, and Kathryn shared the same travel group. Olivia and Elizabeth (Kathryn's sister) also shared a travel group. Annie, Jimmy, and Marie are siblings.

MOON GODDESSES AND BIRTH FAMILIES
by Terry Garlock

THE MORNING AIR HAS TURNED FROM SUMMER MUGGY TO COOL AND CLEAR, THE LEAVES ARE TURNING COLORS AND THE CHINESE MID-AUTUMN FESTIVAL, THE MOON FESTIVAL, IS JUST AROUND THE CORNER AGAIN. Melanie will be ten years old next April, and she already knows some of the Moon Festival legends. Her little sister, Kristen, will soon be five.

I started researching Chinese celebrations to help our girls learn as much as possible about the people and culture that gave them birth. Along the way I realized there are two other good reasons to do this.

First I have found that studying Chinese history and legends creates a deeper connection to China and its people, for me as well as for Melanie and Kristen. The richness and depth of the oldest continuous civilization on earth is fascinating, a reminder that our own country is still a young experiment.

The second reason is that it will help make our girls strong. Think about this. Our children lost their birth family and culture and country, and are growing up as a racial minority. As adolescents they will come to realize they were abandoned by their birth families and may face deep feelings of rejection and loss. Outside our family circle, they could feel adrift, not belonging anywhere. How can they overcome these burdens? I believe the answer is inner strength. By learning as much as they can about Chinese history and culture, they are more likely to be proud to be Chinese as well as American, better equipped to be grounded with a strong sense of self, confident in who they are.

The legends of the Moon Festival are just one tiny part of this journey. As we sit on the front steps, Melanie may ask, "Dad, tell me again the legend of Chang Er." So I will her the story again about how Chang Er had been an immortal up in the heavens and got into trouble along with her husband, Hou Yi. The Jade Emperor, ruler of the heavens and immortals, banished Hou Yi to the sun and Chang Er to the moon, and he allowed them to be together on the moon just one night each year—on the 15th night of the 8th lunar month. Chinese people say the love of Chang Er and

THE LUCKIEST PEOPLE IN THE WORLD
by Barbara Rappaport

SIX YEARS AGO TODAY ANNA WAS PLACED INTO MY ARMS AND I BECAME A MOMMY TO THE MOST INCREDIBLE DAUGHTER. That was the most amazing and important day of our lives, and we both are so thankful every day to have each other and love each other.

This morning when my alarm rang, I heard Anna running out of her room and down the hall toward my room yelling, "*Happy Anniversary, Mommy!!!*"

She flew onto my bed, threw her arms around me, and hugged as tightly as we could without hurting each other. Then she said, "Isn't this just the best, Mom? Aren't we the luckiest people in the world?!!" And with tears, I said, "Yes… yes, we are."

Anna Olivia (age 7),
Shantou, Guangdong—
at a performance with the
Atlanta Chinese Dance Company.

Sisters— Sarah (age 9), holding Charlotte (age 11 months), Tai He, Jiangxi, and Erin (age 14).

Hou Yi is what makes the moon shine its largest and brightest on that night—the night of the Moon Festival.

As we sit on the front steps, recount the legend of Chang Er, and gaze at the moon, we will talk about how this is a special night of family gathering in China, and we will talk about Melanie's birth family.

Melanie will ask where they are, what they are doing, where they live, what they look like; and to all questions we will answer, "We don't know." She knows she can talk about her birth family at any time, but the Moon Festival is a reminder, a special time, to wonder about them.

"Dad, do you really think they will be looking at this very same moon tonight?"

"Yes, I think so because families gather in China on this night for dinner. Then later they go outside to look at the moon and all the pretty lanterns."

Melanie might be a little quiet as she gazes at the moon, thinking about them, and I might say:

"Maybe, just maybe, like you are thinking about them, tonight when they gaze at the moon, they might think about you."

I can't heal the hurt in Melanie's heart from the things she has lost. I can't take away the rejection she might always feel from having been abandoned, and I can't protect her from a harsh world that will try now and then to make her feel bad about herself.

But I can learn some things about China and do my best to teach her to be proud of who she is. I can encourage her to talk about her birth family and let her know it is up to her alone to decide how to feel about them. I can encourage her to be proud of the person of strong character she has become, to be confident in who she is and where she belongs.

Melanie's little sister, Kristin, will be five years old in December. Maybe it is time she learns more about Chang Er, the Moon Festival, and her birth family. Maybe that will be the beginning of her inner strength.

Photo taken by photographer Marie Clark.

(Back) Rachel (age 18), Mom, Dad, and Meili (age 4), Gaoyou, Jiangsu. (Front) Luke (age 10), Yangquan, Shanxi; Raegen (age 5), Loudi, Hunan; Breanne (age 7); and Jake (age 9).

Above: Ellie Wen's referral photo and a note from her big sister, Sophie.

Below: Sisters forever—Ellie Wen (age 3), Kunming, Yunnan, and Sophie (age 8).

YOU ARE CHINA
by Melanie O'Neill

I WANT YOU TO KNOW EVERYTHING POSSIBLE ABOUT THE PLACE OF YOUR BIRTH. I have read books and bought DVDs and decorated our home with silk paintings and antique wedding boxes. We've bought pandas and chopsticks and a rice cooker as well. The dragon head we made of papier-mâché sits silently on your bookshelf, and paper lanterns twinkle at night over your bed. My husband thought I had gone a bit too far when the Terra Cotta warriors arrived by freight truck. Maybe he was right.

My cooking skills have definitely improved since your arrival. I have learned to make egg rolls and dumplings and how to gently wash rice. We are learning Mandarin even though I have always known that language is *not* my gift. We gaze at the autumn moon, and celebrate the New Year with silk clothes and fireworks. I can quote the Chinese zodiac in exact order so quickly that our Chinese friends laugh and say we know more about the holidays than they do. I want to know everything about China, Emi, because I want to know everything about you.

My darling daughter, I want to give you what I feel I have partially taken away. I want you to know your heritage and your history. Through you, I have been granted the greatest gift on earth, of being your mommy. Now I want to give you everything possible in return.

I know I cannot raise you "Chinese" since I was raised Irish, but I look at your incredible face which reflects the beauty of the most ancient country on earth, and I know I have to try.

John William Yuyan (age 4½), Beijing, with Mom and Dad.

GIVING BACK
by Maureen Brogan Gealey

I HAVE HAD THREE RECURRING DREAMS IN MY LIFE—
TO BECOME A NURSE, TO TRAVEL TO ANOTHER COUNTRY
TO USE MY NURSING SKILLS TO HELP CHILDREN THERE,
AND TO HAVE A DAUGHTER. I became a R.N. in the
midst of giving birth to and raising four sons. When
my marriage ended, I was immersed in raising the
boys and working. I set aside my dreams of traveling
as a nurse. As I approached 40 I decided to fulfill
my dream of a daughter and adopt from China. Her
adoption led me to the fulfillment of that third set-
aside dream, to travel and use my skills as a nurse to
help children.

I adopted Heather in 2002. I fell in love with China
and sobbed in the Guangzhou airport as I left with
her. I realized what a great gift China had given me
to allow me to adopt this amazing child. I vowed
to myself that I would return to her homeland to
participate in a cleft mission. For the next few years
I was busy with Heather, but, as I cut back my work
schedule after remarrying, I looked for opportunities
to "give back." I spoke with several different
organizations but felt especially comfortable with Love
Without Boundaries.

I had volunteered with my agency's special needs
program and noticed that files of the cleft-affected
boys were rarely requested. Their eyes spoke to me
and reminded me of my sons. I was told there was an
organization, made of all parent volunteers, who could
arrange surgeries in China. I contacted them and was
soon fundraising for surgeries.

I signed up for LWB's cleft mission to Luoyang,
Henan, China. The summer was filled with
excitement as I sent for a visa and gathered donations
of handmade quilts and toys to take with me. The
plan was that we would take the top floor of the
Luoyang orphanage and turn that space into pre-
op rooms, a surgery suite, a recovery room, post-op
rooms, and a dental suite. I had no idea how much
work this was going to be! I packed scrubs, medical
equipment, and the donations and flew by myself
from San Francisco to Beijing. I was nervous, scared,

and excited when I landed in Beijing. I had no idea of
what to expect.

In the morning I rose early and joined the rest
of the team as we walked across the tarmac to our
waiting plane. It was wonderful to finally meet, in
person, all of the people I had met online. We landed
at a small airport and once again hiked across the
hot tarmac to the terminal. The orphanage had
sent a bus and driver to pick us up. When I saw the
dusty, old green bus with the orphanage name, it
suddenly became real. I was going to be working
in an orphanage filled with hundreds of children. I
would get a chance to see how my daughter may have
lived before I adopted her. We were given permission
to interact with the orphanage children and I was
anxious to get started.

On arrival to Luoyang we quickly checked into our
hotel rooms, changed into scrubs, and headed off to
the orphanage. We discovered that no boxes had been
unpacked or rooms prepared; so we quickly started
unpacking, cleaning, and organizing. The "hospital"
was set up in a matter of hours thanks to the work of
many hands.

We left for dinner just as the first patients were
arriving. The foster parents and children were
from my daughter's home province, and it was very
emotional to greet them in person. That night I
had a hard time sleeping and was up early. I was
scheduled for the evening shift and had the days free
to explore. I had made friends with several other
nurses at dinner. We planned to visit and explore
Luoyang in our free time but first wanted to meet
the orphanage children.

I was touched by the warm welcome the director
gave us, along with permission to play with the
children. How to describe the emotional impact of
room after room filled with beautiful children? I can't.
There were too many infants to count and the rooms
seemed endless. Most of the infants and toddlers were
terrified at their first sight of big nosed, white people.
Some screamed and hid their faces, while others just
stared with wide eyes. I picked up and cuddled a few
newborns and then decided to go upstairs to meet

little ones long enough, I thought.

I bumped into a teenaged boy on the stairs, and he happily showed me the older children's dorm rooms. The kids were proud to show me their rooms and happily posed for pictures with us. Many spoke English, and it was fun to get to know them. All too soon it was time to leave and go upstairs.

My first shift flew by as did the rest of the days. I assessed the children after surgery, administered pain medications, instructed family and caregivers in how to syringe feed the children, and reassured them on their many concerns. I learned to comfort children with "hulla, hulla, hulla"—"okay, okay, okay"—and greeted the new arrivals as they settled in for the night in a pre-op room or on the roof where it was much cooler.

My memories are filled with the incredible people I met: the medical team that traveled using vacation time so they could help these children; the non-medical volunteers always ready to rock, feed, or play with a baby or child; all the patients who had their smiles and lives changed; the foster parents who cared for their foster children with total devotion and little concern for their own comfort; the ayis who sang lullabies and worried about their babies; and especially the rural people who started arriving after the newspaper announced that an organization was doing free cleft surgeries at the Luoyang Orphanage.

I had never really thought about my daughter's birthfather. In my readings and in discussion of the birthmother, there is little mention of the birthfather. The images I carried away from Luoyang include the gentle love of all the fathers I met, whether they were biological, foster, or adoptive fathers. They all loved and cared deeply for the children. There were men who would yell at me across a busy street, "Xie xie, Ai"—"Thank you, Love." I met men who walked miles, leaving crops and harvest behind, to take the chance their child could be healed. I met rice farmers who had found cleft-affected babies abandoned in their fields and who then decided to keep those children and raise them as their own. I heard stories of fathers who quietly cried after being told that their

children were too small for surgery, no longer caring about "saving face." I watched a group of men, who had traveled together with a child with cleft lip and palate, gently bathe and dress him on the roof as they laughed and cared for him. I watched an elderly, frail foster father stand and rock his heavy foster child for hours after surgery, refusing all offers of help. I knew the family that was adopting that sturdy two-year-old would reap the benefits of the love that had been poured into him by this gentle, old man.

I heard the story of the parents who were on a train preparing to abandon their cleft baby when they were told of the team in Henan doing surgeries. They arrived and their child received surgery. An abandonment plan was abandoned as they smiled and took him home, his smile now complete. There was a birthmother who had left her house during her 30 day confinement to beg on her knees for her newborn daughter's cleft surgery. The baby was too young and too small for surgery, but still the mother pleaded.

Seventy-five volunteers from the USA and Canada traveled to Luoyang over the two-week period. One hundred and nine cleft-affected children were healed, and 69 orphaned children received dental care. I stayed as a transition person to bridge between the two teams. I met people I will never forget.

I left China feeling I was the one who had received the most from my trip. I had so many memories that I would take back with me. The memories of the amazing transformation of the cleft children's smiles; of taking 21 children from the orphanage to McDonald's for the first time and introducing them to automatic flushing western toilets, hot running water, and blow dryers; of two children sitting on my lap as we rode home from our adventure, singing softly "Mama Hao"—reminding me that even the eight- and nine-year-old girls and boys long for a mother of their own; of the smiling faces of the people of Luoyang. I will never forget the joy, compassion, and tireless hours of devotion and love that surrounded me there as I got to have my third and final lifetime wish finally come true.

Above: Calissa (age 4).

Left: Sisters—Calissa (age 3) and Jilaina (age 5), Fuzhou, Jiangxi—with their dad.

Left: Jessica Taoli (about age 4 months).

Right: Kaitlyn Taomei (about age 4 months).

Below: Sisters forever.
Jessica Taoli (age 9), Ashley Heejung (age 4), and Kaitlyn Taomei (age 9). Jessica and Kaitlyn are identical twins from Nanchang, Jiangxi. Ashley is from South Korea.

Grace Ann-Yin (age 7½),
Changde, Hunan.

Above: A dream come true. Lainey Ting (age 11½ months), Wuwei City, Gansu, with Mom, along the bank of the Yellow River.

Right: Lainey (age 4)— at her dance recital.

Below: Lainey (age 4) drew this picture and dictated the story to her preschool teacher. When the teacher shared it with me, I was incredibly touched. We are DTC 12-13-05. The wait has been a long one, especially for Lainey. She is so looking forward to being a big sister.

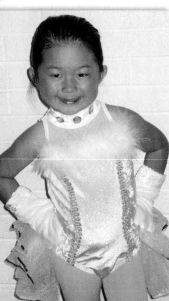

There are three rainbows and a sunshine. And here's my mom and my baby and me.
By: Lainey

A DIFFERENT KIND OF RED THREAD STORY
by Tina Evans

WAITING FOR MY DAUGHTER, GRACE, IN 2003, I JOINED THE YAHOO DTC GROUP FOR THE "AUGUST MOONS." It was there that I met my most treasured friend, Nancy Brown. As the group members emailed to get to know each other, Nancy and I found that we had much in common. During the long wait we corresponded frequently. Nancy and I both verbalized our hope that we would be able to travel together. We knew it was a long shot, as not only did we live in different states but also used agencies in different states. We laughed and said how great it would be if our girls were from the same orphanage and that would be just another thing that we shared.

Our referrals came many months later. Our daughters were not from the same orphanage, nor the same province, but were both from the southern coastal region. Nancy received her travel approval first, along with her consulate appointment. Days passed without word of our travel approval. I panicked to think that our dream of being in China at the same time would not become a reality. In the end our consulate appointments ended up on the same day. Nancy and I were not only able to be in China at the same time, we traveled to and from China on the same flights, spent two days touring in Beijing, and we spent our days together in Guangzhou. We got along so well and enjoyed our time together. After our return home Nancy and I kept in touch, and our families got together once a year. Our husbands and our children all enjoyed each other's company as well.

Nancy and I both kept up with the Yahoo adoption groups and began reviewing the lists of children with special needs. When my husband and I decided to pursue another adoption, this time of a special needs child, the Browns were not even considering another child. But not long afterward they decided to bring home another sweet angel also. Guess what? They also found her on a waiting children list! Not surprisingly, our daughters were from the same province. Nancy received her travel approval and consulate appointment first, but again our consulate appointments were scheduled on the same day. We again traveled to and from China together and spent time in Beijing prior to meeting our daughters.

This summer our families vacationed at the beach together. We know that our friendship was meant to be. Our children are great friends, our husbands are similar in so many ways and enjoy each other's company, and Nancy and I marvel at how God's plan unfolded for us. We continue to be amazed at the similarities we share. We do not share the same parents, but we love each other as only sisters do.

Wind Horse
by Rebecca Nance

Wind horse, carry my lullaby
To China, where my baby sleeps;
Over the cities and over the mountains,
Over the forests, the clouds, and the seas.
I cannot be there to rock her tonight.
Bring her my song on the wings of your flight.
Sleep, my baby, sleep.

She's had a busy day; she's growing every day,
Learning and listening and watching her world.
Tell her this family is waiting here, incomplete,
Until we can welcome our own precious girl.
I could not be there to praise and to play.
Bring her my comfort from so far away.
Sleep, my baby, sleep

Sing of the day I cross over to find her;
Follow the heart that already flies,
Over the ocean, the lakes, and the villages,
To smile into my baby's eyes.
The moment I see her I'll know that sweet face;
I've waited so long for that moment of grace.
Sleep, my baby, sleep.

Mom and daughters. Analiese Qiuxia (age 3), DeYang, Sichuan; Sarah (age 8); and Grace Feizhen (age 5), Wenzhou City, Zhejiang.

When she comes home, I'll always be
Ready to comfort, to love, and to play.
Over the years she'll learn she'll never be alone,
In good times and hard times that life brings her way.
And you'll blow that promise right over the blue,
To a mother in China who blesses her too.
Sleep, my baby, sleep.

They say a red thread connects certain hearts
And draws them together, wherever they start.
Wind horse, carry my song and my prayers
Across all of the threads of those still far apart;
And bring for the others that we leave behind
Fathers and mothers and everything fine.
Sleep, my baby, sleep.

The wind horse is a symbol thought to be older than Buddhism itself. The wind horse image is often seen on prayer flags. It is the sender's hope that her prayers will be carried with the strength of a horse and the speed of the wind, and that they will bring success and good fortune, not only to a specific venture but to all the people of the world. We put up some of these flags when we received approval for our daughter and watched them change through three seasons as we waited to bring her home. It was some comfort to imagine our loving thoughts— and this lullaby—carried on the wind over half the world.

Lucinda Qiu Ying (age 6), Shenzhen, Guangdong, with Dad modeling his Valentine's Day gift.

CHANGING PERCEPTIONS, IMPROVING SMILES
by LWB Medical Volunteers

ONE OF THE PEOPLE WHO TOUCHED OUR HEARTS THE MOST ON OUR CLEFT SURGERY TRIP TO HENAN IN 2005 WAS A 19-YEAR-OLD GIRL WHO HAD LIVED HER WHOLE LIFE WITH A SEVERE BILATERAL CLEFT LIP AND PALATE. Despite not having a normal smile, this courageous young woman set a goal for herself that she would study every day and someday be accepted to the university, even though her loving parents, who had adopted her as a baby, were extremely poor.

Shortly after we did surgery, we received a letter from Cui that brought all of us to tears. A portion of that letter is shared here:

I am almost completely recovered now. I believe that it will not be long to see a true me living freely like other ordinary girls. These are my dreams for so many years. Thinking about possibilities and future life, I am very happy and grateful from the bottom of my heart because I know all these changes were given to me by warm hearted people. I still don't know who are my own biological parents; it's my adopted parents, who picked me up from the road when I was abandoned, that gave me a new life. They are very poor, but I can feel their love. Recollecting the old time, I got used to harsh ridiculous remarks, cold eyes, and snobbish comments from ignorant bystanders. Weeping and sleeplessness in dark nights are still vivid in my memories. Life, year after year, has taught me a lot and made me stronger and now more optimistic. In the past, even though I had never said anything about cleft operation to my current adopted parents, I knew that they were anxious but all helpless. I could only accept this as my fate. I am like other girls who love to have sweet and beautiful dreams. Just before I went to LuoYang, I dreamed that I would meet good-hearted people some day. This miracle appeared unexpectedly and came to me in an unbelievably fast way. To tell the truth, it was nothing more than trying my luck when I went to LuoYang. My past living experience taught me not to expect miracles; that they only appear in storybooks. But everything went smoothly. Thinking about all these now, I still feel that I myself was in the dream of fantasy. The pain and burden in my heart has disappeared; only a happy smile is left.

We were fortunate to meet this young woman again in January 2006, and she told us she would be sitting for the college exam this summer. We were thrilled to learn that Cui was accepted to University. This inspiring young woman had beaten all the odds and is now in college.

Eliana (age 2), Xiushan, Chongqing, with Mom. One year home!

Siblings—(Back) Ryan (age 16) and Tyler (age 14). (Front) Elizabeth ("Ellie") (age 5), Changchun, Jilin; Anna (age 7), Wuchuan, Guangdong; and Trevor (age 12).

New Connections
by Deb Como-Kepler

It took me six years to get back to China. I was determined to return to China to give something back. Thanks to a client who unknowingly planted the idea in my head, I arranged for 18 college students from the University of Southern Maine to do a service learning course at two Chinese orphanages.

Since adopting my first daughter from Huainan, I've had an obsession with China: movies, books, paraphernalia, etc. I can't get enough! When we were in China getting our daughter, we insisted on visiting the orphanage. We were discouraged to do so, but we felt we wanted to get as much information for our daughter as we could. Seeing all the children, especially the older ones, touched my husband and me in a way we could never forget. I had to go back.

So two colleagues and I took 18 students back to China with donations in hand and our knowledge of psychology and occupational therapy. We took 20 orphaned kids on their first shopping excursion to buy their first pair of new shoes, visited a zoo, and bought several wheelchairs and therapeutic toys. In a whirlwind trip we did what we could, but, most importantly, we made new friends and new connections.

Long story short, I got back to China with my family and did a little to help. As with our first adoption trip, I came away with so much more. I'll be back.

Lily Dayle Chang (age 28 months), Dongguan, Guangdong—sharing a beautiful smile with her mommy.

Sweat Equity
by Peggy Lee Scott

In the spring of 2002 three Bay Area single moms traveled to Chengdu, Sichuan Province, with their daughters to participate in a Half the Sky Foundation "build." Half the Sky has several programs designed to improve the quality of life for children in orphanages, which typically involve building new preschool classrooms or infant nurture centers. Parent volunteers from the U.S. pay their own way to China, where they complete a specific orphanage project. Jia Giuliano and Bin Bin Sullivan had lived together at Chengdu SWI for ten months. Although moms Kim Giuliano and Debbie Sullivan thought their children might be a bit young for this adventure, when Half the Sky scheduled a build in Chengdu, off they flew on "the journey of a lifetime."

"This was my first look at where Jia had lived," Kim explained. "We were able to see the room where she and Bin Bin slept. From all over the institution, teachers and caregivers came to greet Jia and Bin Bin. They were so happy to see the girls. Two different caregivers told us they used to take Jia home for overnight visits. It was wonderful to thank these women for taking such good care of my daughter."

For several days, as local workers built furniture and installed new lighting, the parents sanded and painted walls and furniture and assembled toys. Their children played in the reception room, drawing, reading books, and playing dress-up. They sang in English and Mandarin, and when they ran out of steam they helped their parents paint. There were bumpy days for some of the kids, who may have been too young for this experience or who had strong feelings crop up that surprised them all. Some kids had a hard time seeing their parents playing with the young residents. When Kim voiced that she hoped each child at the orphanage would find a family, Jia reminded her sternly, "Yes, but not my mama."

Lauren Grace Jinjuewan (age 2), Wanzai, Jiangxi, with her parents.

Molly (age 1), Yangxi, Guangdong, with her daddy.

On the last day, the volunteers filled the new rooms with all the accoutrements: art supplies, musical instruments, puppets, pretend-kitchen items, dolls, cars, dress-up clothes, and Legos. The nannies on the baby floor loved the new rocking chairs. As a special springtime treat, Kim and Debbie had brought 200 plastic eggs. They filled these with candy and showed the kids how to hunt for them.

The children were overwhelmed. One little girl asked if she could "trade her shoes for some dress-up shoes." They didn't understand that everything was staying; everything was for them. Then this same little girl pulled her egg out of her pocket and offered a piece of candy to Jia. This child who had so little still knew how to share.

Kim adamantly states, "This experience forever changed my life. And Jia now knows for sure that there were people there who really cared for her." Half the Sky volunteers contribute in a very real way while they are on a build, but it is anybody's guess who gains more from these projects—the orphanage or the parents who get the opportunity to give back. Through the labor of their own hands they see their good work put to use. Then they come home with a sense of accomplishment, coupled with priceless memories of China.

WHAT DO YOU WANT?
by Wendy Quick

"WHAT DO YOU WANT?" That is a question that we hear every day, and we all know exactly what we want. Everyone's favorite game is always "What Would I Do if I Won the Lottery!" We want a plasma television. We want a big home. We want to take expensive trips. But if we sat down and really examined our list of wants, would those really be the things we need?

Need is what, I think, encourages so many people to build their families through adoption. A couple needs to have a family. A person needs to be a parent. Yes, you could say that these are wants, but it is so much more than that. Some people need to be a parent, just like we need to eat, or breathe, or sleep. Each adopted child also has a need: to have a family who will love them.

When I started the process to adopt from China, I would have to say that it was a want. I wanted to be a parent. I wanted to adopt a child from China. I distinctly remember the day that my desire to adopt changed from a want to a need. I was at one of my very first meetings with my agency discussing the paperwork and the process. The agency director was explaining about what I could expect when I came home with my daughter. That was the first time I had ever heard anyone say those two words out loud to me. I had never realized how beautiful that could sound. My *daughter*! At that point, I knew that this was something I needed to do, but not just for me. I needed to do this for my daughter. I needed to give her all the love that I had been given as a child. I needed to teach her all the things that I had learned from my parents. We needed to be a family.

The first time I saw my daughter in person, she was being thrust into my arms. The other families that I had traveled with were all holding their daughters, and the room was filled with all kinds of commotion. In that moment, as my daughter was handed to me, she looked into my eyes. I knew that in that very moment I had all I ever really needed. And by the shy, crooked little grin on her face, I hoped that she felt the same way too.

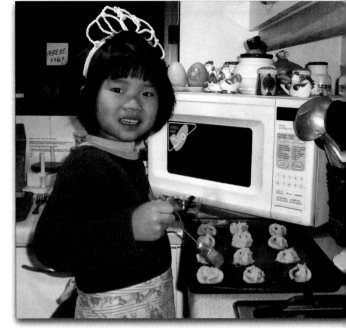

Emili Lizheng (age 5), Lishui, Zhejiang.

Cornwall, England, play group. Evie (age 3), Jiangsu; Elsie (age 18 months), Jiangxi; Faith (age 20 months), Gansu; Mary (age 1), Hubei; Rosie (age 18 months), Guangdong; Shunxi (age 1), Guangdong; and Lulu (age 1), Guangdong, with their moms.

We have shared waiting for referrals, bringing our girls home, birthdays, holidays, baptisms, play dates, baby showers, laughter, tears, frustrations, joys, and good-byes.

Jing-Jing (age 10 months), YangJiang, Guangdong, with caregiver.

ALWAYS WELCOME
by Debbie Smith

ON DECEMBER 19, 2004, THE DAY THAT I RECEIVED MY JING-JING, I asked her caregiver, Ging Yi, if there was anything special that she would like me to tell Jing-Jing when she was old enough to understand. Although Ging Yi seemed momentarily surprised to be asked this question, tears sprang to her eyes and she spoke without hesitation. "Please don't let her forget that she is Chinese. Please tell her to come back. When she comes back, she should visit those of us who cared for her. She will always be Chinese and we will always welcome her."

Sisters—Maggie (age 10), Jiujiang, Jiangxi, and Caroline (age 7), Shanghai—visiting the Great Wall on a heritage tour.

Siblings—(Corner photos clockwise from lower left) Johnny (age 19); Theresa Lin (age 5), Xianyang, Shaanxi; Faith (age 12), Xian, Shaanxi; and Abby (age 3), Suixi, Guangdong.

MOTHERS' HEARTS FOREVER BOUND
by Kimberlie Meyer

Dear Birthmother,

In six days my husband and I will be boarding a plane for China. We will be traveling to pick up our son, for he was your son before it became possible for him to become ours. You are an intimate and intricate part of our family's own red thread story. I've thought about you often over the past nine months of anticipating Zach's arrival. That's the name we have chosen for him. It means "God has remembered" and is a good, strong name. The link between your nine month wait to birth him and our own nine month wait to become parents to him seems significant. I have so many questions I wish I could ask you, but I know it is impossible. I wonder, do you think about him at all? I imagine you do. I can tell you he has been well cared for both in the orphanage and by his foster family. He is tall, strong, and his foster mother says he's the fastest in his class. I wonder, does he get his height from you or from his father? He is smart and has been in school for 18 months now. I have only one picture of him smiling, but from it I imagine that when he smiles, he lights up the room.

I think our boy might be a little scared and sad when he first meets us. That's okay. We are a little scared too. We have the advantage in that we have known about him a lot longer than he has known about us. I didn't think I could ever love a person that I had never met, never touched, or hugged. But I love our son so fiercely it surprises me at times. I long to be there to hug him, comfort him, and keep him safe. My heart aches for him so much sometimes. I wonder, does yours? I think maybe it does.

I don't know anything about you, but I can imagine a few things. You must be brave and courageous because you gave life to our son, and you made sure he would be taken care of even though you could not do so yourself. You must have loved him fiercely too, because you made sure he was safely found. You must be beautiful because our son is so very handsome. I recently came across a song written for the daughters of China, who like my son are finding homes far from the families who gave them life. There is a part of the refrain that sums up my feelings about what you have done for us. It goes something like this: "… they [the daughters] are gifts to those who cherish them by those who just could not. Acts of hope and faith and love, we never will forget." * I will forever be grateful to you for giving me my son. He is truly a gift I will forever cherish—a gift of hope and faith and love. I will think of you often and maybe even cry a few tears for you. I will say a prayer for you whenever I think of you. For even though we will never meet, within our son's red thread story, the mother's heart in me will forever be bound to yours.

*Copyright 2003 Tim Chauvin
 Used with permission.

Above left: Picture drawn by Chloe Jessica (age 9) while waiting for her Chinese cousin.

Above right: Picture drawn by Lauren Rebecca (age 8) for her future Chinese cousin's bedroom.

Below: Chloe and Lauren hard at work creating their artwork.

Friends—(Clockwise from front) Ava, Leizhou, Guangdong; Maya, Lily, Anne, and Grace, all from Youxian, Hunan. All the girls are age 3.

March 8, 2005 (Tuesday) Orphanage Visit
Excerpted essay by Wanda McCormick

I AM AT A COMPLETE LOSS AS TO HOW TO SHARE A DAY THAT NO ONE COULD EVER EMOTIONALLY PREPARE FOR. Today we drove to YangJiang City to visit Mia's orphanage and her finding spot. The emotional impact of walking through the doors of the orphanage, holding our daughter possessively in my arms, while I tried to take in the enormity of over a hundred upturned faces gazing back at me from aluminum barred cribs, will forever be imprinted on my mind's eye and my heart! The faces were scrubbed clean with shiny cheeks and bright inquisitive eyes—some shy, some curious, some seeking that human connection that every heart cries out for. My heart cried back, as I tried to take pictures of the little ones whose families had yet to travel to China for them, and I tried desperately to smile at and touch and hug as many as I could. My mind could not comprehend the sight of 150 babies under the age of one year old, standing, sitting, playing in walkers, sucking thumbs, sleeping peacefully—and waiting patiently, hoping for that one family whose arms long to hold *them*. My arms grew three feet, I'm sure, as I tried to hug as many as possible. They are not unhappy; most of them know no other life. Our visit changed nothing for most of them, but it changed us forever!

Mia (nearly age 2), YangJiang, Guangdong— celebrating Chinese New Year at the Portland, Maine, festival.

SPONSORING LEADS TO LIFELONG FRIENDSHIPS
by Cheri Helsel, American "Auntie Cheri" to Ada Min

IT STARTED AFTER OUR ADOPTION OF OUR DAUGHTER FROM CHINA. The "feeling" that sticks with you after you have returned home and life is complete, and yet you have this feeling that is calling you back to China. The question in my mind was, "Is there another little girl in China waiting for me to adopt?" "Why do I have this feeling?" I would ask myself.

We had just returned home from China at the end of November 2001, and our three biological sons, along with our new daughter, were forming our family well. But yet I had this feeling. After discussing sponsoring a child from China with my husband to fill the void, we filled out our paperwork with Holt International and waited to hear of a child to sponsor. We were sent the paperwork and a photo of a little sweetheart living in Nanchang. Ironically she shared my birthday! Every four months we would receive an updated photo that we would proudly display on our refrigerator door. The medical report would be read through carefully, and her growing personality would be shared with family and friends.

This continued for over a year. We watched this little girl grow before our eyes.

A couple of months went by and we heard nothing. No photo, no medical report. What happened to this sweetheart?

One morning I was on the computer and came across a post entitled, "Looking for the sponsor of Hong Xin Min from America." Amazing how there are so many posts every day on this site, and which I don't check often, but yet this morning I found this post for me!

She was to be adopted by a family in Spain! This little girl that I loved and wished was mine was going to be in a family of her own. I was thrilled. In no time at all I found myself emailing her mom-to-be. I sent her all the photos and medical reports that I had received. She mailed me lots of information about the area that Min would be living. She was adopted in January 2004 at the age of two years old.

It is now the fall of 2006, and we are now nearing Min's fifth birthday. The relationship is continuing to grow between our families, as well as with Ada Min herself. We are hoping to meet one day in person. Until then we will continue to send videos, photos, and email via the Internet from America to Spain. It has been a thrill to watch her grow.

Stella (age 2), Liangping, Chongqing.

Ada Min (age 5), Nanchang, and Auntie Cheri finally getting to meet.

EYES WIDE OPEN
by Suzanne Mabee

I WAS ON MY WAY TO THE AIRPORT TO LOOK FOR A CHINESE TEENAGER AND HIS BRITISH ESCORT COMING IN ON A FLIGHT FROM CHICAGO. I wondered if I would recognize him from the photo. Since February everything in our family's lives had been focused on one thing—the orphaned teenager we were about to welcome into our home for the next six months.

In January I had introduced my husband, Kevin, to Zheng Qi over coffee. Zheng Qi had been born in China with his bladder on the outside of his body. Normally corrected within a day after birth, he had somehow made it to age 19 with the condition uncorrected. The somber look on Kevin's face as he took in the explicit photos showing just how badly the boy was suffering told me all I needed to know. For both of us, "do something" meant that we had to be personally involved.

We talked about getting him a corporate sponsor. We talked of who could be effective getting him treatment. Love Without Boundaries already had a written opinion from a local pediatric urologist, and we pored over it as we brainstormed a plan. We finished our bagels and decided to make this happen. He could stay in our house of five, and we would take care of him after a major surgery. Later that week I sat in the urologist's office, talking about the procedure he recommended, and answering his questions about why someone Zheng Qi's age had gone untreated for so long. I left with his promise to do the surgeries for free, and within a week the local children's hospital had called approving the application I put in for free care.

Suddenly, in a blur of phone calls and forms, a final plan was made to heal Zheng Qi. "He could already have cancer in there or he could live forever," the urologist had said. None of us, including the medical community, could believe he had survived. That's the reason that we all felt

Annah Blu ("Qing Qing") (age 1), Nanchang, Jiangxi.

compelled to do something. He would be here for six months—an orphaned teenager, a young adult man with history and possible unknown behavior issues. Could we trust him? Could we take care of him? Would China even let him come? How would we communicate? The next weeks brought loads of doubt. It was like referral day, sort of, except the baby wouldn't even be a teenager much longer.

He was easy to spot. My 5'7" frame towered over him. He looked excited and nervous. When we got home he took in every detail of our house, and I remember clearly his fascination with the tile covered table, the instant water in the fridge, the wall colors, glasses in the cabinet, and my crazy hand gestures.

Zheng Qi spoke no English but did his best to understand our broken Chinese. Still I couldn't talk to him the way I can talk to my own kids. He told our Chinese friends that he was a great chess player, and how he had once been on a long bike ride carrying a friend on his back. He had been in charge of keeping the lawn mowed and had often slept under the stairs in the orphanage because of the loneliness his body caused.

Over the next six months this shy, careful boy was transformed with attention, endless smiles, pillow fights, and unconditional love from our kids. His surgery was grueling and the recovery long, but he began to fit in—enough for me to feel comfortable nagging him about brushing his teeth. In a very short time he experienced Southern cuisine, warehouse superstores, a wedding in the woods, the beach, bagpipes being played in the Appalachians, the insanity of big city traffic, the summer movie season, back-to-school frenzy, grandparent surprises, and Halloween.

When he boarded the long flight home, he was no longer a patient or a guest. He was part of our family, and he changed lives. A friend told me soon after Zheng Qi returned that one day this young man would look us up and would want to introduce us to his own family. I'll be waiting for that call.

Jade FuBi (age 5), Macy-Meng (age 8), Lyla BaoBao (age 8), Nina Joy FuCai (age 11), all from Yangjiang, Guangdong.

(Fourth from left) Zheng Qi (age 19), with his American foster dad and siblings— Joshua (age 4), Juliana (age 9), and Ally (age 5).

The Roommates of YangJiang
by Kara Post

Over time they arrived, without love or trust,
Haunted by losses and fears.
But this was a place of promise and hope
And sweet aunties to wipe away tears.

Four little girls all alone in the world
'Til the moments they came through the gates.
Here they found friendship, comfort, and peace
Through everlasting bonds as roommates.

They might have felt lonely, or empty, or hurt
With their pasts and their futures unknown.
But the girls forged a family as "sisters" so true
And for them, this felt like a home.

They created their childhood together each day
Playing games, braiding hair, singing songs.
Sharing their dreams of a family forever
And a home where they knew they belonged.

Then came the days they had held in their hearts
As "forever" Moms and Dads took them home!
They left through the gates with courage and hope,
Facing new fears and unknowns.

The girls made new lives with their families and homes,
But never forgetting their past.
There were phone calls, letters, and pictures exchanged
And they knew that their friendship would last.

Love can transcend any distance and time
So a reunion was held for the girls;
A celebration of life, of their loyalty and dreams
That began on the other side of the world.

The roommates gave the gifts of themselves to each other
During their darkest and loneliest of times.
Their journeys are glimpses of God's amazing love
And how precious they are in His sight.

Big brother, little sister.
Alex (age 13) and Carly Jade (age 2), Guiping, Guangxi.

Reese Mackenzie (age 3),
Xinyu, Jiangxi.

BIRTHDAY WISHES
by Michelle Miller

CARLY'S SECOND BIRTHDAY… FEBRUARY 12, 2006. Wow!

I can't believe my little sweetie is two years old! I'm so excited about her birthday, but at the same time a piece of my heart is grieving. Two years ago today Carly came into the world, not knowing what was in store for her.

I can't fathom the sorrow Carly's birthmom must have felt when she laid her newborn daughter down that day. I wonder what she said to her little angel baby as she told her good-bye. I wonder if she turned to look at her sweet face one last time, knowing she would likely never see her again. I wonder if her heart broke that day.

One thing is for sure—it is because of her sacrifice that I have my dear daughter today. So while I feel an incredible sadness about how Carly's life began, I also feel an overwhelming, indescribable sense of gratitude for the two people who brought Carly into this world.

I wish there was a way for her birth family to see Carly now and to know how much she is loved. She is a beautiful, vivacious, happy, loving, compassionate, intelligent, adorable little girl. She is part of my heart and soul. She is so much a part of our family that it is hard to remember what life was like without her.

Circumstances may have dictated the things that happened two years ago today, but fate and destiny brought our lives together. People often say, "What a lucky girl" when they hear Carly's story. But in all reality, she isn't the lucky one at all; we are.

To my precious daughter, Carly: Happy second birthday, sweetie! I love you with all my heart.

Poem to My Birthparents
by Xiu Xiu Cooney

I wonder if you remember me!
Even though I think to myself
Where could you be?
Where would I be if you didn't leave me?
Was I not good enough for you
Or for anyone else?
But I can't think that.
I have to say to myself
That you love me and always will,
No matter what had happened.

People say that I am the lucky one
Because I was adopted,
Even though my Mom is the lucky one,
Who I should give all the credit to.
Without her
My life would not be filled.
The love I have is stronger
Than anything you could imagine
For my birthparents and my mother.

I know you have been protecting me
And watching me
Wherever I go,
Like a red thread clinging to my heart
And not letting go,
No matter what happens.

I would give anything
To see what you look like,
And I would stop the world
And melt with you
Just to have our moments,
No matter how long it would take.
The forever love.

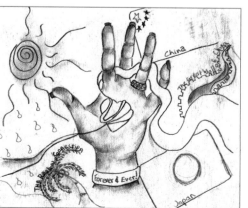

"Red Thread." Original artwork by AiXiu ("Xiu Xiu") (age 14), Nanjing, of her first three homes in Nanjing, Japan, and Hawaii.

Above: Jasmine and Kristen (both age 8)—travel sisters from Tongling, Anhui.

Below: Written by Jasmine (age 8).

I Have a Dream

From the study of Martin Luther King, Jr.

My dream is when I am older I will help chinese babys to found a home.

Jasmine Grade 2 Feb-2008

Sisters—Jaden (age 5), Shaoyang, Hunan, and Jasmine (age 8), Tongling, Anhui.

家庭

Georgia Kaye (age 11 months), Xui Shui, Jiangxi.

Amelia (age 10), Zhanjiang, Guangdong, has danced for seven years and loves it.

PLANS COME TOGETHER
by Annette Nicholson

HOW CAN ONE TRULY EXPRESS IN WRITING THE DELIGHT A CHILD BRINGS INTO ONE'S LIFE? I was 39 years old when she was placed in my arms, never thinking I would feel the love radiating from my own child. There she was—mine. My husband, Charlie, was equally delighted in her presence. She even liked him best.

Our story is no different than others. Every step in a long road led us to China—from having dinner with a friend who knew someone who had adopted from China to reading an article in a magazine. This friend had a business where the adoptive family just happened to come in the very next day. No surprise to me as God's plans are right on target. She asked them the proverbial question, "How did you do that?" They gave her the information, and she was on the phone to us. It snowballed from there. This was all in 1996 when international adoptions were first happening in China.

Our wait was relatively short; we got a referral in November 1996 and traveled two months later. We have loved and adored her from the beginning. She has brought so much joy into our lives and into the lives of our respective families. I know that a divine plan brought us together. We look forward to the many days ahead as we go through life together. We are so proud of China and the wonderful gift they gave us—*our daughter!*

Sisters—Georgia Kaye (age 2½), Xui Shui, Jiangxi, and Abigail Grace (age 4½), Lianyungang, Jiangsu.

Abigail Grace (age 18 months), Lianyungang, Jiangsu.

THE YU YU SISTERHOOD: A STORY OF FOREVER FRIENDS
by Nancy Krebs

IN AUGUST 2003, 12 FAMILIES, ALL STRANGERS TO ONE ANOTHER, CONVERGED IN CHINA TO ADOPT THEIR DAUGHTERS. The girls all lived in the Yulin Orphanage in Shaanxi. They were all given the last name of Yu; hence the name of our group. To celebrate "Gotcha Day," every August the Yu Yu Sisterhood and families gather in different locations in Pennsylvania. We spend an entire weekend together at a hotel—swimming, eating, and letting the girls get to know one another again. Last year we rented a hospitality room and had a dress-up party. We brought dress-up clothes, the girls had their faces painted and nails done, we did craft projects, and we danced. The girls played in the pool together, and we also spent a day at the zoo. In the above photo, 11 of the 12 families were able to attend the reunion. Our hope as parents is that these "sisters," who began their tiny lives in the orphanage together, will continue to reunite and develop friendships that will last a lifetime.

妈爸

Sisters—Saraphina Jing-Li (age 2½), Yangchun, Guangdong and Vanessa Shu-Lien (age 6), Wuchuan, Guangdong.

Above: Sisters—Bella Jane, Yongfeng, Jiangxi, and Vivi Claire, Foshan Nanhai, Guangdong (both age 2).

Left: Playgroup friends—Jada, Yangxi, Guangdong; Katharine, Hengdong, Hunan; Vivi, Foshan Nanhai, Guangdong; Kailee, Fengcheng, Jiangxi; Christine, Yangjiang Guangdong; Olivia, Qingcheng, Guangdong; Anna, Loudi, Hunan; Christina, Shanggao, Jiangxi; and Libby, Yangxi, Guangdong.

My Hometown: The Fengcheng City Project
by B. L. Padilla

About a year after adopting our daughter from Fengcheng City in southeast China, I joined an Internet group that gathers together families who share that point of origin. Soon I realized that it might be nice to share the information I was collecting about our daughter's first hometown. However, as I searched for information about this small, relatively unknown city, I felt frustrated that I had so many more questions than answers. Then it struck me that many of our group members had visited the town. Surely many of us had different pieces of the same puzzle; if we all shared impressions and information, we could provide a more complete picture of the city than any one of us could alone.

I put out a call for information with a list of questions and suggestions for people to write about: memories of traveling to Fengcheng—the people, cuisine, culture—basically anything they might know that could be of interest to the rest of us. The response was not immediately overwhelming, but I have been pleased to see information and descriptive recollections trickle in steadily, as well as plenty of offers to share photos. My job has been to weave it all together into one big report, together with bits and pieces of interesting information I have gleaned from surfing the Internet.

Hopefully one day our children will enjoy finding this report in their memory chests and reading about the fascinating place they come from.

Kaylee Ann (age 3), Shantou, Guangdong.

Sisters—Lydia JiuBao, Nanchang, Jiangxi; Audrey Mariah JingBo (age 7), Nanchang, Jiangxi; and Eliza Grace JiQiu (age 4), Yujiang, Jiangxi—celebrating Lydia's 16th birthday.

Lia Grace Jianqing (age 2), Nanfeng, Jiangxi—in Welsh costume on St. David's Day.

Bethany Mei Juan (born August 2000), Zunyi, Guizhou—at Huangguoshu Waterfall in Guizhou, with Mom.

A Most Wonderful Gift
by Christina Danner
Written on One Year Referral Day Anniversary

One year ago today, our long wait was over.
The mystery of who you were and where you were was solved.
We finally knew about you, our daughter, in faraway China.

Tao Mei Juan—"beautiful, graceful,"
Waiting for your forever family in Zunyi City, Guizhou Province.

Our first look at you was a fax of a fax—
"Isn't she beautiful?!" your mama exclaimed.
"Looks like one of those sonogram pictures!" your baba said.
"She's so cute," your gege said.
A baby's face peered out—not the 20-month-old you already were.
With your pouty lips and wide eyes, you stole our hearts immediately.
More recent pictures brought the realization of how much we had already missed.
Your look said "Are you coming?"
We couldn't wait for you to be home with us.

The most wonderful gift we have ever been given
Came from strangers on the other side of the world.
Although we didn't know it at the time,
God had spoken to us about you when He found you.
The reason for our long wait became clear.
You were meant to be a part of our family and our hearts forever.
You have already added so much joy to our lives.
We love you, Bethany Mei Juan Danner!

Kaizi Marie (age 2),
Zhangshu, Jiangxi.

FOREVER CONNECTED
by Dana Gong

THERE IS A REASON, WHATEVER IT BE, THAT YOU FOUND YOURSELF AT THE BUS STATION THAT DAY. I think of you often when Natalie does something cute or even sometimes as I watch her sleep. I wish you could experience this. And though you may not know, I think of you each May. The anniversary of my family coming together is almost the anniversary that yours was physically separated. The day we celebrate Natalie's birth is the day I reflect on her growth and the day you wonder how she has grown. And the anniversary of that morning at the bus station is the day that both our lives changed forever. Though we will never meet, we are thinking of one another and share these bittersweet thoughts at the same time. And when she is old enough, Natalie will share these with us as well. We will think of you always, particularly those days in May. We are forever connected.

Left: Sisters—Meilyn (age 5), Yueyang County, Hunan, and Laley (age 11 months), Xiushan, Chongqing.

Right: Ella (age 3), Yuanling, Hunan.

Below: Meilyn (age 5), Yueyang County, Hunan; Miriam (age 5), Chongqing; Mia (age 5), Zhanjiang, Guangdong; Yue Yue (age 3), USA; Lily (age 4), Ruijin, Jiangxi; Laley (age 14 months), Xiushan, Chongqing; and Autumn (age 3), Yizhou, Guangxi—participating in a weekly Chinese language and culture class.

Red Threads of Love
by Lucinda Renfree

They say an invisible red thread connects those
   destined to be together
How true it is
As I sit and watch you peacefully sleep,
   I see how much we belong together
You are so much a part of our family, our life,
   our reason to be
We are connected on a soul level

You are a gift
An angel here to deliver joy and happiness
   and experience all life has to offer
My darling girl, you have given me more tears,
   laughter, and love than anyone else I know
You have re-ignited my emotions and shown me
   the meaning of unconditional love

I remember the first time I held you in my arms,
   and you cried a thousand tears
Tears of loss and pain, and I cried too
Now three years on, we still cry, but we also laugh,
   we love, and we sing

I thank your birthparents who gave you life
   and in turn gave me life
They are truly special people who will always be
   a part of you and of us

I can't imagine my life without you
You are such a gorgeous girl: beautiful, intuitive,
   and strong-willed
Your inner beauty shines deeply from within
   and like a shining star could light up the night sky

We belong together, we just do
This red thread has made sure we found each other
   and were united as a family

My love for you grows stronger all the time
Just when I think I'm full up with love,
   my heart grows bigger and the love expands
That love continues to grow from strength to
   strength and will continue to grow as you do

My beautiful daughter, De Ang Fu, I love you!

TIES TO BIRTH FAMILIES
by Patti Kellett

OUR DRIVER, KNOWN AS MARIO ANDRETTI, WAS DETERMINED THAT HE WOULD FIND THE CLINIC IN NORTHERN XI'AN. He had driven me, my friend Barb, and my agency facilitator from the airport in Xi'an to the hotel where I would meet and stay with my new son, Joel. Mario became quite a great friend to the smiling boy who had risen above all obstacles. Joel had resided on the fourth floor of the Xi'an Social Welfare Institute for the first 20 months of his life. He had been found as a newborn infant in front of a medical clinic, cold from the winter chill and weak from lack of food. Joel is cleft affected and had a rather wide opening in both his lip and palate. He was lucky to be taken in by a part of the orphanage run by an international charity which cares for special needs children. They cleaned him up, fed him, and put him into an incubator to keep him warm. They then proceeded to love and care for him for his first 20 months of life.

Two days after I met Joel, Mario drove us to the orphanage on the outskirts of the city in a small village. We had the privilege of meeting his caregivers and some of the babies and older children who lived on this floor. Mario visited with us, and, like me, he appeared to be trying to understand why these beautiful children were abandoned by their families. We learned that the children with clefts are often abandoned several days to a few weeks after birth as their parents realize their inability to care for the child. While this saddened me, it also helped me to understand the anguish of a mother and father who wanted to care for their baby, yet did not know how to feed him and often were not financially able to provide the simple surgeries that could heal him.

I needed so much to find the place that Joel was left so that I could connect further with his parents. Mario seemed to understand my need, and he wrote the finding site address down so he could search for this important spot after he left us at the hotel. The next day after visiting the Terracotta Soldiers, he drove us to this village lined with homes with noodles drying in courtyards. We stopped at the medical center. I photographed it and dried some tears while Joel slept in the car, oblivious to the meaning of this spot. While we walked around, several grandparents came out of the shop with their grandbabies. Although I knew that it was likely that Joel was not from this village, I had the sense that Joel could have been there too, being cared for by his grandparents while his parents worked, and that these children could have been his playmates. I am so grateful for the chance to visit and to connect with Joel's family because we are each a part of the miracle that is his life. This little boy overcomes obstacles on a daily basis and lives with a delight in his heart that blesses all who come into contact with him.

Sisters and friends—Shoshana (age 2), Chenzhou, Hunan; Cleo (age 2), Chenzhou, Hunan; Anna (age 2½), Changsha, Hunan; and Emily (age 2), Chenzhou, Hunan.

Joel (age 20 months), Xi'an, Shaanxi.

Sisters—Eva Xiuxia (age 6), Jinjiang, Fujian, and Helen Lichun (age 4), Yiyang, Jiangxi.

Little Tian, Little Sky
by *Esther Retzer*

Little Tian, Little Sky, how you have changed our lives.

On a gentle evening in December,
With the sky the color of soft navy blue,
And white snow drifting slowly from the sky,
We saw our first picture of your beautiful face,
And the stars shone with our joy.

On a tender February evening in China,
With the sky alive with red and yellow of fireworks,
And celebration sounds of the Chinese New Year filled the air,
We held you in our arms and felt your first caress,
And the red lanterns danced in the wind with our happiness.

On a warm afternoon in China,
With the street alive with music and colors of the dragon parade,
And costumed dancers weaved gracefully through the street,
Your eyes twinkled with wonder but you held our hands so tight,
And the sun warmed our faces to mirror the feelings in our hearts.

And as we continue to share life's journey,
The light in your eyes is as iridescent as the stars,
The joy in your soul dances like the wind,
And the love in your heart has earned the respect of the sun.

Little Tian, Little Sky, how you have changed our lives.

Wuhan "cousins." (Seated on couch) Shana, Emily, Jhenna, Sara, Catie, and Jenna.
(On floor) Ana, Sara, Piper, Lily, Brynna, Klaire, and Meredith.
All are from Xiaogan, Hubei, except twins Ana and Sara, from Huanggang,
and Jhenna, from Hong Hu City, Hunan. All the girls are approximately age 1.

How Did This Family Happen?
by *Yvonne Hillier*

FIVE OR MORE YEARS AGO MY FAMILY AND TEN OTHER FAMILIES MADE PERSONAL DECISIONS TO ADOPT CHINESE DAUGHTERS. We all went through mounds of paperwork and many anxious moments awaiting our daughters' arrival. Each family made their own individual journey to China in hopes of expanding their family by one. Unbeknownst to the families, after our first meeting a strong bond started to form. While in China we all became one large extended family. All of our Chinese born daughters were "cousins" bonded by adoption. This bond of family continues today. Our extended family gathers together every other summer for one magical week. Our daughters and other family members catch up with each other and solidify our bonds. Who would have ever imagined adoption would increase our family size by more than forty?

2nd annual Wuhan "cousins" reunion. (Standing) Shana, Brynna, and Catie. (Sitting on bench) Lily, Sara, Ana, Jenna, and Emily. (Sitting on floor) Piper, Klaire, and Jhenna. All the girls are age 4½.

Mabel XiFeng (age 2), Hefei, Anhui, with Mommy in China.

Soul Sisters
by *Pam and Jim Kelly, Holly Phillips and Jim Johnson*

SOUL SISTERS—YES, THAT IS WHAT OUR TWO CHINESE DARLING GIRLS ARE—IN THE ORPHANAGE AND NOW FOUR YEARS LATER. Two families… two babies from the Yangchung orphanage… two four-year-olds growing up together in Kansas City… two soul sisters celebrating life and pre-kindergarten together. Two soul sisters forever bound by love and friendship and destiny.

Our girls, Faith Kelly and Kassi Johnson, were adopted on the same day, February 19, 2003, in Guangzhou, China. They have truly become best buds as we all celebrate "Gotcha Day" yearly, have "Girls Day Out" frequently, and coordinate Halloween and other festivities. Our girls cultivate their sisterhood daily at school activities. They truly love each other like sisters—arguing, hugging, giggling, even wearing matching outfits with matching make-up.

Our girls are a blessing to us. Their love has been inspiring not only to us, but to all of the people that they come into contact with. Their teachers marvel that they are so similar and have such a strong connection and bond between them. They are truly soul sisters forever.

Above: Mabel XiFeng (age 3), Hefei, Anhui—
at home in South Carolina.
Right: Sisters—Mabel (age 3) and
Lucy (age 6), Changde, Hunan.

Sisters—Chloe FuYen (age 3), Mother's Love, Guangxi, and Lindsey YaQin (age 6), Anqing, Anhui.

TEDDY AND EMY
by Myndee M. Reed

WE FIRST MET JIM AND NANCY BREWER THROUGH A YAHOO INTERNET GROUP FOR FAMILIES WHO ADOPTED THEIR CHILDREN FROM THE JIANDE SOCIAL WELFARE INSTITUTE IN THE ZHEJIANG PROVINCE. The Brewers brought home their dear daughter, Teddy, in December of 2002, and we adopted our Emy in March of 2003. We planned to meet when the Brewers traveled to see family close to our hometown in Kansas. We met at our local Chinese restaurant, where we enjoyed good food and great company. The girls had a ball playing together while the Brewers and I visited about our girls and our adoption experience.

It was at that time that I told Jim and Nancy that Emy was documented as having a heart condition, but, after we brought her home, we discovered her heart was perfect! Nancy looked in awe at her husband and asked, "Could it be?" Nancy explained that while in China adopting Teddy, they were given the privilege of visiting the orphanage where their daughter resided. Nancy recalled a baby who was introduced to them as Teddy's cribmate and who was described as being the orphanage's "heart baby."

I was immediately intrigued and excited at the thought that perhaps we had located Emy's cribmate. As promised, Nancy emailed me pictures as soon as they arrived home. One glance was all I needed to confirm that Emy and Teddy were indeed cribmates! Our daughters had spent their first year of life together sleeping, cuddling, and playing; then had traveled halfway around the world to be reunited once again!

United again. Friends—Emylee and Teddy (both age 3), both from Jiande, Zhejiang.

Sisters—Emalie Quinn (age 4) and Kyleigh Maree (age 7)— at Chinese New Year.

Libby Grace RuiYu (age 1), ZhangYe, Gansu, with Dad.

Abigail Qianhui (age 6), Anqing, Anhui.

Sisters—Lydia Rose (age 5), Bengbu, Anhui, and Adeline Rose (age 1), Zhuzhou, Hunan.

AMERICAN WORKING IN CHINA
by Jessica Cushman

BY SEPTEMBER 2004 I HAD SPENT LESS THAN ONE MONTH OF MY YEAR-LONG ADVENTURE IN SHANXI, CHINA. I was there to teach English but was delighted at the prospect of helping at the city's orphanage. As the taxi drove my friends and me down the dirt road that very first time, we spotted a little cardboard box on the side of the road. Inside that box lay the most frail but beautiful soul that my eyes had ever seen. He had not yet been cleaned after his birth, and, as I untied his restraints to give him his first hug, I realized why he had been abandoned. Baby Aniah had a partially formed Siamese twin attached to his left side. Death seemed imminent, but many miracles were about to happen. Anyone looking at him would never imagine that Aniah would live through the night, but indeed he made it. He needed surgery quickly, though, to remove the other baby in order to give him a chance. Within days he was sent to Beijing where surgery was performed immediately. There was no earthly reason he lived that first week, and certainly no reason that he survived the surgery, yet he began to grow and thrive. He came back to Shanxi the following March to live with a foster family. As he turns three this year, he is more beautiful and special than ever. He is still waiting to be united with a most fortunate family, but for now he happily lives with my husband and me. The scar on his left side will always be a reminder to me of the grace of God. The smile on his face will always remind me that prayer is powerful and miracles still happen.

Brianna Liang (age 4), Dianjiang, Chongqing.

Corban Huiyan (age 1), Chenzhou, Hunan.

WE GIVE OUR LOVE
by Mary Anne Castranio

WE GIVE OUR LOVE. We give our love and promises to the little ones who come to us from China and other faraway places. They need our love and support and strength to blossom and bloom into the amazing adults we dream and hope and strive for them to be.

What we receive in return is so much more than we expected. We receive a family—longed for, cherished, challenging, unbelievably wonderful, funny, and endlessly entertaining. We receive the gifts of a fascinating country and heritage to explore, a new set of friends joyously engaged in the same life's journey, and a whole community of well-wishers we never knew had such big hearts.

We seek to discover the nuances of China's culture and history and do our utmost to help our children learn to honor its intricacies and treasures. We freely share our deep, deep love with these new little persons and rejoice in all they become.

And we are transformed.

Megan Anna (age 2½), Shantou, Guangdong.

Olivia Faye (age 7½), Gaoyou, Jiangsu.

Sophia Sage (age 7), Gaoyou, Jiangsu.

Abigail Paige (age 9), Linchuan, Jiangxi.

RECOLLECTIONS OF CHINA
by Stephen Rogers

ONE YEAR LATER THE THING I REMEMBER MOST ABOUT CHINA IS PEOPLE STOPPING ME TO PRACTICE THEIR ENGLISH, all of us standing next to the inevitably unmarked hole in the sidewalk, the thunder of traffic broken by the tinkle of bikes, the various scents of dim sum flavoring the air.

Bridget (age 2), Dingyuan, Anhui, with her grandmother, "Muh."

Birthday Wish
by Maureen Maginn

On our daughter's birthday, before she wakes,
I step outside to look at the sky,
dawn here in Missouri,
evening there in China.

Someone once told me that the body
feels anniversaries, feels in its bones
the echo of what happened last year
even if the mind has forgotten, or
tried to.

Last year on this day, you gave
birth to our daughter.

Someday our daughter will look to the sky
and honor you herself on this day,
but for now I am here by proxy,
here instead of her,
here instead of you.

And my wish is this, on this anniversary,
that you know:

Your baby is safe with me.

Zoe Elizabeth (age 4), Gaozhou, Guangdong.

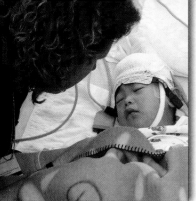

Jared YunDong ("YuYu") (age 5), Yuncheng, Shanxi. Six months after returning home, YuYu had a stroke and received brain surgery, reminding us that, just as with biological children, there can be unknowns. Through all of his time in the hospital and scary procedures, YuYu never complained or lost his sweet nature.

Brother and sister forever! Jared Yun Dong ("YuYu") (age 5) and Alia ManLi ("LiLi") (age 4), Jinchang, Gansu.

Happy cowboy! Jared YunDong ("YuYu") (age 5).

Siblings—Tyler John (age 5), Mother's Love, Guangxi; Jordan; Gracie Faith (age 5), Huzhou, Zhejiang; Cody; and Noah Paul (age 5), Shenyang, Liaoning.

Charlotte (age 1), Shanggao, Jiangxi.

HOSTING A CHINESE TEACHER
by Patti Kellett

IN THE FALL OF 2001, A FEW MONTHS AFTER MY TEN-MONTH-OLD DAUGHTER, LAUREL, AND I RETURNED HOME FROM OUR ADOPTION TRIP, I MADE THE DECISION FOR US TO PARTICIPATE IN THE SISTER CITY PROGRAM. The two cities, Liuzhou in Guangxi Province and Cincinnati in Ohio, have developed a teacher exchange program. English teachers from Liuzhou come to Cincinnati for about five months for instruction in English and live with host families. We had the privilege of hosting Irene, who had the most adventurous spirit of the students that year. She fully integrated herself into our family and became a fast friend to Laurel and me. Irene taught me so many things about China and the culture that Laurel came from. I learned the fact that anything can be stir-fried, including leftover meatloaf; that one can make a bath of ginger, green onions, and Epsom salts for a child with an upper respiratory infection and it really works; how to make paper cuts; how Chinese families live; and how to build a bridge to Laurel's homeland. Irene had the experience of living with an adopted child from her culture, learning about independent American women, going to Tupperware parties, attending different church services, eating pizza and liking it, and so much more. Irene and I bonded over late night discussions about September 11, growing up in China or America, families, marriage, parenting, school, religion, and politics. This deep and meaningful experience was such a great way to build a friendship and to share in the red thread of Laurel's Chinese heritage.

Sisters—Cate Xue He (age 2), Fengcheng, Jiangxi, and Cara Lin Xin (age 4), Xiaogan, Hubei.

Sisters—Melissa Rose (age 10), Fuzhou, Fujian, and Beth Min (age 8), Yueyang, Hunan.

Dorisa Quan-Yu (age 18 months), FengCheng, Jiangxi.

Sisters—Caitlyn Peng (age 3),
Fuling, Chongqing,
and Lauren Ping (age 6),
Anyuan, Pingxiang City, Jiangxi.

How Do I Stop?
by Jill McLaughlin

WHEN MY HUSBAND AND I BEGAN OUR ADOPTION JOURNEY, I THOUGHT WE WOULD ADOPT ONE CHILD, TWO AT THE MOST. The adoption process is long and arduous, and it is so difficult to wait patiently, placing our hearts and all of our hopes in the hands of a foreign government.

Little did I know our trip to China to adopt our first daughter would permanently change my soul. I fell in love with the Chinese culture and the Chinese people. I love the exotic food, smells, and architecture. But the children of China have forever claimed my heart.

Visiting the babies and older children residing in the orphanage irreversibly altered my point of view. Seeing all of those beautiful children convinced me our adoption journey would not be complete anytime soon. Since our first adoption trip, we have traveled to China three more times, and each trip was as unique and wonderful as the child who came home with us.

Our home is now bursting at the seams with both love and activity—so much activity that we draw attention wherever we go, eliciting sympathetic comments like, "Wow! You really have your hands full," or, "Are all those children yours?" Our home and backyard are full of toys. Rather than dust bunnies, we have tumbleweeds. The housework just doesn't seem as important as it used to. Our bank account is empty from paying for adoption trips and adoption fees, although our hearts are abundantly full.

But instead of feeling satisfaction in knowing our family is complete, I still feel the excruciating pull of the children left behind.

Every time I see a child lingering on a waiting child list, it tears at my heartstrings. In that small picture I recognize so much potential just waiting to be released by the love of a permanent family. Would this child be resilient, smart, and athletic like my Rose? Perhaps this child would be funny and fiercely loyal like my Ginger or a happy little charmer like my Michael. Or maybe she would be loving and perceptive like my Emma.

My head knows we have exhausted our emotional and financial resources, and I can't adopt them all. My head knows I should be satisfied advocating for adoption. But my heart, oh my heart. I look into each little face, and I see the faces of my own beloved children. Will she ever know what a unique and exceptional person she is? Will he ever grow strong and confident knowing a family's love and support? How do I reconcile my head with my heart? How do I stop?

Siblings—Emma (age 3), Hubei; Rose (age 6), Anhui; Michael (age 4), Chongqing; and Ginger (age 4), Jiangxi—celebrating Emma's first 4th of July in the USA.

Sisters—Sasha Mengfeng
(age 8 months), Yugan, Jiangxi,
and Olivia Meishao
(age 3½), Anqing, Anhui.

Lilly Xinrong (age 2), Yangxin, Hubei.

If I were a butterfly I would fly to china and eat noodls. Laura

Created by Laura Joy Xin (age 6), Honghu, Hubei.

RETURNING WITH A PURPOSE
by Christine Mei Louise Minor (age 8½)

MY FAMILY TRAVELED TO CHINA THIS SUMMER. We each picked one special place we really wanted to go in China. I had two places that were very memorable. First was sleeping on the Great Wall in Jin Da Ling in one of the towers. It was so awesome. We had to pee off the side because there was no bathroom. We had to get up at 4 a.m. to see the sun rise. The long morning was kind of boring; so I counted all the bricks in the perimeter wall of our tower. I counted the rows across and the rows down. It took most of the morning, but I did it. There were 2,996 bricks! Finally it was breakfast—the biggest bowl of Top Ramen I have ever seen. I was happy.

We decided to walk from Jin Da Ling to Si Ma Tai—32 towers and six miles of walking along the Great Wall. My brother and I were always ahead of Mom and Dad. We were the scouts on lookout for the Mongols. I loved seeing how the huge wall built so long ago still stands today. Along the wall are characters carved into the stones. These are the names of the people who built the wall 2,000 years ago. What a hard job—100 degrees in the summer and freezing in the winter.

Besides visiting my little sisters in China, I wanted to do something to help in my orphanage. So before we went to China we talked about how I could raise money to get something they needed. I went to work. I wrote a letter to my friends and my family's friends telling about my orphanage and that I wanted to raise money for them. I said I would read for three hours a week for three months and exercise for 30 minutes four times a week. I asked for donations to help buy clothes, books, and toys. My dad made me a website so people could see what I was doing. My mom helped me with the letter, and her friend said she would make t-shirts for raising money too. I designed the t-shirt myself. I did a brush painting of pandas and bamboo on the front and a Ying and Yang on the back with a picture of me as a baby in China and a picture of me now. I was able to reach my goal and more. I raised over $2,000 and bought a commercial dryer for my orphanage. It was very exciting to see it at the orphanage. It was really big. I felt very proud of myself and a little shy. We gave the orphanage staff my t-shirts too.

I want to go back to my hometown and volunteer at my orphanage and even live in China when I get older. It might be hard, especially trying to learn how to speak Mandarin, but I can learn.

Kiarra Nicole (age 2), Xiushan.

Lilian Mei Zu (age 2), Shanggao, Jiangxi.

Sisters—Josie (age 5), Yangzhou, Jiangsu, and Lucy (age 3), Fuling, Chongqing.

Above: Marie (age 2), Xiushan, Chongqing—borrowing from Monet.

Below: Cousins—Grace and Kaili (both age 5), both from Guiping—together for a week at Dillon's International Culture Camp.

CIRCLING
by Trudy Miller

I AM VISITING THE TOWN OF MY DAUGHTER'S BIRTH FOR THE VERY FIRST TIME. When I adopted her three years ago, I was not able to visit her hometown and only stayed in the provincial capital, which was five hours away by bus.

My daughter has grown into a beautiful four-year-old girl with many questions about the first year of her life, which she spent in the orphanage in one small baby room. She asks me all the time about "her" city and her caregivers. I can give her no real answers, as everything I think I know about her hometown is from the Internet.

My husband finally convinced me that I should return to China, to help find some of the answers that Mia so truly needs. I know in my heart that I need these answers as well. I want to meet those who cared for my beloved daughter. I want to thank them in person and memorize their faces. I want to be able to tell my daughter with certainty that, yes, she was loved and is still remembered.

And so here I am, circling above her hometown in an airplane. Out the window I see a small river and lots of farmland. There is a man plowing with an ox, and I see an older woman turning the earth with a hoe. As we get closer to the ground, I can suddenly feel my heart beating faster and faster, and I am holding my breath. I have just realized that somewhere below me, somewhere in the city that is spread under the plane's wings, are my daughter's first parents. This is my daughter's birthplace. Four years ago, somewhere below me, a woman gave life to the child I now love completely. And then I realize I am crying as I begin to understand that I need to memorize everything for Mia. I want her to know it all. This is her story, her homeland, her beginning.

Elizabeth Qiongfei (nearly age 2), Hengyang County, Hunan—riding her mom's childhood tricycle.

Siblings— Elizabeth Leone Qing (age 2), Fengcheng, Jiangxi, and Thomas AnAn (age 3), Hangzhou, Zhejiang.

OUR FCC GROUP
by Susan Knispel

INCLUDING CHINESE CULTURE IN OUR LIVES HAS BEEN ONE OF THE MOST REWARDING AND ENLIGHTENING PARTS OF THE ADOPTION EXPERIENCE. Our local FCC group is just fabulous. We live in southern New Jersey, near Philadelphia, where so much is available to us, and we are part of an incredibly nurturing community. My daughter, Lia, now five years old, has taken Chinese language lessons and is part of a dance troupe of Chinese adopted children called the Mei Mei Dancers. The troupe performs at many cultural events in the area.

These activities not only involve her in Chinese culture but also create an incredible bond with other children adopted from China. One highlight for both of us was the program we presented to her preschool class last Chinese New Year. I read a story to the class about Chinese New Year, and then the class did a Lion Dance with a beautiful costume handmade by our dance teacher. It was the hit of the year; the children and their parents were talking about it for some time afterwards. It made Lia so proud of her heritage and was a learning experience for everyone.

Lillian
by Deana Groves

Yesterday.
Today.
Tomorrow.
On my mind,
in my heart.

Home.
Relax.
Routine.
Two cultures,
new family.

Explore.
Play.
Learn.
Constant awe,
ever-changing child.

One daughter.
Two continents.
Four parents.
Forever love,
forever in love.

Neighborhood friends—Liam (age 7), China; Jared (age 5), Korea; Brooke; Royce; Gabriel (age 8), Korea; Nicholas (age 3), China; and (standing) Josepha (age 12), Korea.

ALIVIA XIAN
by Kimberly Kohus

FOR US ADOPTION REALLY WAS NOT A SECOND CHOICE. Ultimately we likely could have conceived, but it was something that both my husband and I longed to do. Everything about it just seemed right.

I don't think a week has passed in the past year that I have not gone back and looked at all of our pictures from China. I look at her face, and I almost can't believe that this is the same child. When we received our referral picture, my husband and I cried our eyes out. We had just never seen anyone so beautiful. When we looked at her eyes in the photo, it just felt as though she was staring right back at us saying, "Come get me."

Weeks passed and the day finally came—our Forever Family Day. We held her in our arms for the first time and promised to love and protect her always. Again there were many tears. She stared back up at us, just like in the photo, but this time we could see so much more. Although she seemed skeptical, we got her to smile and laugh quite quickly.

It has been just over a year, and I now look at my life before and realize that we have completed each other. When people say to me, "She's a lucky baby," I tell them, "No, we are the lucky ones."

Left: Alivia Xian (age 12 months), DianBia, Guangdong, with Mom.

Below: One year later— Alivia Xian (age 2).

Where I'm From
by Tessa Howard (age 11)
(written when 7 years old)

I am from all across the world.
I am from chicken fried rice and noodles.
I am from Chinese New Year.
I am from Mom and Dad saying, "We love you."
I am from a *big* family that's nice.

Siblings—Aileen Ling (age 13), Luoyang, Henan; Celeste Di (age 5), Beijing; Julia Jiang (age 11½), Jiangyin, Jiangsu; and Melody Lu (age 12½), Luoyang, Henan.

Loving sisters—Anne (age 18 months), Youxian, Hunan, and Katie (age 10).

Aileen Ling (age 12)—playing chess with another sibling, Christopher Mark (age 13).

Dreaming of Home
by Lisa Kaden

I SAT LAST NIGHT IN FRONT OF MY COMPUTER FOR MORE THAN AN HOUR READING MY OWN ADOPTION JOURNAL. We have been home for two months, and I am still in awe of our whole experience. This was our second adoption trip to bring home our fourth daughter. I read my writings of our experiences in China and being united with our sweet little girl. I closed my eyes and could still see her hometown so perfectly.

We drove 4½ hours each way for a glimpse of her first home. When I breathed in deeply, I could feel the rhythm of this place. The distinct smell from the street vendors, the chaos of traffic, the people—her people— strolling and chatting on the sidewalks. A 30 minute drive took us away from the city to a dusty, one-road township. In contrast it was quiet and somewhat lonesome. There, in front of a small clinic, is where her story began. Beautiful karst formations framed the setting, and I could hear hushed voices in the distance behind doorways. It was just as hard to leave this place in my mind as it was the day we visited. I remember turning in circles trying to drink it all in—not ever feeling like I had seen enough. My throat tight and my chest heavy, I knew it was time to leave. I turned and took one last gaze over the scene. Remember, Lisa; remember it all.

This place is now a part of me, and a part of our entire family, as are many other sites in China relating to our daughters' history. When I stepped off the plane in China, I had an overwhelming feeling I was returning home. Even though I obviously stood out as "not belonging" on the outside, in my heart I was home. My daughters' culture is woven into our family's identity. As their mother I feel I am part Chinese. I love their first homeland, and I embrace it as my own. This is not something I planned or expected; it is just something that happened when I gave my heart away and received this treasure greater than gold in return. They became a part of me, and now a part of me will always long for home.

Alex (age 9) and Avery (age 6), both from Shantou, Guangdong— reunited as brother and sister.

Zoey SiLing (age 15 months), Chongyang, Hubei.

Above: "A Nanny's Loving Care." Painting by Michela (age 13)— dedicated to all of the hardworking nannies doing all they can to care for the children in the social welfare institutes.

Below: "The Grand Welcome." Painting by Alexis (age 10)— conveying the excitement in the hearts of friends and family who wait to welcome the sweet child home.

Siblings—Julia Jiang (age 11), Jiangyin, Jiangsu; Celeste Di (age 5), Beijing; and Phoenix Li (age 7), Dongguan, Guangdong.

Selah Faith QingMu (age 19 months), Yizhou, Guangxi.

A very happy John Michael (age 2), Shang Rao Ling, Jiangxi, and Daddy. Photo taken while riding a bus in China six days after being united with his family in July 2007.

GRACE'S BIRTHFATHER
by Larry Vandenbergen

I SAW GRACE'S BIRTHFATHER LAST NIGHT. I always wondered what her birthparents looked like and if my visions of them would be the same as hers.

I was giving Grace her bottle before bed. This time is special because it is the last quality time that I get with her that day. Most nights I look her square in the face, look deep in her eyes, and let time stand still until she closes her eyes. Last night she rolled around in my arms until she found a comfortable spot. And as I looked closer, my vision of her birthfather came to life.

He is in his mid to late 20s, about 5'6" tall, with striking, straight black

Sisters—Grace Guanying (age 11 months), Shanggao, Jiangxi, and Sarah (age 7).

hair that is cut short and parted on the side. He has fair skin, brown eyes, high cheekbones, and a protruding jaw. He has a sly, but happy, smile and maybe a few hints of facial hair scattered about his face.

As I watched Grace, I saw his eyes look into the skies, as if he was thinking about something or someone from a long time ago. I saw him working in the fields—a strong, young man, who liked taking care of his crops, providing a meager living for his family. I saw a man who came home at night to his young wife and his parents, who were now in his care. I saw a man who was proud of who he was and where he was from. I saw him look to the heavens and wonder about where life had taken him, and what was in store for him in the future.

I wonder if Grace was his first child. I wonder if he cried the day that she was born, loving his first child but knowing the undoubting task that he needed to do just a few minutes after she was born. I wonder about his last final seconds with her—tenderly wrapping her clothes around her to keep her warm before he left her in that special place. I wonder if he hid in the shadows, looking to make sure that she was found, to finalize his duties for her well-being. Or, I wonder, if he had done this before and if the feelings were as deep this time as they had been in the past.

The vision only lasted a few seconds, but it could have been a lifetime, for both her birthfather and me. As Grace finished her bottle, she rolled over toward me and pushed the bottle away, along with the vision that had me transfixed for what seemed like an eternity. I put Grace to bed, fervently hoping that I would meet her birthfather again and be able to tell him that his daughter is just fine.

Marit (age 6), Huangmei, Hubei, with sister, Mattie (age 4), Jianxin, Jiangxi Province—receiving an impromptu lesson in fan painting at the Qingyan Temple in Chengdu, Sichuan.

Sophia Qing Liu
(age 2½), Anqing, Anhui.

喜

Katie (age 2),
MaoNan, Guangdong,
and sister, Sara (age 4),
Kunming, Yunnan—
at a reception in
Washington, D.C.
for the director
of the Kunming SWI.

Abby Mei Hope (age 6) and Marie Jeannine (age 7), both from Guixi City, Jiangxi.

We found Marie's picture on the Guixi SWI website and knew the likeness with Abby
was remarkable. DNA testing showed that they are indeed sisters. We were blessed
to be able to reunite Marie and Abby and to get to know each other's families.

Sisters—Caroline Lishu (age 5),
Zhuzhou, Hunan, and
Elizabeth Qiongfei (age 1),
Hengyang County, Hunan,
with Mom.

TRAVEL GROUP 67 IS STILL TRAVELING
by Kelly Savage

OUR TRAVEL GROUP, AMERICA WORLD ADOPTION ASSOCIATION'S GROUP NUMBER 67, TRAVELED TO CHINA IN JANUARY 2002 TO ADOPT OUR CHILDREN. Most of us were first-timers, and we met in Chicago, toured Beijing, split up to the various provinces, and reassembled in Guangzhou. This group came together at a particular time and place to share the intense and unforgettable experience of adoption in China. In those two weeks we became "friends for life."

The summer after we traveled, four of our 15 travel families reunited at Point Pleasant Beach in New Jersey. We formed an e-group on Yahoo, naming it "PtPleasant" after the first reunion site. Through this group we have pooled our knowledge; shared prayer requests; rejoiced through births, marriages, subsequent adoptions, and a discovered Chinese sibling; and cheered and been awed at each other's charitable and professional successes. Through this travel group we have shared our lives.

We had a reunion again in June 2005 at Hawks Nest State Park in West Virginia. Twelve families—much larger families—attended. We had an amazingly blessed time. Recognizing the role of the Internet in facilitating this group's cohesiveness, I stopped to thank Al Gore for inventing the Internet, but everyone just laughed at me. We're all thankful for what God has done in our lives.

Though we're diverse geographically (New York to Florida to Nebraska), professionally (single working moms, business owners, teachers, linemen, engineers, politicos), and in many other ways, we're united in purpose and faith and friendship.

Travel Group 67 is still traveling.

Cousins—Markiana Yang Yu, Chengdu,
and Anna BaoChun, Chenzhou (both age 6).

Bailee (age 3), Guilin, Guangxi, and Dakota (age 5), Shihezi, Xinjiang, with Dad and Mom.

Katie Min, (age 1½), Tonggu, Jiangxi, with her dad.

Sisters—Dana Qiang (age 11), Zhejiang, and Jamie Qiao (age 9), Jiangxi.

SISTERS RETURN

by Jamie Qiao Murphy Soika (age 9)

GOING BACK TO CHINA WAS AWESOME! It was fun to see all of the land that I was born on. It was exciting meeting all of the new people who were also adopted from China. All of China is magnificent! I wish I could go more often.

by Dana Qiang Murphy Soika (age 11)

SEEING CHINA AGAIN WAS REALLY COOL! It made me feel at home there. It was also very cool eating there! I thought that eating there was very different. Seeing my orphanage was awesome too! Just seeing where I lived for maybe one year. It was exciting seeing all of the Chinese writing! Even though I couldn't read it, it was so cool seeing it.

Walking on the Great Wall of China was just so *magnificent*—looking out and seeing a lot of the beautiful land of China! Hearing about some of the legends of China was very interesting and learning about the history was amazing!

Going to China was a really, *really*, *really* great experience. I really hope I can go see China again soon!

Chrissy (age 11), Nanchang, Jiangxi.

Betsy (age 9), Suzhou, Jiangsu.

Ann (age 10), Changsha, Hunan.

Mary Kate (nearly age 12), Shangrao, Jiangxi.

Nancy (age 32 months), Lily (age 33 months), MeiXi (age 31 months)—all from Dingyuan, Anhui, and adopted on the same day to families in the United Kingdom.

Siblings—Luke Nicholas (age 5); Ciana Angang (age 2), Bengbu, Anhui; and Claire Rachel (age 8).

Amy Faith (age 4), Anqing, Anhui.

Zoe Xi (age 4), Huazhou, Guangdong.

Dingyuan Friends
by Janet Potts

It was the end of October 2002, and three families in the United Kingdom, strangers to one another, had been awaiting their referrals for nearly 15 months. They were really starting to doubt that their referrals would ever arrive. They did, of course, and the wait was instantly forgotten as envelopes were eagerly ripped open in Essex, Gloucestershire, and Cheshire, and pictures were pored over, reports were faxed to translators, and tears were shed.

Unusual for U.K. referrals at that time, many of the children matched to families that month were from the same social welfare institute—a relatively small, new institute in Anhui Province called Dingyuan SWI. These three families were amongst the group receiving the pictures of their Dingyuan girls that weekend. This group remains the only group of U.K. families ever to be referred children from Dingyuan. A couple of days later, through the magic of the Internet and the kindness of the translator, three mums were new friends. Travel dates were coordinated, and we all finally met—moments before we met our daughters—in a hotel lobby in Hefei on December 9, 2002.

Once home the communication continued, and we have managed to get together at least once a year since then for our three Dingyuan girls—Lily, Nancy, and MeiXi—to spend some time together. Whenever and wherever we meet, there is a special bond between our girls, who love to spend time together. The three mums remain firm friends, and it is lovely to see our girls continuing their special friendship.

AbbyLiz ZiYang (age 3½), Anqing City, Anhui.

Gracie (age 4), Yuanling, Hunan.

My Hunan Family
by Ellen Harlow
Submitted by Jenny Rogers

A Tribute to the AFTH/CAS Yuanling, Hunan, September 23, 2003, Adoption Group

My mom traveled all the way to China
She knew I'd be waiting for her there
She took me in her arms and held me tight
I could feel her love and I could feel her care

I knew she was taking me back home with her
There were nine of my sisters there too
Some had moms and some had moms and dads
It was quite an adventure how we grew

From the Hunan province a family of ten
Traveling and bonding along the way
We still meet and have play times together
Looks like my sisters and I are here to stay

God has truly blessed me with my mommie
He has made me as happy as I can be
I now have eight uncles and nine aunts
The Hunan family are we

喜

Caitlin (age 10), Anhui—at Yangshuo Mountain Retreat in Guilin.

Siblings—Isabella Grace Yile (age 6), Chenzhou, Hunan; Noah Benjamin(age 10), The Philippines; and Abigale Rose Haiqing (age 3), Dainbai, Guangdong.

MY HOMELAND TRIP
by Caitlin Riccio (age 10)

IN MARCH OF 2006 MY PARENTS AND I WENT TO CHINA FOR A HOMELAND VISIT. You see, I was born in Tongling, China, and my mom and dad and I met when I was two years old. I am now ten years old. Our flight was 14 hours long, but we were so anxious to get to China that it was not really too bad. Here is some of what we saw and did in China.

We stayed in Beijing first. It was fun to be eating noodles for breakfast! Tiananmen Square is so big with the picture of Chairman Mao; that is the first thing that you really notice there. The Forbidden City is so amazing—all 999 rooms of it!! I cannot imagine life there. The Summer Palace is just as amazing and so peaceful and pretty. Empress Cixi's marble boat on Kunming Lake is so impressive. The Temple of Heaven was closed for renovations, but Temple of Heaven Park was fun—couples dancing, ladies ribbon-dancing, families together enjoying the time with each other, people singing and playing all kinds of games. This was a great day; we really enjoyed being with the people in the park.

We went on a Hutong tour and rode in rickshaws. We visited a school and a family and saw life in the Hutong. We saw the Beijing Acrobats show, which was real good too. The Great Wall was a site I had wanted to see for a long time, and I was so excited to finally get there. We rode up to the Wall on ski lifts and came down on one-person toboggans—such fun. I really liked being at the Wall and walking on it.

We left Beijing and flew on to Hefei and then drove to Tongling. We visited at the Tongling Social Welfare Institute where I used to live. We had a really nice visit and met the directors and took pictures with them. I had a photo album of pictures of me for them that they really liked. We saw the children and played with them, and we saw my old room. We walked around the grounds, and it was nice to be there. Then the directors took us to lunch. We talked and ate a lot. We had a great time with them.

We flew on to Chengdu and went to the Panda Research Center. It was really fun seeing all the pandas and we didn't want to leave. On to Guilin, where we took the Li River Cruise. It was so beautiful! We stayed at a lovely bed and breakfast type place. It was so beautiful, quiet, and peaceful. It was nice without televisions. We visited a very poor village and the Silver Caves. We also went on a tea plantation tour and a silk factory tour. They were both interesting and fun too.

Next on to Guangzhou. We got to stay at the White Swan and did a lot of shopping. It was fun to barter with the shopkeepers on prices. Then we were overnight to Hong Kong and on our way home. The two weeks that we were in China flew by. We met a lot of nice people, ate delicious food, and saw a lot of my birth country. China will always be a part of me, and I am glad and proud.

Sisters—Madelyn (age 4), Qingyuan, Guangdong, and Olivia (age 3), Desheng, Guangxi.

BETTER
by Deborah Amazon

WHILE MY FIVE-YEAR-OLD DAUGHTER WAS PLAYING HER FAVORITE DRESS-UP GAME ON A RAINY SUMMER DAY IN VERMONT, she suddenly said, "I want to go back to China."

Stunned, I asked, "Why?"

She replied, "The weather is better there."

She is right.

Leah Ruth Zi (age 4), Yang Dong, Guangdong—winning another ribbon at the local horse show.

Dream of a Family
by *Lisa Kaden*

My story unfolds
Back many a day,
Round a corner,
Tucked away.

My story continues,
A policeman found,
A tiny wrapped bundle
With no one around.

My story moves forward
In a large room,
A place filled with children
Praying home would come soon.

My story adds chapters
Under my nannies' care,
With hope and a dream
Of belonging somewhere.

My story fills pages
As more months unfold,
I stand by the window
Will my volume be told?

My story knows sadness
And joy all in one,
I bid good-bye to friends
Their new lives begun.

My story is open
For people to see,
Will someone read,
Take a journey to me?

My story holds promise
Oh, I do long to dance,
In the arms of a family
I just need a chance.

My story needs verses
I'm waiting for you,
I may be the child
Of your heart beating true.

Sisterhood. Olivia (age 3) and Gwen (age 3), Guangxi; Katie (age 5), Jadyn (age 4), Grace (age 4), Mya (age 6), Madelyn (age 4), Marla (age 4), and Catherine (age 5), Guangdong.

Cate Xue He (age 2), Fengcheng, Jiangxi.

Above: Anna Meng (age 6).
Below: Lauren Min (age 5).

Kelly Xuemei (age 8), Kunming, Yunnan.

Sisters—Anna Meng (age 6), Changsha, Hunan, and Lauren Min (age 5), DongYang, Zhejiang.

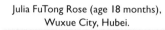

Julia FuTong Rose (age 18 months), Wuxue City, Hubei.

Above: Friends since two weeks of age—Katelyn Fuxiao and Reegan Fujing (both age 4), both from Desheng, Guangxi.

Left: Lianna Tingting (age 22 months), Desheng, Guangxi.

Emily Grace Yu Yang (age 2), Huai Hua, Hunan.

Sisters—(Bottom to top) Elena Myah (age 5), Anhui; Sophia Kay (age 3), Dianjiang; and Abigail Elizabeth (age 2), Chonqing.

Siblings—Mose (age 2), Donnea (age 9 months), and Samantha (age 3½), Hengdong, Hunan.

Jayme (age 5), Maoming City, Guangdong, with cousins, Aly (age 10), Andrew (age 11), A. J. (age 11), and James (age 9).

Meeting their new brother. Camille (age 4), Hengyang, Hunan; Clayton (age 20 months), Wuhan, Hubei; and Lillian (age 7).

Cousins and best friends—Lauren and Mikaela, Sanshui, Guangdong (both age 4).

Hannah (age 3), Miluo, Hunan.

Lucy Mae Ji Chun
(age 2), Fuzhou, Jiangxi.

Sisters—Mikaela (age 5), Sanshui, Guangdong, and Hannah (age 2), Miluo, Hunan.

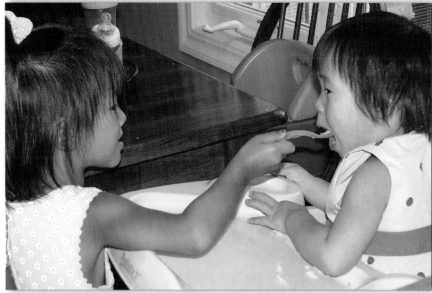

Sisters—Amy-Hui Carmichael (age 3), Yangjiang City, Yangjiang, Guangdong, and Anna Chenghao (age 1), JiangCheng District, Yangjiang, Guangdong.

Right: Annie Fei Fei (age 2), Shantou, Guangdong.

Below: Annie Fei Fei (age 2), with Mom at the Guangzhou Zoo.

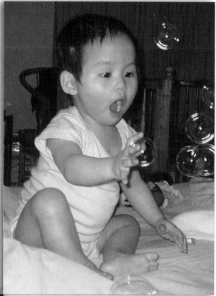

THINKING THE UNTHINKABLE
by Lori Melton

I HAVE TO ADMIT THAT MY DEEP-THINKING DAYS OF MY CHILDREN'S BEGINNINGS HAVE LONG SINCE PASSED. I'm a coward; to that I will confess. When talking in general about the circumstances that bring children to orphanages, I am able to discuss it in abstract terms: "those" circumstances for "those" children. But when I am forced to confront the reality that "those" children are in fact the children that I love so dearly, the children that I would give my last drop of blood or the last breath from my lungs, I turn around and run.

I remember Raegen's second birthday. She turned two years old nine months after coming home. Suddenly the abstracts were no longer abstract, but they were the reality of this child that had fully and forever won my heart. Suddenly I mourned that I did not get to experience her growing inside me. I grieved that I did not get to thrill at her movements or speak to her with every expectation that she could hear and understand me. I did not get to anticipate her birth or marvel at her tiny, newborn face. Something had happened during those months; something I didn't even realize was happening. As my love for her grew, we became one. She wasn't my Chinese daughter, my child from China, my adopted daughter, or any other words of description that others might use for her. She was just, purely and simply and wholly... mine. No descriptives or explanations— just mine... all mine... forever mine... totally mine. My deep thinking about her possible circumstances was no longer possible without deep pain.

As I lay in bed last night I wondered why. Why didn't I want to think about that? I decided that when I think in those terms I start getting defensive. She is worthy, lovable, valuable, and perfect. Any suggestions that she might be otherwise and the momma bear in me bares her sharp teeth and is willing to defend her cub with a fierce slap from mighty claws. That, of course, is just the front to hide the emotion that forms in the pit of my stomach, travels up through my throat, and threatens to rush out my eyes in the form of tears. How can this child I love with every ounce of my being have ever been abandoned or alone? She was vulnerable, and I was not there to comfort or protect her. How close did we come to never meeting? What if I had said "no" when God called me out of my comfort zone and into the unknown of international adoption? What would have become of her then? And me? How close did I come to missing out on this miracle called Raegen? My mind won't take me there. I am a coward.

Myleigh YiXin (age 2), Zhuzhou, Hunan.

Above: Anna-Marie Jia-Mei (age 4), Changde, Hunan.

Right: Savannah GuYan (age 23 months), Kunming, Yunnan.

Hong Xiatong (age 12), Hefei, Anhui.

Laura Louise Axing (age 21), Hangzhou, Zhejiang. Adopted at eight years old, Laura is now starting nursing school.

Sisters—Lydia (age 3), Shangrao, Jiangxi, and Kathryn (age 6).

Siblings—Terence Xiatie (age 2) and Margaret Yangyuan (age 8), both from Hanzhong City, Shaanxi.

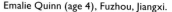

Emalie Quinn (age 4), Fuzhou, Jiangxi.

To My Daughters, Jenna and Allysa
by Vicki Leihgeber

You've
Stirred within my heart such joy and peace
Brought laughter and giggles that never cease
Showed me how to dream and hope
Taught me to persevere and cope

You've
Awakened in me a new purpose for living
Shown me the pureness and sweetness of giving
Expanded my world to reach across oceans
Connecting with others who share my emotions

You've
Stilled in my heart a deep longing and yearning
Brightened each day with your thirst for learning
Opened my eyes and caused me to see
How I'm more than just me, I'm a family of three

You've
Forever changed my journey on this earth
Given it purpose and meaning and worth
Shown me the wonder that each moment holds
Making sweet memories as our life together unfolds

You've
Connected me to a love so much larger than life itself
Filled me with blessings and given me true wealth
Your beauty, courage, and perfect grace
Speak of unconditional love that's reflected in your face

God has graced me with the two of you—
    my priceless treasures.
How you have changed and blessed my life,
No one, no words can ever measure.

Sisters— Allysa (age 3), Suixi, Guangdong,
and Jenna (age 5), Yangjiang, Guangdong, with Mom.

Sisters—Leah Catherine; Emma Charlotte, Nanning, Guangxi; Sarah Elizabeth; and Julia Claire (all age 2).

Above: Lauren Yuan (age 15 months), Yangjiang City, Guangdong, with Mama.

Left: Siblings—(Clockwise from top) Austin (age 11); Lindsay (age 14); Lauren (age 17 months), Yangjiang City, Guangdong; and Gavin (age 7).

EmmaLi Xiaozhuang (age 3), Anqing City, Anhui.

Sisters—Serena Xiu Jin (age 2), Xiushan, Chongqing; Maya Elizabeth (age 4); and Alison Kathlyn (age 7).

William Chepil, great grandfather of Ella Li Xia, Guangxi—standing at the Great Wall in 1946.

OUR GRANDDAUGHTER
by *Marsha Wong*

I CRADLED OUR GRANDDAUGHTER IN MY ARMS LAST NIGHT AND THOUGHT OF YOU. Halfway across the world, in the shadow of a bamboo forest, perhaps you were thinking of her too—the baby girl who was with you for so brief a time. Was she well? Was she happy? Where was she? On many such a night I pray that somehow you will know that the little one, born to your family and who is now a part of mine, is happy and doing very well indeed. She was anticipated with great longing and greeted with much joy and thanksgiving by family and friends.

Our granddaughter is a healthy, smiling little girl with a sense of humor and a sometimes mischievous grin—a real charmer! She has a bright, inquiring mind and delights in discovering the world around her. She has a vivid imagination and pretend-plays for her own and everyone else's pleasure too. She brightens our hearts with her presence.

The invisible red thread that brought your daughter to my family undeniably connects you and me as well. And, as the ancient belief proclaims, the thread will never break. I know you will remember our granddaughter all your days. And I will remain grateful through all of mine for the blessing you have given us. My goodnight kisses will be from both of us. Our granddaughter will always be cherished and loved.

OUR LINK TO CHINA
by *Karen Alexander*

MY HOUSE HAS THE TYPICAL COLLECTION OF FAMILY PHOTOS, BUT ON ONE WALL WE HAVE A "SHRINE" TO THE GREAT WALL OF CHINA. This collection all started with a sepia-toned image of my grandfather posing at the wall in 1946. The most recent photo is that of my husband and me on top of the wall, freezing in the December cold and a little shell-shocked because the following day we would meet our daughter, Ella Li Xia, who was living in an orphanage over 1,000 miles to the south.

The photo that started our collection shows my grandfather at a more desolate wall than the tourist-filled one we visited more than five decades later in 2002. In the photo my grandfather stands proudly near grass-covered steps, the Great Wall winding behind him, disappearing into diaphanous hills.

As a professor of agronomy, my grandfather spent almost two years (1946–47) as a soil reclamation specialist with a United Nations Relief and Rehabilitation Administration team, helping Chinese farmers along flooded areas of the Yangtze River.

Growing up I wasn't fully aware of the significance of the Chinese artifacts in my grandparents' house. Their home contained a rich collection of items representing their Ukrainian heritage and Chinese mementos from my grandfather's travels. As a child I remember being fascinated by two brush paintings of Chinese horses, but more because of a typical pre-pubescent girl's fascination with horses than with their being from China. I used to play with a Chinese wooden doll my grandfather brought home for my mother. The doll had an intricate papier-mâché headdress and a fierce, green dragon embroidered on his silk tunic, making quite a regal suitor for my comparatively flimsy plastic Barbie dolls.

As an adult I've been fascinated by the many black-and-white photos my grandfather took of 1940s Shanghai, as well as of leather-faced farmers in the Hunan, Anhui, and Jiangsu Provinces. Letters chronicle my grandfather's work and life in China, his many Chinese friends and international colleagues, as well as his adventures, including being transported by mule cart to Nanjing with a case of acute appendicitis.

Someday I hope my daughter will also appreciate this legacy handed down through generations of our family. On occasion I let Ella hold the wooden doll, now safely preserved behind glass, and tell her about how her great-grandfather brought the doll home for her nana. As a girl playing with my doll from Shanghai, how could I have known that someday I would have a daughter from China? How could I have known how our lives would be enriched by our adoption as well as by our daughter's heritage?

My family's connection to China is a deep and personal one. Someday when we return to China, we will take a family portrait on the Great Wall to add to our collection. I'm sure my grandfather would have been proud of this family tradition he unwittingly helped to start so many years ago.

Photo by Fang Fang Wu Lee.

The magnificent Great Wall (photo courtesy Gute family).

Photos by Zhang Ming.

Above and below photos by Fang Fang Wu Lee.

Hong Hu
by R.P. BenDedek

I first became aware of the Hong Hu Adoptees Group when Linda Mitchell contacted me in 2004 after seeing some of my photographic articles about Hong Hu. She asked if I could take some special photos so that the group's children might be able to see something not just of their birthplace, but the locations in which they were found.

I visited many places in order to get specifically requested photos, and sometimes local people would ask why I was taking a photo of something banal. Once informed, many showed tremendous interest, and sometimes they asked for very specific information about the circumstances relating to the child for whom I was taking photos. I sometimes would wonder at their expressions of happiness at knowing that a child had found a good home.

I originally undertook the task as a matter of courtesy, but, with each new contact with Linda and others, I grew more and more interested in the issue of international adoption. In December 2004 I published an article on behalf of the Hong Hu Adoptees group so that their children will have something to read later that will give them a sense of personal connection to their hometown. I ended that article in the *Magic City Morning Star News* with two sentences I would like to repeat for the benefit of all adoptees:

"Always remember that God has given you a gift. Use it wisely. I send you my very best wishes, and hope that my articles have helped you to discover who you truly are—your mom's and dad's daughter."

Above and below photos by R.P. BenDedek.

Photo by Zhang Ming.

RED THREADS
by Linda Mitchell

SO OFTEN WE IN THE CHINA ADOPTION COMMUNITY SPEAK OF THE RED THREADS THAT ARE SPUN AND CONNECT US TO THE CHILDREN WE MEET, FALL IN LOVE WITH, AND MAKE OURS. Those are beautiful, treasured red threads to be sure. Sometimes those threads take us to someone unexpected, but also miraculous and significant. The red threads between parents of my daughter's orphanage group and an Australian journalist living in China are a perfect example.

There are only eight members of my daughter's Yahoo group. Collectively we know of relatively few families in the world who have adopted from Hong Hu Community Social Welfare Institute in Hubei Province. Each of us keeps our eyes open for other parents who adopt from there. We periodically scan referrals on APC and Google for leads to connections to our daughters' small, rural birthplace to share with each other.

Two years ago one of our members discovered a series of news stories about life in China in an online newspaper by R.P. BenDedek. What was most exciting to us was that R.P. lived in Hong Hu and was writing of his experiences as an English teacher in the town's public high school. R.P.'s stories were a gold mine of information for us and our daughters.

Not long after reading his articles online, I emailed R.P., asking if parents of Hong Hu children could ask him some questions. R.P. was most gracious and generous. Not only was he open to answering questions about our daughters' first home, he listened to our adoption stories, found them interesting, and became our friend and ally in gaining information from an area very few adoptive parents have been able to visit or learn about.

Using our questions, R.P. brought up the subject of international adoption among his students and learned that none of them knew there was a social welfare institute that housed orphans in their hometown. Students shared with him and us their feelings about international adoption and what it meant to them to be male or female members of their community. One teenage girl in particular shared a poignant story of how she was not wanted by her grandparents, but that her parents had decided to keep her and raise her anyway. R.P. wove this information and experience into his news articles and even wrote an article specifically for our children.

R.P. also took photos, hundreds of photos, of Hong Hu for our families. He walked about the town and surrounding area taking everyday shots of life on the farm, market day, the canal and river, cemeteries, schools, and finding places of our daughters. These photos are priceless to us, and we are so fortunate to have found and been befriended by R.P. None of us has met R.P. in person, but we are forever grateful that our red threads exist and have led to each other.

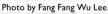

Above and below photos by Zhang Ming.

Photo by Fang Fang Wu Lee.

Fuzhou, Jiangxi, girls at the 6th annual LaLaFuLooza reunion held in Colorado.

A MAGNIFICENT COUNTRY
Excerpted essay by Toni Daniels

IN MAY, AFTER YEARS OF INEXPLICABLE RED TAPE, I TRAVELED WITH ANOTHER BRITISH FAMILY ADOPTING FROM THE SAME SOCIAL WELFARE INSTITUTE and experienced an event that was incomprehensibly monumental to my life and that of my family. Most of them had long lost hope of this day ever occurring.

I know that I speak for many when I find myself at a loss of words to describe the indelible mark that my daughter and the magnificent country of her birth have left on my soul. China is a great land, and words simply cannot describe the awe I have for its history, people, art, and landscapes. China is sometimes criticized for some of its policies, but they are forward thinking enough to allow children and families the joy and love to join together in families through adoption when many other countries will not.

Indeed my daughter and I were meant to be together, and I so look forward to all we have yet to become and the contributions we can make as individuals and as a family to our immediate community and China alike.

Pacific Northwest Sweet Peas 2nd Annual Reunion.
(Top row) Aleah (age 24 months), DiangJiang, Chongqing, and Susanna (age 19 months), Yangjiang, Guangdong. (Middle row) Kaeli (age 15 months), Xiangtan, Hunan; Caroline (age 19 months), Huaihua, Hunan; Joy (age 16 months), Xiangtan, Hunan; and Malia (age 17 months), Xiangyin, Hunan. (Bottom row) Ruby (age 11 months), Leping, Jiangxi; Anthony (age 11); Mille (age 3), Maoming, Guangdong; Mimi (age 16 months), Miluo, Hunan; Mariah (age 18 months), Miluo, Hunan; and Savannah (age 19 months), Yihuan, Jiangxi.

A LETTER TO MY DAUGHTER AS SHE BEGINS HER ADULT LIFE
by Martha Osborne
Editor, RainbowKids.com
International Adoption Magazine

My dearest daughter, Jennifer WuQin:

Where have the years gone? When I look at you now, I can still see the image of a little girl, shyly staring into the camera, ponytails framing your face. This was our first look of you—one tiny photo and a few sentences saying that you had had heart surgery years before. You were eight years old then and turned nine just before you bravely walked away from your orphanage, your hand in mine, and into your new life. You traded one future, in a land where you knew the language, culture, and customs and had many friends, for an entirely different future.

All at once you became a big sister, a daughter, an American, a minority. All at once I became the mother of a pre-teen, a teacher of English as a Second Language, and the keeper of your memories. You were so ready for a mom, and I felt incredibly inadequate. Together we worked it out. As you discovered extended family, your joy grew. Grandparents, you realized, have focus, time, and energy to teach you how to make the perfect piecrust, knit a blanket, or can jam after you spent all day picking the berries. Cousins run with you through the sprinkler and teach you to walk on stilts.

I wonder now if you knew then that I could hear your muffled tears during those first months through your bedroom door. I would rest my head against the wall near your door and pray that your heart would heal. When I walked in your room, you would light up and smile, never wanting me to know how much you missed your other "home."

So many years have now gone by. What an amazing, wonderful person you are. How much I love you. If I could go back in time now, I would

Sophronia Snow HuiJu (age 2), Guixi, Jiangxi.

tell myself, "It will be okay! You and Jenni will have such wonderful times, filled with laughter and love." Whoever said time flies, oh, how I wish I would have listened to them closer. Time has flown, and now you are such a beautiful young lady.

You are now entering your final year of high school, and already you know that next summer you will be in China. You want to travel, to see your original homeland, learn the language again, and possibly find a way to give part of what you have gained here—as part of a family who loves you deeply—back to the children who still wait to find their own dream of a family become reality.

Before you go, my daughter, I want to tell you this: Letting you spread your wings, letting you go, is the hardest thing I have ever had to do. But it is not enough for me to tell you this. You must also know that I am the third set of people to let you go. This is a sorrow, a hope, a wish, a prayer that I also share with many others. We all are here, all with our red threads of light and love surrounding you—your birthparents, your caretakers, and this family who loves you as our own.

You have your roots planted firmly in all of us. Now use your wings and fly. Soar high and fly strong, my beautiful daughter. Our love will never let you fall.

Sophronia Snow HuiJu (age 2½), with brother,
Samuel Erik Tao Hua (age 2½), Zunyi, Guizhou.

Friends—De Ang Fu (age 4) and Lucy May Deran (age 5),
both from Fuling, Chongqing. The red thread of friendship
has brought them together from China to Australia.

My Promise to You
by Helen Rigelsford
July 18, 2005, 2:18 a.m.,
thinking of my child-to-be

I promise to take care of you—from now on we're together
I promise to be with you for longer than forever
I promise I'll be near you to protect you from all harm
I promise you'll have food to eat and clothes to keep you warm

I promise not to leave you and not to cause you doubt
I promise to be open and not to shut you out
I promise to respect you and learn to know your will
I promise that I'll comfort you if you are sad or ill

I promise to defend you if there is ever cause
I promise to admire you and to accept your flaws
I promise to instill in you a sense of your own worth
I promise to explore with you and celebrate your birth

I promise that I'll teach you to be gentle, fair, and kind
But also that at times you need to say what's on your mind
I promise that you'll go to school and learn to work and play
I promise to be patient and not to force my way

I promise you lightheartedness—I want to see you dance
I promise you will learn to live and grasp at every chance
I promise to remind you of where your life did start
I promise you that China will be special in your heart

I promise to return with you so you can know the land
I promise to be there for you if you should need my hand
I promise your birth mother that she'll always be in mind
You'll know she loved you so much that she dared leave you behind

I promise to say sorry when I fall short of these vows
I promise you the confidence security allows
I promise to have fun with you—I want to hear your laughter
But most of all, I promise you my love forever after.

Dedicated to Lily Jing Mei

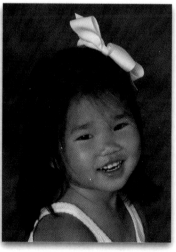

Photos by photographer David Clapp.
www.davidclapp.com

(Clockwise from upper left) Jada, Fengcheng, Jiangxi; Abbey Grace, Gaoyu, Jiangsu; Claire, Chenzhou, Hunan; Allie, Yangxi, Guangdong; Aly, Guangchang, Jiangxi; and Eliza, Shuidong, Guangdong.

Remembering

When joining the China adoption community, one becomes part of a very unique, extended family. One becomes part of a caring group of individuals who support each other during the paperchase, encourage each other during the wait to referral, cheer with joy each and every time a child comes home, and most definitely cry together when great sorrow occurs.

The following pages are in remembrance of some very special members of our adoption community who have now passed on. They have all left a permanent and beautiful mark on this world, and their memories will be held in our hearts forever.

The One You Have Chosen For Me
by Donna Barthel
written for her daughter, Lily

Who is this little girl of mine
Her face I cannot see
And yet I feel I know her soul
And I know that she knows me
I cannot help but ask, Lord,
Just why You have chosen me
To receive such a precious life
The one You have chosen for me
So until I touch her little face
And kiss her soft sweet cheeks
I lay here and wonder
Just why You trusted me enough
To loan this little one to me
I pray to always remember
The questions I ponder this eve
To do my very best
Your plan for her life to heed
And return to You one day
The child You gave to me
The special young lady
You knew that she would be

Donna Barthel, with her daughters, Lia and Lily, both from Shantou, Guangdong.

DONNA BARTHEL,
LOVE WITHOUT BOUNDARIES CO-FOUNDER
by Amy Eldridge

IN EARLY 2003 I RECEIVED A PHONE CALL FROM A FELLOW ADOPTIVE PARENT FROM THE SHANTOU ORPHANAGE IN GUANGDONG. She called and said, "I know you don't know me, but this is Donna Barthel, and God has really laid it on my heart that I am supposed to go to China with you." A few weeks later we were on our way. There were four of us on that trip. When we first met up with Donna at the Hong Kong airport to catch our flight into mainland China, we immediately were drawn to her joy-filled ways and her infectious laugh. All during that unforgettable trip we saw her heart for children. While many of us stayed busy with the loud and noisy babies who were cooing to be picked up, Donna was drawn to the quietest and most solemn. Every time I would look her way, she would be sitting on the ground with a baby in her lap, gently rocking and quietly talking or singing to them.

We left China as new and dear friends, and we all felt as if we were destined to meet. Following that trip, in August of 2003, we made a pact with each other that we were going to form a foundation to help bring assistance to orphaned children and that we were going to do it completely as volunteers. We agreed that in everything we did, we would try to bring them the most loving and compassionate care possible. Donna's wisdom and insight during this period was invaluable in the forming of Love Without Boundaries. She told us over and over again that we could keep doing the busywork because she would be covering the foundation with her prayers. And she most certainly did just that. She would listen to us talk for hours about the children we were trying to help, and then she would calmly tell us that she was going to get on her knees to pray for the right answer. Donna's passion and pure desire for goodness set the standard for what we wanted this foundation to be. Her heart for those who are hurting inspired all of us to try harder. Whether she was running our very first school program or soothing babies post surgery on a cleft mission, Donna poured her life out to anyone in need.

On April 14, 2007, Donna Bennett Barthel passed away at the age of 53, following a tragic car accident. The news of her passing stunned everyone who knew her, and we mourned the loss of a truly great woman. Our thoughts and prayers went immediately to her family, as Donna was a devoted wife and the loving mother of seven children. She was a mentor, a friend, an encourager, and a gift to all who knew her. As a founding member of LWB, Donna Barthel is a part of every single child that we have ever had the privilege of helping. We will miss you forever, Donna. We are certain that you are now in heaven holding those babies who also had to leave the earth too soon. Rock them gently for us, and know that we will carry your memory always in our hearts.

ANDIE MEI XIANG MEDER,
APRIL 28, 1997–DECEMBER 13, 2000

Andie Mei
by Gina Meder

You were born in our hearts one very special day
We loved you so much no words can ever say
You gave us joy and happiness in every kind of way
You will be with us forever, our little Andie Mei

Love,
Mommy and Daddy
and every life you have touched

Chaya Su and her baba.

INCOMPLETE
by Angela Taylor

IN JANUARY 2004 I ATTENDED A QUIET CEREMONY AT MY DAUGHTER'S SCHOOL. Chloe and I sat together, eyes closed, with the lights turned out and a single candle glowing dimly, the sweet smell of oranges and cloves in the air. In this sacred space a single thought unexpectedly intruded on my quiet mind: "You have a daughter in China and she needs you." My eyes flew open, and I looked around to see if anyone else had heard what I had so clearly heard. This wasn't an audible voice, though; it was a message I felt in my body. We already had two daughters and a son, but there was no debating the message. I returned home and, with trembling voice, told my husband what had happened. Through my tears, coughs, and other choking sounds, he pieced together what I had experienced. He took my hands in his and said, "Let's make it happen."

He began signing up for overtime shifts while I scoured the waiting child lists searching for our daughter. There were so many beautiful children, each one compelling in his or her own way, but each time we considered a child we were guided to say no. One night in the spring of that year, a still, small voice let me know, "You have a daughter in China, and she needs you. Something is wrong with her heart, and she needs you." I see dozens of photos of children from China every week, but I knew then that my daughter would have a heart condition. Months went by, and we looked at every list we could find, searching for her.

In September 2005 my husband and I traveled to China on a volunteer mission to provide surgeries for orphans. We were part of a large and extraordinary group of people dedicated to giving back to the children of China. We were helping in an orphanage which was home to countless beautiful faces, and we spent stolen moments playing with the children and cuddling with the babies. The day before we were scheduled to leave, I made the rounds once more and was pulled down a hallway I hadn't noticed before. Inside one of the rooms I saw a row of cribs… and

there she was. I recognized her as soon as I saw her. Her eyes were filled with the knowledge of the ages, and she gazed up at me as if to ask why it took so long for me to find her. The tears began to flow before I ever even touched her. I scooped her up and held her, cradling my sweet baby at last. This was the child I had grown to love, even as she was still in the womb. I was overwhelmed with emotion, trying my best to keep my composure so that I wouldn't concern the nannies. How could I possibly explain to them the profundity of this moment? How could I explain that I had been searching for this child, my child, for more than a year? There are 1.3 billion people in China, and in the past week I had seen and held countless babies. Yet, here she was. I wanted to fall to my knees right there and thank God for leading me to her, but I didn't want to frighten the nannies; so instead I whispered quiet words of thanks while staring into my daughter's eyes.

After holding her for a few minutes, speaking softly to her and letting her get to know my voice, my smell, and my touch, I reluctantly gave her to a nanny and trudged up the stairs to resume my work. I could hardly concentrate on what I was doing—my mind was racing, my heart was pounding… and where was my husband? I had to find him and tell him that at long last I had found our daughter! A couple of hours passed, and I looked up from my paperwork to see him walking toward me. As usual, he held a small bundle in his arms. As often as possible, he picked up the babies who were having surgery and comforted them as he paced the floors with them.

Drawing near, I noticed that he had tears in his eyes. "Come meet your daughter," he said, and held her out to me. All of the air was sucked out of my chest as he handed me the same baby that I had found earlier in the day. She was our daughter, no doubt about it. On the same day, but at different times, we each had found her and recognized her as ours.

Our daughter was very sick. She was lethargic, and her lips and fingertips were blue. We asked about her and were told that she had something wrong with her heart. For the next 24 hours we divided our time between packing to return home, carrying out our volunteer responsibilities, and bonding with our daughter. We named her "Chaya," which means "life." This served not only as her name, but also as a mantra. I told Chaya that we would do everything we could to come back for her one day and trusted the same God who led us to her would also bring us back for her.

The following month Chaya had heart surgery. She was fortunate to receive care from one of the best pediatric heart surgeons in China. Back home in California my husband and I held each other and clung to family and friends as we awaited news of the outcome. It was excruciating not to be there with her. The call finally came: Chaya's heart surgery was successful. Unfortunately she was just too sick to recover. Chaya died in China just a few hours after her heart surgery was completed. I don't remember the words that came after that or hanging up the phone.

I do remember collapsing to the floor and screaming when I got the news. I screamed the primal scream of a mother who has just lost her child. I continued screaming until there was nothing left in me. I never told my husband that she had died; I didn't have to. He held me as I screamed; he let me hit him over and over again in my despair. He cradled me like a baby. He cried with me. I descended into a rabbit hole of pain from which I didn't think I could ever recover. I got through the following days one agonizing second at a time, reminding myself to breathe and being coerced into eating and sleeping.

A year has now come and gone since the day that Chaya died, and I am still in that rabbit hole, trying to climb my way out. Through the fog I have glimpses of joy each day—when I help my children with their homework, when I watch them play, when I see them sleeping on their Baba's chest. The same chest that Chaya slept on just a year ago. The same strong chest that held me as I wept for our daughter gone to dance with the angels.

I remember Chaya's eyes and the way that she looked directly into my soul. She held my gaze without blinking. I remember her soft whimper as she snuggled into her baba's chest as she slept and am so thankful to have that whimper on video. I remember how she held onto me as tightly as I held onto her, and I remember how she got annoyed with us when we touched her fingers and toes. I remember searching for her bottom lip, which was so small we laughed that we couldn't find it to kiss. I remember 21 months of loving this child before I ever laid eyes on her, and I remember the most precious gift of the 24 hours when we were united with our daughter and I could hold her at last. I think Chaya was a Great Teacher, a Sage, who came into this world with a purpose—to touch the lives of others, so that they would in turn feel compelled to show compassion to even more children in China.

It has now been a year since Chaya died, and on the fifth floor of her orphanage there is now a brand new critical care unit, which cares for the most chronically ill and terminally ill children. Our closest friends and family members came together and sponsored "Chaya's Kitchen," where nutritious meals are lovingly prepared by staff members and given to the babies and children who need the most specialized attention.

Chaya will live on in our hearts forever, and her legacy to shake the world in her own gentle way has only just begun. She is proof of the incredible power of each individual to impact the world, and she serves as an inspiration to live a more meaningful life, to live life unconditionally, and to give back to others.

As time passes people occasionally ask me when we will adopt again. I don't know if we will. I do know that our family is incomplete. It will always be incomplete with Chaya gone. I don't know if there is another child out there somewhere who is meant to join our family. I don't know if I have it in me to risk that kind of love and loss again. Chaya's adoption was incomplete. Her assimilation into our family was incomplete. Our ability to mourn for her was incomplete. Everything still feels so unfinished, and, when I think of adopting another child, I just want my child, my sweet Chaya Su, and no other. Perhaps one day, perhaps not, but for now I remain Incomplete.

Love's Debut
by Tom Fisher

On the Sixth of July she was born
In the year Two Thousand and Two
A Chinese girl came into this world
It was her first debut.

Thirteen months had come and gone
The year Two Thousand and Three
It was that August she found herself
Upon her new Daddy's knee.

Her second debut was in the States
A brand new family formed
Her Mom and Dad had brought her home
Their lives at once transformed.

An attachment of hearts grew deeply
They soon fell more in love
A family now was growing strong
With help from God above.

Thirteen months soon quickly passed
Two years eight months from birth
Two debuts for one so young
Her time had passed on Earth.

Her third debut was glorious
In Heaven's grandeur stands
This little one from China
With God, now holding hands.

Our prayers are with the family
She's in their hearts to stay
The answer seems too simple
God wanted her that day.

IN MEMORY OF LYNN MEI ROCHELEAU, JULY 6, 2002–MARCH 4, 2005

Lynn Mei (age 2), Xinyu, Jiangxi.

A Woman's Life is Like a Rose
by Mark Frazer, loving husband to Denee

She grew in the sun bloomed in glorious splendor,
  with such a pleasing fragrance.
A beauty unsurpassed!
Bringing joy, love, and happiness.
But, starts to fade too soon, in a short lifetime gone…
Leaving a memory of her life in the fragrance
  of her petals left behind.

DENEE FRAZER—A LEGACY OF LOVE
by JoAnn Stringer

DENEE FRAZER LOVED ANGELS AND ROSES, AND ON APRIL 1, 1998, SHE GOT BOTH—in a tiny bundle she and her husband, Mark, named Angelica Rose.

In the hallway of the Lakeview Hotel in Nanchang, a very concerned foster mother handed over a squirming bundle to the 4'11" woman with the Texas drawl. At that moment Denee realized her lifelong dream of becoming a mother. Mark had children from a previous marriage, and they also raised Denee's godchild. Denee loved them all dearly, but this tiny child with tanned skin and large black eyes was the love of her life—her destiny and what she had been waiting for all her life.

In 2003 the circle of love widened to welcome Autumn Jade, a spitfire of a child from Wuhan, with penetrating eyes and an impish grin.

Denee was described as "everyone's best friend," and her concern and love for the children adopted from China, as well as the children left behind, was evident in her worldwide network of friends she knew only by email. Some of us were lucky to know her in person. I'm especially blessed to also have been there in the hallway of the Lakeview when our daughter was handed to us, and we became "Fu Families Forever."

Denee christened our annual get-together of Fu families "LaLaFuLooza," which she founded along with myself and Sue Mladenik.

Denee and Mark worked passionately for the children of China, promoting and supporting Love Without Boundaries and the Amity Foundation. They supported the work of Orphan Allies, which helps to fund surgeries as well as find temporary homes for orphans getting reconstructive surgery. As a family they stood in front of department stores and asked for donations of shoes for Shoes for Orphan Souls. Denee used her position as an employee of KXII television in Sherman, Texas, to promote international adoption.

Denee was diagnosed with ovarian cancer in July 2006 and passed away on May 20, 2007. She leaves a legacy of friendship and love to all who knew her. She will never be forgotten, and the seeds of love she has planted will grow and blossom in our children from China.

Denee Frazer, with her daughters, Angelica Rose (age 8), Fuzhou, Jiangxi, and Autumn Jade (age 5), Wuhan, Hubei.

For Mikey
by Holly Bombria

On July 6, 2002
A baby boy was born
In China's province: Jiangsu.

The tiny boy
Was brought right away
To the SWI
For 3 years to stay.

He was named Xi Neng
He was growing strong
His heart needed surgery
It wouldn't take long.

On September 14, 2004
His ventricle was repaired
He was ready for more.

His file was readied
By the CCAA.
CHI went to work
"Noah" was on his way.

Noah's lovely photo
Posted to list number 10
Many gazed upon him
One family looked again.

That family saw the eyes
Of their baby boy!
Yes, little Noah
Would bring them so much joy!

Mama Lisa and Baba Stephen
Rushed through the paperchase
As they moved forward
They gazed on Noah's sweet face.

In late spring of 2005
They got their TA!
With hearts aflutter
They held Mikey one June day!

Lisa held him close
She sang him a song
"Summertime" floated in the air
The family's love was strong!

Two months later
Katrina came along
The battered family was together
In Atlanta, they stayed strong.

July 6th
In 2006
Back in New Orleans
Fourth birthday tricks!

A trip to the zoo
To celebrate the day
The trials they faced
Were melting away.

The Cronvich family
Five precious members
Were building memories
Each always remembers.

Sisters Lauren and Morgan
Such precious girls!
They had longed for a brother
To enhance their world.

And enhance he did!
Mikey's light shone bright!
Each of them recalls
A treasured day or night.

Although we all feel
That time was too brief.
God has perfect timing!
In this faith, we have belief.

We know that the time
With Mikey along
Has filled many hearts
With his special song!

We cannot go backward.
We cannot change time
We are so very grateful
That the Cronvichs called Mikey "Mine."

For "mine" he was
And always shall be
Though his physical body
We no longer can see.

We can close our eyes
And feel his love.
We can look to the heavens
And see him above.

For we shall never lose him
As long as Love remains
For that is Mikey!
And we have all gained.

In Memory of Mia Mei Qi Ryan, April 23, 2004–November 14, 2005
by Michele Ryan

On Mother's Day 2005 our family was blessed with the addition of our beautiful "Lotus Blossom," Mia Mei Qi, into our lives and family.

Just as soon as she entered our lives, she was suddenly taken and kissed us good-bye on the afternoon of November 14, 2005.

In just the short time that we had Mia on this earth, she taught us many valuable things, but the one thing she *didn't* have to teach us was "*how to love*." Mia was an extremely easy child to love and she gave back to us the same unconditional love and affection that we gave to her. Every kiss, every cuddle was given to us with such warmth and meaning that it was a true honor to have her as our daughter and sister.

Mia had a tough struggle to survive the first 12 months of her life, and it took a while for her to become accepting and open to the love that we wanted her to experience and enjoy as she truly deserved.

Mia has left us tremendously heartbroken and sad that she is no longer with us, but equally as much, she has left us tremendously *proud* and honored to have been her "forever" family. We are forever grateful that God chose *us* to be her mama, dada, and big brother. Even had we known what lay ahead for her, we would have *still* taken her as our daughter because, to us, she *was* our flesh and blood and *will always be.*

Mia was loved by many, including her grandparents, great grandparent, uncles, aunts, nieces, nephews, and friends. She brought joy to all of those who knew and loved her.

May she now rest in peace and always know the love and joy that she brought into our lives and hearts on a daily basis.

We love you, Mia, and send you "kisses in the wind" when we think of your love for us. At night when we look up into the sky, we see the moon and *know that you are "home."*

Xie xie, Mia… xie xie.

Mama, Dada, and
big brother Ethan

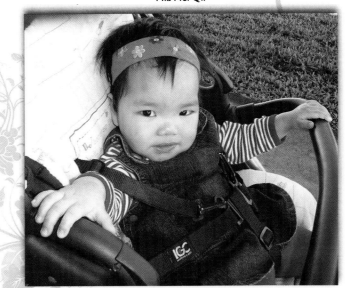

Mia Mei Qi.

Cheryl Grinton, with her daughter,
Sarah Grace XiaDi (about age 20 months), Daye, Hubei.

Cheryl Lynn Terrell Grinton
by Jerry and Sarah Terrell

We traveled to China with Cheryl and Steve in January 2002 when they went to get their precious daughter, Guo Xia Di, Sarah Grace Grinton. It was one of the happiest days of Cheryl's life. She and Grace bonded immediately. From that day forward Cheryl became Grace's dear mother, and Grace became Cheryl's beloved daughter. Grace has brought blessing and joy into all the lives of the Grinton and Terrell families.

Cheryl has cultivated Grace's Chinese heritage in culture, Mandarin language, and music. Cheryl was a talented pianist, and she wanted to impact the lives of those children still waiting in Chinese orphanages through her gift of music. She recorded a piano CD of classical lullaby music which was given to orphanages throughout China and which helped raise funds to begin a music program in Guangdong. Cheryl was a strong advocate of adoption and talked frequently about returning to China with her daughter.

Our beloved daughter, Cheryl Lynn Terrell Grinton, passed away on July 13, 2006. Her beautiful heart and loving spirit will never be forgotten.

In Memory of Mark Morse, 1953–2006
by Kristi Morse

LOVE AND THANKS TO A WONDERFUL AND CARING HUSBAND AND FATHER. Mark was the father of three loving children—Dustin, Katie, and Jade—and husband to Kristi for 26 beautiful years. Mark leaves a legacy of caring for the children of Asia. Along with two daughters adopted from Korea and China, he also sponsored the education of two young students from Qinghai Province and helped with the school building in RenZhen. These two students will continue their education, thanks to his memorial fund, along with three additional students from China.

Mark Morse, with his daughter, Jade.

IN LOVING MEMORY OF DAISY'S DADDY, KENT PHILLIPS, 1959–2005

Kent Phillips and his daughter, Daisy (age 11 months), Zhaoqing, Guangdong—strolling along the Pearl River.

Our Forever Angel
by Deb Birge

HER SMILE WAS INFECTIOUS, HER HEART WAS PURE. She taught us so much in the very short time she was here. She was our China angel, literally. This is the story of Qu Bo Yang—Madison Aleyce BoYang.

The world came crashing down around me upon receiving a phone call on April 2, 2000. While out of town I had been told by my husband that our 13-year-old daughter, Kaylee, had died in a skiing accident. Life was no longer simple, and I now had to adjust to the fact that we were a family of four, not the family of five that I had become so accustomed to.

My angels began to talk to me shortly thereafter, and my heart was bombarded with messages that another child was out there for us. Eventually, after much soul searching, failed ideas, and failed procedures, I pleaded with God: "How in the world am I supposed to parent another child? If we are to do so, please send me a sign." My sign arrived that evening while watching a newscast. A story was aired of a family that adopted from China after losing their biological child. There was no looking back from that point on. So, during a cold November of 2000, our pursuit of little Madison began. After a long and tedious wait, Madison Aleyce BoYang was finally placed in our arms on July 4, 2002.

She felt so light in my arms, this little ten-month-old child. A blank stare covered her face as her little fingernails dug into the flesh of my arms. Magical is the only word to explain this day. The pain of losing Kaylee lightened. My life now had meaning. I thanked Kaylee.

Once home I was mesmerized by this little girl. Having parented children before, I knew this child was different. Or perhaps I was different. All I knew was that I was consumed by this child, telling my husband, Dave, that I loved this child so much I wanted to gobble her up. I worked with her intensely, trying to make up for all that she lost in the orphanage and perhaps for all that I had lost through the death of Kaylee. I taught her to play with me when she didn't want to

MADISON ALEYCE BoYANG, QUZHOU, ZHEJIANG, AUGUST 20, 2001–SEPTEMBER 22, 2003

play, and I taught her to not be afraid of airplanes when she wanted to be afraid.

However my list of what I taught her was short compared to what she taught us and everyone around her. Her message was tolerance and love. She would insist everyone give hugs and kisses and always had a wave for those she would see in a restaurant or mall.

Madison was to be our only adoption. After all we were older parents. However, it was after being home with Madison nine months, I was consumed with the "knowing" that I needed to go back to China. This feeling was so strong; I told Dave that I had to go to China, with or without him.

Sadly, this "calling" was very much meant to be. We had submitted our dossier to our agency and learned that it was on its way to China. At this same time Madison developed a light runny nose. Shortly thereafter she became more seriously ill with a high fever and rash all over her body. The doctors insisted she was fine and that it was just viral, no matter how many frantic calls I made. Five days later I held my precious child in my arms. The machines were turned off, and the bed that coldly cocooned my child was empty. My beautiful baby, Madison, was silent; death had taken her little soul. Madison's illness was not viral, but rather she died of undiagnosed Strep A. My angel child was no more on this earth. It seemed like a cruel joke. Once again my life ceased to exist.

We knew, however, that we were going to have to pull ourselves together quickly as we were waiting for our referral from China. We discovered two days after Madison's death that our dossier had been logged into China on September 18, 2003. On July 5, 2004, Hannah Claire XiaoMei was placed in our arms. She was a beautiful little toddler who clung to me as much as I clung to her. Together we were inseparable. God had given me the perfect, most divine gift, once again.

Dave and I have gone on to adopt two more times: a beautiful waiting child, Ellie Olivia SiJia, who makes us giggle every day, and now we anxiously await Carson Luke LuSong, another waiting child. Many people have questioned this adoption; however, this little boy has given me peace, a tranquillity I have not experienced since Madison's death. My children give me the reason for living.

Madison was bigger than life, and I cannot think of a more fitting tribute to this beautiful child than to add to our forever family—Maddi's forever family. We are no longer a family of "four" but a fabulous family of "nine!" We are truly blessed.

Maggie, Anhui.

MAGGIE
by Anne Ainsworth

ZHANG CHUN JIA WAS MY DAUGHTER. I chose her from my agency's waiting child list and gave her the name of Maggie. In February of 2004 I received approval from China to bring her home. However I learned just two months later that Maggie had become too ill to be adopted. Her adoption file was withdrawn by the orphanage when her kidneys began to fail. I was able to send her packages and was able to pay for the special care she required until she passed away in June. In this way I felt I never lost "touch" with the child I would never be able to hold in my arms. My girls, Maeve, Clare, and Kate, and I will hold her forever in our hearts.

REMEMBERING
by Sherry McKellar

WHEN OUR THEN 18-MONTH-OLD LITTLE GIRL JULIA LIJING APPEARED ON THE WAITING CHILD LIST FOR CHILDREN'S HOUSE INTERNATIONAL (CHI) IN APRIL 2004, many kind and generous people noticed her need for surgery for spina bifida and quickly arranged to have it done and raised the money for it. We were very touched by their love and kindness. Shortly after we were chosen to be her forever family, we found out that she was in the advanced stages of cancer and had very little time left to live. Oh, how our hearts ached to hold her and comfort her! The money that had been raised for her surgery was donated in her name to help several other children instead. My friend, Kimber Bakos, wrote the following poem when we first found out that our sweet Julia was sick. She expressed very well the emotions we felt.

For Julia
by Kimberly Bakos

My sweet birthday girl,
My heart weeps for you,
All around the world,
What can I do?

I long to hold you tight,
And hug away your pain,
I wish with all might,
That wouldn't be in vain.

So instead, each day I'll pray
And lift you up on High
That the pain will go away
And you don't have to cry.

Your little life means so much,
The spark is seen in each eye,
You've reached many with your touch,
And now all we can do is cry.

But we can do much more,
And your light will show us how,
To see that this is an open door,
To help others starting now.

You little life will be too brief,
And we may not understand,
Why we must all feel such grief,
As you slip from our hands.

But in our heart you will always be,
And may it inspire us each day,
To look for opportunity,
To help the others in some way.

I'll miss you, my sweet Jing Jing,
And the joy your face brings to me,
But soon you'll hear the angels sing,
And be running and so free.

So as you prepare to leave us here,
You leave something special at the door.
You've changed us, Julia dear,
And make us want to do even more.

So go, my sweet one, to where the angels wait,
For you to dance and run and play,
We only want the best for you,
And it seems this is the way.

Calla Elise.

CALLA ELISE CHRISTOPHERSON
Born July 13, 2004, Hubei Province, China
Adopted June 28, 2005
Passed Away August 22, 2006

by Holly Christopherson

Calla was a daughter and a sister.
She was a granddaughter, a niece, and a cousin.
She was a playmate and a friend.

Calla loved to blow bubbles, paddle in her pool, and take baths with her big sister.

Calla loved to snuggle with her mom and keep up with her big sister—even if it meant climbing to the top bunk or standing on the table.

Calla loved her special visits from Grandma Bev and her Thursday afternoons with Papa and Grandma Betsy!

Calla loved rice, spaghetti, and candy.

Calla loved to color and paint, even if her canvas was her own arms and legs… or Mama's walls and furniture.

Calla had a smile that could light up a room and a heart that knew true love.

Calla loved to love, and she loved to be loved.

Calla's life was too short, but her memory and spirit will live on in the hearts of her mama, her big sister, Kiah, and the many people who will always love her.

Debbie Lyne, with her daughters,
Allison Lirong (age 6½), Daye, Hubei, and
Olivia Xiaoji (age 3½), Yangxi, Guangdong.

IN MEMORY OF DEBBIE LYNE,
JANUARY 2, 1962–MARCH 24, 2007

by Debbie Lyne

I'm your mommy and I love you.
I couldn't stay with you
As long as I wanted to.

I wanted to see you grow up and
Have babies of your own.
But God called me to heaven
And I had to go.

But though I am in heaven
And not with you,
I will never leave you.

When you lie in the green grass and
Look up at the clear blue sky,
I will be looking down from heaven
And waving to you.

When you feel
The warm sunshine on your cheek,
It will be me kissing you.

When you hear the mama robin
Singing to her babies,
It will be me singing your praises.

When you feel
The rain on your shoulders,
It will be me crying tears of joy
For the wonderful girl
You've become.

When you feel
The cool breeze on your arms,
It will be me hugging you tightly.

When you see
A rainbow reach across the sky,
It will be me smiling
From ear to ear.

When you see a flower bloom,
It will be my love for you,
Always growing.

When you see
The snowflakes start to fall,
It will be me.

When you see the leaves
Turn crimson and gold,
It will be me.

When you see a butterfly
Emerge from its cocoon,
It will be me watching you
Grow into a woman.

When you see
A horse race across the field,
It will be me
Trying to catch up to you.

When you see
The moon glow at night,
It will be me
Shining with pride for you.

When you see
The stars twinkle in the night sky,
It will be me
Giggling at your silly jokes.

I will never leave you if you
Keep me alive in your heart.
I will always love you.
You are loved.

KALAIAH RAGSDALE,
NOVEMBER 23, 1999–OCTOBER 29, 2004

Kalaiah (age 4), Guangdong. During her stay in the hospital, Kalaiah enjoyed her bathtime, especially since it meant that the doctors would leave her alone there.

Kalaiah loved fall festivals. She would go to several each fall. Here she's dressed as Little Red Riding Hood and is enjoying her snack.

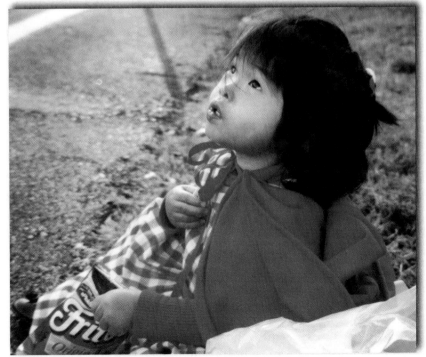

DOUBLE BLESSING
by Zea Ragsdale

WE ADOPTED OUR BEAUTIFUL DAUGHTER, KALAIAH, FROM THE GUANGDONG PROVINCE IN CHINA ON SEPTEMBER 19, 2000, WHEN SHE WAS NINE MONTHS OLD. It felt like Kalaiah had always been a part of our family. We played at bath time, explored Guangzhou, and involved her in everything. God gave us one of the greatest gifts we've ever known, and He chose to do it through the vibrant, rich, and diverse culture of China.

Once home the ecstasy never seemed to end. Kalaiah loved to play, and she loved to learn. She roller skated at age two, went straight to a princess bike with training wheels, and at age four got a scooter. We celebrated Chinese New Years with special dinners, red envelopes, and fireworks. We celebrated the moon festival with other families. We celebrated Kalaiah's adoption day with a special present from China each year and by dressing up. Birthdays were huge celebrations, and, because KK's birthday fell around Thanksgiving, we celebrated her "half" birthday too. With Kalaiah every day was a celebration. Truly her laughter and joy and sense of humor permeated every hour of the day.

We experienced a double blessing: We had the most precious child in the world (to us) to love and to cherish, and we realized how blessed we were—both then and now.

In January 2004 Kalaiah asked Jesus into her heart. In April, at 4½ years of age, she started running high fevers. After a month of doctor's visits and another month in the hospital, the doctors finally found the extremely rare form of cancer, NK Lymphoma. We spent most of the next four months in the hospital doing everything we knew to help Kalaiah fight for her life.

The most amazing thing was that Kalaiah was still joyous. She shot silly string at doctors, watched Sleeping Beauty more times than I can count, laughed, played games, and loved. She did not like all the shots and slept a lot when she was really sick, but life was still a beautiful blessing because Kalaiah was in it.

Sadly for her dad and me, Kalaiah won her battle with cancer on October 29, 2004, when she went to Jesus' party. We were and are devastated, but we are also enriched and blessed forever by having the precious Chinese jewel we call Kalaiah as our daughter.

Acknowledgements

We express our sincere gratitude to all those who helped create this book. First and foremost, we thank all of the contributors who shared their hearts and submitted stories, poems, photos, journal entries, and drawings. Over 4,000 submissions were received, which made it difficult to narrow down the entries to be included in the book. We enjoyed each and every submission, whether or not we were able to include it. We appreciate the patience and assistance of the contributors during the book creation process. We have done our best to eliminate mistakes but apologize in advance for any we may have missed.

We additionally wish to thank:

Bruce Sherman—for his vision of the "red thread" theme.

Kimber Bakos—for her efforts in soliciting submissions.

Angela Carswell, Mary Anne Castranio, Jan Champoux, Suzanne Damstedt, Nancy Delpha, Lori Dubbs, Kate Finco, Donna Goodrich, Lisa Kaden, Tracie Linne, Junie Maggio, Kyle Messner, Lori Melton, Michele St. Martin, Angela Taylor, and Anthony Thornton—for their assistance in editing and proofreading the numerous submissions.

Carla Kennedy—for her seemingly endless hours spent reviewing and editing photos for the book.

Jolaine Chatham—for her talented design of the book.

Andy Huff and Canterbury Press—for their generous spirits and efforts in publishing the book.

Bao, Helen, Ming, Stephanie, Tingting, Winnie, and Yvonne—our wonderful facilitators in China—for working tirelessly to carry out our programs to help orphaned children.

We especially wish to acknowledge our children and all of China's children, who are the inspiration for this book.

From tired to angry to bemused, each baby has such a different look and expression that it truly sums up our motto of "Every Child Counts"—whether young or older, little or big, healthy or with special needs. Love Without Boundaries Foundation is privileged to work with you to help the children in China. We share the belief with each of you that every child on this earth is important and deserves to know love.

Photo by Mui Koh.

Author Index